CRUMBS

SHORT DEVOTIONS

FOR

EVERY DAY OF THE YEAR

By C. M. ZORN

Original German Edition Rendered into English
by the Author's Son,

H. M. ZORN

ST. LOUIS, MO.
CONCORDIA PUBLISHING HOUSE
1914

Note of the Translator.

To meet the demand for brevity, the hymn-verses have not been copied in full, but are merely represented by numbers which refer the reader to the "Evangelical Lutheran Hymn-Book" published by Concordia Publishing House. These verses are translations, where such were to be had, or selections that have a trend similar to those of the German edition.

FIRST PART.
THE FESTIVAL SEASON.

First Week in Advent.

SUNDAY.

Rejoice greatly, O daughter of Zion! Shout, O daughter of Jerusalem! Behold, thy King cometh unto thee: He is just, and having salvation.—Zech. 9, 9.

This is a word of prophecy written at a time when the Savior had not yet come. It is a word of prophecy given to the Daughter of Zion, the Daughter of Jerusalem. Who was the Daughter of Zion, the Daughter of Jerusalem? It was the congregation of believers in Israel, who desired to lift up their eyes to Mount Zion towering forth in Jerusalem, for upon that mount stood David's royal palace, and it was from David that the eternal King, the Savior, was to descend according to His human nature. And the desire of the believers was not to be put to shame. Through the Holy Spirit the Prophet cried: "Rejoice greatly, O Daughter of Zion; shout, O Daughter of Jerusalem! Behold, thy King cometh unto thee," thy King, thy eternal King! And He "is just, and having salvation": through His justice and righteousness, the righteousness which He procured for thee, a poor sinful people, He will help thee forevermore.

Christians, believing Christians, the Savior has come. By His bloody merit He has procured for you tl.at righteousness wherewith ye can stand before God. He hath holpen you. Say:

> Jesus' blood and righteousness
> My jewels are, my glorious dress,
> Wherein before my God I stand
> When I shall reach the heavenly land,

Ye are now the Daughter of Zion, the Daughter of Jerusalem. And now rejoice greatly, O Daughter of Zion; shout, O Daughter of Jerusalem! Behold, thy King cometh unto thee: He is just, and having salvation. Christians, ye believe in Him, ye are righteous before God, ye are holpen.

PRAYER.—Lord Jesus Christ, dear Savior, I give thanks unto Thee that Thou hast fulfilled Thy Word, given through the prophets, that Thou hast truly come. Even me, a poor sinner, hast Thou made righteous before God; unto me, too, hast Thou opened heaven; me, too, hast Thou holpen. Continue to help me, Lord Jesus, through Thy Word and Thy Holy Spirit, that in true faith I may firmly hold Thee; that I may rely upon Thy merit wrought for me; that I may serve Thee, my King, willingly and gladly, and finally enter the blessed realms above. Amen.

Hymn 146, 1. 4.

MONDAY.

I will put enmity between thee and the woman, and between thy seed and her seed; it shall bruise thy head, and thou shalt bruise His heel.—Gen. 3, 15.

Adam and Eve, and in and with them all men, had been deceived by the devil, concealed in the serpent. And they had fallen into sin, death, and damnation. And Satan triumphed. Then came the Lord, the eternal Son of God. And in the hearing of Adam and Eve He first said to the devil: "I will put enmity between thee and the woman, and between thy seed and her seed." So, after all, the devil's victory was not to be final. There was to be another battle, another strife, between him and his hosts on the one hand, and mankind on the other. And furthermore the Son of God said: "It shall bruise thy head, and thou shalt bruise His heel." The outcome of this battle and strife was to be that the Seed of Woman, a man born of woman, should, in bloody, mortal combat, completely overcome the devil and rescue man from his power, from sin, death, and damnation. And by saying "His seed," the Son of God spoke of Himself, who should become man and accomplish all these things.—This is the first Advent message, the very first message concerning the coming of the Savior. Herewith Adam and Eve and many of their offspring comforted themselves, until other prophecies were added.

Ye Christians, look unto Bethlehem and unto Golgotha and into the empty grave, and there see how the Son of God made good His word. And believing in Him, let your souls be comforted.

PRAYER.—Lord Jesus Christ, Thou eternal Son of God, I give thanks unto Thee that Thou didst become true man, and by Thy bitter suffering and death, and also by Thy victorious resurrection, hast redeemed me and all mankind from all sins, from death, and from the power of the devil. Grant me, I beseech Thee, that in true faith I may at all times find true comfort in Thee, and remain steadfast in such faith against all the temptations of the Prince of this World, who, withal, is judged already, until by a blessed death Thou wilt lead me into eternal life. Amen.

Hymn 146, 8. 9.

TUESDAY.

In thy seed shall all the nations of the earth be blessed.—Gen. 22, 18.

When God blesses a poor sinful man, I say, when He blesses, must not every curse vanish; must not all sin be forgiven, death become life, damnation be turned into salvation? Most certainly.

Now, bearing in mind yesterday's meditation, listen to something of olden times.—Men had multiplied on earth. But nearly all had cast the prophecy of the Seed of Woman, the Savior, to the winds, and had become wicked. The doom of the Flood had come upon them. Noah only, and his family, had been spared. Even the descendants of Noah had soon become wicked. Then, about the year 2000 after the creation of man, God chose unto Himself Abraham, the descendant of Shem, the son of Noah. Out of Abraham's descendants He wanted to raise up a people unto Himself. To this people He desired to give His Word. Of this people, as concerning the flesh, the promised Savior should come. And He said to Abraham: "In thy seed shall all the nations of the earth be blessed." By the Seed of Abraham Christ is meant. Through Christ God's blessing was to come unto all men.

Christ has come, and the blessing has come with Him. Thou knowest this, O Christian. Now bow before Christ in faith, O sinner, O poor and lost sinner, and receive His blessing, that every curse may be taken from thee, thy sins be forgiven thee, death turned into life, and damnation into salvation. God wants to bless thee. Dost thou not desire to be blessed?

PRAYER.—Yea, Lord, I indeed desire to be blessed, O my God. I bow down before Thee, Lord Jesus Christ, my Savior. Grant me Thy blessing. Make every curse vanish. Forgive me all my sins, turn death into life for me, grant me eternal life for Thine own sake. Perform unto me Thine old unchanging promise. I know Thou wilt do it. I give thanks unto Thee; I desire to give thanks unto Thee in all eternity, for Thy blessing. Amen.

Hymn 107, 5.

WEDNESDAY.

Behold, the days come, saith the Lord, that I will perform that good thing which I have promised unto the house of Israel and to the house of Judah. In those days, and at that time, will I cause the Branch of Righteousness to grow up unto David; and He shall execute judgment and righteousness in the land. In those days shall Judah be saved, and Jerusalem shall dwell safely. And this is the name wherewith He shall be called, The Lord, our Righteousness.—Jer. 33, 14-16.

The promise which said that through his seed, which seed is Christ, all the nations of the earth should be blessed, had passed from Abraham upon Isaac, from Isaac upon Jacob, called Israel, from Israel upon Judah, and from Judah upon King David, who lived a thousand years before Christ. And henceforth the believers called the expected Messiah, or Christ, the "Son of David." The prophets then often foretold many things concerning Him. And about six hundred years before Christ the Prophet Jeremiah spoke the words found at the head of this lesson. The Lord Jehovah would become the Son of David and help His people by becoming their righteousness wherewith they might stand before God. And then, as their rightful King, He would execute judgment in the land, and for time and eternity clothe them with righteousness and salvation. And the children of Israel sang: "Hosanna to the Son of David! Blessed is He that cometh in the name of the Lord; Hosanna in the highest! Blessed be the kingdom of our father David, that cometh in the name of the Lord: Hosanna in the highest! Blessed be the King that cometh in the name of the Lord: peace in heaven and glory in the highest!" And when Christ had come and was now entering Jerusalem, the people sang, and the children in the temple sang unto Him this song of praise. And do thou, O Christian, also sing it unto Him with heart and mouth, just as now our own children also sing unto Him, "Hosanna in the highest!"

PRAYER.—I give thanks unto Thee, Lord Jesus Christ, Thou great Lord Jehovah and Son of David, that Thou hast come to us miserable and lost sinners, and hast established for us eternal help and deliverance. In Thee we have that righteousness wherewith we stand before God, and eternal salvation. Now help us, Thy beloved Christians, that in true faith we honor, laud, and praise Thee, our true King, and serve and obey Thee with cheerful hearts as long as we live. And finally take us where we shall praise Thee forevermore with the choir of angels, O Lord Jesus. Amen.

Hymn 135, 3. 4.

THURSDAY.

The Lord hath laid on Him the iniquity of us all.—Is. 53, 6.

Thus did Isaiah prophesy concerning Christ, the promised Messiah. He spoke as if these things were then already long past. And now they are long past. The Lord did lay on Him the iniquity of us all, and we are free and saved eternally. These are the glad tidings brought us now.

But how few there are that believe these glad tidings! Many are offended at Christ Crucified. Flesh and blood, in looking at Him, behold no form nor comeliness, no beauty such as they would fain see. He is despised and rejected of men, a man of sorrows and acquainted with grief. Man, as it were, hides his face from Him; natural man esteems Him not. Yet the Lord laid on Him the iniquity of us all. Surely, He hath borne our griefs, and carried our sorrows. He was wounded for our transgressions, He was bruised for our iniquities. The chastisement of our peace was upon Him, and with His stripes we are healed. We are all as sheep gone astray; but the Lord hath laid on Him the iniquities of us all. He was the blameless and patient Lamb of God that bore the sins of the world. It pleased God so to bruise Him. He has made His soul an offering for sin. They who are born of God know this, and behold this, and delight in it. And even He, our Savior, delights in the congregation of believers which has sprung from His sowing of blood and from the travail of His soul. By His knowledge He, the righteous Servant of God, justifies many; for He bore their iniquities. Despite the unbelief of many, the portion of His spoil is large, because He has poured out His soul unto death, and was numbered with the transgressors, and bore the sin of the world, and made intercession for the transgressors.— And thou, too, O Christian, art of the portion of His blessed spoil. Thy sin, also, did the Lord lay upon Him.

PRAYER.—I give thanks unto Thee, Thou crucified Redeemer, because Thou didst bear my sin, and didst make me righteous in the sight of God. I thank Thee for the blood Thou didst shed and for Thy death upon the cross. When I contemplate this, my soul is delighted in Thee. For this is my salvation. I thank Thee that through Thy most precious Gospel Thou didst pluck me, a poor sinner, from out of the unbelieving world, and through faith in

Thee didst make me a portion of Thy spoil, and art satisfied with a great satisfaction. Hold me fast, Lord Jesus, and take spoil upon spoil from unbelief and destruction, O Jesus. Amen.
Hymn 145, 6. 12.

FRIDAY.

Thou wilt not leave my soul in hell; neither wilt Thou suffer Thine Holy One to see corruption. Thou wilt show me the path of life; in Thy presence is fullness of joy; on Thy right hand there are pleasures forevermore.—Ps. 16, 10. 11.

These words were spoken *by* David, but not *concerning* David. It was the eternal Son of God, who wanted to become the promised Son of David, the Messiah, that spake these words by the mouth of David. Two infallible exponents of the Bible tell us this, the Apostles Peter and Paul, as you may read in Acts 2, 25-31 and 13, 35-37. With these words the Son of God spoke of His resurrection, which was to follow soon upon His death on the cross. And the Son of God actually did what He had promised to do. On the third day after His death He arose. And thereby He, as our Savior and Substitute, did away with our death entirely, together with its fearful causes and terrible consequences, and utterly destroyed it. Through the resurrection of Christ we sinners have been made righteous before God; dying, we have been brought to life; damned, we have been saved. This was foretold by the prophets in the Old Testament, and proclaimed by the evangelists and apostles in the New Testament. And whoever, through the Holy Ghost, in true faith accepted this in ages gone by or whoever accepts it now; whoever comforted his soul with it then, or does so now, really possessed all these things then, and possesses them now. My dear Christian, look alone unto Christ in faith, and rejoice in what He has done for thee.

PRAYER.—Not I, O Lord Jesus, not I must overcome, nor can I overcome, the cruel power of my sin and of death and of judgment and of damnation, and save myself. Nay, all this Thou, Thou, hast done for me. For this I render Thee heartfelt thanks. Grant, I beseech Thee, O Jesus, that I may look alone unto Thee, and trust and rely on what Thou hast done for me, and what Thy sacred Word doth say. Thus Thy righteousness shall be my righteousness, Thy life shall be mine, Thy blessedness my own. O Thou risen and living Lord and Savior, I put my trust in Thee. Amen.

Hymn 218, 4. 5.

SATURDAY.

The Lord said unto my Lord, Sit Thou at my right hand.—Ps. 110, 1.

Thus David, the prophet and king, from whose seed Christ should be born, foretold the final ascension of Christ, both his and our Lord. Through the Holy Ghost he heard in advance how God the Father, after Christ's great victory of our salvation was accomplished, would say to Christ: "Sit Thou at my right hand." And so it came to pass. Christ, true God and man, our Substitute and Savior, ascended into heaven, and—note well—opened heaven for us, which had been barred against us. When He ascended into heaven, He reopened unto us the door of Paradise that day. The cherub guards the gate no more: to God our thanks we pay. And He, true God and man, our Substitute and Savior, sat at the right hand of God. And thus He prepared a place for us where we shall be in the most intimate communion with God forevermore, and where the glory of God will illumine our entire being, both soul and body. He has accomplished all things for us. He has prepared all things for us. And He, true God and man, our Savior and Substitute, now sitteth at the right hand of God, and filleth all things with His presence and omnipotence. Or is there a space where the right hand of God is not? And He that sitteth at the right hand of God, the Father Almighty, ruleth over all. In this way our dear Savior is with us alway, even unto the end of the world. And thus He guards, guides, leads, directs, and rules us that we may obtain the salvation of our souls. Let us receive Him, let us trust in Him, and rely on Him, on Him who secured us every blessing, and brings us to the blissful abodes of heaven.

PRAYER.—Jesus, Thou exalted Savior, Thou callest me, a poor sinner, unto that glory which Thou hast procured for me, which Thou hast prepared for me, which Thou hast taken possession of for me. O Lord Jesus, I trust in Thee alone. O Thou my Righteousness, Thou my Life, Thou my Salvation, protect me against Satan, against the wicked world, and against my own evil flesh and blood. Keep me in the true faith and trust in Thee, and open wide heaven's door for me when from this earth my soul shall flee. Amen.

Hymn 557, 5.

Second Week in Advent.

SUNDAY.

This same Jesus who is taken up from you into heaven shall so come in like manner as ye have seen Him go into heaven.—Acts I, 11.

Thus spake the two heavenly messengers to the apostles while they looked steadfastly toward Jesus as He went up into heaven. That same Jesus who, visibly before the eyes of the apostles, ascended into heaven shall one day come again from heaven, visibly, with great power and glory, and all His holy angels with Him. And then shall He judge the quick and the dead. And then shall He establish that eternal and glorious Kingdom of God unto which God has created us in the beginning, saved us through Christ, and sanctified us through the Holy Ghost. The scorners shall not always scorn Him, nor shall the scoffers always scoff at Him. He shall come and put them to silence. And He shall satisfy the eager desire of His children. For those, too, who expired with Jacob's dying prayer on their lips: "I have waited for Thy salvation, O Lord!"—shall He come, and He will fill their mouth with laughter and their tongue with singing. Thus God shall from all evil forever make us free, from sin and from the devil, from all adversity, from sickness, pain, and sadness, from troubles, cares, and fears, and grant us heavenly gladness, and wipe away our tears.—Dear Christian, wrap thyself entirely in His merits, His righteousness by faith, and always remain a sheep of His fold, so that when He, who is thy salvation, shall come, it may be to bring thee eternal salvation.

PRAYER.—O my Lord and Savior Jesus Christ, I thank Thee most heartily that Thou so faithfully remindest me of Thy coming in glory, and teachest me to be ready therefor, and vouchsafest unto me to know the great and eternal comfort thereof. Grant, I beseech Thee, unto me Thy Holy Ghost, that my conversation may be in the fear of Thee, in true faith, and with a good conscience, and that I may, with a joyful heart and wakeful eye, hope and wait for Thy coming in glory: Thou who livest and reignest and wilt come a Judge and a Redeemer, blessed forever. Amen.

Hymn 136, 10.

MONDAY.

But the day of the Lord will come as a thief in the night, in the which the heavens shall pass away with a great noise, and the elements shall melt with fervent heat, the earth also and the works that are therein shall be burned up.— 2 Peter 3, 10.

Thus writes St. Peter concerning the coming of the Lord. It will be a terrible event indeed. Everything will topple. Everything will perish where now we live and have our being. Terrors worse than those of death will seize upon flesh and blood. And what will be the state of mind of those who have rejected their Savior? "Behold, He cometh with clouds; and every eye shall see Him, and they also who pierced Him: and all kindreds of the earth shall wail because of Him. Even so. Amen." (Rev. 1, 7.) And yet, behold! those who, through faith, are His own, in spite of all, will know through the Holy Ghost that it is their beloved Savior coming in the midst of all these terrors, coming to deliver them from every evil work, and to preserve them unto His heavenly Kingdom. And right quickly will they lift up their heads, and their fear will be turned into consolation, peace, and joy. How canst thou be afraid when amidst all these fearsome things thou seest thy Savior coming? Only be ready at all times, and own Him as thy Redeemer at all times, that on yonder great day, too, He may be thy beloved Savior. And thou knowest not when that great day will come.

PRAYER.—Jesus, my Lord, Thou art my beloved Redeemer. O indeed, I am not afraid of Thee; I trust in Thee and rely upon Thee. Thou art my very best Friend. Thou hast redeemed me and received me as Thy own; Thou richly and daily forgivest unto me all mine iniquities; Thou healest all my diseases; Thou speakest unto me words of grace and love and comfort and life and eternal blessedness. O Lord Jesus, I know Thee. Keep me in the knowledge of Thee until Thou shalt come, that I may rejoice in Thee and greet Thee, saying, Jesus, Jesus, O my Savior! Amen.

Hymn 553, 4.

TUESDAY.

The hour is coming in the which all that are in the graves shall hear His voice and shall come forth: they that have done good unto the resurrection of life, and they that have done evil unto the resurrection of damnation.—John 5, 28. 29.

Thus says the Lord Jesus. He speaks of the hour of His second coming. Then all the dead, without exception, shall hear His voice calling them, and shall come forth from the grave, and from the dust, and from all mixture and fusion with the elements of the earth. True, death has an awful power, and no man, nor any other creature, can awake us therefrom. But the voice of Jesus is almighty, and even the dead must hear it.—There is a difference among the dead. First, there are those who have done good on earth, poor sinners, who believed in their Savior, and showed that their faith was true by resisting sin and serving their Lord. These shall rise unto eternal life and blessedness. Then there are those who have done evil on earth, who rejected the Savior, and lived according to their own thoughts and desires. These shall come forth unto eternal damnation.—Christians, how powerfully does this call and admonish us that to-day, while we live, we turn in faith unto our Savior and to His grace offered us freely and without price, and turn away from sin, and serve Him.

PRAYER.—Jesus, my beloved Lord, I believe; help Thou mine unbelief. Grant that I may live and die firmly believing in Thee, my Savior, and that I may not fall into the snares and pitfalls of unbelief and sin. O Thou Love of my love, draw me unto Thee that I may follow Thee! Grant me a blessed end and a joyful resurrection unto eternal life. Keep me from the wrath of the Judgment to come, and from eternal damnation, O Lord Jesus! Amen.

Hymn 348, 7.

WEDNESDAY.

He that believeth and is baptized shall be saved; but he that believeth not shall be damned.—Mark 16, 16.

Christ will come to judge the quick and the dead. Do we know exactly how and according to what rule He will pass sentence? Yes, indeed. He will not pass sentence upon us according to the law of Moses, not according to our works. If He did that, we should be lost. How, then, will He rule? According to faith and unbelief. Seest thou His Word at the head of this lesson? If thou, a poor, miserable, sinful being, dost in faith accept the things which Christ doth give thee in His Word and doth seal unto thee in Baptism: the salvation which He has earned, and which consists in the forgiveness of sins, in life, and salvation,— then thou shalt be saved. If, on the other hand, thou, a poor, miserable, sinful being, dost in unbelief reject the things which Christ doth give thee in His Word: the salvation which He has earned, and which consists in the forgiveness of sins, in life, and salvation,—then thou shalt be damned. That is the great law, the law of mercy, according to which judgment shall be pronounced. Not according to the law of Moses, not according to our works, will He judge us. And yet, He will make His ruling according to our works too. But only in so far as by works He will publicly establish faith or unbelief. He that believes begins to serve Him with His deeds; he that does not believe does not serve Him with a single deed. Thus by works will He establish faith or unbelief. But that which turns the scales of judgment is faith or unbelief alone.—What a blessing that even now we know exactly according to what rule we shall be judged! There is no doubt nor uncertainty here.

PRAYER.—Lord Jesus, I, a poor sinner, believe in Thee. My soul longeth, yea, even fainteth for Thy salvation. I rely upon Thy Word. O Thou everlasting Father, Thou wilt not enter into judgment with Thy child; Thou Good Shepherd wilt not damn Thy poor sheep. Look not upon my sins: Thou hast atoned for them. Look only upon that new thing which Thy Spirit hath created within me. Thou wilt surely do this, Thou Faithful One. And so with joy and confidence will I approach the day of judgment. I shall not be damned. I shall be saved. Amen.

Hymn 133, 3. 4.

THURSDAY.

Therefore, being justified by faith, we have peace with God through our Lord Jesus Christ:—and rejoice in the hope of the glory of God.—Rom. 5, 1. 2.

We who believe in our Lord Jesus Christ are justified in the sight of God, and have forgiveness of sin. Because God forgives us our sin and justifies us, we have peace with God through our Lord Jesus Christ. God has no further charge against us. He is with us altogether. Because we have peace with God, He will surely not condemn, or damn, us. He will save us, give us eternal life and glory. This is so divinely certain that even now we greatly rejoice in such hope.—This is what Dr. Martin Luther expresses in the words of the Small Catechism: "Where there is forgiveness of sin, there is also life and salvation." Thou, believing Christian, hast forgiveness of sin. Thou knowest that God forgiveth thy sin unto thee. How, then, is it possible that thou shouldst still be damned, since it is only for sin that one can be damned? And that has been forgiven thee. Nothing but sin could prevent thee from obtaining life and salvation. And thou hast forgiveness of sin. Hence thou hast life and salvation also. Thou needst not concern thyself about life and salvation if thou hast forgiveness of sin. Thou art absolutely sure of life and salvation, and needst not fret nor fear, if only thou hast forgiveness of sin. Where there is forgiveness of sin, there is also life and salvation. Do but hold fast to the forgiveness of sin offered thee freely and without price for Christ's sake, and life and salvation will come inevitably. Look cheerfully and confidently beyond death and the judgment, and rejoice in the hope of the glory of God.

PRAYER.—Most heartily I thank Thee, Lord Jesus, that Thou hast merited and given to me forgiveness of my sin. Now I have peace with God and rejoice in the hope of the glory of God. Amen, my God, so let me have life and salvation. O my God, Thou wilt surely do this, for Thou hast forgiven me all my sin. Preserve in me, O Thou faithful God, true faith in my Lord Jesus Christ through whom I have forgiveness of sin. Amen, Thou wilt hear me. Amen.

Hymn 316, 5.

FRIDAY.

Behold, I create new heavens and a new earth; and the former shall not be remembered, nor come into mind.—Is. 65, 17.

Thus God prophesies through the Prophet Isaiah. And again He says: "As the new heavens and the new earth, which I will make, shall remain, saith the Lord, so shall your seed and your name remain," Is. 66, 22. And the Apostle Peter, when speaking of the passing of the heavens and the earth at the second coming of the Lord, continues:

"Nevertheless we, according to His promise, look for new heavens and a new earth wherein dwelleth righteousness," 2 Peter 3, 13. And John, the holy seer, writes: "And I saw a new heaven and a new earth; for the first heaven and the first earth were passed away," Rev. 21, 1. And St. Paul writes: "The creature itself also shall be delivered from the bondage of corruption into the glorious liberty of the children of God," Rom. 8, 21.—These are the last and abiding things which Christ will bring at His second coming, to give unto us, unto His beloved Church, unto all those who from the beginning of the world to the last hour have believed in Him: a new heaven and a new earth. Then shall the former not be remembered, nor come into mind. These shall remain, even as the congregation of the redeemed. There righteousness shall dwell. The creature itself shall partake of the glorious liberty of the children of God, of their freedom from the bondage of corruption, and of their glory. There shall be everlasting joy and blessedness. Heaven shall descend to earth, and earth shall rise to heaven, and heaven and earth united shall be our paradise. O what great things hath the gracious God prepared for us!

PRAYER.—O my God, Thou dost enrapture me. Shall I see, and own, and enjoy, all these things, and forever? Forsooth, Thou sayest it, and Thou Faithful and Almighty One wilt fulfill Thy Word. For Jesus' sake graciously grant me Thine help, O Lord, that I may always remain in the company and congregation of those to whom Thou hast given these great and wondrous promises, that I, too, may bless Thine almighty grace in never-ending rapture. Amen.

Hymn 559, 1.

SATURDAY.

Surely, I come quickly.—Amen. Even so, come, Lord Jesus.—Rev. 22, 20.

When will the Lord Jesus come again in His glory and unto our glory?—"Of that day and hour knoweth no man,"

Second Week in Advent.

says He, "no, not the angels of heaven, but my Father only," Matt. 24, 36. But even John wrote: "Little children, it is the last time," 1 John 2, 18. And Peter: "The end of all things is at hand," 1 Peter 4, 7. And James: "The coming of the Lord draweth nigh. Behold, the Judge standeth before the door," James 5, 8. 9. And St. Paul speaks of the Christians of his own time as such "upon whom the ends of the world are come," 1 Cor. 10, 11. And the Lord Jesus Himself says to the Apostle John: "Surely, I come quickly." Thus, well-nigh nineteen centuries ago the coming of the Lord was declared to be at hand, to be coming soon.—But how about this? Have not centuries upon centuries elapsed since then? Has not generation upon generation returned unto the dust since those days? Does not the old and wretched world still stand? How is this? Has God's Word and Bible come to naught? God forbid! Peter writes: "Beloved, be not ignorant of this one thing, that one day is with the Lord as a thousand years and a thousand years as one day," 2 Peter 3, 8. And furthermore remember that death transports thee in a moment into the presence of the Lord. In death thy body knows of no time, though it is still within the bounds of time. And thy living soul will then no longer dwell in time, but in eternity. And what on earth is a long time is but a moment in eternity. Thus, as I have said, death transports thee in a moment into the presence of the Lord. How near at hand is the coming of the Lord Jesus! "Surely, I come quickly," saith He. And do thou, in joyous, blessed faith, say: "Amen. Even so, come, Lord Jesus."

PRAYER.—Amen. Even so, come, Lord Jesus! Come in that glorious last Advent, or, if so be that I shall not be among the living then, come to meet me at my blessed end. Ah, Lord Jesus, how quickly and speedily, as in a moment, shalt Thou then transport me to that hour when all things shall become new, and a new heavens shall smile upon a new earth. Lord Jesus, grant me grace to be ready at all times. Surely, Thou wilt come quickly. Amen. Even so, come, Lord Jesus! Amen.

Hymn 549, 2.

Third Week in Advent.

SUNDAY.

In all places where I record my name I will come unto thee, and I will bless thee.—Exodus 20, 24.

In the first week of Advent we heard how the Lord, the Son of God, according to His promise, became man and accomplished the work of redemption. In the second week we learned that our dear Lord will come again to judge the quick and the dead, and to establish His eternal Kingdom of Glory. In this week we shall learn how our Savior comes to us now, in this vale of tears, with His salvation and His grace.

God the Son, the Lord, had descended upon holy Sinai with an innumerable company of His heavenly hosts, and had given His Law with flaming fire.* And the people trembled greatly. There the Lord appointed unto the people the sacrifice which, until the fullness of time, was to typify His atoning death on the cross of Golgotha. And in this connection He said: "In all places where I record my name I will come unto thee, and I will bless thee." So wherever man, according to God's ordinance and institution, would remember Him as the Atoner, Redeemer, and Savior, there He would come to Him with His gracious salvation, with His saving grace, and bless him.— This word of the Lord is valid even in New Testament times, in our day. Wherever the Gospel of Christ, the Savior of sinners, is read, taught, preached, and heard, and wherever by His command men baptize and administer Holy Communion, there our Lord and Savior comes to us with His grace, His salvation, and blesses us. There we must salute Him in trusting faith, and confidently accept His salvation, His grace, His blessing.

PRAYER.—Lord Jesus, my Savior and my eternal King, now I know where I, a poor sinner, haunted with sorrows, shall find Thee and all Thy grace and all Thy salvation,

---

* Compare Ps. 68, 17. 18, with Eph. 4, 8-10.

Thou comest unto me in Thy Word and in Thy holy Sacraments, and blessest me with an everlasting blessing. Grant me grace, O Lord, to continue steadfast in the right and true faith, that at all times I may seek Thee and Thy salvation in these Thy blessed means of grace, and hold fast unto Thee, until Thou shalt come to take me where I shall see Thee in everlasting joy and blessedness. Amen.

Hymn 142, 2.

MONDAY.

But the righteousness which is of faith speaketh on this wise, Say not in thine heart, Who shall ascend into heaven (that is, to bring Christ down from above)? or, Who shall descend into the deep (that is, to bring Christ up again from the dead)? But what saith it? The word is nigh thee, even in thy mouth and in thy heart: that is, the Word of Faith, which we preach.—Rom. 10, 6-8.

What do these words teach? They teach this: If thou wouldst have Christ and, with Him, the righteousness that availeth before God, be undismayed, and say not, How shall I ascend into heaven to get Christ down from above? or, How shall I descend into the deep to bring Christ up again from the dead? But this is what thou must say, right cheerfully and confidently: I have the *Word,* the word of faith in Christ. I have that Word in my Bible; that Word is preached to me; that Word is in my heart: I believe it; that Word is in my mouth: I confess it; that Word is very near to me and is my own. And just so near, and just so my own, is Christ, and, with Him, the righteousness that availeth before God. Indeed, so shalt thou say. For Christ has put Himself, and the righteousness which He procured and wherewith thou canst stand before God, into the Word, that thou shouldst take it, yea, Him. So thou needst not join in the lament of those recent hymn-writers who tell of their great pain and sorrow and loss of peace at not finding Jesus, and who long for wings, that they might soar o'er hill and valley to seek Him. On the contrary, thou mayest shout and say: Lord, Thou art with me, Thou art with me in Thy Word.

Third Week in Advent.

PRAYER.—Indeed, O my Lord Jesus, my **righteousness** wherewith I, a poor sinner, may stand before God, my life and my salvation: Thou art with me. Thou hast put Thyself and all Thy salvation into the Word, and thus Thou comest unto me, and art very near to me, and dost embed Thyself in the inmost recesses of my heart, to make me sure that Thou wilt be mine in all eternity. I give unceasing thanks unto Thee for this Thy great mercy and gracious kindness. Grant me Thy Holy Spirit that at all times I may hold Thee and never leave Thee, Lord Jesus. Amen.

Hymn 117, 4.

TUESDAY.

Ye are all the children of God by faith in Christ Jesus. For as many of you as have been baptized into Christ have put on Christ.—Gal. 3, 26. 27.

Faith is the only means through which Christ and His salvation becomes our own, and through which we thus become the children of God in time and eternity. Therefore the Holy Ghost saith to the believing Christians: "Ye are all the children of God by faith in Christ Jesus." Such is the strength of faith, but not because it is a noble virtue, and a beautiful and good work on the part of the Christians; no, such is the strength of faith, because it is merely the acceptance of what God gives. First comes God and gives us Christ and His salvation, and then we accept Christ and His salvation, that is, we believe. And as through the Word, so also through *Baptism,* does God give us Christ and His salvation. Word and Baptism belong together. Through Baptism God has steeped us into Christ and His salvation, so that the floods of grace and salvation compass us about. Through Baptism God has clothed us sinners with Christ, as with the garment of salvation and the robe of righteousness. And now me must willingly suffer the love of God to do so, and say: Amen, O God; thanks, thanks be unto Thee, my God! That is faith. Through such faith Christ and His salvation actually become our own, Christ and His salvation given us in Baptism.—Through Baptism Christ has come to thee also, O Christian, with His salvation. Now consider thy Baptism with the eyes of faith, and the things which God there has given to thee, and say: "I am a child of God through faith in Christ Jesus, for I have been baptized and have put on Christ." With such words of faith thou wilt surely prevail in time and eternity.

PRAYER.—Lord Jesus, Thou art the flood of grace and salvation into which I have been steeped in Baptism. Thou art the garment of salvation and the robe of righteousness with which I have been clad in Baptism. This I believe, Lord Jesus. Keep me in such faith! Grant that against all the horrors of sin and of death and of hell I plead my baptism. For do I not know that God will never retract what He so solemnly has certified to me? Nay, my God, Thou wilt most certainly not withdraw what in Baptism Thou hast given to me. Amen.

Hymn 544, 9.

WEDNESDAY.

And David said unto Nathan, I have sinned against the Lord. And Nathan said unto David, The Lord hath also put away thy sin; thou shalt not die.—2 Sam. 12, 13.

If, like David, penitent and athirst for mercy, thou confessest thy sin, where, then, is the prophet to forgive thee thy sin in the name of the Lord, and to make thee sure of obtaining life, eternal life? Or where is Jesus Himself to comfort thee thus?—If in the church-service which we call "Confession" thou confessest thy sin before the confessor, that is to say, the called minister of the Word, as before God Himself; and if the confessor thereupon pronounces absolution, or forgiveness, unto thee in the name of the Lord, then this is as valid and certain, in heaven also, as if Christ, thy dear Lord, dealt with thee Himself, and thou must never doubt, but firmly believe, that thereby thy sins are forgiven before God in heaven. For thus writes the holy Evangelist John, chapter 20: "The Lord Jesus breathed on His disciples and saith unto them, Receive ye the Holy Ghost: whosesoever sins ye remit, they are remitted unto them." Thus the Lord Jesus has given unto His disciples

Third Week in Advent.   23

the power to remit sins, so that thereby the sins are actually forgiven. His believing disciples exercise this power publicly in their congregations through their called ministers of the Word. Thus in "Confession" Christ, the Lord, is Himself truly present, and by the mouth of His called minister of the Word declares unto thee the forgiveness of thy sins, and assures thee of eternal life. O wondrous mercy, wondrous consolation! Do but open the eyes of faith and see how mercifully near unto thee thy Savior is. And comfort thyself with this mercy of His.

PRAYER.—Lord Jesus, I, a poor sinner, athirst for mercy, do not fall short of David as regards mercy and consolation. Thou, even Thou, my Savior, through Thy minister of the Word, dost proclaim unto me a complete absolution of all my sins. And such mercy, such consolation, I may have as often as I desire it. The river of Thy mercy runs forever. For this I give Thee most hearty thanks. Draw me poor sinner through Thy Holy Ghost to come again and again, and to receive grace for grace from Thee, my ever-present, gracious, and blessed Savior. Amen.

Hymn 426, 6. 10.

THURSDAY.

And as they were eating, Jesus took bread, and blessed it, and brake it, and gave it to His disciples, and said, Take, eat; this is my body. And He took the cup, and gave thanks, and gave it to them, saying, Drink ye all of it; for this is my blood of the new testament, which is shed for many for the remission of sins.—Matt. 26, 26-28.

Thus was *the Lord's Supper* instituted, which Christians are to continue celebrating until the coming of the Lord Jesus. For the Holy Ghost saith through Paul the Apostle: "As often as ye eat this bread, and drink this cup, ye do show the Lord's death till He come," 1 Cor. 11, 26. Just as in the Word, and in Baptism, and in Confession, so our Lord also comes to us in Holy Communion, giving us His salvation, which is forgiveness of sin, life, and eternal salvation. How clearly do we behold particularly in the Lord's Supper that our dear Savior, though unseen, yet bodily and truly, communes with us in this sad world. In Holy Communion, under the bread and wine, He gives us His body and His blood,—the body which was given into death for us, the blood which was shed for us for the forgiveness of sins. He gives us His body and His blood that it may be unto us the most solemn and trustworthy pledge of the free forgiveness of our sins, and of life and eternal salvation. Could He do more to prove His loving-kindness and gracious condescension? How eagerly, therefore, ought we poor, but highly favored sinners hasten to receive Him who so kindly visits us, and bestows such gracious gifts upon us!

PRAYER.—Of a truth, my dear Lord Jesus, Thou dost not leave me to myself here below. Thou visitest me, and in the most wondrous way dost give Thyself wholly unto me, that I, poor sinner, might be saved through Thee. Thou lavishest Thy grace upon me. For food and drink unto eternal life Thou givest me Thy body and Thy blood. Thou wouldst render me utterly firm in faith, and confident that Thou wilt surely save me. Why should I stand back, or even stand at a distance, when Thou so kindly beckonest and callest? Through Thy Holy Spirit draw me to accept Thy great mercy. Amen.

Hymn 432, 2.

FRIDAY.

Lo, I am with you alway, even unto the end of the world. Matt. 28, 20.

Thus spake the risen Savior to the congregation of His disciples which, together with the eleven Apostles, had been assembled on a mount in Galilee. "You" means all His disciples unto the end of the world. He comes to us through His Word and Sacrament, and is with us alway. But only through His Word and Sacrament does He make Himself known unto us; and there we take Him, Him and His salvation. He is with us alway, in great mercy, love, and truth. He does not leave His own to themselves, comfortless, in this wicked world: He is with us. Thanks be unto

Thee, Lord Jesus! And what is it, above all, that He wants to accomplish by His presence? By means of our word and testimony He wants to gain more men for His blessed kingdom; and us, and all those so gained, He wants to keep in faith unto the end, unto salvation. That is His chief aim. And what could be better? What does all other gain profit us, if we do not remain in the faith and finally will not be saved? To this end He governs our whole life, and causes all things to work together for good to them. Thanks be unto Thee, Lord Jesus! He is with us alway, the Almighty, the All-merciful. He is with us with a tenderness greater than that of a mother. He has given His angels charge concerning us to keep us in all our ways. But the watch His angels keep is as nothing compared with His. He is with us when we sleep, when we wake, when we weep, when we laugh, when we err, when we fear, when we cry and yearn for Him. He is with us alway, and guards us against the devil, the world, and ourselves,—against our wicked heart, which forever wants to err. He is with us alway, until, at last, we shall be with Him forevermore.

PRAYER.—Thanks be unto Thee, Lord Jesus, that Thou art with me alway. I rejoice now that I know this, now that I know I am in Thy care, in Thy keeping, in Thy protection. Abide with me, Lord Jesus, and do not leave me unto myself. Keep me as the apple of Thine eye, Lord Jesus. Into Thy trusty saving hand I wholly commend both my body and soul. I cannot find the way to heaven alone, nor can protect myself against mine enemies. But Thou art with me. Thanks be unto Thee, dear Savior! Amen.

Hymn 9, 6.

SATURDAY.

Behold, I see the heavens opened, and the Son of Man standing on the right hand of God.—Acts 7, 56.

When our last hour comes, the crisis will be at hand, the great crisis, as physicians call that turning-point of a sickness which makes it plain whether recovery or death will be the final outcome. All who in the hour of death will be found to believe in Christ will be saved; those, however, who will lack this faith will be damned. And it is just in the hour of death, the most important and critical hour, that we are very weak, most exceedingly so, least able to accomplish anything ourselves. It is just then that the Evil Foe will see his opportunity for making the last and fiercest assault upon us. And what then?—When Stephen knew that his last hour was at hand, he, being full of the Holy Ghost, looked up into heaven and saw the glory of God, and Jesus standing on the right hand of God, and he said: "Behold, I see the heavens opened, and the Son of Man standing on the right hand of God." He saw that Jesus was going to be with him in death and to help him.—I tell thee, Christian, just when thou needest the Savior most, He will be nearest to thee, to rescue thee. Then will His strength be made perfect in thy weakness. And thou shalt conquer all, yea, all the terrors of death. This is most certainly true.—But let no man defer his conversion to that hour when reason, sense, and thinking fail like a flickering light that to and fro doth waver, ere 'tis extinguished quite. To-day thou livest, to-day repent! Be His own now, that in thy last hour Jesus may own thee and deliver thee.

PRAYER.—Lord Jesus, grant that through Thy Word and Holy Ghost now and always I may believe in Thee and be Thine own. And when my last hour shall come, then do come, Thou faithful Savior, and grant me Thy strength, and keep the devil from me, and receive my spirit as Thou receivedst that of Stephen. Amen. Thou wilt do this, Thou faithful Savior, who sayest regarding Thy sheep: "I give unto them eternal life; and they shall never perish, neither shall any man pluck them out of my hand." Amen, Lord Jesus, Amen.

Hymn 201, 9.

Fourth Week in Advent.

SUNDAY.

When the fullness of the time was come.—Gal. 4, 4.

We will now speak of the time when God, according to His eternal counsel, began to fulfill all the prophecies and promises regarding the coming of the Savior. For four thousand years the congregation of believers had waited for this time to come. Many a time they had yearned for the Savior, crying: "Oh, that Thou wouldest rend the heavens, that Thou wouldest come down!" Many a time their eager, anxious question was, "Watchman, what of the night? Watchman, what of the night?" The stars of prophecy and promise shone bright and clear, and filled the night with splendor. But, withal, it was night. The light of dawn did not yet brighten the eastern sky, and the Sun, the eternal Sun, did not yet rise. Generation upon generation of believers had been gathered to their fathers, waiting, hoping, trusting, that the fullness of time would come. And their waiting, hope, and trust was not to be put to shame. The fullness of time did come. The Apostle says, inspired by the Holy Ghost: "When the fullness of the time was come." He speaks of that which has actually come to pass. The dawn has appeared, the Sun has arisen, fully 1900 years ago. The present-day congregation of believers, looking back in faith upon what has come to pass, joyfully shouts: Hallelujah! Christ has come! All the promises of God in Him are yea, and in Him Amen, unto the glory of God. God always makes good His promises. He will surely also fulfill all the promises pertaining to the eternal kingdom of Christ, the Kingdom of Glory. No promise shall fail. Meanwhile, may His Word uphold us!

PRAYER.—Lord God, Thou hast fulfilled Thy promise. Thou hast sent Thy Son. Thou hast sent us our Savior. The Sun did arise, and He giveth light to us in Thy Word. Therefore we are glad. Hallelujah! O Jesus, my Sun, my Lord, shine within my heart, and dispel all the shades of night! O Thou Spirit of the Father and of the Son, let me live and die in faith, and thereafter let me arise with joy and enter eternal life. Amen.

Hymn 146, 2. 3.

MONDAY.

Behold, I will send my messenger, and he shall prepare the way before me.—Mal. 3, 1.

Immediately before the appearance of Christ a messenger, or preacher, was to come who, by most impressively preaching repentance, should prepare the Savior's coming into the hearts of men. This had been prophesied three times. (Is. 40, 3-5; Mal. 3, 1; 4, 5. 6.) And when God in a miraculous way sent word that this preparer of the way should be born, there appeared the first glimmer of the dawn of breaking day, the day of the fulfillment, of all prophecies. Hear how it was done.

In the days of King Herod there lived in the land of Judea a priest named Zacharias, and his wife's name was Elisabeth. They were both sincerely pious. And they had no child, and were now well stricken in years. One day, while Zacharias was burning incense in the temple, and the multitude of the people prayed without, in the court of the temple, there appeared to him an angel of the Lord standing on the right side of the altar of incense. When Zacharias saw him, he was troubled. But the angel said to him: "Fear not, Zacharias; for thy prayer is heard, and thy wife Elisabeth shall bear thee a son, and thou shalt call his name *John*. And thou shalt have joy and gladness; and many shall rejoice at his birth. For he shall be great in the sight of the Lord, and shall drink neither wine nor strong drink; and he shall be filled with the Holy Ghost, even from his mother's womb. And many of the children of Israel shall he turn to the Lord, their God. *And he shall go before Him in the spirit and power of Elias* to turn the hearts of the fathers to the children and the disobedient to the wisdom of the just, *to make ready a people prepared for the Lord."* Zacharias said: "Whereby shall I know this? For I am an old man, and my wife well stricken in years." The angel answered: "I am Gabriel, that stand in the presence of God, and am sent to speak unto thee, and to show thee these glad tidings. And, behold, thou shalt be dumb, and not able to speak, until the day that these things shall be performed, because thou believest not my words, which shall be fulfilled in their season." And Zacharias remained speechless until his son John was born. (Luke 1, 5-25.)

O ye Christians, do not disdain to contemplate, both with eye and heart, the time when the precious, wondrous deeds of God for our salvation were accomplished!

PRAYER.—Most heartily do I give thanks unto Thee, most merciful and true God, for having fulfilled Thy Word given through the prophets, and for causing that day of salvation to dawn which so gladdens my heart. Let this Thy work, I beseech Thee, be the light of mine eyes, and the joy of my heart, that my faith may be true and well grounded, not on anything that I may have done, but solely on what Thou hast graciously perfected, and on Thy Word, which is firm and unchanging, even as Thou art, God, blessed forever. Amen.

Hymn 147, 4.

TUESDAY.

Behold, a virgin shall conceive, and bear a son, and shall call His name Immanuel.—Is. 7, 14.

Six months after the events told yesterday, the angel Gabriel was sent from God into a city of Galilee named Nazareth, to a virgin of the house and lineage of David, espoused to a man whose name was Joseph, also of the house of David: and the virgin's name was Mary. And the angel came in unto her and said: "Hail, thou art highly favored; the Lord is with thee: blessed art thou among women." And when she saw him, she was troubled at his saying, and cast in her mind what manner of salutation this should be. And the angel said unto her: "Fear not, Mary; for thou hast found favor with God. *And, behold, thou shalt conceive in thy womb, and bring forth a son, and shalt call His name JESUS.* He shall be great, and shall be called the Son of the Highest. And the Lord God shall give unto Him the throne of His father David. And He shall reign over the house of David forever; and of His kingdom there shall be no end." Then Mary said unto the angel: "How shall this be, seeing I know not a man?" And the angel answered and said unto her: "The Holy Ghost shall come upon thee, and the power of the Highest shall overshadow thee; therefore also that holy thing which shall be born of thee shall be called the Son of God. And, behold, thy cousin Elisabeth, she hath also conceived a son in her old age: and this is the sixth month with her, who was called barren. For with God nothing shall be impossible." And Mary said: "Behold the handmaid of the Lord; be it unto me according to thy word." And the angel departed from her. (Luke 1, 26-38.) —Thus was the above prophecy fulfilled. The eternal Son of God had become man in the womb of the Virgin Mary, conceived of the Holy Ghost.

PRAYER.—Lord God, Heavenly Father, I thank Thee for Thine unspeakable grace, that Thou hast regarded us poor sinners, and has sent Thy Son into our flesh, and hast caused Him to become man for us. I pray Thee so to illumine my heart with Thy Holy Spirit, that I comfort myself with His incarnation, suffering, and death, and know and accept Him as my Lord and eternal King, and that through Him I may live with Thee and the Holy Ghost in eternal blessedness. Amen.

Hymn 148, 1-3.

WEDNESDAY.

Blessed is she that believed.—Luke 1, 45.

In those days, when the angel Gabriel had made the great annunciation to Mary, she arose and went with haste from Nazareth, in Galilee, into that city of Judea where Zacharias and Elisabeth lived. And she entered into the house of Zacharias and saluted Elisabeth. And it came to pass that, when Elisabeth heard the salutation of Mary, the babe leaped in her womb. And Elisabeth was filled with the Holy Ghost; and she spoke out with a loud voice and said: "Blessed art thou among women, and blessed is the fruit of thy womb. And whence is this to me that the mother of my Lord should come to me? For, lo, as soon as the voice of thy salutation sounded in mine ears, the babe leaped in my womb for joy. And blessed is she that believed: for there shall be a performance of those things which were told her from the Lord." And Mary, also, was filled with the Holy Ghost, and uttered that beautiful psalm, the "Magnificat," which begins with the words: "My soul doth magnify the Lord, and my spirit hath rejoiced in God, my Savior," and which thou mayest read in the Bible. And Mary abode with Elisabeth three months, and returned to her own house. (Luke 1, 39-56.)

Oh, I know of no story which breathes such glorious faith as this. Consider! Elisabeth called Mary "the mother of my Lord." She blessed Mary, she blessed the fruit of her womb. She was full of faith and joy, in the Savior. And Mary, in blessed rapture, blessed God, that God who now had become her Savior—and her child. And even unborn John, as the angel had foretold, was filled with the Holy Ghost in his mother's womb, and saluted his Savior. What blessed believers! God grant us His Holy Ghost, that we, likewise, may rejoice in the fullness of faith!

PRAYER.—Behold, O faithful God, the pitiful condition of my heart. Indeed, by Thy grace I believe in Thee, my Savior Jesus Christ. But my poor sinful heart is so barren, quick to grasp earthly, slow to grasp heavenly things. God Holy Spirit, Thou my only Strength, quicken my faith through Thy Word, that the divine fire may burn brightly within me so that I may experience heartfelt joy and gladness in my Savior and great love for Him. Amen.

Hymn 152.

THURSDAY.

The dayspring from on high hath visited us to give light to them that sit in darkness and in the shadow of death, to guide our feet into the way of peace.—Luke 1, 78. 79.

And Elisabeth brought forth a son. And she rejoiced greatly, and her neighbors and her cousins rejoiced with

Fourth Week in Advent.

her. On the eighth day they came to circumcise the child, and meant to call him Zacharias, after his father. But his mother exclaimed: "Not so; but he shall be called John." They marveled and called his father. Asking for a writing-table, he wrote: "His name is John." And straightway his mouth was opened, and, filled with the Holy Ghost, he prophesied and said: "Blessed be the Lord God of Israel; for He hath visited and redeemed His people, and hath raised up a horn of salvation for us in the house of His servant David, as He spake by the mouth of His holy prophets which have been since the world began, that we should be saved from our enemies, and from the hand of all that hate us; to perform the mercy promised to our fathers, and to remember His holy covenant; the oath which He swore to our father Abraham, that He would grant unto us, that we, being delivered out of the hand of our enemies, might serve Him without fear, in holiness and righteousness before Him, all the days of our life." And turning to the babe, he said: "And thou, child, shalt be called the prophet of the Highest; for thou shalt go before the face of the Lord to prepare His ways, to give knowledge of salvation unto His people by the remission of their sins, through the tender mercy of our God, whereby the dayspring from on high hath visited us, to give light to them that sit in darkness and in the shadow of death, to guide our feet into the way of peace." (Luke 1, 57-79.)

PRAYER.—Lord Jesus Christ, Thou art the dayspring from on high; Thou art the eternal Son of the Father, our Light and Salvation; Thou hast appeared and dost give light to us who sit in darkness and in the shadow of death, and hast guided our feet into the way of eternal peace. In Thee, Lord Jesus, is our salvation, the forgiveness of all our sins. What tender mercy of our God! Thou, our God, hast truly kept Thy Word, Thou hast raised up a horn of salvation for us, which is Jesus Christ, our Lord, the Son of David; through Him Thou hast saved and delivered us out of the hands of all our enemies, that now we are Thine own, and may serve Thee with joyful, childlike hearts all the days of our life, until Thou shalt take us home. Praise and glory be unto Thee, O God of mercy! Grant that I may always keep Thy Word through which Thou impartest unto me all Thy salvation, divine power to firmly believe what Thy Word teaches me regarding this salvation. Amen.

Hymn 147, 5.

FIRST CHRISTMAS DAY.

Unto us a Child is born, unto us a Son is given. And the government shall be upon His shoulder; and His name shall be called Wonderful, Counselor, The mighty God, The everlasting Father, The Prince of Peace.—Is. 9, 6.

This is the prophecy the fulfillment of which Christendom celebrates to-day.

Joseph had been told by God, through an angel, that Mary, his espoused wife, was that virgin of whom Isaiah had spoken (7, 14), and in obedience to the command of God he had taken her unto himself. But that was in Nazareth of Galilee, and, according to the prophecy of Micah (5, 1), Christ was to be born in Bethlehem of Judea. And so it came to pass in those days that there went out a decree from Cæsar Augustus that all the world should be taxed. This was the first taxing of its kind. And all went to be taxed, every one into his own city. And Joseph also went, with Mary, his espoused wife, to Bethlehem, the city of David, because he was of the house and lineage of David. And while they were there, the days were accomplished that Mary should be delivered. And she brought forth her first-born son, and wrapped Him in swaddling clothes, and laid Him in a manger, because there was no room for them in the inn. (Luke 2, 1-7.)

Christians! Unto us this Child is born, unto us this Son is given—to be our Redeemer. A poor babe He lay there in the manger, but the government of heaven and earth was upon His shoulders. Was not that wonderful? This Child Himself is the Wonderful, for He is God and He is man, and His conception and birth were supernatural. This Child is the Counselor who counsels and helps us lost and condemned sinners when we are utterly at a loss for counsel and help. He is the mighty God who bruises the devil's

Zorn, Crumbs.

head and saves us. He is the everlasting Father unto us, His redeemed; we are to be His blessed children, here in time and hereafter in eternity. He is the Prince of Peace; for His subjects have peace of heart and conscience, until the rivers of eternal peace shall refresh them forevermore. O ye Christians, embrace this Child in true faith!

PRAYER.—Lord God, Heavenly Father, I give thanks unto Thee for Thy great mercy and kindness in having Thine only-begotten Son become flesh, thus graciously saving us from sin and eternal death. I pray Thee, enlighten my heart by Thy Holy Spirit, that I may remain thankful for such grace and comfort myself with the same in every tribulation and temptation, and so be eternally saved through Him, my Savior. Amen.

Hymn 156, 2. 3.

SECOND CHRISTMAS DAY.

Thus saith the Lord: The people that walked in darkness have seen a great light; they that dwell in the land of the shadow of death, upon them hath the light shined.—Is. 9, 2.

And there were in the same country shepherds abiding in the field, keeping watch over their flock by night. And, lo, the angel of the Lord came upon them, and the glory of the Lord shone round about them; and they were sore afraid. And the angel said unto them: "Fear not; for, behold, I bring you good tidings of great joy which shall be to all people. For unto you is born this day in the city of David a Savior, who is Christ the Lord. And this shall be a sign unto you: Ye shall find the Babe wrapped in swaddling-clothes, lying in a manger." And suddenly there was with the angel a multitude of the heavenly host praising God and saying: "Glory to God in the highest, and on earth peace, good will toward men."—And it came to pass, as the angels were gone away from them into heaven, the shepherds said one to another: "Let us now go even unto Bethlehem, and see this thing which is come to pass, which the Lord hath made known unto us." And they came with haste, and found

Mary and Joseph and the Babe lying in the manger. And when they had seen it, they made known abroad the saying which was told them concerning this Child. And all they that heard it wondered at all those things which were told them by the shepherds. But Mary kept all these things, and pondered them in her heart. And the shepherds returned, glorifying and praising God for all the things that they had heard and seen, as it was told unto them. (Luke 2, 8-20.)

In these words we, too, see heavenly glory and eternal salvation, for we see the Savior. Here all darkness must vanish. All fear is turned to gladness. Let us seek and see the Savior in His Word, that we may be sure of being His in faith. Let us tell others of Him. Let us keep His Word and ponder it in our hearts. Let us joyously glorify and praise God for His great mercy.

PRAYER.—Gracious and merciful God, I give thanks unto Thee, that Thou didst not leave us poor, lost sinners in darkness, but didst send us the promised Savior, the true and eternal Light, and didst cause Thy Word to be preached to us. O faithful God, cause this light to shine into my poor heart, that, enlightened by true faith, I may constantly magnify and praise Thee through the same Thy Son, Jesus Christ, our Lord and Savior. Amen.

Hymn 141, 6. 7.

Week of Sunday After Christmas.

SUNDAY.

And when eight days were accomplished for the circumcising of the Child, His name was called JESUS, which was so named of the angel before He was conceived in the womb. Luke 2, 21.

Circumcision in the Old Testament signified that all mankind is conceived and born in sin, and consequently under the wrath of God and lost forever, unless saved and cleansed by the blood of Christ. And through this same circumcision God imparted the saving and cleansing power of the blood of Christ which was to be shed in the fullness of time. Herewith the believers in the Old Covenant were to comfort themselves always, and thus to become and remain partakers of such grace. Thus circumcision in the Old Testament was what Holy Baptism is to-day.—When the Christ-child was eight days old, He was circumcised, although He was without sin. But upon Him lay the sin of the whole world, and He was made to be under the Law for us. Circumcision for the Christ-child was a pledge that He would surely save the whole world from all its sins through His blood. For that reason He received the name JESUS when He was circumcised in accordance with the instruction given by the angel; for Jesus means Redeemer, Savior. Unto this name, to this Child, to this Redeemer and Savior, we must look in life and death. Then we shall be His own and partakers of His salvation.

PRAYER.—Lord Jesus, Thou hast borne the sins of the whole world, and mine also; with Thy blood Thou hast blotted out the sins of the whole world, and mine too. Thou art my Redeemer, my Savior, my Jesus. Write, I beseech Thee, this name Jesus upon the tablet of my heart, that it may forever glow and glisten there, in life and in death. Amen.

Hymn 178.

MONDAY.

Lord, now lettest Thou Thy servant depart in peace, . . . for mine eyes have seen Thy salvation.—Luke 2, 29. 30.

When Christ was born, there was a man in Jerusalem named Simeon. He was just and devout, waiting for the consolation of Israel, the promised Savior; and the Holy Ghost was upon him. And it was revealed unto him by the Holy Ghost that he should not see death, before—O what blessing!—he had seen the Lord's Christ. Now, six weeks after the birth of Jesus, when Joseph and Mary brought the Child to the temple at Jerusalem to present Him unto the Lord, and to offer the sacrifice of purification, as prescribed

Week of Sunday After Christmas.   37

in the law of Moses (Exod. 13, 2; Lev. 12), this aged Simeon, moved by the Spirit, also came to the temple. As soon as he saw the Child, he took Him up in his arms, and blessed God, and said: "Lord, now lettest Thou Thy servant depart in peace, according to Thy word; for mine eyes have seen Thy salvation which Thou hast prepared before the face of all people, a light to lighten the Gentiles, and the glory of Thy people Israel." Joseph and Mary saw and heard this, and were filled with holy and increasing wonderment. (Luke 2, 22-23.)

God is just as gracious to us as He was to Simeon. We can likewise see the Savior while we live, to wit, in His Word. We also can take Him in our arms, to wit, in His Word and holy Sacraments. Our hearts, too, shall rejoice in Him in blissful joy, to wit, through the Holy Ghost who is given us. And so we, too, shall one day depart in peace; for he that sees and embraces his Savior in true faith, and rejoices in Him, has eternal life.

PRAYER.—I thank Thee, Lord Jesus, my only Savior, my Life and my Salvation, that I may see Thee, and embrace Thee, and rejoice in Thee. Now I know that when my last hour shall come I shall depart in peace. Grant me Thy Holy Spirit, that at all times I may look unto Thee, and, embracing Thee, may always find in Thee my greatest joy. And when my last hour cometh, give, O give, unto me that eternal peace which Thou hast earned for me, O Jesus! Amen.

Hymn 190, 2. 4.

TUESDAY.

This Child is set for the fall and rising again of many in Israel.—Luke 2, 34.

Aged Simeon, of whom we read yesterday, finally blessed Joseph and Mary. And then he prophesied concerning the Christ-child, saying to Mary, His mother: "Behold, this Child is set for the fall and rising again of many in Israel, and for a sign which shall be spoken against, (yea, a sword shall pierce through thine own soul also,) that the thoughts of many hearts may be revealed."—Jesus is the corner-stone of that temple of God which shall grow until the last day, His redeemed and believing Church. Those who in unbelief stumble and are offended at Him shall fall into eternal destruction. But those poor and prostrate sinners who in faith lay hold on Him, and strengthen themselves in Him, shall rise to new and eternal life. Jesus is the great sign demonstrating the grace of God toward us poor sinners. But how did they gainsay Him! Think of His cross! There the sword, as prophesied, pierced deepest through the soul of Mary. When men so gainsay Him, now as ever, then the thoughts, the wicked, godless thoughts of hearts, are revealed in their nakedness. Judgment Day will show this. O thou that readest this, let the Spirit of Jesus Christ govern thee to believe in the Savior, and to strengthen thyself in Him, and to stand in the grace of God, and to enter eternal life!

PRAYER.—Lord God, dear Heavenly Father, who through holy Simeon didst foretell that Christ, Thy Son, is set for a fall and rising again of many in Israel, enlighten my heart, I beseech Thee, through Thy Holy Ghost, to know Thy Son Christ to be my Savior, always to stay with Him, and to rise in Him, but not, like the blind and careless world, to stumble at Him and fall. Grant, O Lord, that I may ever be a living stone of Thy temple which is built on Christ, the only corner-stone, and which is Thy habitation, Thou gracious Triune God. Amen.

Hymn 190, 5.

WEDNESDAY.

We have also a more sure word of prophecy, whereunto ye do well that ye take heed as unto a light that shineth in a dark place.—2 Peter 1, 19.

In the East, for centuries, there had been a caste of learned men devoted to the sciences. In times past the Prophet Daniel had been master of them, and to him and his book they owed the knowledge of Christ, the expected "King of the Jews," which was common among them. When the time of Jesus' birth was at hand, God caused these men to

Week of Sunday After Christmas.

see a peculiar star, and gave them to know that this star indicated the birth of Christ which was now to come to pass.—Hence, when Jesus was born, the Wise Men came from the East to Jerusalem, saying: "Where is He that is born King of the Jews? for we have seen His star in the East, and are come to worship Him." When Herod the King heard these things, he was troubled, and all Jerusalem with him. And when he had gathered all the chief priests and the scribes of the people together, he demanded of them where Christ should be born. And they said to him: "In Bethlehem of Judea; for thus it is written by the prophet, And thou Bethlehem, in the land of Juda, art not the least of the princes of Juda; for out of thee shall come a Governor that shall rule my people Israel." Then Herod privily called the Wise Men, and enquired of them diligently at what time the star had appeared. And he sent them to Bethlehem and said: "Go and search diligently for the Child; and when ye have found Him, bring me word again that I may come and worship Him also." When they had heard the king, they departed; and, lo, the star which they saw in the East went before them, till it came and stood over where the young Child was. When they saw the star, they rejoiced with exceeding great joy. And when they were come into the house, they saw the young Child with Mary, His mother, and fell down and worshiped Him. And when they had opened their treasures, they presented unto Him gifts, gold and frankincense and myrrh. And being warned of God in a dream that they should not return to Herod, they departed into their own country another way. (Matt. 2, 1-12.)

We have something better and more sure than the star which the Wise Men saw. We have the Word of God, which points to Christ and leads us to Christ. Let us look there. Let that be our guiding star.

PRAYER.—Lord God, Heavenly Father, who guidest us through Thy Word, which is the true star, pointing to the Child Jesus, we pray Thee, endue our hearts with Thy Holy Spirit, that we who are called Christians may receive that light, make blessed use of it, and thereby be led to Jesus, our Savior, and thus into eternal light. Amen.

Hymn 179, 6.

THURSDAY.

They are dead who sought the young Child's life.—Matt. 2, 20.

When the Wise Men had departed from Bethlehem, behold, the angel of the Lord appeared to Joseph in a dream, saying: "Arise, and take the young Child and His mother, and flee into Egypt, and be thou there until I bring thee word; for Herod will seek the young Child to destroy Him." And Joseph arose and took the young Child and His mother by night, and departed into Egypt.—When Herod saw that he was mocked, as he called it, by the Wise Men, he was exceeding wroth, and sent forth, and slew all the children that were in Bethlehem and in all the borders thereof, from two years old and under, according to the time which he had diligently enquired of the Wise Men. Then was fulfilled that which was spoken by Jeremy the prophet, saying: "In Rama was there a voice heard, lamentation and weeping and great mourning, Rachel weeping for her children, and would not be comforted, because they are not." But when Herod was dead, behold, an angel of the Lord appeareth in a dream to Joseph in Egypt, saying: "Arise, and take the young Child and His mother, and go into the land of Israel; for they are dead who sought the young Child's life." And he arose, and took the young Child and His mother, and came into the land of Israel. But when he heard that Archelaus reigned in Judea after the death of his father Herod, he was afraid to go to Bethlehem. And being warned by God in a dream, he turned into the parts of Galilee, and dwelt again in Nazareth. Thus two prophecies were fulfilled: "Out of Egypt have I called my Son," and: "He shall be called Nazarene." (Matt. 2, 13-23.)

Carnal-minded Herod meant to kill the Christ-child, but God rescued Him. The carnal-minded world means to destroy the Church, Christendom; but God will keep it, and when it comes to the utmost, will take it to Himself in heaven.

as He did with the infants at Bethlehem. To the world, however, that saying applies: "They are dead who sought the young Child's life." And what then? Ah, fear not the impotent rage of Christ's enemies!

PRAYER.—Christ Jesus, true God and man, bring to naught the counsels of all who persecute Thy holy name, that their wicked machinations may be put to shame with them. But let us, whom Thou hast taken into Thy gracious favor, enjoy the protection of the holy angels, that we, being protected in body and soul, may lastly, with joy, enter eternal life, which Thou hast merited for us by Thy willing death upon the cross. Amen.

Hymn 279, 1. 3.

NEW YEAR'S DAY.

I will not leave thee until I have done that which I have spoken to thee of.—Gen. 28, 15.

To-day thou enterest a new year, O Christian, and thou knowest not what it hath in store for thee. In Christ God hath given thee the most solemn assurances of His grace, of protection, of guidance on your pilgrimage to the eternal home. Enemies will waylay thee, oppose thee, enemies cruelly armed with deep guile and great might. But God will stand between thee and them. And if thine eyes were opened as were Jacob's (Gen. 32, 1. 2), thou wouldst see the angels of God meet thee, and thou wouldst shout: Mahanaim, this is God's host! Open thine eyes, see, and shout! He hath given His angels charge over thee to keep thee in all thy ways. And yet, it may come to pass that thou wilt fear, fear greatly, because of some threatening danger or other. For thy flesh fainteth and is despondent. Then shalt thou pray and cry anxiously, and remind God of the promises which He gave thee. That is the proper thing to do. And yet, it may be that God will meet thee as an enemy, as He did Jacob (Gen. 32, 24-30), in order to try thee. Oh, then hold fast to God, as Jacob did, and say: "I will not let Thee go except Thou bless me." And He will bless thee, and thou shalt shout again: Peniel, the face of God! My life is preserved! And God will help thee and lead thee in the paths of righteousness, and lastly, this year or another, bring thee home, home! All this He promiseth thee. And He saith: "I will not leave thee until I have done that which I have spoken to thee of." Now, with joy and confidence do thou say, Amen.

PRAYER.—Lord God, dear Heavenly Father, I thank Thee for the sure and comforting promises which Thou hast given me in Christ Jesus, and that Thou hast faithfully fulfilled them hitherto. I pray Thee to continue to do so, and not to leave me, until Thou hast done that which Thou hast spoken to me of. O Lord, Thou art faithful. Give me Thy Holy Spirit, that, trusting in Thy Word, and led by Thy hand, with all joy and confidence I may enter upon the new year, indeed, face the whole future before me, hastening unto my eternal home. Amen.

Hymn 169.

SATURDAY.

The Lord whom ye seek shall suddenly come to His temple.—Mal. 3, 1.

The parents of Jesus went to Jerusalem every year at the Feast of the Passover. And when Jesus was twelve years old, they went up to Jerusalem after the custom of the feast. And when they had fulfilled the days, as they returned, the Child Jesus tarried behind in Jerusalem; and Joseph and His mother knew not of it. But they, supposing Him to be in the company, went a day's journey; and they sought Him among their kinsfolk and acquaintance. And when they found Him not, they returned to Jerusalem, seeking Him. And after three days they found Him in the temple, sitting in the midst of the doctors, both hearing them, and asking them questions. And all that heard Him were amazed at His understanding and His answers. And when they saw Him, they were amazed. And His mother said unto Him: "Son, why hast Thou thus dealt with us? Behold, Thy father and I have sought Thee sorrowing." And He said unto them: "How is it that ye sought me? Wist ye not that *I must be about my Father's business?"* And they understood not the saying which He spake unto them. And He went down with them, and came to Nazareth, and was subject unto them. But his mother kept all these sayings in her heart. And Jesus increased in wisdom and stature, and in favor with God and man. (Luke 2, 41-52.)

This is the only story we have of Jesus' youth. We here see a ray of His divine glory shining forth from His voluntary lowliness. "Wist ye not that I must be about my Father's business?" said He, being the only-begotten Son of the Father. So in Him there had come to His temple the Lord for whom they had waited, whom they had sought so long. In this light thou must know the Child Jesus.

PRAYER.—Jesus, Jesus, Thou poor infant in the manger, Thou obedient Son of Thy lowly parents, who didst take upon Thee the form of a servant, and wast made in the likeness of men, and being found in fashion as a man, didst humble Thyself and becamest obedient unto death, even the death of the cross: Thou art nevertheless the Lord, the true God, begotten of the Father from eternity. I thank Thee that Thou, great Lord, didst become man, a lowly man, and didst save us miserable sinners. Grant, O Lord, that I may know Thee aright, and in true faith may call Thee my Lord and Savior, until I shall behold Thee in Thy great glory. Amen.

Hymn 147, 5-7.

Week of the Sunday After New Year.

SUNDAY.

Repent ye, for the kingdom of heaven is at hand.— Matt. 3, 2.

When Jesus entered upon His thirtieth year, John the Baptist appeared, preaching in the wilderness of Judea and saying, "Repent ye, for the kingdom of heaven is at hand!" Jesus has come! Realize your sinful ruin, and believe in Him, your Savior,—that was his meaning. There was a great commotion among the people. All flocked to see John. They confessed their sins and were baptized by John for the remission of their sins for Jesus' sake, who now had appeared. John then taught them how to serve God with the simple works of faith which their calling and station required of them. But when he saw many self-righteous Pharisees and wicked Sadducees come to his baptism, he said to them: "O generation of vipers, who hath warned you to flee from the wrath to come? Bring forth, therefore, fruits meet for repentance; and think not to say within yourselves, We have Abraham to our father; for I say unto you that God is able of these stones to raise up children unto Abraham. And now also the ax is laid unto the root of the trees; therefore, every tree which bringeth not forth good fruit is hewn down and cast into the fire. I indeed baptize you with water unto repentance; but He that cometh after me is mightier than I, whose shoes I am not worthy to bear; He shall baptize you with the Holy Ghost and with fire; whose fan is in His hand, and He will thoroughly purge His floor, and gather His wheat into His garner; but He will burn up the chaff with unquenchable fire." (Matt. 3, 1-12.)

The kingdom of heaven is near, very near at hand, for us, too. We must repent and believe in the Savior, and seek forgiveness of sins in the Word and in Baptism and in the Lord's Supper. Then we must bring forth fruits meet for repentance. But woe unto the self-righteous and wicked who depend upon mere outward church-membership! Christ, who, through the means of grace, gives the fire of the Holy Ghost unto true faith, will finally purge His congregation of such hypocrites, and judge them.

PRAYER.—Lord God, Heavenly Father, I pray Thee, through Christ, Thy dear Son, my Savior, do at all times graciously bestow upon me Thy Holy Spirit through Thy Word and Sacrament, that in true repentance I may realize my sin, and take comfort, in true faith, in my Savior, and bring forth fruits meet for repentance, and hereafter be saved, through the same, my Savior, Thy dear Son, Jesus Christ. Amen.

Hymn 307.

MONDAY.

Repent, and be baptized, every one of you, in the name of Jesus Christ for the remission of sins.—Acts 2, 38.

In the days when John preached and baptized, as shown yesterday, Jesus came from Galilee to John at the Jordan to be baptized of him. But John forbade Him, saying, "I have need to be baptized of Thee, and comest Thou to me?" And Jesus, answering, said unto him, "Suffer it to be so now; for thus it becometh us to fulfill all righteousness." Then he suffered Him. And Jesus, when He was baptized, went up straightway out of the water; and, lo, the heavens were opened unto Him, and he saw the Spirit of God descending as a dove and lighting upon Him; and, lo, a voice from heaven, saying: "This is my beloved Son, in whom I am well pleased." (Matt. 3, 13-17.)

On sinless Jesus rested the sin of the whole world. Therefore He was baptized, even as once He was circumcised, for the remission of sins which, by His suffering and death, He would merit for Himself, that is, for the whole world. And so the Father was well pleased with Him, His dear Son. And the Holy Ghost came upon Him, according to His human nature, for the performance of His great work.—And what about our Baptism? We have been baptized into Him, into His merit, and have received forgiveness of sin. When we were baptized, the Holy Ghost came, entered our hearts, and effected in us the new birth of children of God. God the Father then said to every one of us: "Thou art my beloved child in whom I am well pleased." And in true repentance, that is, in true confession of sin and in a living faith, we must always comfort ourselves with our Baptism. So help us God!

PRAYER.—I give thanks unto Thee, O Lord, Triune God, for my blessed Baptism. There Thou, Lord Jesus, didst become my own with all Thy merit. There Thou, Lord Holy Ghost, didst create faith within me and make me a child of God in Christ. And there Thou, God the Father, didst graciously receive and proclaim me Thy dear child. Grant now, O merciful God, that in faith I may hold fast to such grace obtained in Baptism, and, living and dying as Thine own, may enter eternal life. Amen.

Hymn 401, 1.

TUESDAY.

He was in all points tempted like as we, yet without sin. Hebr. 4, 15.

After His Baptism, Jesus was led up of the Spirit into the wilderness to be tempted of the devil. And when He had fasted forty days and forty nights, He was afterwards an hungered. And when the Tempter came to Him, he said: "If Thou be the Son of God, command that these stones be made bread." But He answered and said: "It is written, Man shall not live by bread alone, but by every word that proceedeth out of the mouth of God." Then the devil taketh Him up into the Holy City, and setteth Him on a pinnacle of the temple, and saith unto Him: "If Thou be the Son of God, cast Thyself down; for it is written, He shall give His angels charge concerning Thee; and in their hands they shall bear Thee up, lest at any time Thou dash Thy foot against a stone." Jesus said unto him: "It is written again, Thou shalt not tempt the Lord, thy God." Again the devil taketh Him up into an exceeding high mountain, and showeth Him all the kingdoms of the world and the glory of them; and saith unto Him: "All these things will I give Thee if Thou wilt fall down and worship me." Then saith Jesus unto him: "Get thee hence, Satan; for it is written, Thou shalt worship the Lord, thy God, and Him alone shalt thou serve." Then the devil leaveth Him, and, behold, angels came and ministered unto Him. (Matt. 4, 1-11.)

In, and together with, our first parents we were tempted by the devil, and fell into sin. To make restitution for all this, our Savior, being the Substitute of all mankind, was in all points tempted like as we, yet without sin. In His holy human nature He truly felt how Satan tempted Him to doubt God, haughtily to tempt God, and to serve the devil in vainglory. But He armed Himself with the Word of God and did not sin, no, not with the faintest thought and desire. This we should consider and believe, and account it our righteousness, since God wants to impute to us what the Savior did for us.

PRAYER.—O my Savior! In Adam and Eve, and in a thousand ways myself, I have fallen into temptation, but Thou hast overcome all temptations. I am a miserable sinner; Thou art without spot, holy, and righteous. Thy righteousness is my righteousness, wherein I stand before God. Most heartily do I give thanks unto Thee that Thou hast done this and much more for me, a poor sinner, and so didst make amends for my evil condition. Help me by Thy Holy Spirit that in faith I may always take comfort in this blessed fact, and rejoice therein against all the terrors of an evil conscience, O Thou blessed Conqueror of Satan! Amen.

Hymn 310, 6. 7.

EPIPHANY.

Ye are the light of the world.—Matt. 5, 14.

This day, since olden times, has been especially devoted to the consideration of Heathen Mission.

"Ye are the light of the world," says Jesus to His believing disciples. Light is salvation. And salvation, the salvation of the world, surely is none other than Christ, the Savior, and He only. When, therefore, Jesus says to His believers: "*Ye* are the light of the world," He thereby says that believing Christians are to be the bearers of the light, the bringers of salvation, for the world. We, who through His Word and Holy Ghost know and own Him who is our Light and Salvation, are to bring Him, His name and His Word, to those who are in spiritual gloom and darkness, and who do not know the Savior. This is His fixed and express will. Therefore He says to us: "Go ye therefore, and teach all nations, baptizing them in the name of the Father and of the Son and of the Holy Ghost," and again: "Go ye into all the world, and preach the Gospel to every creature." And prophesying even through Isaiah the Prophet, He says to the Christian Church: "Arise, shine; for thy light is come, and the glory of the Lord is risen upon thee. For, behold, darkness shall cover the earth, and gross darkness the people; but the Lord shall arise upon thee, and His glory shall be seen upon thee. And the Gentiles shall come to thy light." (Is. 60, 1-3.)

So let the obedience to His will and the compassionate love wrought by the Holy Ghost, as well as the promise that our labors shall not be in vain, let all this move us to bring to the heathen the light of salvation which has saved our souls.

PRAYER.—Lord God, Heavenly Father, who hast caused us to believe in Thy dear Son Jesus Christ, who is our Light and our Salvation, and hast made Him to be our own, enlighten us, we beseech Thee, by Thy Holy Spirit that we may duly appreciate such grace and thank Thee for the same with all our heart, and also communicate our light and salvation to those who still sit in darkness and in the shadow of death. This grant, O merciful God, who wilt have all men to be saved and to come to the knowledge of truth. Amen.

Hymn 179, 1.

THURSDAY.

Behold the Lamb of God that taketh away the sin of the world.—John 1, 29.

At the time when John the Baptist, by his preaching and baptizing, caused so great a commotion in Israel, the Chief Council sent messengers to him, asking who he was. They asked him whether he were not the Christ; and when he denied it, whether he were Elias; and when he denied that too, whether he were the promised Prophet. When he denied that also, they demanded him to tell them who he was. He answered: "I am the voice of one crying in the wilderness, *Make straight the way of the Lord,* as said the Prophet Esaias." Then they asked him why he baptized. He answered that he baptized because he was the forerunner of Christ, who was standing among them, whom they knew not.—The next day John saw Jesus coming to him, and he publicly testified: "Behold the Lamb of God that taketh away the sin of the world." And again he testified and said: "This is the Son of God." (John 1, 19-34.)

This is the true, and only true, testimony concerning Jesus Christ, and this is the true, and only true, knowledge of Jesus Christ: He is the Lamb of God that taketh away the sin of the world, and He is the Son of God who became man. Let this be thy faith, O Christian, thy comfort, the source of thy defiant trust and confidence in life and death, that the eternal Son of God has become man, and has become the Lamb of God, of whom all the lambs sacrificed in the Old Testament were but types, that He is the right and true Lamb of God that hath taken away the sin of the world and, therefore, also thy sin. I say unto thee, this Lamb is mighty and strong so to take away thy sin that it no longer burdens thee.

PRAYER.—Lord Jesus, Thou eternal Son of God, my Savior and my Lord! I, a poor sinner, am now entirely free from all my sin, and its grievous, unbearable, and damning burden no longer lies upon me; for Thou, my dear Lord, didst become the Lamb of God and hast taken away altogether the sin of the whole world, and also my sin; Thou hast paid for it, atoned for it, and utterly abolished it. Praise and thanks be unto Thee! Endow me with Thy Holy Spirit, that in such true faith I may nevermore fear nor faint, but joyfully appear before the face of God, and be blessed forevermore. Amen.

Hymn 102.

FRIDAY.

Follow me.—John 1, 43.

On the next day John was standing, and two of his disciples with him. And Jesus walked by. And again John said, "Behold the Lamb of God." And the two disciples followed Jesus. It was four o'clock in the afternoon. Jesus turned and asked them, "What seek ye?" They said, "Rabbi, where dwellest Thou?" He said, "Come and see." And they went with Jesus and abode with Him that day. It was *Andrew* and *John*. Andrew found his brother Simon, and said to him, "We have found the Messiah." And he brought him to Jesus. And Jesus surnamed him Cephas, or *Peter,* that is, rocklike man. Then John brought his brother James to Jesus. The day following, Jesus found Philip, who, like the four just mentioned, was of Bethsaida in Galilee, and said to him, "Follow me." And Philip, in turn, found Nathanael, called Bartholomew, and said to him, "We have found Him of whom Moses and the prophets did write, Jesus of Nazareth, the son of Joseph." Nathanael said, "Can there any good thing come out of Nazareth?" Philip said, "Come and see." When Jesus saw Nathanael, He said, "Behold an Israelite indeed in whom is no guile." Nathanael saith unto Him, "Whence knowest Thou me?" Jesus answered, "Before that Philip called thee, when thou wast under the fig tree, I saw thee." Nathanael answered and said to Him, "Rabbi, Thou art the Son of God; Thou art the King of Israel." Jesus said, "Because I said unto thee, I saw thee under the fig tree, believest thou? Thou shalt see greater things than these." (John 1, 35-51.)

To thee also doth the Gospel of Jesus say, "Behold the Lamb of God." To thee, too, doth Jesus say, "Follow me." Learn to know Jesus in the Word, which tells of Him, and follow Him. Proclaim Jesus in word and deed. Do thy part in bringing others to say to Jesus: "Thou art the Son of God, Thou art the Lamb of God."

PRAYER.—Lord Jesus, Thou art indeed the Son of God, the Lamb of God that taketh away my sin and the sin of the whole world. Thee will I follow. With Thee alone do I find life and salvation. Draw me to Thee in true faith through Thy Word and Thy Spirit. Fill my heart with fervent love for those who do not yet know Thee, open my lips to a frank confession of Thy sweet name Jesus! O Jesus, Jesus, save me and mine and many others through faith in Thee! Amen.

Hymn 234, 3. 5.

SATURDAY.

And Jesus manifested forth His glory; and His disciples believed on Him.—John 2, 11.

After Jesus had been baptized by John, and tempted by the devil, and gathered His first disciples, He returned with these to Galilee. And there was a marriage in Cana of Galilee; and the mother of Jesus was there. And Jesus and His disciples were invited to the marriage. And there was a lack of wine. And the mother of Jesus said to Him, "They have no wine." He said to her, "Woman, what have I to do with thee? Mine hour is not yet come." His mother had no right to tell Him how or when He should manifest His divine glory. Mary now said to the servants, "Whatsoever He saith unto you, do it." Now there were six waterpots of stone set there after the Jews' manner of purifying, containing two or three firkins apiece. Jesus said to the servants: "Fill the waterpots with water." And they filled them up to the brim. And He said unto them: "Draw out now, and bear unto the ruler of the feast." And they took it there. And when the ruler of the feast tasted the water that was made wine, and knew not whence it was (but the servants who had drawn the water knew), he called the bridegroom and said to him, "Every man at the beginning doth set forth good wine; and when men have well drunk, then that which is worse; but thou hast kept the good wine until now." This was Jesus' first miracle. Thus did He manifest forth His divine glory which hitherto had been hidden. And His disciples believed on Him the more firmly. (John 2, 1-11.)

Christian, thou believest in thy Savior and art His disciple. Blessed art thou. But to remain in this faith, and to grow ever more firm and deeply rooted and grounded therein, so as to overcome all temptation and lastly to be saved, thou must read the Word of Jesus always, and see how there His glory is revealed, the glory of the only-begotten Son of the Father, who became thy Savior. Without such use of the Word of Jesus thy flesh will stifle the faith within thee, and thou wilt be lost. May God keep thee from such a fate!

Week of the First Sunday After Epiphany.

PRAYER.—O God the Holy Ghost, thou Spirit of Christ, who glorifies Christ within the hearts of Thy believers, create, I beseech Thee, within me a mind that gladly readeth and contemplateth Thy Word, beholding there the glory of my Savior, and clinging to Him in ever stronger faith, until in my last hour Thou wilt glorify His gracious image within my soul unto eternal bliss. Amen.

Hymn 103, 2.

Week of the First Sunday After Epiphany.

SUNDAY.

Go thy way; thy son liveth. The man believed the word. John 4, 50.

The time had now come that Jesus was to appear in public, and by preaching and working miracles was to manifest Himself as the Son of God and Savior of the world. He did this first in Judea, in Jerusalem and the country south of Jerusalem, for more than half a year. Then He went to Galilee, coming again to Cana where He had performed His first miracle. In Capernaum, about five or six hours' walk from Cana, there lived at this time a certain nobleman, a government official, whose son was at the point of death. When he heard that Jesus was at Cana, he went to Him and besought Him that He would come down to Capernaum and heal his son. Jesus said to him, "Except ye see signs and wonders, ye will not believe." But the man kept on entreating Him and said, "Sir, come down ere my child die." Jesus said to him: "Go thy way; thy son liveth." The man believed the word that Jesus had spoken to him, and went his way. The next day his servants met him, saying, "Thy son liveth." Then enquired he of them the hour when he began to mend. And they said: "Yesterday at the seventh hour (one o'clock in the afternoon) the fever left him." So the father knew that it was in the same hour in which Jesus had said to him, "Thy son liveth." And he himself believed, and his whole house. (John 4, 46-54.)

Thus did Jesus manifest His divine glory: by a mere word spoken from a distance He healed the sick. And thus did the nobleman prove his faith: he relied upon the word of Christ. Through His written Word, Jesus now gives thee the forgiveness of sin, life, and salvation, for the sake of the redemption wherewith He hath redeemed thee. Believe this Word, go thy way, and rely upon this Word in life and death, rest and depend upon this Word, though thou feel or see naught of its power. Jesus' Word will not deceive thee.

PRAYER.—Almighty, eternal God, who through Thy Son didst promise us forgiveness of sin, righteousness, and everlasting life, I pray Thee that by Thy Holy Ghost Thou wouldst so rule and quicken my heart that in daily prayer, and especially in all temptation, I may seek such help of Him, and, firmly believing His Word and promise, surely find and obtain it, and lastly be saved through Him. Amen.

Hymn 311, 10.

MONDAY.

What manner of man is this that even the winds and the sea obey Him!—Matt. 8, 27.

From Galilee, Jesus had returned to Jerusalem, for the Passover, and in the temple, before a mighty concourse of people, He had preached a most powerful sermon regarding the divine majesty of His eternal Sonship; but the Jews had rejected Him and had threatened to kill Him. So now He went to Galilee, there to manifest Himself as the true Prophet foretold by Moses. John the Baptist's activity had now come to an end. Jesus chose for His home the city of Capernaum, situated on the Sea of Gennesaret. And of an evening, at the close of an extremely busy day, He entered a ship, to go to the eastern shore of the lake. His disciples followed Him. And, behold, there arose a great tempest in the sea, insomuch that the ship was covered with the waves; but Jesus was asleep. And His disciples came to Him, and awoke Him, saying, "Lord, save us: we perish!" Then said

He to them, "Why are ye so fearful, O ye of little faith?" And He arose, and rebuked the winds and the sea; and there was a great calm. But the men marveled, saying: "What manner of man is this, that even the winds and the sea obey Him!" (Matt. 8, 23-27.)

This tired man, whom, however, the winds and the sea obey, is the incarnate Word, the eternal Son of the Father who has become man. He is thy Savior, who then was in the state of humiliation, but now is exalted to the right hand of God the Father. It is He who has all power in heaven and in earth, and most graciously is with thee at all times. Why, then, dost thou fear so often? Fear not, neither in life nor in death, but trust His gracious omnipotence.

PRAYER.—O true Man and true God, Jesus Christ, whom winds and sea and all things obey, I acknowledge mine infirmity and diffidence, mine inability to weather the tempests of this world without Thy consolation. O help me, that I perish not! Keep the ship of Thy Church against all the powerful enemies who threaten it, comfort all fearsome hearts, strengthen all such as are weak of faith. Be with us, our only, but almighty Helper in need, blessed forever! Amen.

Hymn 523.

TUESDAY.

Thy sins be forgiven thee.—Matt. 9, 2.

When Jesus returned to His own city, Capernaum, and was in His dwelling, they brought a man to Him who was sick of the palsy and was lying on a bed. They had great difficulty in bringing him because of the crowd that blocked the street. Jesus, seeing their faith, said to the sick of the palsy: "Son, be of good cheer; thy sins be forgiven thee." The Searcher of Hearts saw that the sick man sought the grace of God and the forgiveness of sins above all things. But certain of the scribes who were present said within themselves: "This man blasphemeth. Who can forgive sins but God only?" Jesus, knowing their thoughts, said: "Wherefore think ye so evil in your hearts? For whether is easier, to say, Thy sins be forgiven thee; or to say, Arise, and walk? But that ye may know that the Son of Man hath power on earth to forgive sins (then said He to the sick of the palsy,) Arise, take up thy bed, and go unto thine house." And he arose, and departed to his house. When the multitude saw it, they marveled, and glorified God, who had given such power unto men. (Matt. 9, 1-8.)

Here the Son of Man proves by a divine miracle that He is the eternal Son of God, having all power, and also the power to forgive sins on earth; and He gladly exercises it. Here thou seest that above all things thou must seek forgiveness of sins with Him. For what good will all things do thee if thou hast not the forgiveness of sins and the grace of God? But if through the forgiveness of sins thou hast the grace of God, thou canst at all times call upon God, even as a dear child calls upon its dear father, and He will give thee what is best for thee in time and eternity.

PRAYER.—Lord God, grant me the forgiveness of all my sins, for the sake of Jesus Christ, my dear Savior. Thou hast solemnly promised to do this. Fulfill the promise Thou hast given me. Let me abide in Thy grace. O my God, then naught will have power to harm me, then shall I be able to comfort myself with Thee, almighty God, and rejoice in all need, yea, even in death. Through Thy Holy Ghost, O God, vouchsafe unto me the salutary knowledge of true faith unto eternal life. Amen.

Hymn 122, 2. 3.

WEDNESDAY.

Talitha, cumi.—Mark 5, 41.

At one time, when a great multitude crowded about our Lord at the sea shore of Capernaum, one of the rulers of the synagogue, Jairus by name, sought Him. And when he saw Him, he fell down at His feet, and besought Him greatly, saying: "My little daughter is at the point of death: I pray Thee, come and lay Thy hands upon her, that she may be healed and live." And Jesus went with him. And a great multitude followed Him. Now when they approached the house of Jairus, some of his people said to him: "Thy daughter is dead; why troublest thou the Master any further?" But Jesus heard it and said to Jairus: "Fear not, only believe." And He suffered no man to follow further, save Peter and James and his brother John. And He cometh to the house, and seeth the tumult, and them that wept and wailed greatly, and the minstrels that played in a mournful strain. And He confronted them, saying: " Why make ye this ado, and weep? The damsel is not dead, but sleepeth." And they laughed Him to scorn, knowing that she was dead. And Jesus put them all out, and He taketh the father and the mother of the damsel and the three disciples, and entereth in where the damsel was lying. And He took the damsel by the hand and said unto her: " Talitha, cumi," which, in English, is, Damsel, I say unto thee, Arise. And straightway the damsel arose and walked. She was twelve years old and an only daughter. And they were astonished with a great astonishment. And Jesus charged them straitly that they should tell no man. And He commanded to give her to eat. (Mark 5, 21-43.)

In the sight of the Lord Jesus death is a mere sleep, even thy death and that of thy loved ones. Right easily can He awaken all His own from death unto eternal life, and He certainly will do it. Let thy dead who died in the Lord be at rest, and rejoice that they are sleeping peacefully. Jesus will waken them unto eternal life when He will come again. And do thou, thyself, remain with Jesus, and when death approacheth thee, then say: Thou art but a sleep from which my Savior shall awaken me.

PRAYER.—Lord Jesus Christ, our Savior, who with Thy blood didst cancel all our sins, and turnedst bitter death into a peaceful sleep, grant that the tumult of carnal reason and of the scoffers of this world may not prevent me from believing nor confound me, but, rather, that I may lay hold on Thee in Thy Word, and keep Thee securely in faith, and through Thee be saved forever, for Thy name's sake. Amen.

Hymn 528, 5.

THURSDAY.

Verily, I say unto you, I have not found so great faith, no, not in Israel.—Matt. 8, 10.

After a long sermon tour through Galilee, Jesus one day returned to His own city, Capernaum. And the centurion, a heathen, commanding the Roman garrison there, sent the elders of the Jews to Him, beseeching Him and saying through them: "Lord, my servant lieth at home sick of the palsy, grievously tormented." And Jesus saith: "I will come and heal him," and went toward the centurion's house. But the centurion sent friends to Him, saying: "Lord, I am not worthy that Thou shouldst come under my roof; but speak the word only, and my servant shall be healed. For I also am a man under authority, having soldiers under me: and I say to this man, Go, and he goeth; and to another, Come, and he cometh; and to my servant, Do this, and he doeth it." As if to say: As my servants obey my word, so all things must obey Thy word. When Jesus heard this, He marveled, and said to them that followed: "Verily I say unto you, I have not found so great faith, no, not in Israel. And I say unto you, That many shall come from the East and the West, and shall sit down with Abraham and Isaac and Jacob in the kingdom of heaven. But the children of the kingdom shall be cast into outer darkness; there shall be weeping and gnashing of teeth." And Jesus sent word to the centurion: "Go thy way; as thou hast believed, so be it done unto thee." And his servant was healed in the self-same hour. (Matt. 8, 5-13.)

The heathen centurion, with eyes wide open in faith, saw the Savior's divine glory hidden under the form of a servant, and with great confidence, though in deep humility, he comforted himself therewith. God be praised that a great number of all ages and nations have had such true and simple faith. But is such faith found often in Christendom to-day? Ah, no! And thinkest thou that all who from their childhood have been brought into the kingdom of God, and still are looked upon as children of the kingdom, will actually be saved? Ah, no! Only through the faith which knows Jesus and truly lays hold on Him do we become righteous before God and shall we be saved. And in no other way.

PRAYER.—Almighty Lord, Jesus Christ, before whom all must humble themselves, and to whose word and command all must yield, grant me grace to come to a true knowledge both of my unworthiness and Thy kindness and mercy, in firm faith to hold fast to Thee, to remain in Thy kingdom, to comfort myself with the assistance Thou hast promised me in all need, and finally to be saved: O Thou, who art the Lord and Helper of all mankind, blessed forever. Amen.

Hymn 260, 1. 4.

FRIDAY.

He will swallow up death in victory; and the Lord God will wipe away tears from off all faces.—Is. 25, 8.

On the day after the event of yesterday's lesson, Jesus went into the city of Nain, seven or eight hours' walk from Capernaum. And many of His disciples went with Him, and a great multitude. Now when He came nigh to the gate of the city, behold, there was a dead man carried out, the only son of his mother, and she was a widow; and much people of the city was with her. And when the Lord saw her, He had compassion on her and said unto her: "Weep not." And He came nigh and touched the bier; and the bearers stood still. And He said: "Young man, I say unto thee, Arise." And he that was dead sat up and began to speak. And He gave him unto his mother. (Luke 7, 11-15.)

This is a picture of now and hereafter. Now death reigns, the wages of sin. It swallows up young and old. How much misery and grief does it cause! But the Lord, whose glory Thou beholdest in this story, our Savior, who conquered sin and death, shall one day come again and oppose Death; and He will touch this old earth, which once was Nain, "The Beautiful," "The Lovely," but now has become a huge burying-ground, and will awaken His own therefrom unto eternal life, and will swallow up death in victory, and will wipe away tears from off all faces, He, the Lord God; and He will restore us to one another; and He will create a new Nain, where there shall be fullness of joy, and at His right hand rivers of pleasure forevermore. So must thou view death, Christian, and so behold thy Savior. Let this be thy sure and joyful hope in faith.

PRAYER.—Omnipotent Lord, Jesus Christ, Thou Conqueror of Death, who hast compassion with all that mourn because of death, comfort all the sorrowing by the knowledge of Thee, keep all the dying in true faith, and give me, too, Thy Holy Spirit that I may commend my soul into Thy hands, and at all times know and acknowledge Thee to be the Lord God who wilt forever abolish death, and on the last day give unto me and all the elect eternal life with endless joy and glory, wherein Thou, Lord, now livest and reignest, world without end. Amen.

Hymn 216, 5. 6.

SATURDAY.

Give us this day our daily bread.—Matt. 6, 11.

A year before His death, about the time of the Passover, Jesus crossed the Sea of Galilee with His disciples, seeking a little recreation on the eastern shore after much hard work. But a great multitude followed Him, because they saw the miracles which He did on those who were diseased. And so He could find no rest. Toward evening He went up into a mountain, and there He sat with His disciples. And when He saw the great multitude, He said to Philip: "Whence shall we buy bread that these may eat?" This He said to prove him; for He Himself knew what He would do. Philip answered: "Two hundred pennyworth (*denarii*, about 30 dollars' worth) of bread is not sufficient for them, that every one of them may take a little." One of His disciples, Andrew, Simon Peter's brother, saith unto Him: "There is a lad here who hath five barley loaves and two fishes; but what are these among so many?" Jesus said: "Make the people sit down." Now there was much grass in the place. So the men sat down, in number about five thousand. And Jesus took the loaves; and when He had given thanks, He distributed to His disciples, and the disciples to them that were set down; and likewise of the fishes as much as they would. When they were filled, He said to His disciples: "Gather up the fragments, that nothing be lost." Therefore they gathered them together, and filled twelve baskets with the fragments of the five barley loaves, which remained over unto them that had eaten. (John 6, 1-13.)

All four evangelists tell this story. Two of them were eye-witnesses. It was an exceedingly great divine miracle. It shows us Christ's divine glory. It also reveals His compassionate heart. He wants to give daily bread to those who follow Him. Thou seest that He is able to do it. He even says that we should pray: "Give us this day our daily bread." Why, then, do we worry or fret? When He tells us so to pray, will He not hear us?

PRAYER.—Lord Jesus, almighty God, give us, we beseech Thee, our daily bread and grant us Thy Holy Spirit, that we may cheerfully rely on Thee, and nevermore offend against Thy Gospel, Thy glory, and our conscience for the sake of our bread and body. Give Thy grace also to me, so weak in faith, that at all times in faith I may look upon Thy bountiful hand, there finding hope and cheer, and, above all, seeking the imperishable good with Thee, who livest forever and forever and aye wilt be our great Benefactor. Amen.

Hymn 22, 4. 5.

Week of the Second Sunday After Epiphany.

SUNDAY.

Be of good cheer; it is I; be not afraid.—Matt. 14, 27.

When our Savior had miraculously fed the five thousand, He straightway constrained His disciples to get into a boat, and to go before Him unto the other side, while He sent the multitudes away. And when He had sent the multitudes away, He went up into the mountain apart to pray. When the evening was come, He was there alone. But the boat was now in the midst of the sea, tossed with waves; for the wind was contrary. And in the fourth watch of the night, Jesus went unto them, walking on the sea. And when the disciples saw Him walking on the sea, they were troubled, saying: "It is a spirit." And they cried out with fear. But straightway Jesus spoke unto them, saying: "Be of good cheer; it is I; be not afraid." And Peter answered Him and said: "Lord, if it be Thou, bid me come unto Thee on the water." And He said: "Come." And when Peter was come out of the boat, he walked on the water to go to Jesus. But when he saw the wind boisterous, he was afraid; and beginning to sink, he cried, saying: "Lord, save me!" And immediately Jesus stretched forth His hand, and caught him, and said unto him: "O thou of little faith, wherefore didst thou doubt?" And when they were come into the boat, the wind ceased. (Matt. 14, 22-32.)

Indeed, Jesus is of a truth the Son of God, the only-begotten Son of the Father. His divine eye sees when His own are in trouble. He hastens to succor them. But when He comes, His own ofttimes do not know him and His wondrous ways, and rather think that hell is near. And great fear takes hold of them. Then they must listen to the voice of His word: "Be of good cheer; it is I; be not afraid." And they must take courage and good cheer, and fear nothing, relying only on Him and His Word. But how easily such consolation of faith does vanish again! When new waves of disaster threaten, how little in faith are they! Then naught remains but to cry: "Lord, save me!" And the faithful Lord will not refuse to do so. He will stretch out His hand and help, help alway, unto eternal life.

PRAYER.—Jesus Christ, Thou great and faithful Lord, I am a poor being, weak of faith, easily perplexed, soon despairing. Have patience with me. Cast me not away from Thy presence; and take not Thy Holy Spirit from me. Restore unto me the joy of Thy salvation; and uphold me with Thy free Spirit. Do not leave me nor forsake me. For Thy name's sake, O Lord, guide me amid all temptation from

within and without until I shall obtain eternal life, where I shall bless and glorify Thee forever. Amen.
Hymn 373.

MONDAY.

He that believeth shall not make haste.—Is. 28, 16.

When Jesus' activity in Galilee was at an end, He went with His disciples into the parts of Tyre and Sidon, cities of Syrophenicia. And behold, a Canaanitish woman, a heathen, cried unto Him, saying: "Have mercy on me, O Lord, Thou son of David; my daughter is grievously vexed with a devil." But He answered her not a word. And His disciples came and besought Him, saying: "Send her away; for she crieth after us." But He answered and said: "I am not sent but unto the lost sheep of the house of Israel." In Israel, and not among the heathen, Jesus was to manifest Himself through miracles while sojourning visibly on earth. But the woman came and worshiped Him, saying: "Lord, help me." But He answered and said: "It is not meet to take the children's bread, and to cast it to the dogs." And she said: "Truth, Lord; yet the dogs eat of the crumbs which fall from their masters' table." Then Jesus answered and said unto her, O woman, great is thy faith: be it unto thee even as thou wilt. And her daughter was made whole from that very hour. (Matt. 15, 21-28.)

"He that believeth shall not make haste." Call upon Jesus in every trouble of body and soul. Ask Him for every deliverance in time and eternity. When He pretends not to hear thee, and when He upbraids thee on account of thine unworthiness, and thy conscience says it is even so, then do not make haste and flee from Him. *Thy faith must not be based upon thy worthiness, but upon Christ's mercy pledged thee in His Word.* Plead that, and continue in prayer. He cannot deny Himself—His mercy and His Word. He will give thee what thou desirest. "He that believeth shall not make haste."

PRAYER.—O Lord and Savior Jesus Christ, Thy great tender mercy so often fains harshness toward us who believe and set our hope in Thee. Nevertheless, Thou art our Father and Redeemer; Thy name is from everlasting. Grant that I may learn to know Thee aright, taking Thee at Thy Word, and when in temptation and affliction Thou contendest with me, grant me grace to conquer Thee, yea, Thee, in exulting faith and in the end to feel that Thou art with me. Hear me, O Savior, for the sake of Thy most trustworthy loving-kindness. Amen.

Hymn 498, 4. 5. 7

TUESDAY.

I will behold Thy face in righteousness. I shall be satisfied, when I awake, with Thy likeness.—Ps. 17, 15.

When the time of His suffering and death drew nearer and nearer, Jesus began to prepare the disciples for the shock which flesh and blood would experience. He told them of His impending suffering and death and of the consequent resurrection. And He did more. One day He took Peter and James and John, and took them up to a high mountain. There He was transfigured before them; and His face did shine as the sun, and His raiment was white as the light. For a while He laid aside the lowliness of His human nature and caused it to glow in His heavenly, divine, glory. And, behold, there appeared unto Him Moses and Elias talking with Him. Then Peter, as in a dream, said to Jesus: "Lord, it is good for us to be here; if Thou wilt, let us make here three tabernacles; one for Thee and one for Moses and one for Elias." While he yet spake, behold, a bright cloud overshadowed them; and behold a voice out of the cloud, which said: "This is my beloved Son, in whom I am well pleased; hear ye Him." And when His disciples heard it, they fell on their faces and were sore afraid. And Jesus came and touched them, and said: "Arise, and be not afraid." And when they lifted up their eyes, they saw no man, save Jesus only, in old familiar form. (Matt. 17, 1-8.)

What is it we see here? We see that Jesus, the Son of Man, is the very God of Glory, our Savior. We see that after this life there is in store for us another life, when

Week of the Second Sunday After Epiphany.

our quickened body shall be like unto His glorious body. It is very good for us to be there. We shall be restored to one another, and recognize each other. We see that here on earth we must put all our hope in Jesus only and in His Word: that is the Father's pleasure. Let this be our song in the land of our pilgrimage: "I will behold Thy face in righteousness; I shall be satisfied, when I awake, with Thy likeness."

PRAYER.—Almighty God, Heavenly Father, who didst glorify Thy dear Son Jesus Christ before the face of all the world, glorify Him, I beseech Thee, also within my frightened heart by Thy Holy Spirit, that I may cling to Him only and trust in His Word altogether, until at last, quickened from death, I shall be glorified forever with all the elect, and dwell with Thee in eternal joy and blessedness. Grant this, O God, to me, a poor sinner, for the sake of Thy dear Son, Jesus Christ, my Lord and Savior. Amen.

Hymn 520.

WEDNESDAY.

I am not come to call the righteous, but sinners, to repentance.—Matt. 9, 13.

We have so far, since Epiphany Day, beheld Jesus' *divine* glory, from His miracles. We shall now view His *saving* glory, the glory of His mercy toward poor sinners.

When our Lord had healed the man sick of the palsy in Capernaum, He went to the Sea of Galilee with His disciples. And He saw a man named Levi Matthew sitting at the receipt of custom. This was one of the justly ill-famed and proverbial publicans, who were guilty of so much injustice. Jesus said to him: "Follow me." He became the Apostle Matthew. This same Matthew then made a great feast in his own house for Jesus and His disciples, and there was a great company of publicans and other sinners that sat down with them. And when the self-righteous, sanctimonious Pharisees saw it, they said to His disciples after the feast: "Why eateth your Master with publicans and sinners?" When Jesus heard this, He said to them: "They that be whole need not the physician, but they that are sick. But go ye and learn what that meaneth, I will have mercy and not sacrifice; for I am not come to call the righteous, but sinners, to repentance." (Matt. 9, 9-13.)

Jesus has come expressly for us poor and condemned sinners, and not for the good and righteous. And us He calls to repentance, that penitently we acknowledge our sin, and believe in Him, and take full and lasting comfort in Him. Not a single sinner is excepted, however wicked he may be.

PRAYER.—Dear Heavenly Father, who through Thy Word hast called us miserable sinners to Thy kingdom, where there is forgiveness of sins, which Thy dear Son hath merited, and every grace and mercy, I beseech Thee so to enlighten my heart by Thy Holy Spirit that like Matthew, the publican, I may always follow that call, ceasing to sin, bettering my life, and looking confidently to Thy dear Son, Jesus Christ, for all grace, and thus finally entering heaven. Amen.

Hymn 318, 1-4.

THURSDAY.

Come unto me, all ye that labor and are heavy laden, and I will give you rest.—Matt. 11, 28.

One day a Pharisee, in one of the cities of Galilee, desired that Jesus would eat with him. And Jesus went into the Pharisee's house and sat down to meat, but was not shown the customary courtesies. And, behold, there was a woman in the city who was a notorious sinner. When she knew that Jesus sat at meat in the Pharisee's house, she brought an alabaster box of ointment, and stood at His feet behind Him, weeping, and began to wash His feet with tears, and wiped them with the hair of her head, and kissed His feet, and anointed them with the ointment. Now when the Pharisee saw this, he spake within himself: "This man, if He were a prophet, would have known who and what manner of woman this is that toucheth Him; for she is a sinner." Jesus said to him: "Simon, I have somewhat to say unto thee." And he said: "Say on." Jesus said: "A certain creditor had two debtors: the one owed him 500 pence and the other 50. And when they had nothing to pay, he frankly forgave them both. Tell me therefore, which of them will love him most?" Simon answered and said: "He, I suppose, to whom he forgave most." And He said unto him: "Thou hast rightly judged." And He turned to the woman, and said to Simon: "Seest thou this woman? I entered into thy house, thou gavest me no water for my feet; but she hath washed my feet with tears, and wiped them with the hair of her head. Thou gavest me no kiss; but this woman, since the time I came in, hath not ceased to kiss my feet. My head with oil thou didst not anoint; but this woman hath anointed my feet with ointment. Wherefore I say unto thee, Her sins, which are many, are forgiven, for she loved much; but to whom little is forgiven, the same loveth little. And He said unto her: "Thy sins are forgiven." And they that sat at meat with Him began to say within themselves: "Who is this that forgiveth sins also?" But Jesus said to the woman: "Thy faith hath saved thee; go in peace." (Luke 7, 36-50.)

Dost thou see our text above? Dost thou see from this story how Jesus fulfills it? Dost thou see how Jesus receiveth sinners? Dost thou see how those who know that Jesus has forgiven them much also love Him much? And dost thou see how those who think they need but little forgiveness have but little love for Jesus? Dost thou know thy sins? Dost thou know the Savior's compassion? And dost thou love Him much?

PRAYER.—Lord Jesus, who didst forgive many sins to the sinful woman, and thereby didst reveal the great love Thou dost bear us sinners, give me, I beseech Thee, a penitent heart, that my tears, too, may bear witness of the sorrow for my sins. Grant that, relying on Thy Word in true faith, I may come to Thee, and ever again find forgiveness of sins and peace and joy of heart, and that I love Thee, O merciful Savior, above all things. Amen.

Hymn 318, 5. 6.

FRIDAY.

This man receiveth sinners.—Luke 15, 2.

This was a word of derision with the self-righteous Pharisees. With us it is a word of praise and blessing. The following story is the origin of it.

All the publicans and sinners were drawing near unto Jesus to hear Him. And the Pharisees and scribes murmured, saying: "This man receiveth sinners and eateth with them." And He spake this parable unto them, saying: "What man of you, having a hundred sheep, if he lose one of them, doth not leave the ninety and nine in the wilderness, and go after that which is lost until he find it? And when he hath found it, he layeth it on his shoulders, rejoicing. And when he cometh home, he calleth together his friends and neighbors, saying unto them, Rejoice with me; for I have found my sheep which was lost. I say unto you that likewise joy shall be in heaven over one sinner that repenteth, more than over ninety and nine just persons who need no repentance." (Luke 15, 1-7.)

Jesus receives sinners; He seeks the straying sheep. Jesus has much power and a thousand means to seek. Knowest thou of a lost sheep? Commit it to Jesus. Jesus deals kindly with the sinner, to seek and find him. Do thou likewise, in Jesus' name and with His Word. And when Jesus has found a sinner, when the sinner repents, He takes him to His bosom and absolves him through His Word, comforts him, quiets his fears, and gives him the free Spirit who works confidence of faith within him. And all heaven rejoices, yea, rejoices more over that one sinner than over all the dearly beloved who already have the precious righteousness of faith. O the Savior's love! O the grace of God! Jesus receives sinners!

PRAYER.—Dear Lord and Savior Jesus Christ, rich in mercy, who hast come into the world to seek and to save that which was lost, and art found conversing with poor sinners, I give thanks unto Thy great mercy and grace, and I beseech Thee, vouchsafe unto me true repentance and daily continuance in the same, that there may be joy in heaven over me, and that my joy may be eternal and perfect. Amen.

Hymn 105.

SATURDAY.

Likewise joy shall be in heaven over one sinner that repenteth.—Luke 15, 7.

A certain man had two sons. And the younger of them said to his father: "Father, give me the portion of goods that falleth to me." And he divided unto them his living. And not many days after the younger son gathered all together, and took his journey into a far country, and there wasted his substance with riotous living. And when he had spent all, there arose a mighty famine in that land; and he began to be in want. And he went and joined himself unto a citizen of that country; and he sent him into the fields to feed swine. And he would fain have filled his belly with the husks that the swine did eat; and no man gave unto him. And when he came to himself, he said: "How many hired servants of my father's have bread enough and to spare, and I perish with hunger! I will arise and go to my father, and will say unto him: Father, I have sinned against heaven and before thee, and am no more worthy to be called thy son; make me as one of thy hired servants." And he arose and came to his father. But when he was yet a great way off, his father saw him, and had compassion, and ran, and fell on his neck, and kissed him. And the son said unto him: "Father, I have sinned against heaven and in thy sight, and am no more worthy to be called thy son." But the father said to his servants: "Bring forth the best robe, and put it on him; and put a ring on his hand and shoes on his feet; and bring hither the fatted calf and kill it; and let us eat and be merry: for this my son was dead, and is alive again; he was lost, and is found." And they began to be merry. (Luke 15, 11-24.)

This parable spake Jesus. "Likewise joy shall be in heaven over one sinner that repenteth." Thou mayest be perfectly sure that God receiveth thee, when, trusting in

Jesus and His Word, thou comest to thy heavenly Father, against whom thou hast so often offended. Jesus Himself brings thee to the Father through His Word and Holy Ghost.

PRAYER.—Lord Jesus, when I have sinned, yea, when I have strayed and lost my way, and fallen grievously, then do not leave me, O my Savior, but create repentance within me through Thy Word and Holy Ghost, so that I say: "I will arise and go to my Father, and will say unto Him: Father, I have sinned against heaven and before Thee, and am no more worthy to be called Thy son." Do Thou thus lead me to the Father, my Savior, who hast atoned for me with Thy blood and death, and intercede for me. Then shall the Father surely receive me, and love and caress me, and make me His child for time and eternity. Leave me not, Lord Jesus, leave me not, until I reach Thy Father's eternal mansions. Amen.

Hymn 107, 1.

Week of the Third Sunday After Epiphany.

SUNDAY.

Likewise joy shall be in heaven over one sinner that repenteth, more than over ninety and nine just persons who need no repentance.—Luke 15, 7.

To-day we will continue the parable of Jesus which we did not conclude yesterday.—Now the elder son was in the field; and as he came and drew nigh to the house, he heard music and dancing. And he called one of the servants, and asked what these things meant. And he said unto him: " Thy brother is come; and thy father hath killed the fatted calf, because he hath received him safe and sound." And he was angry, and would not go in; therefore his father came out and entreated him. And he, answering, said to his father: " Lo, these many years do I serve thee, neither transgressed I at any time thy commandment, and yet thou never gavest me a kid, that I might make merry with my friends; but as soon as this thy son was come, who hath devoured thy living with harlots, thou hast killed for him the fatted calf." And he said unto him: "Son, thou art ever with me, and all that I have is thine. It was meet that we should make merry and be glad; for this thy brother was dead, and is alive again; and was lost, and is found." (Luke 15, 25-32.)

Here thou seest how there is joy in heaven over one sinner that repenteth, more than over ninety and nine just persons who need no repentance, need no new repentance after some great fall from grace. Here thou seest how children of God are assailed by wicked thoughts, and their eye becomes evil because God is so good. Here thou seest how promptly and most kindly God sets His children right again through His Word and Holy Spirit. And here thou seest how the children of God must join in the joy which is in heaven over one sinner that repenteth.

PRAYER.—Lord, my God, I thank Thee that Thou hast graciously adopted me as Thy child and lettest me dwell with Thee, so that all that Thou hast is mine and I lack no truly good thing. O my God, this is naught but mercy which Thou showest me in Christ, my Savior, and of which I am altogether unworthy. Now when Thou quickenest to new life some poor lost child of sin and takest him to Thy bosom, then grant that I may not be forgetful of the grace on which alone I subsist, and that I may have no evil eye. And though such dark thoughts assail me, do Thou set me right again, that I, too, may rejoice with Thee and the holy angels over my brother who was dead and is alive again, who was lost and is found. Grant this, O merciful God, for the sake of Jesus Christ, my Savior. Amen.

Hymn 99, 2.

MONDAY.

So the last shall be first, and the first, last.—Matt. 20, 1-15.

Another warning parable in addition to that of yesterday.—The kingdom of heaven is like unto a householder who went out early in the morning to hire laborers into his vine-

Week of the Third Sunday After Epiphany.

yard. And when he had agreed with the laborers for a penny a day, he sent them into his vineyard. And he went out about the third hour, and saw others standing idle in the market-place and said unto them: "Go ye also into the vineyard, and whatsoever is right I will give you." And they went their way. Again he went out about the sixth and ninth hour, and did likewise. And about the eleventh hour he went out, and found others standing idle, and saith unto them: "Why stand ye here all the day idle?" They say unto him: "Because no man hath hired us." He saith unto them: "Go ye also into the vineyard; and whatsoever is right, that shall ye receive." So when even was come, the lord of the vineyard saith unto his steward: "Call the laborers, and give them their hire, beginning from the last unto the first." And when they came that were hired about the eleventh hour, they received every man a penny. But when the first came, they supposed that they should have received more; and they likewise received every man a penny. And when they had received it, they murmured against the goodman of the house, saying: "These last have wrought but one hour, and thou hast made them equal unto us, who have borne the burden and the heat of the day." But he answered one of them and said: "Friend, I do thee no wrong: didst not thou agree with me for a penny? Take that thine is, and go thy way; I will give unto this last, even as unto thee. Is it not lawful for me to do what I will with mine own? Is thine eye evil because I am good?" (Matt. 20, 1-15.)

"So the last shall be first, and the first last," said Jesus at the end of this parable. In the kingdom of God naught but grace avails. And it is God's will of His great goodness to make the last equal to the first. And he that, knowing this, forever has an evil eye and would boast of his own pitiful merit, shall be last in such a way that he cannot remain in the kingdom of God. From this may God defend us!

· *PRAYER.*—Lord God, dear Heavenly Father, who from childhood in manifold ways hast effectually called and invited us into Thy kingdom of grace, as into Thy vineyard, I thank Thee for such Thine unmerited favor bestowed upon me. And I beseech Thee that through Thy Holy Ghost I may not only follow Thy voice, but also, trusting purely and solely in the merit of Thy dear Son Jesus Christ, continue in Thy grace, until, through the same, I enter eternal bliss. Amen.

Hymn 328.

TUESDAY.

Neither do I condemn thee: go, and sin no more.—John 8, 11.

In the last autumn of His earthly sojourn Jesus went to the Feast of Tabernacles at Jerusalem. On the day after the feast, early in the morning, He came into the temple. And all the people came unto Him. And He sat down and taught them. And the scribes and Pharisees brought unto Him a woman taken in adultery; and when they had set her in the midst, they said unto Him: "Master, this woman was taken in adultery, in the very act. Now Moses in the law commanded us that such should be stoned; but what sayest Thou?" This they said, tempting Him, that they might have to accuse Him. But Jesus stooped down, and with His finger wrote on the ground, presumably to indicate that it was not His business to interfere with the administration of civil justice. So when they continued asking Him, He lifted up Himself and said unto them: "He that is without sin among you, let him first cast a stone at her." And again He stooped down, and wrote on the ground, now, perhaps, to let His simple word take effect. And they, when they heard it, being convicted by their own conscience, went out one by one, beginning at the eldest, even unto the last. And Jesus was left alone, and the woman standing in the midst. (John 8, 1-11.)

Here we see the Savior in His official capacity. He did not come to condemn the world, but to save the world. He did not condemn the woman, but met her as her Redeemer: He forgave her sins unto her. And He said: "Sin no more." And so He meets us. He forgives us all our sins. We must believe this. And then we must go, and serve sin no more.

Week of the Third Sunday After Epiphany.   73

PRAYER.—Kind Savior, to me also dost Thou forgive all sins. Of this I am fully assured. Thy Law condemns me, my conscience condemns me, men condemn me,—but not Thou. Now grant me also Thy Holy Spirit to the end that from a heart filled with gratitude to Thee I may hate sin, and love and serve Thee. Forgive my sins unto me daily, yea, always, give me daily, yea, unceasingly, Thy Holy Spirit, that I may continually hate sin, and love and serve Thee, kind Savior. Amen.

Hymn 48.

WEDNESDAY.

This man went down to his house justified.—Luke 18, 14.

Who went down to his house justified? Who had forgiveness of sins? Who was absolved and pronounced entirely free and rid of all his sins? Who thus had the righteousness of God,—who?

Jesus spake the following parable unto certain who trusted in themselves that they were righteous, and despised others: Two men went up into the temple to pray, the one a Pharisee and the other a publican. The Pharisee stood and prayed thus with himself: " God, I thank Thee that I am not as other men are, extortioners, unjust, adulterers, or even as this publican. I fast twice in the week, I give tithes of all that I possess." And the publican, standing afar off, would not lift up so much as his eyes unto heaven, but smote upon his breast, saying: " God be merciful to me, a sinner." —In conclusion Jesus added: " I tell you, this man went down to his house justified rather than the other; for every one that exalteth himself shall be abased; and he that humbleth himself shall be exalted." (Luke 18, 9-14.)

Now thou knowest who is justified: not he that parades his own righteousness before God, despising others and exalting himself. No, his own righteousnesses are as filthy rags; in these no man can stand before God. And whoever means to boast of them before God shall be abased, rejected, damned. *He* is justified, he ever was and ever shall be justified, that humbles himself, acknowledges his sins, knows that he is an abomination unto God, but looks to Christ and, quickened by the Holy Ghost through the Gospel, imploringly says: God, for Christ's sake be reconciled to me, a sinner; be merciful to me, a sinner! Thus the worst sinner is justified before God and exalted to the heart of God. And this is the grace of our Lord Jesus Christ.

PRAYER.—Righteous God, merciful Father, in whose sight naught in all the world availeth anything save only the blood and death of Thy beloved Son, whereby Thou hast established eternal righteousness for all mankind, Thou that hatest all that trust in their own works: I give thanks unto Thy great mercy and heartily beseech Thee graciously to keep me from unbelief, pride, and arrogance, as well as from despair and other vices, lest my prayer become an abomination before Thee, but rather grant that I may take true comfort in the merit of Thy dear Son, and honor Him by leading a Christian life: through the same Thy dear Son Jesus Christ, our Lord. Amen.

Hymn 325, 2. 3.

THURSDAY.

The Son of Man is come to seek and to save that which was lost.—Luke 19, 10.

Our Lord, when on His way to Jerusalem, where He was to suffer and die, passed through Jericho. And, behold, there was a man named Zacchaeus, the chief among the publicans, and rich. And he sought to see Jesus who He was: but he could not for the crowd, because he was little of stature. And he climbed up into a sycamore tree to see Jesus; for He was to pass that way. And when Jesus came to the place, He looked up, and saw him, and said unto him: "Zacchaeus, make haste and come down; for to-day I must abide at thy house." And he made haste, and came down, and received Him joyfully.—What a blessed hour that must have been for Zacchaeus!—But when the people saw it, they all murmured, saying: "He is gone to be a guest with a man that is a sinner." And Zacchaeus stood and said unto the Lord: "Behold, Lord, the half of my goods I give to the poor; and if I have taken anything from any man by false accusation, I restore him fourfold." Thus Zacchaeus proved his faith in the Savior. And Jesus said unto him: "This day is salvation come to this house, forasmuch as he also is a son of Abraham. For the Son of Man is come to seek and to save that which was lost." (Luke 19, 1-10.)

Such is the grace of God in Christ Jesus: the Father draws poor sinners to Jesus through their hearing of Him. Jesus receives poor sinners most kindly, and continues to manifest Himself to them as their Savior and Redeemer. Through the Holy Spirit the poor sinners rejoice in their faith and begin to lead a new life; they are true sons of Abraham, the father of believers. And in such grace God will not be restricted by the enormity of the sins. For the Father hath sent the Son, and the Son of Man is come to seek and to save that which was lost.

PRAYER.—Lord, my God, I rest on Thy grace, O Heavenly Father, always draw me to Thy Son, my Savior. O Jesus, always receive me kindly and give me Thy salvation. O Holy Spirit, always make me rejoice in my faith and create a new heart within me. O God, let me never fear nor faint in such faith and trust in Thee, never let me doubt nor waver, never let me be deceived nor led astray therefrom. Grant that I may steadfastly trust in Thy grace, that I may obtain the end of my faith promised me by Thy grace, my soul's salvation, for Christ's sake. Amen.

Hymn 325, 1. 4.

FRIDAY.

This is my beloved Son in whom I am well pleased; hear ye Him.—Matt. 17, 5.

Nothing on earth, dear reader, can possibly be of greater consequence for thee than becoming fully assured of the fact that Jesus Christ is the eternal Son of God and thy merciful Savior and Redeemer. One thing only can give thee this certainty: *hearing and reading His Word.* Recall the story we read on Tuesday of the second week after Epiphany. There God the Father said concerning Jesus: "This is my beloved Son in whom I am well pleased; *hear ye Him."* Referring to this, St. Peter writes: " For we have not followed cunningly devised fables when we made known unto you the power and coming of our Lord Jesus Christ, but were eye-witnesses of His majesty. For He received from God the Father honor and glory, when there came such a voice to Him from the excellent glory, This is my beloved Son in whom I am well pleased. And this voice which came from heaven we heard when we were with Him in the holy mount. We have also a more sure word of prophecy, whereunto ye do well that ye take heed, as unto a light that shineth in a dark place, until the day dawn, and the day-star arise in your hearts: knowing this first that no prophecy of the Scripture is of any private interpretation. For the prophecy came not in old time by the will of man, but holy men spake as they were moved by the Holy Ghost,", 2 Peter 1, 16-21.

Hear, read, and heed the Word of Jesus, the Word concerning Jesus. Thou wilt find it in the word of the prophets, who prophesies concerning Him, and in the word of the apostles and evangelists, who proclaim His power and His coming again. That is God's Word, God's Word concerning Jesus, given by inspiration of the Holy Ghost. Thus, and thus only, will the day dawn, and the day-star arise in thy heart: the divine certainty that Jesus Christ is the eternal Son of God and thy merciful Savior and Redeemer. For by this Word the Holy Spirit, who is God, works faith within thee. And faith is certainty.

PRAYER.—Almighty and eternal God, I thank Thee that Thou hast given unto wretched mankind Thy holy Word, the Word concerning Christ, as a bright light for the darkness of our hearts. Grant me, I humbly beseech Thee, Thy Holy Ghost, that at all times I heed this Word, that the day may dawn within my heart, and that the true morning-star may lead me unto Christ, until I shall see Him in eternal light. Amen.

Hymn 257, 2.

SATURDAY.

One thing is needful.—Luke 10, 42.

Now it came to pass, as Jesus went with His disciples, that He entered into a certain village: and a certain woman named Martha received Him into her house. And she had a sister called Mary, who also sat at Jesus' feet, and heard His Word. But Martha was cumbered about much serving, and came to Him and said: "Lord, dost Thou not care that my sister hath left me to serve alone? Bid her therefore that she help me." And Jesus answered and said unto her: "Martha, Martha, thou art careful and troubled about many things; but one thing is needful; and Mary hath chosen that good part, which shall not be taken away from her." (Luke 10, 38-42.)

The one thing needful is, that Jesus' Word be preached and heard. Nothing at all on earth is as important and necessary as this, and, certainly, nothing is more important and more necessary than this. For only through the preaching and hearing of the Word of Jesus is that faith wrought and sustained within us—sustained, I say—wherein we sinners stand before God and are justified and saved. Without this faith, which is sustained only and exclusively through the Word of Jesus, even the best of our works can by no means please God, for without such faith we ourselves cannot please God. So the preaching and the hearing of the Word of Jesus is the one thing needful. Let no one take this from thee, O Christian!

PRAYER.—I thank Thee, my God, that Thou hast graciously given me Jesus' Word, the holy Gospel. Preserve it unto me and mine and unto all believers! Let it have free course and increase upon earth! Give unto me and all believers Thy Holy Ghost, that we may sincerely consider it the one thing needful, and gladly, diligently, and eagerly hear and learn it. Awaken hearts everywhere that heed the Word of Jesus and are thereby converted and saved. For Thou, God, art most good, and dost earnestly want all men to be saved through faith in Christ Jesus, the only Savior. Amen.

Hymn 83, 3. 4.

Week of the Fourth Sunday After Epiphany.
SUNDAY.

They have Moses and the prophets; let them hear them. Luke 16, 29.

There was a certain rich man who was clothed in purple and fine linen, and fared sumptuously every day; and a certain beggar named Lazarus was laid at his gate, full of sores, and desiring to be fed with the crumbs which fell from the rich man's table; moreover, the dogs came and licked his sores. And it came to pass that the beggar died, and was carried by the angels into Abraham's bosom. And the rich man also died, and was buried. And in hell he lifted up his eyes, being in torments, and saw Abraham afar off, and Lazarus in his bosom. And he cried and said: "Father Abraham, have mercy on me, and send Lazarus that he may dip the tip of his finger in water and cool my tongue; for I am tormented in this flame." But Abraham said: "Son, remember that thou in thy lifetime receivedst thy good things, and likewise Lazarus evil things; but now he is comforted, and thou art tormented. And besides all this, between us and you there is a great gulf fixed, so that they who would pass from hence to you cannot; neither can they pass to us that would come from thence." Then he said: "I pray thee therefore, father, that thou wouldst send him to my father's house; for I have five brethren, that he may testify unto them, lest they also come to this place of torment." Abraham saith unto him: "They have Moses and the prophets; let them hear them." And he said: "Nay, father Abraham; but if one went unto them from the dead, they will repent." And he said unto him: "If they hear not Moses and the prophets, neither will they be persuaded though one rose from the dead." (Luke 16, 19-31.)

We sinners must turn to Jesus while we live; then shall we obtain salvation. Who does not turn to Jesus will be damned. To the end that we turn to Jesus, God has given us the Word of Jesus through which the Holy Ghost operates within us. Other means of conversion God does not give. Nothing else could convert us. This is most certainly true.

Week of the Fourth Sunday After Epiphany.

PRAYER.—God, who hast given to me the Word of Jesus, have mercy upon me, and grant that I may gladly and properly use this Word and at all times turn to my Savior, in order that I may not be lost, but obtain eternal bliss with all the elect. Help me, help me, O my Lord! Amen.
Hymn 552, 4.

MONDAY.

Which things also we teach, not in words which man's wisdom teacheth, but which the Holy Ghost teacheth.— 1 Cor. 2, 13.

To the end that His Word and Gospel may be preached on earth until the last day, Jesus, having prayed to His heavenly Father, chose twelve from among His disciples, whom He also called *Apostles,* or ambassadors. They were the following: *Simon Peter,* and his brother *Andrew, James* and his brother *John, Philip* and *Bartholomew, Matthew* and *Thomas, James,* the son of Alphaeus, *Simon,* called Zelotes, *Judas,* the brother of James, and *Judas Iscariot,* the traitor. (Luke 6, 12-16.) After the sad end of Judas Iscariot, *Matthias* took his place. (Acts 1, 26.) These men, who had been with the Lord during His sojourn on earth, from the baptism of John unto the day that He was taken up into heaven, were to be His witnesses to all the earth of those things which they had seen and heard, and witnesses of His resurrection. Later *St. Paul,* who had received special revelations, was added to their number. (Rom. 1, 1; Gal. 1, 11. 12.) These men, by word of mouth and by their writings, were to proclaim the Gospel, the Word of Jesus, to all the world. For this work they were to receive the gift, the special gift, of the Holy Ghost, so that the things which they spoke and wrote were not in the words which man's wisdom teacheth, but which the Holy Ghost teacheth, as our text above says. Others besides them received this special gift (Acts 2, 1-4); thus also the evangelists *Mark* and *Luke.* So in the writings of the evangelists and apostles, which we have in the Bible, we have the Word of God, the Word of Jesus, just as divinely pure, unalloyed, and certain as if Jesus, our Lord, stood before us and preached. And this, even this, we must hear and read.

PRAYER.—I give thanks unto Thee, merciful God and Father, that in the Bible Thou hast given me Thy Word, Thy Gospel, so that I may know my Savior aright, believe in Him, and through faith obtain salvation. I pray Thee, vouchsafe unto me Thy grace, that by the power and operation of Thy Holy Ghost I hold Thy Word sacred, and gladly hear and learn it, and be confirmed in faith, until in eternal joy and bliss I shall see what here I have believed. Do this for Jesus Christ's sake. Amen.

Hymn 2, 1. 2.

TUESDAY.

He that heareth you heareth me; and he that despiseth you despiseth me; and he that despiseth me despiseth Him that sent me.—Luke 10, 16.

Besides the apostles the Lord Jesus appointed other disciples, seventy in number, and sent them two and two before His face into every city and place whither He Himself would come. And He said unto them: "The harvest truly is great, but the laborers are few; pray ye therefore the Lord of the harvest that He would send forth laborers into His harvest. Go your ways: behold, I send you forth as lambs among wolves." And furthermore He instructed them not to be concerned about their food, but to let those provide for them who would receive them and their message. But if the people of a city would not receive them, then were they to say publicly: "Even the very dust of your city which cleaveth on us we do wipe off against you; notwithstanding be ye sure of this, that the kingdom of God is come nigh unto you." And lastly Jesus said: "He that heareth you heareth Me; and he that despiseth you despiseth Me; and he that despiseth Me despiseth Him that sent Me." (Luke 10, 1-16.)

This word of the Lord applies to all preachers of His Word at all times, that is, to those who preach His Word right and pure throughout. Observe that well! If thy preacher, be he eloquent or not, preaches the Word of Jesus,

Week of the Fourth Sunday After Epiphany.

then thou must hear him as if thou heardst Jesus Himself. Thou must listen to the Word, not to the person. Dost thou understand? If, however, thou despisest such a preacher, then in reality thou despisest Jesus; and if thou despisest Jesus, thou despisest the great God that sent Him. And what will then become of thee?

PRAYER.—Lord God, Heavenly Father, I thank Thee that Thou hast given us Thy Word and hast also appointed the holy ministry. I pray Thee in the name of Thy dear Son Jesus Christ, and at His command, to send forth faithful laborers into Thy vineyard, and to grant that those whom Thou hast may abide in the true doctrine and lead a Christian life unto their end. And give unto me and to all Christians Thy Holy Spirit, that at all times we may gladly receive the Word which they preach, assiduously follow its teachings, and in the end obtain eternal life, through Jesus Christ, Thy dear Son, our Lord. Amen.

Hymn 110, 9.

WEDNESDAY.

So will I compass Thine altar, O Lord, that I may publish with the voice of thanksgiving, and tell of all Thy wondrous works. Lord, I have loved the habitation of Thy house, and the place where Thine honor dwelleth.—Ps. 26, 6-8.

Surely, this text was in the mind of Anna. Anna was a daughter of Phanuel, of the tribe of Aser. She was of a great age, having lived with her husband seven years from her virginity, and was now a widow of about fourscore and four years. She was a prophetess, a woman endowed with especial gifts of the Holy Spirit. But though she was a prophetess, yet, unmindful of her great age, she departed not from the temple, but served God with fastings and prayers night and day. And for this she received a great and blessed reward: she found Jesus in the temple. And when she had found Him, she gave thanks to the Lord and spoke of Him to all that looked for redemption in Jerusalem. (Luke 2, 36-38.)

What a pattern for old Christians! They look back upon a long pathway of life which they have traversed. Soon they must pass through the valley of death to their eternal home, where heavenly peans resound, where all the wonders of God's grace are seen and fully known, where the glory of God shall be upon them. Meanwhile, what better thing can they do than to compass God's altar, where they publish with the voice of thanksgiving, where they tell of all His wondrous works, where His honor dwelleth, yea, where they find Jesus and His Word and Sacrament? Oh, may God grant His Holy Spirit to all old Christians, that, leaning upon their staff, if need be, they regularly wend their way to the house of God. And oh! may they also pray, and speak of Jesus to their kin and to other Christians. This is a fitting habit for aged pilgrims whose goal is heaven.—Much more, however, ought *young* Christians to be found where God would equip them for the perilous way through this life to heaven.

PRAYER.—Lord God, Heavenly Father, grant me, I beseech Thee, Thy Holy Spirit, that I may publish with the voice of thanksgiving, and tell of all the wondrous works which Thou hast done for our salvation and wilt do for our eternal happiness, and that I may love the habitation of Thy house, and the place where Thine honor dwelleth. And there bless me, O God, with blessings from on high, that I may know my Savior ever better, and believe in Him ever more firmly, and finally finish my course joyfully, and through Him enter my eternal home. Amen.

Hymn 78, 2-4.

THURSDAY.

The seed is the Word of God.—Luke 8, 11.

Yes, the seed from which the fruit of faith and salvation grows is the Word of God. But why, O why do so many that hear the Word of God nevertheless not believe and obtain salvation?—It is with the Word as it is with the seed which a sower went out to sow. As he sowed, some fell by the wayside; and it was trodden down, and the fowls of the air devoured it. Thus many who hear the Word do not allow this divine seed to enter their hearts; it lies loosely upon the surface. Then cometh the devil and taketh it away, lest they believe and be saved. And some of the sower's seed fell upon a rock; and as soon as it was sprung up, it withered away because it lacked moisture. Thus many receive the Word with joy; but they do not let it take root; for a while they believe, but in time of temptation they fall away. Still other of the sower's seed fell among thorns; and the thorns sprang up with it and choked it. Thus many allow cares and riches and pleasures of this life to choke the Word of God, so that it brings no fruit to perfection. Hence it is not the Word's fault that so many do not believe and are not saved, but it is their own fault.—Some seed, however, fell on good ground, and brought forth fruit a hundredfold. Thus some hear the Word of God, and keep it in an honest and good heart, and bring forth fruit with patience: they become believing children of God, and in the end obtain salvation. This is not owing to their good conduct, but to the grace of God and the divine power of the Word. (Luke 8, 4-15.)

O my dear reader, which ground dost thou resemble?

PRAYER.—Almighty God and Father, who madest heaven and earth and who hast prepared salvation and eternal blessedness, and didst profusely scatter the heavenly seed of Thy divine Word among us, I give thanks unto Thee for these Thy gracious gifts and treasures. I beseech Thee to so prepare my heart by Thy Word and Spirit that I may be good land, guarding myself against false confidence, indifference, instability, care, avarice, and lust, taking firm root in Thy gracious Word, and patiently enduring every heat, storm, temptation, and tribulation that may afflict me, that in an honest and good heart I may bring forth rich fruit, praising and honoring Thee now and forever. Amen.

Hymn 248, 5.

FRIDAY.

We have heard Him ourselves, and know that this is indeed the Christ, the Savior of the world.—John 4, 42.

In the first year of His public career, while He was going from Judea into Galilee, and must needs pass through Samaria, Jesus had come to Jacob's well, before the city of

Sychar, and there met a sinful woman of Samaria, whom, through His words, which are spirit and life, and through the wonderful manifestation of His divine glory, He converted from a life of sin to faith in Him, the promised Christ. (Thou mayest read this in John 4, 1-26.) Then the woman went into the city with haste, and said to the men: "Come, and see a man who told me all things that ever I did; is not this the Christ?" She wanted others to share the joy she had found in her faith. And they, at once inclined to believe on Jesus because of what the woman said, went out of the city, and came unto Him, and besought Him to tarry with them. And He abode there two days and proclaimed unto them the salvation which had appeared in Him. And many more believed in Jesus because of His own Word, saying to the woman: "Now we believe, not because of Thy saying; for we have heard Him ourselves, and know that this is indeed the Christ, the Savior of the world." (Read this in John 4, 27-42.)

This is the proper way to obtain true faith in Jesus: see Him for thyself, and hear His Word. And true faith is to be fully assured that Jesus is indeed the Christ, the Savior of the world. Thou, too, canst come to true faith in Jesus and attain to firmness in this faith in this way. In thy Bible thou hast His faithful image and His pure Word. May God graciously work perfect assurance within thee, that thou, too, mayest say: Henceforth I believe, not because of the saying of others; for I have heard Jesus myself, and know that He is indeed the Christ, the Savior of the world. This is the faith through which thou shalt conquer all and enter heaven.

PRAYER.—God, my God, grant me Thy Holy Spirit, that I may at all times seek, see, and hear Jesus myself in His Word, which Thou hast so graciously given me. And thus, my God, let me grow ever more firm and ever more certain, yea, become firmly established in my faith and fully assured that Jesus is indeed the Christ promised in the Old Testament, the world's and my, even my, Redeemer and Savior. Amen.

Hymn 83, 9.

SATURDAY.

And he said, Lord, I believe. And he worshiped Him.— John 9, 38.

In the last year of His visible sojourn on earth, when He had come to Jerusalem to celebrate the Feast of the Tabernacles, Jesus restored a man's eyesight who had been born blind. He did it on a Sabbath day. The man born blind knew, indeed, that it was Jesus who opened his eyes, but he did not know Jesus as he should. Now when the Pharisees, who were hypocrites and hated Jesus, said to the man born blind that Jesus could not be the Son of God because He did this on a Sabbath day, he answered: "He is a prophet." And when they continued to revile Jesus, and said that He was a sinner, and that they knew not whence He was, the man born blind answered: "Why, herein is a marvelous thing, that ye know not from whence He is, and yet He hath opened my eyes. Now we know that God heareth not sinners; but if any man be a worshiper of God, and doeth His will, him He heareth. Since the world began was it not heard that any man opened the eyes of one that was born blind. If this man were not of God, He could do nothing." Then the Pharisees said to him: "Thou wast altogether born in sins, and dost thou teach us?" And they cast him out.—Then Jesus found him and said to him: "Dost thou believe on the Son of God?" that is, on Christ, the promised Messiah, who, according to the testimony of John the Baptist, was now to appear. He answered: "Who is He, Lord, that I might believe on Him?" Jesus said unto him: "Thou dost both see Him, and it is He that speaketh with thee." Then said the man that was born blind: "Lord, I believe." And he worshiped Him. (John 9.)

All the angels of God worship our Lord and Savior. And the hour shall come in which all must bow their knees before Jesus, whether they will or no. Now, then, O sinner, whom Jesus has redeemed, and whom He so kindly approaches through His Word, revealing Himself as the Savior, believe in Him and worship Him with exceeding great joy through the Holy Ghost, that when He shall appear in His glory, thou mayest exult and cry: "My Savior!"

PRAYER.—Lord Jesus, true God and man, my Savior and Redeemer, I believe in Thee, I love and praise and glorify Thee, I worship Thee with all the angels and the elect in heaven and on earth. Preserve my faith through Thy miraculous Word, through Thy gracious Holy Spirit. Bring me where believing shall be turned to seeing, where my love shall be perfect, my praise and glorifying shall be heavenly, my worship an everlasting joy. Amen.

Hymn 394, 2.

Week of Septuagesima Sunday.

SUNDAY.

I am the Resurrection and the Life.—John 11, 25.

Now that Passover drew nigh when Jesus was to suffer and die. He was in Perea, east of the Jordan, several days' journey from Jerusalem. In Bethany, near Jerusalem, Lazarus, the brother of Martha and Mary, lay at the point of death. The sisters sent word to Jesus, saying: " Lord, behold, he whom Thou lovest is sick. But Jesus, who loved Lazarus and his sisters, remained two days in the same place where He was. Then He went to Judea with His disciples, to raise Lazarus, who, meanwhile, had died.—When Martha heard that Jesus was near Bethany, she went to meet Him and said to Him: " Lord, if Thou hadst been here, my brother had not died. But I know that even now, whatsoever Thou wilt ask of God, God will give it Thee." Saith Jesus: " Thy brother shall rise again." Martha saith: " I know that he shall rise again in the resurrection at the last day." Saith Jesus: *" I am the Resurrection and the Life. He that believeth in Me, though he were dead, yet shall he live; and whosoever liveth and believeth in Me shall never die.* Believest thou this?" She saith: " Yea, Lord; I believe that Thou art the Christ, the Son of God, that should come into the world."—Now Martha went and called Mary secretly, saying: " The Master is come, and calleth for thee." Quickly

Mary came to Jesus and fell down at His feet, weeping and saying: " Lord, if Thou hadst been here, my brother had not died." Many Jews had come along and wept also. Jesus was troubled and said: " Where have ye laid him? " They said: " Lord, come and see." Jesus wept. And they came to the tomb, the entrance of which was closed with a stone. Jesus saith: " Take ye away the stone." Martha saith: " Lord, by this time he stinketh; for he hath been dead four days." Jesus saith: " Said I not unto thee that, if thou wouldst believe, thou shouldst see the glory of God? " Then they took away the stone. But Jesus lifted up his eyes and said: " Father, I thank Thee that Thou hast heard Me. And I knew that Thou hearest me always; but because of the people which stand by I said it, that they may believe that Thou hast sent Me." And He cried with a loud voice: " Lazarus, come forth." And he that was dead came forth, bound hand and foot with grave-clothes; and his face was bound about with a napkin. Jesus said unto them: " Loose him and let him go." (John 11, 1-44.)

Jesus is the Christ, the Son of God, who came into the world. He is the Resurrection and the Life. He has given His life into death for us. He has arisen and lives. He that believes in Him, receives Him in true faith, shall live though he die. And he that lives and believes in Him shall nevermore die, shall never know what death really is. Believest thou this?

PRAYER.—I believe this, my Lord and Savior. Jesus, I believe in Thee. When my last hour comes, I will, trusting in Thee, laugh at death and see life. When I rise, I shall see Thee, and exult in the glory of eternal life. Grant this, Thou Conqueror of Death, Thou Prince of Life, Thou merciful Savior. Amen.

Hymn 544, 11.

MONDAY.

It is expedient for us that one man should die for the people, and that the whole nation perish not.—John 11, 50.

Many of the Jews who had witnessed the raising of Lazarus believed in Jesus. But some of them went away to the

Pharisees and told them what Jesus had done. Then the chief priests and Pharisees gathered a council and said: " What do we? for this man doeth many miracles. If we let Him thus alone, all men will believe on Him; and the Romans shall come and take away both our place and nation." And one of them, named Caiaphas, being the high priest that same year, said unto them: " Ye know nothing at all, nor consider that it is expedient for us that one man should die for the people, and that the whole nation perish not." And this spake he not of himself; but, being high priest that year, he prophesied that Jesus should die for that nation, and not for that nation only, but that also He should gather in one of the children of God that were scattered abroad. The latter are God's elect, whom God's eye seeth. So from that day forth they took counsel together that they might put Jesus to death. Jesus therefore walked no more openly among the Jews, but went thence to a country near the wilderness, into a city called Ephraim, between Bethel and Jericho, and there continued with His disciples.—And the Jews' Passover was at hand. (John 11, 45-55.)

Yes, indeed, it is expedient that the *one* Jesus should die for us all, and that we all perish not. Indeed, according to the counsel of God, Jesus should die for all men, and gather together a blessed congregation of God's children. Indeed, Jesus has died for us, and we who believe in Him shall live through Him. Believe, O believe in Him, Christian!

PRAYER.—I believe in Thee, my Savior. Help me always to believe in Thee. Thou hast died in my stead, and hast procured salvation for me. Help me to seize on Thy salvation. Help me into heaven, help me into eternal life, Lord Jesus! Amen.

Hymn 530, 3.

TUESDAY.

Behold the Lamb of God!—John 1, 36.

Now came the Feast of the Passover. Jesus now arose and went with His disciples from Ephraim to Jerusalem by way of Jericho. And on the road between Ephraim and Jericho He took the twelve disciples apart and said to them:

"Behold, we go up to Jerusalem, and all things that are written by the prophets concerning the Son of Man shall be accomplished. For He shall be betrayed unto the chief priests and unto the scribes, and they shall condemn Him to death, and shall deliver Him unto the Gentiles to mock, and to scourge, and to crucify Him; and on the third day He shall rise again." And they understood none of these things, and this saying was hid from them, neither knew they the things which were spoken. (Matt. 20, 17-19; Luke 18, 31-34.) Before the vision of Jesus all that should happen to Him in Jerusalem was clearly unfolded. And willingly He went to suffer all. For He knew that He was the Lamb of God that should suffer all these things for the salvation of mankind, by the eternal and determinate counsel of God, and according to the prophecies and types of the Old Testament. But at that time His disciples could in no wise comprehend this.

If thou wouldst truly know Jesus, thou must know Him in His death and resurrection. Thou must know Him to be the Lamb of God that taketh away and—conquereth thy sin and that of the whole world. This is the true and saving faith.

PRAYER.—I thank Thee, Lord Jesus, Thou Lamb of God, that Thou so willingly didst atone for my sin through Thy bitter suffering and death, and didst so utterly abolish the same through Thy victorious resurrection, so that it can in no wise harm me any more. Give me, I beseech Thee, Thy Holy Spirit, that I may truly know this, comforting myself with Thee, and in faith pleading Thee before God to be the real sacrifice by which my propitiation has been effected. Amen.

Hymn 191, 3.

WEDNESDAY.

She is come aforehand to anoint my body for the burying.—Mark 14, 8.

Six days before the Passover, on Saturday, Jesus came to Bethany, where Lazarus was, who had been dead, whom Jesus had raised from the dead. There they made Him a

Week of Septuagesima Sunday.

supper. And Martha served; but Lazarus was one of them that sat at the table with Him. Then took Mary a pound of ointment of spikenard, very costly, and anointed the feet of Jesus, and wiped His feet with her hair; and the house was filled with the odor of the ointment. Then saith one of His disciples, Judas Iscariot, Simon's son, who should betray Him: "Why was not this ointment sold for three hundred pence and given to the poor?" This he said, not that he cared for the poor, but because he was a thief, and had the bag, and carried what was put therein. And the other disciples were persuaded to agree with him. Then said Jesus: "Let her alone; against the day of my burying hath she kept this. She is come aforehand to anoint my body for the burying. For the poor ye have always with you; but me ye have not always." (John 12, 1-8.)

Jesus went to meet His death most willingly. That is seen from this story. And I think that Mary, ever a silent, thoughtful listener of Jesus' Word, knew more of Jesus' impending sacrifice in death than all the others. And her great and fervent love for her Savior moved her to do as she did. And her Savior would not let them chide her.—Surely, thou, O Christian, knowest what thy Savior did for thee, how He loved thee, and still loves thee. Do thou love Him! Do for Him as thy love bids thee do. He will take pleasure in it. It will please Him most if thou surrenderest thyself wholly to Him, that He may bring thee to eternal bliss.

PRAYER.—O my dear Savior Jesus Christ, who of Thy great love didst give Thy life into death for me, and dost love me now and always with a boundless love: I love Thee. But it grieves me sorely that I cannot love Thee as I should. But what is it Thou askest? Thou wilt have me, poor sinner, and save me. That is the reward Thou demandest for Thy love, O merciful Savior. So, then, take me, and bring me to eternal salvation, where I shall surely love Thee truly and fully. Amen.

Hymn 191, 5.

THURSDAY.

Hosanna to the Son of David! Blessed is He that cometh in the name of the Lord; Hosanna in the highest!— Matt. 21, 9.

The following day, on Sunday, Jesus arose to go to Jerusalem together with His disciples and a great number of people from Bethany. Bethany was situated on the eastern slope of the Mount of Olives, and this was immediately east of Jerusalem. And when they approached the hamlet of Bethphage, still on the east side of the mountain, Jesus sent two of His disciples, saying: "Go into the village over against you, and straightway ye shall find an ass tied, and a colt with her: loose them and bring them unto me. And if any man say aught unto you, ye shall say, The Lord hath need of them; and straightway he will send them." All this was done that it might be fulfilled which was spoken by the prophet, saying: "Tell ye the daughter of Zion, Behold, thy King cometh unto thee, meek, and sitting upon an ass, and a colt, the foal of an ass." And the disciples went, and did as Jesus commanded them, and brought the ass and the colt, and put on them their clothes, and set Him thereon. And a very great multitude that had come to meet Him from Jerusalem spread their garments in the way; others cut down branches from the trees and strewed them in the way. And the multitudes that went before, and that followed, cried, saying: "Hosanna to the Son of David! Blessed is He that cometh in the name of the Lord; Hosanna in the highest!" And when He came into Jerusalem, all the city was moved, saying: "Who is this?" And the multitude said: "This is Jesus, the Prophet of Nazareth of Galilee." (Matt. 21, 1-11).

It was Jesus' will, before His suffering and death, to be publicly proclaimed the Christ by and before all the people that had come to the Passover at Jerusalem from all the ends of the earth. And so it was done. But soon the Hosannas were turned into "Crucify Him, crucify Him!" Do thou, however, in constant faith, hail thy Savior, who has come in the name of the Lord to save thee through His suffering and death.

PRAYER.—Lord Jesus, I, a poor sinner, praise and magnify Thee that Thou hast presented Thyself a sacrifice also for my redemption and salvation. Thou art indeed the Savior of the world, promised since the world began, eagerly expected of so many a believing heart. Open, I beseech Thee, my heart and lips by Thy Holy Spirit, that I, too, poor sinner though I be, may join in the praises of Thy people whom Thou hast redeemed. Amen.

Hymn 136, 1.

FRIDAY.

My house shall be called the house of prayer.—Matt. 21, 13.

On the morning after His entry into Jerusalem, Jesus, with His disciples, went from Bethany—for there He spent the nights of His last week on earth—to the temple at Jerusalem. And what did He behold? The spacious courts of the temple resounded with the noisy tumult of a public fair. Those who yesterday had cried Hosanna were now bartering and jollifying—all "for the good of the cause," as is said in our day on similar occasions. And Jesus, in righteous indignation and irresistible majesty, cast out all those that bought and sold in the temple, and overthrew the tables of the money-changers, and the seats of those that sold doves, saying to them: "It is written, 'My house shall be called the house of prayer'; but ye have made it a den of thieves." —And the blind and the lame came to Him in the temple; and He healed them. And the children hailed Him, singing: "Hosanna to the Son of David." But when the chief priests and the scribes saw the wonderful things that He did, and heard the children crying in the temple, saying: "Hosanna to the Son of David," they were sore displeased,—the hypocrites, who had willingly tolerated the tumult of the fair,— and said to Him: "Hearest Thou not what these say?" And Jesus said unto them: "Yea; have ye never read, 'Out of the mouth of babes and sucklings Thou hast perfected praise'?" And He left them, and went out of the city to Bethany; and He lodged there. (Matt. 21, 12-17.)

All who name the name of the Savior, and who hear His Word and worship Him, must do so seriously and with the simplicity of a child, and not combine worldly and carnal attractions therewith. The Church of Christ must be truly desirous of salvation, and must assemble to hear, to pray, and to praise. The Lord who came to His temple at Jerusalem is present in our assemblies also. And when we do carnal things under the pretense of serving Him, He beholds with grief and indignation that our heart desires Him not.

PRAYER.—Help, O my Lord and Savior, that I, a poor lost sinner, may desire Thee truly for my only Savior. Graciously help me to seek and embrace Thee and Thy salvation in Thy Word, for there, and there only, wilt Thou be sought and found. Grant that I may prize Thy Word above every treasure, and account no obstacle or cost too great to have Thy Word. Grant me grace to praise and magnify Thee in the congregation with newness and singleness of heart. Amen.

Hymn 99, 5.

SATURDAY.

The stone which the builders rejected, the same is become the head of the corner.—Matt. 21, 42.

On Tuesday morning Jesus returned to the temple, and preached to the people assembled there the Gospel, the good tidings that He, Christ, their Lord and Savior, had now come. Then the chief priests and the elders of the people came to Him and said: "By what authority doest Thou these things? and who gave Thee this authority?" And Jesus answered and said to them: "I also will ask you one thing, which if ye tell me, I in like wise will tell you in what authority I do these things. The baptism of John, whence was it? from heaven or of men?" And they reasoned with themselves, saying: If we shall say, From heaven, He will say unto us, Why did ye not, then, believe him? But if we shall say, Of men, we fear the people; for the people regarded John the Baptist, who had testified that Jesus was the Lamb of God, and the Son of God, as a prophet. And they answered Jesus: "We cannot tell," whereupon He said to them: "Neither tell I you by what authority I do these things." They plainly did not *want* to believe in Him, and were hardened in their enmity against Him. This very thing He told them in strong terms and in parables and said: "The publicans and the harlots go into the kingdom of God before you." And furthermore He said: "Did ye never read in the Scriptures, The stone which the builders rejected, the same is become the head of the corner? Therefore say I unto you, The kingdom of God shall be taken from you, and given to a nation bringing forth the fruits thereof." And they sought the more to kill Jesus. (Matt. 21, 23-46.)

Indeed, they, the builders of Israel, were hardened. They rejected Israel's Messiah, the Savior of the world. But the stone which the builders rejected, the same is become the head of the corner of God's eternal temple, the congregation of the redeemed. To-day, also, countless builders of the Church reject Jesus, their Savior. But do thou build thy faith on Him, and thou shalt obtain salvation.

PRAYER.—O Lord Jesus, grant me Thy Holy Spirit, that the contradiction arising against Thee a thousand-fold on the part of chief priests and the elders within the Church may not shake my faith and lead me astray, but rather build my faith on Thee, and through Thee obtain salvation. For Thou alone art the Lord and Savior, and Thou hast given Thy life for me. Amen.

Hymn 312, 1.

Week of Sexagesima Sunday.

SUNDAY.

Many are called, but few are chosen.—Matt. 22, 14.

On Tuesday morning, in the temple, Jesus also spoke the following parable to the chief priests and elders who hated Him: "The kingdom of heaven is like unto a certain king who made a marriage feast for his son, and sent forth his servants to call them that were bidden to the wedding; and they would not come. Again he sent forth other servants, saying: Tell them that are bidden, Behold, I have prepared my dinner; my oxen and my fatlings are killed, and all things are ready; come to the marriage. But they made light of it, and went their ways, one to his farm, another to his merchandise; and the rest took his servants, and entreated them spitefully, and slew them. But when the king heard thereof, he was wroth; and he sent forth his armies, and destroyed these murderers, and burned their city." This part of the parable plainly refers to the unbelieving Jews. The Lord continued: " Then saith he to his servants: The wedding is ready, but they who were bidden were not worthy. Go ye therefore into the highways, and as many as ye shall find, bid to the marriage. So the servants went out into the highways, and gathered together all as many as they found, both bad and good: and the wedding was furnished with guests." This refers to the remnant in Israel and to the converted heathen. " And when the king came in to see the guests, he saw there a man who had not on a wedding-garment; and he saith unto him, Friend, how camest thou in hither not having on a wedding-garment? And he was speechless. Then said the king to the servants: Bind him hand and foot, and take him away, and cast him into outer darkness: there shall be weeping and gnashing of teeth." Here a man is portrayed who maintains outward affiliation with the Church of Christ, but does not, in true faith, lay hold on Christ's merit. Finally the Lord said: " For many are called, but few are chosen." So in this parable He shows that God fervently and with great mercy calls many to His salvation who are still lost through their own fault. And there are but few elect of God who truly comfort themselves with the merit of Christ, and lay hold on His salvation. Dost thou do it, reader?

PRAYER.—Almighty and eternal God, who, from pure and undeserved mercy in Christ Jesus, dost offer righteousness and eternal life to us poor sinners, freely and without price, I beseech Thy mercy graciously to keep me, that I may not despise nor forfeit Thy divine grace; and give unto me Thy good spirit, that I may lay hold on the same in true

faith, and walk worthily of the same in true sanctification: through Jesus Christ, Thy dear Son, our Lord. Amen.
Hymn 545, 1.

MONDAY.

God is not the God of the dead, but of the living.—Matt. 22, 32.

On Tuesday, in the temple, our Lord was tried and tempted a great deal by His enemies, the hardened Pharisees and Sadducees. The latter, who said that there is no resurrection, came and asked Him, saying: "Master, Moses said, If a man die, having no children, his brother shall marry his wife, and raise up seed unto his brother. Now there were with us seven brethren; and the first, when he had married a wife, deceased, and, having no issue, left his wife unto his brother; likewise the second also, and the third, unto the seventh. And last of all the woman died also. Therefore, in the resurrection, whose wife shall she be of the seven? for they all had her." Jesus answered and said unto them: "Ye do err, not knowing the Scriptures nor the power of God. For in the resurrection they neither marry, nor are given in marriage, but are as the angels of God in heaven. But as touching the resurrection of the dead, have ye not read that which was spoken unto you by God, saying: I am the God of Abraham, and the God of Isaac, and the God of Jacob? God is not the God of the dead, but of the living." (Matt. 22, 23-32.)

If through faith in thy Savior thou art a child of God, so that God is thy God and Father, then God will not leave thee in death, but raise thee from the dead; for He will not be the God and Father of the dead, but of the living. This is what Jesus Christ has taught, and His Word also in manifold ways and places teaches the resurrection of the dead. In the resurrection, however, there will be no marrying nor giving in marriage; we shall be no longer subject to the laws and regulations of this terrestrial life, for we shall have spiritual bodies. These the power of God, which is boundless, will give us. So let not the spiteful drivel of those who know neither the Scriptures nor the power of God confuse thee.

PRAYER.—Grant, Thou faithful God, that I may be and remain Thy child through faith in my Lord and Savior, depart this life in blessed peace, holding fast to Thy grace, rest in my grave under Thy protection, rise by Thy power, and thereupon inherit the blessed hope, eternal life, for the sake of Thy dear Son Jesus Christ, to whom, with Thee and the Holy Ghost, be praise, honor, and glory, now and evermore. Amen.

Hymn 534.

TUESDAY.

I, even I, am the Lord; and beside me there is no Savior. Is. 43, 11.

When the Pharisees heard that Jesus had put the Sadducees to silence, they were gathered together. Then one of them, a lawyer, asked Him a question, trying Him, and saying: "Master, which is the great commandment of the Law?" Jesus said unto him: "Thou shalt love the Lord, thy God, with all thy heart and with all thy soul and with all thy mind. This is the first and great commandment. And the second is like unto it: Thou shalt love thy neighbor as thyself. On these two commandments hang all the Law and the prophets." So instead of walking into the open trap, and setting one commandment above the other, our Lord recited the sum of all commandments and of all their explanations, which is the love toward God and toward the neighbor. But who dare boast of this love? Who can thereby become righteous before God and be saved? Not one.—Now, while the Pharisees were gathered together, Jesus asked them: "What think ye of Christ? Whose Son is He?" They said unto Him: "The son of David." He said unto them: "How, then, doth David in spirit call Him Lord, saying: The Lord said unto my Lord, Sit Thou on my right hand, till I make Thine enemies Thy footstool? If David, then, called Him Lord, how is He his son?" And no man was able to answer Him a word. And the trials were at an end. (Matt. 22, 34-46.)

True, Christ is the son of David. But at the same time Christ is He who through the prophet said: "I, even I, am the Lord; and beside me there is no savior." And *Jesus* is the Lord who became David's son and our only Savior. And He, through His vicarious life, suffering, death, and resurrection, procured for us that righteousness which we sinners could never bring about by the fulfillment of the Law. Let us look to Him in faith, then shall we be righteous before God and obtain life eternal.

PRAYER.—O Jesus Christ, my Lord and God, Lord and God of Abraham and Isaac and Jacob and David, and of all who in all ages desired Thy salvation, I give thanks unto Thee, for Thou hast kept Thy gracious Word, and by Thy salutary birth and by Thy bitter suffering and death didst make Thyself our Savior. Verily, beside Thee there is no Savior. Grant that by Thy Holy Spirit I may bow my knees before Thee in firm confidence, and be and remain a partaker of Thy salvation, who with the Father and the Holy Ghost art true God, blessed forever. Amen.

Hymn 93, 3. 4.

WEDNESDAY.

O Jerusalem, Jerusalem, thou that killest the prophets, and stonest them that are sent unto thee, how often would I have gathered thy children together, even as a hen gathereth her chickens under her wings, and ye would not! Behold, your house is left unto you desolate. For I say unto you, Ye shall not see me henceforth till ye shall say: Blessed is He that cometh in the name of the Lord.—Matt. 23, 37-39.

Our Lord and Savior Jesus Christ, by preaching and working miracles, had done so much for the people of Jerusalem in order to reveal Himself to them; but He had always been rejected. On this last Tuesday, in the temple, the chief priests, scribes, and elders of the people had continually harassed and tempted Him. They even held counsel how to kill Him. So now, in presence of all the people, powerfully and repeatedly, Jesus cried woe upon these murderous hypocrites. At last He said: "Wherefore, behold, I send unto you prophets and wise men and scribes: and some of them ye shall kill and crucify; and some of them shall ye scourge in your synagogues, and persecute them from city to city, that upon you may come all the righteous blood shed upon the earth, from the blood of righteous Abel unto the blood of Zacharias, son of Barachias, whom ye slew between the temple and the altar. Verily I say unto you, All these things shall come upon this generation." And then He pronounced upon whole Jerusalem, encrusted in unbelief, self-righteousness, and carnal-mindedness, the stirring as well as portentous words written above. Yea, He often would have gathered Jerusalem, even as a hen gathereth her chickens under her wings; but they would not. As Jerusalem had always been a murderess of prophets, so even now it brooded murder against Him and His witnesses. Therefore an end must be made of Jerusalem and of the temple and of the service and of the people. And Him, the Savior, they were not to see henceforth, not until they shall see and hear Him on Judgment Day, when, with gnashing of their teeth, they shall be constrained to confess that it is He to whom they must say: "Blessed is He that cometh in the name of the Lord." (Matt. 23.)

O thou people that callest thyself a Christian people, even to-day, how recreant art thou and full of hatred toward Christ! How doth thy Savior seek to gather even thee with fervent desire, but thou wouldst not! What dreadful doom will finally come over thee! Christians, Christians, let us accept the Savior!

PRAYER.—Lord Jesus, I thank Thee that through Thy Gospel Thou hast taken me under Thy saving wings and hitherto hast kept me there! Govern me, I beseech Thee, by Thy Holy Spirit, lest, after all, I reject such grace. Grant that I may appreciate the same evermore, and accept it ever more thankfully, gladly hearing and learning Thy precious Word, living according to it, and being governed by it, to the end that now I may know Thee to be my gracious Savior, and when Thou shalt come again, that then I may enter the eternal mansions with Thee. Amen.

Hymn 33, 8.

Week of Sexagesima Sunday.

THURSDAY.

While ye have the light, believe in the light, that ye may be the children of light.—John 12, 36.

To-day let us hear the last words Jesus spoke before the people in public, and in which He testified that He was the Savior. This was on the same Tuesday in the temple.

Thinking of His suffering and death, which was to come to pass so soon, He said: "Now is the judgment of this world; now shall the prince of this world be cast out. And I, if I be lifted up from the earth, will draw all men unto me." After Christ's atoning death this is the judgment of this world, that Satan, the prince of this world, is cast out no longer to accuse us, and that all may find righteousness and salvation with Jesus, who was lifted up on the cross.—"Yet a little while is the light with you. Walk while ye have the light, lest darkness come upon you; for he that walketh in darkness knoweth not whither he goeth. While ye have the light, believe in the light, that ye may be the children of light." Jesus is the light. He shineth upon us through His Word. We must believe in Him before it is too late.—And He cried and said: "He that believeth on Me, believeth not on Me, but on Him that sent Me. And he that seeth Me seeth Him that sent Me. I am come a light into the world, that whosoever believeth on Me should not abide in darkness. And if any man hear my words, and believeth not, I judge him not; for I came not to judge the world, but to save the world. He that rejecteth Me, and receiveth not my words, hath one that judgeth him: the word that I have spoken, the same shall judge him in the last day. For I have not spoken of myself; but the Father who sent Me, He gave me a commandment what I should say, and what I should speak. And I know that His commandment is life everlasting. Whatsoever I speak therefore, even as the Father spake unto Me, so I speak." Jesus was not, as the Jews imagined, a prophet set up by Himself; no, the Father had sent Him. He spoke God's Word, the Word of grace, even as He performed God's work, the work of grace, for the salvation of the world. He, the Savior and Redeemer, will not judge any man. But if a man does not believe His Word, then this Word of divine grace which he rejected will on Judgment Day bear witness to his unbelief, which will condemn him. These were the last words Jesus addressed to His people. How inviting they were! But the masses were hardened. And now Jesus turned away from this people. (John 12, 31-50.)

Oh, while thou hast the light, believe in the light, that thou mayest be a child of the light!

PRAYER.—Lord Jesus, within me and about me there is naught but darkness. Thou alone art Light and Salvation. Thou givest light for me through Thy Word. Thy Word is God's Word. Grant that through this Thy Word I may believe in Thee, lay hold on Thee as my only Savior, and through Thee enter eternal bliss. Amen.

Hymn 34, 1. 3. 5.

FRIDAY.

Watch therefore, for ye know neither the day nor the hour wherein the Son of Man cometh.—Matt. 25, 13.

On Tuesday evening, after He had been beset by His enemies all day long, Jesus sat with His disciples on the western slope of the Mount of Olives, facing Jerusalem. And there He spoke with them at great length about His coming again to Judgment. And this was the burden of all His discourse: "Watch therefore, for ye know neither the day nor the hour wherein the Son of Man cometh." This is meant for us, too, as we also are His disciples. We must do as the virgins did, the companions of the bride, who took their lamps and went forth to meet the bridegroom,—not like the foolish virgins, who took their lamps, but took no oil with them. Not only the name, not only the outward demeanor of Christians must be found with us, we must not merely profess allegiance to Christ and to His Church, no, our hearts must be filled with *faith,* with faith in the Savior, with faith which makes us the Savior's own, with faith which the Holy Ghost through the Word gives, increases, strengthens, and sustains. True, it may be that we become drowsy when the bridegroom delays to come, for our heart, which holds faith's treasure, is but an earthen vessel. And yet, if only faith is there—when the cry is made, "Behold, the Bridegroom cometh!" our faith will not be surprised, but it will be aroused, and brightly will its light shine, and gladly will it hail the Savior; and we shall go in with Him to the heavenly marriage-feast. But who has no faith, his light will then go out, and the door will be shut for him forever. "Watch therefore, for ye know neither the day nor the hour wherein the Son of Man cometh."

PRAYER.—Lord Jesus, Shepherd and Keeper of my soul, so govern me through Thy Word and Thy Holy Spirit, that the oil of true faith in Thee be ever found in the frail vessel of my heart, and that I may be ever watchful and wakeful, in order that I may neither fear nor faint when Thou, O heavenly Bridegroom, comest, but, together with Thee, may joyfully enter the marriage-feast of eternal life, and by Thy grace obtain eternal salvation. Amen.

Hymn 134, 1.

SATURDAY.

And it came to pass, when Jesus had finished all these sayings, He said unto His disciples, Ye know that after two days is the feast of the passover, and the Son of Man is betrayed to be crucified.—Matt. 26, 1. 2.

Tuesday's sun was setting, and, according to Jewish reckoning, Wednesday began. And Jesus arose from the place on Olivet where He sat with His disciples, and went with them to Bethany. And there, as they went, He said to them: "Ye know that after two days is the feast of the passover, and the Son of Man is betrayed to be crucified."

Christian, this is the faith which always must be within thy heart: Christ is crucified; Christ is crucified for *me;* Christ is crucified to atone for my sin; Christ is crucified to reconcile me unto God, to make me righteous before God. In this faith thou canst not fear nor faint: not though the power of death overtake thee; not when the last trumpet shall resound; not when heaven and earth shall pass away; not when the Judge of all the earth, appearing in dreadful splendor, shall assemble all the nations before Him. This faith holds out always and against everything. This is the one true Christian faith. There is none other. There has never been any other, there never will be any other. Keep this faith. Deep within thy heart let the name and *cross* of Christ glow ever and always. Not with hands merely, but through the Holy Ghost, in faith, make the sign of Christ's cross, as it were, upon thyself. This will keep thee eternally.

PRAYER.—Lord Jesus, write, draw, engrave, Thy cross, whereby I am saved, deep within my inmost heart. Do it, O Lord, through Thy Gospel and through Thy Holy Spirit, who worketh effectually upon sinful hearts through the Gospel. Through Thy cross Thou hast overcome all things that can terrify me. Grant that through faith in Thy cross I may overcome all adversity, and whatever causes me to take fright, and enter heaven. Amen.

Hymn 532, 3.

Week of Quinquagesima Sunday.

SUNDAY.

For a truth against Thy Holy Child Jesus . . . were they gathered together, for to do whatsoever Thy hand and Thy counsel determined before to be done.—Acts 4, 27. 28.

Wednesday our Lord passed at Bethany with His disciples, enjoying rest and quiet. The chief priests and scribes and elders of the people, however, were not restful and quiet. They assembled in the palace of the high priest Caiaphas and took counsel together that they might subtly take Jesus and kill Him. But they said: "Not on the feast day, lest there be an uproar among the people." And lo, then one of the Twelve, Judas Iscariot, came to them and said: "What will ye give me, and I will deliver Him unto you?" And they were glad, and covenanted with him for thirty pieces of silver. And from that time he sought opportunity to betray Him. (Matt. 26, 3-5. 14-16.) But it was Satan who ruled the elders in their hatred toward Christ, and who had entered into Judas: he was bent on Jesus' destruction. But Satan and Judas and the Chief Council could only do what God's hand controlled and what God's counsel had determined before to be done. Indeed, God ruled amidst the wickedness of man and the enmity of Satan. God wanted to carry out what His gracious counsel determined before to be done, that the Savior should become the Lamb of sacrifice that taketh away the sins of the world.—And so henceforth all things must serve God to the end that thou mayest be saved. Commit all things into God's keeping.

PRAYER.—Almighty, merciful God, I give thanks unto Thee that Thou didst so turn the evil counsel of the devil and of the elders of the church, as well as of Judas who betrayed Thee, that Thy good and gracious counsel for the salvation of the human race was thereby accomplished. O God, give me Thy grace that in faith in Thy dear Son, my Savior Jesus Christ, I may always commit myself into Thy fatherly hands which will surely rule all things for my good and my eternal happiness. Amen.

Hymn 65, 3.

MONDAY.

If ye know these things, happy are ye if ye do them.—John 13, 17.

On Thursday morning the disciples came to Jesus, saying: "Where wilt Thou that we make ready for Thee to eat the passover?" And He said: "Go into the city to such a man and say to him, The Master saith, My time is at hand; and I will keep the passover at thy house with my disciples." And the disciples did as Jesus had told them; and they made ready the passover. Now when the even was come, He sat down with the Twelve. And there arose also a contention among the disciples which of them should be accounted the greatest. And Jesus rose and laid aside His garment; and He took a towel and girded Himself. After that He poured water into a basin, and began to wash the disciples' feet, and to wipe them with the towel wherewith He was girded. Then cometh He to Simon Peter; and Peter saith unto Him;

"Lord, dost Thou wash my feet?" Jesus answered and said unto him: "What I do thou knowest not now; but thou shalt know hereafter." Peter saith unto Him: "Thou shalt never wash my feet." Jesus answered him: "If I wash thee not, thou hast no part with me." Simon saith unto Him: "Lord, not my feet only, but also my hands and my head." Jesus saith unto him: "He that is washed needeth not save to wash his feet, but is clean every whit. And ye are clean, but not all." For He knew who would betray Him; therefore said He: "Ye are not all clean." So after He had washed their feet, and had taken His garments, and had sat down again, He said to them: "Know ye what I have done unto you? Ye call me Master and Lord; and ye say well, for so I am. If I, then, your Lord and Master, have washed your feet, ye ought also to wash one another's feet. For I have given you an example that ye should do as I have done to you. Verily, verily, I say unto you, The servant is not greater than his lord; neither is he that is sent greater than he that sent him. If ye know these things, happy are ye if ye do them." (Matt. 26, 17-20; Luke 22, 24; John 13, 1-17.)

We Christians are clean through faith in Christ. He merely needs forgive us the sins which defile us on our journey through this life. And this He gladly does. And so we Christians must also be kind to one another, and willingly forgive one another, and serve one another in every way. If we know these things, happy are we if we do them.

PRAYER.—Lord Jesus, my Savior, I thank Thee that by Thy blood Thou hast cleansed me of all my sins, and that Thou richly and daily forgivest me all my sins. Grant me Thy Holy Spirit that I may prove myself Thy disciple, gladly forgiving my neighbor when he has offended me, and loving and serving him. Amen.

Hymn 197, 2. 7.

TUESDAY.

Lord, is it I?—Matt. 26, 22.

Now they ate the passover. And after the blessing Jesus broke the bread for His disciples. And He also took the cup, and gave thanks, and said: "Take this and divide it among yourselves; for I say unto you, I will not drink henceforth of the fruit of the vine until the kingdom of God shall come." ' And while they were eating, He was troubled in His spirit and said: "Verily, verily, I say unto you that one of you shall betray me." Then the disciples looked at each other, and not knowing of whom He spake, they said to Him one by one: "Lord, is it I?" He said to them: "It is one of the Twelve that dippeth with me in the dish. The Son of Man indeed goeth as it is written of Him, but woe to that man by whom the Son of Man is betrayed! Good were it for that man if he had never been born." John, whom Jesus loved, sat next to Jesus, leaning on His bosom. To him Peter beckoned that he should ask who it was of whom Jesus spoke. John said to Jesus: "Lord, who is it?" Jesus answered: "He it is to whom I shall give a sop when I have dipped it." And when he dipped the sop, He gave it to Judas, the son of Simon, the man from Cariot. This man then said shamelessly: "Master is it I?" Jesus answered him: "Thou hast said." And after the sop Satan entered into him. Then said Jesus unto him: "That Thou doest; do quickly." The other disciples did not understand this, because they had not heard what Jesus had said to John. Judas then, having received the sop, went out straightway. And it was night. (John 13, 21-32; Matt. 26, 21-25.)

Woe unto Judas! Woe unto every disciple that falls away from Jesus! Christian, thou must not doubt that thou wilt remain constant in faith and wilt enter heaven. But thou must not ground such thy constancy and eternal blessedness on thy own strength. When looking upon thyself, thy heart and mouth always tremblingly ask, "Is it I?" But when thou thus addressest thyself to the Lord, and dost anxiously look to Him to keep thee, then He will surely do so. Thou mayest safely depend upon Him.

PRAYER.—Lord Jesus, help me and keep me from Satan and from the wiles of my own heart. I cannot remain true to Thee, I cannot obtain eternal salvation, unless Thou sustainest me. Therefore I call upon Thee, my eyes look anxiously unto Thee. Thou wilt not suffer me to be put to

shame. I rely upon Thee, the merciful Savior, doubting nothing. Amen.
Hymn 347, 1.

ASH WEDNESDAY.

As often as ye eat this bread and drink this cup, ye do show the Lord's death till He come.—1 Cor. 11, 26.

As they were eating, when the paschal meal was about over, Jesus took bread, and blessed it, and broke it, and gave a piece of it to each of His disciples, saying: "Take, eat." While thus dividing the bread, and as the disciples were eating, He said: *"This is my body,* which is given for you." And when all had eaten, He said: "This do in remembrance of me." After the same manner also He took the cup, gave thanks, and gave it to the disciple sitting nearest to Him, saying: "Drink ye all of it." And while they all drank, one by one, He said: *" This is my blood* of the new testament, which is shed for many for the remission of sins." And when all had drunk, He said again: "This do ye, as oft as ye drink it, in remembrance of me."

We know that here the Lord Jesus instituted the Holy Communion of the New Testament, which was to take the place of the typifying paschal meal of the Old Testament. And in all Christendom this is to be celebrated to the end of time. In Holy Communion, Jesus, who is the true Lamb of God, under the bread and wine, gives us His body, which was given into death for us, and His blood, which was shed for us. In Holy Communion the Lamb of God, that taketh away the sin of the world, gets into the closest possible communion with us; we receive His body and blood, and with it the forgiveness of sins, life, and salvation. Here we must in true faith joyously hail our Savior, remember His salutary death, and show and by an open profession proclaim His death by virtue of which we have been redeemed. Ah, how well do we own Him who in the fullness of time came to suffer and to die for us!

PRAYER.—O Thou Lamb of God, Lord Jesus Christ, I thank Thee that of Thy great mercy toward me poor sinner Thou hast instituted a supper where I receive the food and drink of eternal life, Thy body, sacrificed for me, and Thy blood, shed for me. Grant that I may often approach this Holy Supper with true hunger and thirst, that I may receive forgiveness of sins, life, and salvation through Thee, and, firmly believing, comfort myself with such salvation. And grant me grace, I beseech Thee, to adorn such faith with a frank profession of Thy blessed name and with a Christian walk, until Thou wilt come to seat me at the tables Thou hast prepared for me in the blissful mansions above.

Hymn 441, 1. 2. 4.

THURSDAY.

I am the Way, the Truth, and the Life: no man cometh unto the Father but by Me.—John 14, 6.

What terror must have seized upon the disciples, the poor sheep, that night in which their Lord was betrayed, in which the Shepherd was slain! For that reason He lingered long with them at the table after the paschal supper, seeking to comfort them, to strengthen and steel them for the approaching hours as well as for every evil hour in days to come. "Let not your heart be troubled," He said kindly. "Ye believe in God, believe also in Me." And at once He directed them to the goal which they were bent on reaching, by saying: "In my Father's house are many mansions." There they are to remain forever. If, however, a doubt should harass their poor soul, He wished to tell them that He was now going to prepare a place for them. And though He is doing this, He assures them that, nevertheless, He will come again and receive them unto Himself, that where He is, they may also be. "And," He continued, "wither I go ye know, and the way ye know." The way to the Father, He would say, is familiar to you. Thereupon Thomas said, disappointed and sad: "Lord, we know not whither Thou goest; and how can we know the way?" Jesus answered him: "I am the Way, the Truth, and the Life. No man cometh unto the Father but by me." Jesus, the Savior, the Sin-Atoner, the Propitiator, the Redeemer, the dear, kind, merciful Lord, whom we know so well·from His Word, and who possesses our hearts, He, yea, He is the Way to the mansions of His Father. Through Him we are saved. If He is ours by faith, we are on the way that surely leads to heaven. He also is the Truth, the only Truth, fixed in God's eternal counsel; if we trust in Him, we cannot fail. And He is the Life, Eternal Life, for us sinners; if we have Him, we have life. But without Him no man cometh unto the Father. He is the only Way, the only Truth, the only Life. Without Him there is no salvation. (John 14, 1-16.)—Dear Christian, will not these words comfort, strengthen and steel you against sin and affliction and death and judgment, in life and death?

PRAYER.—O Lord Jesus, since Thou art the Way, the Truth, and the Life, I, a poor sinner, am of good cheer. I know Thee, and Thou art mine, beloved Savior! Keep me, Thou faithful Lord, lest I stray from Thee and err from the only way to salvation, forgetting the only saving truth, and losing eternal salvation. Let mine eyes in faith be ever fixed on Thee, and I shall assuredly obtain salvation. Amen.

Hymn 88, 6.

FRIDAY.

He that hath seen Me hath seen the Father.—John 14, 9.

Jesus wanted to comfort His disciples because of His departure. He therefore said to them: "If ye had known Me, ye should have known my Father also: and from henceforth ye know Him and have seen Him." Dost thou understand these words, dear Christian reader? · He that knoweth Jesus aright also knoweth the Father aright. And, forsooth, the disciples now knew Jesus aright, hence they also knew the Father. But their fear and sadness had overpowered them now and had dimmed their knowledge. Up, up! the Savior would say, collect your thoughts! Ye know the Father even now, and ye have seen Him. Then Philip said to Him: "Lord, show us the Father and it sufficeth us." Jesus said to him: "Have I been so long time with you, and yet hast thou not known me, Philip? *He that hath seen Me hath seen the Father;* and how sayest thou then, Show us the

Father? Believest thou not that I am in the Father, and the Father in Me? The words that I speak unto you I speak not of Myself; but the Father that dwelleth in Me, He doeth the works. Believe Me that I am in the Father, and the Father in Me: or else believe Me for the very works' sake." (John 14, 7-11.)

Wouldst thou, O Christian, look into the inmost heart of God, to be real sure of Him? Look upon *Jesus* in the Word of Holy Writ. When seeing Jesus, thou seest the Father. The Son is of one and the same essence with the Father. He is the eternal personal Word, the eternal personal image of the Father. Jesus is in the Father, and the Father is in Him. Jesus' Word is the Father's Word. Jesus' work is the Father's work. Yea, Jesus' mind is the Father's mind; Jesus' compassion is the Father's compassion; Jesus' benign goodness is the benign goodness of the Father. As Jesus receives thee, sinner though thou be, so the Father receiveth thee. Oh, why wouldst thou see the Father? Thou hast seen Jesus, thy dear, good Savior, in His Word: thus thou hast beheld and seen the Father. Why dost thou not rejoice? Let thy heart be filled with comfort, trust, and confidence! God is thy Savior. He that has seen Jesus has seen the Father.

PRAYER.—Lord God, Heavenly Father, I thank Thee with a heart filled with joy that in Thy Son, Jesus Christ, Thou hast so clearly revealed Thy gracious will and Thy loving heart toward us poor sinners, and I beseech Thee to graciously grant that I may daily increase in this knowledge, that in every temptation I may comfort myself therewith, and buoyed up with such hope, may overcome all evils that beset me, and in the end be saved. Amen.

Hymn 103, 5.

SATURDAY.

If ye shall ask anything in my name, I will do it.—John 14, 14.

Jesus instilled His despondent disciples with courage in that night by giving them a great and sure promise. He said: "Verily, verily, I say unto you, He that believeth on Me, the works that I do shall he do also; and greater works than these

Week of Quinquagesima Sunday.

shall he do, because I go unto my Father. And whatsoever ye shall ask in my name, that will I do, that the Father may be glorified in the Son. If ye shall ask anything in My name, I will do it." (John 14, 12-14.) Through faith in Him His disciples were to be men of God's power on earth. They were to do the works that He had done, and greater still. For while Jesus preached, and did signs and wonders, and brought people to faith in Him in but a small nook of the earth, they were to go into all the world, and preach the Gospel, and do signs and wonders, and bring many more people to faith in Him than He had done Himself! And such power He would give them when through suffering and death He would enter into the glory of His Father. And if they would pray in His name, trusting in Him and firmly believing His promise, they would always be endowed with such power—by *Him,* in order that the Father might be properly known and glorified in Him, in whom alone the Father is truly revealed and made known to mankind. And again the Lord assured them: "If ye shall ask anything in My name, I will do it."

How is it with us who also believe in Jesus? Does this promise also pertain to us? Most certainly. True, He has not commanded us to do signs and wonders. But we are to do the greatest of all things, we are to bring men to saving faith in Him through the Gospel. And for such power of God we are to pray, and He will surely grant it to us. This is certain. Oh, that we had the true zeal for such work! Oh, that believingly and earnestly we would pray for such power! How much would we then accomplish!

PRAYER.—Lord Jesus, strengthen my faith! Through Thy Holy Spirit grant me true zeal to perform Thy work on earth. Give me fervent love for my erring brother, that I may seek to win him for Thee and Thy salvation. And give unto me, O Jesus, Thy power of God whereby alone such things can be done. Lord, cure me of the paralyzing idleness and indifference of my flesh. Let me be Thy disciple, Thy servant, Thy instrument, the bearer of Thy power, as long as I live on earth. Amen.

Hymn 67, 7.

Week of the First Sunday in Lent.

SUNDAY.

I will not leave you comfortless.—John 14, 18.

Thus spake the departing Savior to His grieving disciples. How, then, would He not leave them comfortless?—"If ye love Me; keep my commandments," He said first. He that truly believes in Jesus loves Him, and he proves his love by keeping, and holding fast to, Jesus' commandments and instructions. Such are Jesus' true disciples. To them the Lord said and says: "And I will pray the Father, and He shall give you another Comforter, that He may abide with you forever." And who is He? "The Spirit of Truth," the Holy Spirit, who proceeds from the Father and from the Son, who through the Word of Truth divinely and mightily strengthens and comforts the hearts of Jesus' disciples, and always directs to Jesus. This Comforter the unbelieving world cannot receive, because they see Him not, neither do they know Him; they are incapable of comprehending His comfort; His Word of Truth, the burden of which is Christ, is altogether foreign to them. But Jesus' disciples know this Comforter. It is He who through His Word brought them to Jesus in faith. And He will abide with them, and be in them, and comfort them, and divinely and mightily strengthen and comfort them, and always direct them to Jesus. It is in this manner that Jesus would not leave them comfortless. Thus He will come to them through the Holy Spirit, and the comfort that the Spirit gives. "Yet a little while," said He to His disciples, "and the world seeth Me no more; but ye see Me," in the comforting light of the Holy Spirit. "Because I live, ye shall live also," in the life of the comfort of faith, which the Holy Spirit worketh in you. "At that day ye shall know that I am in the Father, and ye in Me, and I in you. He that hath my commandments, and keepeth them, he it is that loveth Me," and is my true disciple. "And he that loveth Me shall be loved of my Father, and I will love him, and I will manifest Myself to him," through the Holy Spirit, unto great comfort.

Are the disciples of Jesus comfortless? No, "I will not leave you comfortless," says Jesus. Meditate on this blessed truth. (John 14, 15-21.)

PRAYER.—Lord Jesus, who through cross and death and resurrection and ascension didst enter into the glory of Thy Father, and art no longer visible with Thy disciples and Christians on earth, I thank Thee that, nevertheless, Thou didst not leave us comfortless, but comest to us through Thy Word and the enlightenment of Thy Holy Spirit, and revealest Thyself to us, and abundantly comfortest us with Thy nearness, though unseen, and with Thy great love. Bestow this great comfort upon me too, O Lord, richly and daily, that I may rejoice in Thy love, and exultantly finish the course leading to the mansions of the Father. Amen.

Hymn 248, 3.

MONDAY.

Peace I leave with you, my peace I give unto you.—John 14, 27.

In that night Judas, not Iscariot, said to Jesus: "Lord, how is it that Thou wilt manifest Thyself unto us and not unto the world?" That was a question showing great want of wisdom. For Jesus reveals Himself and the fullness of His grace through His Word, and not otherwise. Now His disciples, who love Him, hold fast to that Word as to their greatest treasure. And the Father loves them, and comes to them with the Savior, and most graciously and lovingly makes His abode with them; and they realize evermore what a treasure their Savior is to them. But a man of the world, who does not love the Savior, neither holds fast to His Word, but despises it. And Jesus' Word is not the word of mortal man, but the Word of the Father who sent Him. How, then, should Jesus manifest Himself to a man of the world?— This His Word the Lord had revealed to His disciples while He was still present with them. Now came the hour of parting. "But," said He, "the Comforter, even the Holy Ghost, whom the Father will send in my name, He shall teach you all things, and bring all things to your remembrance, whatsoever I have said unto you." Thus in us Christians also, who adhere to the written Word of Jesus, the Holy Spirit works the true, inner, heartfelt understanding of this Word, and thereby reveals unto us evermore the fullness of Jesus' saving grace. And then we have peace, precious, eternal peace, that does not perish like the things of this world. Jesus says: " Peace I leave unto you, my peace I give unto you: not as the world gives, give I unto you. Let not your heart be troubled, neither let it be afraid." (John 14, 22-27.)

O thou Christian, disciple of Jesus, hold to Jesus' Word! Meditate on it daily. Then the divine majesty will dwell with thee in love and grace; the Holy Spirit, who is ever present in the Word of Jesus, will reveal the great salvation wrought by thy Savior evermore clearly unto thee; and thou shalt have peace, eternal peace, peace amid the strife of this time, peace in the blessed rest of heaven.

PRAYER.—Lord Jesus, grant through Thy almighty power that I, a poor sinner, may unceasingly hold to Thy saving Word. God Father, love me for Jesus' sake! Lord Jesus, come with Thy Father and the Holy Spirit, and make Thy abode with me! God Holy Ghost, glorify Jesus' gracious and sure Word within my heart, that I may have peace henceforth forevermore! Amen.

Hymn 253, 1-3.

TUESDAY.

Abide in me.—John 15, 4.

Jesus is the true Vine; God the Father is the Husbandman; the believers, the Christians, are the branches. Every branch in Jesus that bears no fruit, that stops to live and to walk in faith, God shall take away from Jesus. But every branch that bears fruit God will purge that it may bring forth more fruit. Dear Christian, now thou art clean through the Word of Jesus which thou hast held in faith. Thereby thou hast been united with Jesus as a branch with the vine, and thou hast the salvation which is in Jesus, His righteousness, His life, and His strength. But *abide in*

Jesus, that Jesus and His salvation may abide in thee. As the branch cannot bear fruit of itself, except it abide in the vine, so thou canst not bear fruit unless thou abidest in Jesus through faith in His Word. Jesus is the Vine, thou art the branch. Thou canst and wilt bring forth much fruit only if thou abidest in Him and He in thee. For without Him, of thyself, thou canst do nothing. Whoever does not abide in Jesus is cast forth as a branch and is withered. And the withered branches are gathered and cast into the fire and must burn. If, however, thou abidest in Jesus, if His Word abides with thee, all that thou askest and desirest will be given thee—all good gifts, all power from on high. For when thou bearest much fruit and art a true disciple of Jesus, the Father is glorified. Listen! As the Father hath loved the Son, so hath Jesus Christ, thy Savior, loved thee. Continue in this His love! Listen! If thou keepest, and holdest fast to, His Word and His commandments, thou wilt abide in His love, even as He kept His Father's commandments and abode in His Father's love. Bear this in mind as a word spoken to thee by—Jesus. These things He says unto thee in order that His joy might remain in thee, and that thy joy might be full and never end. Thus Jesus spoke to His disciples in that night. Thus He also speaks to thee. (John 15, 1-11.)

PRAYER.—O Father in heaven, Thou great heavenly Husbandman, I thank Thee that through Thy Word and the Holy Spirit Thou hast engrafted me in Thy Son Jesus Christ, and hast made me a partaker of the entire salvation wrought by Him. O merciful God, graciously grant that I may always embrace my Savior in His Word and abide in Him, thus being His true disciple and bringing forth fruit meet for faith, that I may continue in my Savior's love, and that He may rejoice in me, and that my joy may be full eternally. Amen.

Hymn 21, 7.

Week of the First Sunday in Lent.

WEDNESDAY.

These things I command you, that ye love one another.—John 15, 17.

The first fruit of a godly life which Christians, as branches ingrafted in Christ, must bring forth is mutual love. In that hour of parting Jesus said to His disciples: "This is my commandment that ye love one another, as I have loved you." The love of Christ toward His own must move us to love one another. Ought we not to love those whom Jesus loves? And how has He loved His own! He says: "Greater love hath no man than this, that a man lay down his life for his friends." He loved them unto death. He calls His own His "friends." And He says to His disciples, and He says to us: "Ye are my friends if ye do whatsoever I command you," if ye love one another. Should not this constrain us to do so? And to us, His disciples, He says: "Henceforth I call you no longer servants; for a servant knoweth not what his lord doeth." A servant must obey implicitly, without knowing his master's motives, without being taken into his confidence. "But I have called you friends; for all things that I have heard of my Father I have made known unto you." Through His Word He has made known unto us the whole counsel of God for our salvation. Indeed, we, His own, are His friends. And He has made us His own, not we ourselves. He says: "Ye have not chosen Me, but I have chosen you, and commanded you that ye should go and bring forth fruit, and that your fruit should remain, that whatsoever ye shall ask of the Father in my name, He may give it you." It is naught but His grace. Even as He laid down His life for us for our salvation, so also, without our seeking, He has chosen and made us His own, His branches, and has given us power to bring forth fruit, abundant fruit. And for such grace we may ask the Father in His name at all times, and He will give it. Thus we must and can bring forth the fruit of loving one another. "These things I command you, that ye love one another," says our dear Lord. (John 15, 12-17.)

PRAYER.—Lord God, dear Heavenly Father, bestow upon me, a poor sinner, I beseech Thee, the power to love my brethren. Consider, I pray Thee, that Thy dear Son has chosen me by grace and has made me His own, and has given me the power of His life, so that I can begin to do what pleases Him; and He calls me His friend. And it is His will that I should love my brethren, whom He loves even as He loves me. O Heavenly Father, I pray Thee, in the name of Jesus and at His command, that Thou wouldst give me the power of Thy Spirit to do my Savior's will. I long for such grace, and Thou wilt not deny it to me. Amen.

Hymn 67, 5.

THURSDAY.

If the world hate you, ye know that it hated Me before it hated you.—John 15, 18.

The disciples of Jesus enjoy the love which loves Jesus, and must endure the hate which hates Him: they are loved by their fellow-disciples and hated by the unbelieving world. In the latter instance they must note the word of Jesus: "If the world hate you, ye know that it hated Me before it hated you." If we disciples of Jesus still were of the world, the world would love us as its own; but because we are not of the world, but our Lord has chosen us out of the world and has made us His disciples, therefore the world hates us, for it hates Jesus. We must remember the word that Jesus said to His disciples on a former occasion: "The servant is not greater than his lord." If they have persecuted Jesus, they will also persecute us; and in the same way in which they accepted His Word, just so will they accept ours also, namely, they will *not* accept it, for it is the same Word. Just for the sake of the name and Word of Jesus the world hates us; for it is their own fault that they do not know God who sent Jesus. True, if the world, which in its unbelief hates Jesus, had not heard His Word, this guilt would not rest upon it, but now it has no excuse for its sin. What sin? The sin of hating Jesus and His Word. He that hates Jesus hates God the Father, who manifests Himself in Jesus. Thus the prophecy of the Son of God is fulfilled: "They hated Me without cause," Ps. 69, 4. Who is it that really testifies of Jesus? It is the Comforter, whom Jesus has sent us from the Father, even the Spirit of Truth that proceedeth from the Father. And we Christians also bear witness of Jesus from the Word which the Holy Spirit has written through the Apostles. And what results? The true witnesses of Jesus are cast out by the unbelieving world, even by that part which decks itself with Jesus' name and calls itself the Church of God. Indeed, there have been times, and they may return, that whosoever killeth the witnesses of Jesus thinketh that he doeth God service. Let no disciple of Jesus be offended thereat. Jesus has foretold it; we must bear it in mind. The unbelieving world, both in secular and spiritual garb, knows not, nor does it want to know, either the Father or our Lord and Savior Jesus Christ. Therefore it hates the disciples and witnesses of Jesus. The hatred which the world bears us because of Jesus' name is testimony to the fact that we belong to Jesus, and that His Spirit rests upon us. (John 15, 18—16, 4.)

PRAYER.—O Lord, almighty Son of God, who carest for Thy children with a loving father's care, and foreknowest all things that will befall Thy Church, and the faithful witnesses of the Truth in particular, we give thanks unto Thee that Thou dost forewarn us of this and insurest us against offense. I pray Thee graciously to grant the Comforter, the Holy Spirit, unto me, too, that I may fearlessly confess Thy truth, suffer gladly for its sake, remain true to Thee and Thy Word, and both in success and adversity praise and magnify Thee. Amen.

Hymn 273, 4.

FRIDAY.

He will reprove the world of sin and of righteousness and of judgment.—John 16, 8.

Thus the Lord spoke to His disciples in the night in which He was betrayed: "But now I go my way to Him that sent Me; and none of you asketh Me, Whither goest Thou? But because I have said these things unto you, sorrow hath filled your heart. Nevertheless, I tell you the truth: It is expedient for you that I go away; for if I go not away, the Comforter will not come unto you; but if I depart, I will send Him unto you." By His going to the Father, by atoning for our sins with His precious suffering and death, our Redeemer has brought it about that the Holy Ghost comes to us and most kindly comforts us with the only, aye, the eternal comfort of God, which is Christ, and makes us bold and confident against all the enmity of the world.—But even with this malignant world, which hates and rejects Christ and His witnesses, the Holy Spirit desires to accomplish something through our testimony. What? He wants to *reprove* the world. What does that mean? He wishes to convince it against its will—of what? Of sin, of righteousness, and of judgment. How so of sin? Through our testimony of Christ the Holy Spirit thrusts this prick into the hearts of unbelievers: If we do not believe in Christ, we remain under the curse of sin. And of righteousness? Thus: By rejecting Christ, who through His death and resurrection and ascension went unto the Father, we reject the only righteousness thus procured for us, and wherein we can stand before God. And, lastly, of judgment? Thus: We who reject Christ serve the prince of this world; but he and all his followers and all his pomp is judged and damned. On the day of Judgment, when God shall bring to light the counsels of the hearts, it will become manifest that by our testimony of Christ this threefold prick has been thrust into the hearts of gainsayers, and that with malice aforethought they kicked against this prick. Thus does the Holy Ghost give us the power of God, and make our testimony divinely effectual. So let us, each on his part, bear firm, undaunted, strong witness of Jesus. (John 16, 5-11.)

PRAYER.—God Holy Ghost, grant me, I beseech Thee, courage and strength to be a true witness of the only Savior of sinners, Jesus Christ. Grant me grace to bring many to the salutary knowledge of Jesus Christ. But thrust a prick into the hearts of malicious gainsayers that they may become aware of the fact that they are rejecting their salvation, the only salvation of their souls. Let Thy almighty Word be

Week of the First Sunday in Lent.

effectual, for Thou truly art He that testifieth of Christ on earth. Amen.

Hymn 247, 5.

SATURDAY.

He will guide you into all truth.—John 16, 13.

In the three years that He was with His disciples, Jesus had declared unto them the whole truth, and told them all things which they had to know for their own and all mankind's salvation. Nothing was wanting. But where was it all now? Fear and sadness covered it all as with a dense veil. This veil the Savior sought to lift in that night with many kind words. But now the time was too short. A spiritual numbness had come over the disciples. Therefore He said: "I have yet many things to say unto you, but ye cannot bear them now. Howbeit when He, the Spirit of Truth, is come, He will guide you into all truth." Into the whole truth which the Savior had already told them, the Holy Spirit would guide them, and make it an inward possession, light, bright, and clear unto faith's divine comprehension. Not "of Himself" would He speak, no new things would He teach, but only those things which He would hear in the eternal and ever-present counsel of God, and which the Savior had already revealed unto them. He would also show them those things to come in time and eternity which the Savior had already foretold them. He was to glorify Jesus alone; for He was to testify of Jesus only, and what He had done for us. All the things that the Father has, His divine being as well as His saving counsel and compassion and operation and work, all, all is Jesus' own, and is in Jesus, and has appeared in Jesus, and is to be found in Jesus. Therefore the Lord said to His disciples: "He shall take of Mine, and shall show it unto you." (John 16, 12-15.) Note this, Christian! For this is said to thee, too. Make diligent use of the Word of Jesus. There all things are revealed that are able to save thee. By means of this Word the Holy Spirit will guide thee into all truth, and glorify Jesus, yea, Jesus, in thee.

PRAYER.—Lord Jesus, my Savior, my entire salvation, grant me, too, Thy Holy Spirit that He may rid me of my faint-heartedness and the numbness of my heart, and so enlighten me with His divine light, that I may behold the whole saving truth of Thy Word with the clear eye of faith. Thou, O Jesus, art the saving Truth. Glorify Thyself within my heart through Thy Word and the Holy Spirit, that I may know Thee aright, firmly believe in Thee, and cheerfully and confidently wait for the things to come; for there I see no gloom, but only blessed light. Amen.

Hymn 9, 3.

Week of the Second Sunday in Lent.

SUNDAY.

Your sorrow shall be turned into joy.—John 16, 20.

In that night of parting Jesus said to His disciples: "A little while, and ye shall not see Me: and again, a little while, and ye shall see Me, because I go to the Father." Then said some of His disciples among themselves: "What is this that He saith unto us, A little while, and ye shall not see Me; and again, a little while, and ye shall see Me; and, because I go to the Father?" They said therefore: "What is this that He saith, A little while? We cannot tell what He saith." Now Jesus knew that they were desirous of asking Him, and He said unto them: "Do ye enquire among yourselves of that I said, A little while, and ye shall not see Me; and again, a little while, and ye shall see Me? Verily, verily, I say unto you, That ye shall weep and lament, but the world shall rejoice; and ye shall be sorrowful, but your sorrow shall be turned into joy. A woman when she is in travail hath sorrow, because her hour is come; but as soon as she is delivered of the child, she remembereth no more the anguish, for joy that a man is born into the world. And ye now therefore have sorrow; but I will see you again, and your heart shall rejoice, and your joy no man taketh from you. And in that day ye shall ask me nothing." (John 16, 16-23.) When Jesus suffered and died, the unbelieving multitude of the Jews rejoiced, for they thought that now there was an end of Him. And the disciples' faith in their beloved Lord collapsed like a dying fire, and they wept and lamented in great sorrow. But when the Risen One came to them, and even more, when the Holy Spirit gave them the true and full knowledge of Christ, their sorrow was turned into joy, into joy which no man and nothing could take from them. And no anxious questions disturbed them any more.—And, dear Christian, when, through His Word and the Holy Spirit, the Father mightily draws Thee to thy Savior, but thou, in the pain of sin and temptation, dost not see that even now thou art in the embrace of Jesus, the True Savior, then thou hast great sorrow. When, however, the Holy Spirit, through the Gospel, anointeth thine inner eye, so that thou dost truly and clearly discern Christ and His grace, then thy sorrow will be turned into joy, into all-conquering and everlasting joy, and then thou knowest all things that thou desirest to know. O Christian, seek the illumination of the Holy Spirit in the Word.

PRAYER.—Lord God Holy Ghost, Thou precious Light, enlighten me by Thy holy Word, that I may know Christ, my Savior, aright, rejoice in Him greatly, and be abundantly satisfied in such knowledge: who with the Father and the Son livest and reignest, true God, in all eternity. Amen.

Hymn 83, 5.

MONDAY.

Verily, verily, I say unto you, Whatsoever ye shall ask the Father in my name, He will give it you.—John 16, 23.

Hearest thou, O Christian, what the Lord assures thee here? Whatsoever thou wilt ask in Jesus' name, trusting in Him who made thee a dearly beloved child of God, grounding thyself on this His promise, but in humble child-like submission to God's fatherly wisdom, He will give it thee. This is glorious! Until then the dear disciples had not prayed thus in Jesus' name. Why not? Because as yet they had no full inward understanding of the Word and speech of Jesus. For the greater part it had remained a dark saying to them. And He had been with them, and had always supplied what they lacked. But now He said: " Ask, and ye shall receive, that your joy may be full." For now the time was to come when, through the Holy Ghost, Jesus would tell them plainly of His Father, the time when the Holy Ghost would make Jesus' Word concerning the Father all light and bright and clear to them, so that it would cease to be a dark saying to them, but that they would be assured that they are God's dear children, to whom the Father gladly gives all good things for Jesus' sake. When this time came, they asked the Father in Jesus' name.—And that time has come for thee, too, O Christian! In Jesus' Word thou hast the Holy Ghost, who enlightens thee. Thou art sure that thou art God's dear child. Thou prayest in Jesus' name. But thou dost not want to ask God for what is not good, as those do who pray foolishly. Thou confidest in God's love and wisdom. And God heareth thy every prayer. And thou rejoicest. And to thee and to all the children of God do the kind and comforting words of the Savior to His disciples apply: " And I say not unto you that I will pray the Father for you; for the Father Himself loveth you, because ye have loved Me, and have believed that I came out from God." Indeed, the Lord Jesus has come forth from the Father, and has come into the world to atone for us, and to make of us God's dear children; again, He has left the world and gone to the Father to gather the fruits of such atonement from His heavenly Father—and for us, that is, to give us the Spirit of blessed sonship of God, so that now with all confidence we ask the Father, who dearly loves us, for all good things. And He gives them to us. And we rejoice. (John 16, 23-28.)

PRAYER.—Lord God, dear heavenly Father, through Thy Son Thou hast made us Thy dear children, and hast told us that in His name we should ask Thee for all good things, and that Thou wouldst hear us. Open our timid hearts through Thy Holy Spirit, that in full confidence we may know Thee to be our loving Father, telling Thee all things, bringing all our complaints to Thee, asking Thee for all things, even as dear children ask their dear father. And then hear us, O Father, according to the firm assurance of Thy dear Son, and at all times give us what Thy kind fatherly heart knows to be best for us; yea, do more than we ask or think, for Jesus' sake. Amen.

Hymn 67, 8.

TUESDAY.

In the world ye shall have tribulation; but be of good cheer: I have overcome the world.—John 16, 33.

When the Lord conversed so kindly with His disciples and promised them that later on they would fully understand His words, they said, in a burst of feeling: "Lo, now speakest Thou plainly and speakest no proverb. Now we are sure that Thou knowest all things, and needest not that any man should ask Thee;" for, they would say, Thou answerest before we ask. "By this we believe that Thou camest forth from God." Ah yes, poor disciples, they believed, believed in their Savior. But their faith was still very weak. Therefore the Lord answered them: "Do ye now believe? Behold, the hour cometh, yea, is now come, that ye shall be scattered, every man to his own, and shall leave Me alone. And yet I am not alone, because the Father is with Me." How manifestly were these words fulfilled but a few hours later!—And His last words were: "These things I have spoken unto you that in Me ye might have peace. In the world ye shall have tribulation; but be of good cheer: I have overcome the world." (John 16, 29-33.)

Have not we, too, tribulation in this world? Does not the devil, as a roaring lion, walk about, seeking whom he may devour? Do not the unbelieving children of the world hate us? Does not our own wicked flesh and blood imperil us? Does not all manner of trouble and adversity threaten? and death? and judgment? and hell? Yea, and do not the trifling, miserable things often frighten us more than the great and serious hostile powers that surround us? And does not our own faith ofttimes grow weak? Do we not often grow faint-hearted and despondent? What are we to

Week of the Second Sunday in Lent. 125

do? We must take refuge in the Word of Jesus. In His Word the Holy Ghost is divinely present, and through it He rules and strengthens us, and makes us mighty in God against every terror, and gives us peace in Jesus, who has overcome the world, and every wicked thing in the world, for us. And He comes and gives us the victory He has gained over everything. And by His Word and the Holy Spirit He gives us sure knowledge of this, and good cheer. Indeed, let us take refuge in the Word of Jesus and be of good cheer. Then the storms of life will not be able to engulf us. And lastly we shall enter the abodes of eternal peace.

PRAYER.—Lord Jesus, Thou knowest how frail I often am, and of so little faith. And yet I am Thine and believe in Thee. Help me, my Savior! Strengthen me, for I am so weak; endow me with courage, for I am so timid. Give me Thy peace! O Lord, Thy help is at hand already, indeed, in Thy Word. Thy Word is a divine power. Thanks be unto Thee for Thy Word! Draw me unto Thy Word, and let me experience its power. O Lord Jesus, Thou great Conqueror, give me Thy victory unto eternal peace, unto eternal comfort. Amen.

Hymn 107, 4.

WEDNESDAY.

And this is life eternal, that they may know Thee the only true God, and Jesus Christ, whom Thou hast sent.—John 17, 3.

In the night in which He was betrayed, after the parting words which John records had been spoken, Jesus lifted His eyes up to heaven and, with a loud voice, in the hearing of His disciples, prayed to His Father. First He prayed for Himself, saying: " Father, the hour is come; glorify Thy Son, that Thy Son also may glorify Thee, as Thou hast given Him power over all flesh, that He should give eternal life to as many as Thou hast given Him. And this is life eternal, that they might know Thee the only true God, and Jesus Christ, whom Thou hast sent. I have glorified Thee on the earth; I have finished the work which Thou gavest Me to do,

And now, O Father, glorify Thou Me with Thine own self with the glory which I had with Thee before the world was." (John 17, 1-5.)

Dear Christian! The Father has sent the Son to be the Savior of the world. All men are in the Savior's hand. Without Him no man can have eternal life. He gives eternal life to all whom the Father gives to Him, whom the Father makes His own through faith. Through His work and through His saving Word the Son glorifies the Father; He truly reveals the Father in His great tender mercy. And, again, the Father glorifies the Son by presenting Him to the world as the only Savior, and by highly exalting Him, after His work of salvation was accomplished, into the eternal glory which He had with the Father before the world was, from everlasting. And now He who thus through faith knows the Father to be the only true God, and Jesus Christ, whom He sent to be the Savior, has eternal life. May the Holy Spirit ingraft this in thy heart, O Christian, so that thou mayest always remain in such knowledge, which is eternal life.

PRAYER.—O Father in heaven, I give thanks unto Thee that Thou hast granted me grace to know Thee according to Thy tender mercy, which was manifested in Christ Jesus, Thy dear Son, our Lord and Savior. O Father, grant me Thy Holy Spirit that I may abide in the Word which tells me of such compassion, trusting in the same unto my end, and thus inheriting eternal life which Thy dear Son, my Savior, has merited for me at so great a price. Amen.

Hymn 67, 2.

THURSDAY.

Sanctify them through Thy Truth; Thy Word is Truth. John 17, 17.

And now the Lord prayed for His disciples, the Apostles. He prayed thus: "I have manifested Thy name unto the men whom Thou gavest me out of the world. Thine they were, and Thou gavest them Me; and they have kept Thy Word. Now they have known that all things whatsoever

Thou hast given Me are of Thee. For I have given unto them the words which Thou gavest Me; and they have received them, and have known surely that I came out from Thee, and they have believed that Thou didst send Me. I pray for them. I pray not for the world, but for them which Thou hast given Me; for they are Thine. And all Mine are Thine, and Thine are Mine; and I am glorified in them. And now I am no more in the world, but these are in the world, and I come to Thee. Holy Father, keep through Thine own name those whom Thou hast given Me, that they may be one as We are. While I was with them in the world, I kept them in Thy name: those that Thou gavest Me I have kept, and none of them is lost but the son of perdition, that the Scripture might be fulfilled. And now come I unto Thee; and these things I speak in the world, that they might have my joy fulfilled in themselves. I have given them Thy Word; and the world hath hated them, because they are not of the world, even as I am not of the world. I pray not that Thou shouldst take them out of the world, but that Thou shouldst keep them from the evil. They are not of the world, even as I am not of the world. *Sanctify them through Thy Truth; Thy Word is Truth.* As Thou hast sent Me into the world, even so have I also sent them into the world. And for their sakes I sanctify myself, that they also might be sanctified through the Truth." (John 17, 6-19.)

To "sanctify" means to set apart for God. Only through God's Truth, received in faith, is man sanctified; and the Word of God is this Truth. And the Word of God is the Word concerning Christ, who has sanctified Himself for a sacrifice of the world's atonement. Thus sanctified, the Lord sent His Apostles into the world to preach His Word. And His prayer kept them.—Christian, never forget that thou, too, art sanctified unto God through the truth of the Word of Christ received in faith. Thou art God's, and God will make use of thee in His service. And He will keep thee.

PRAYER.—I thank Thee, my God, that out of pure grace, for Christ's sake, Thou hast sanctified me through Thy Word, which is the eternal Truth. Let me be and remain Thine own eternally. Let me be Thy servant, useful unto Thee,

thoroughly furnished unto all good work. Keep me, O God; for I trust in Thee. Amen.
Hymn 252, 4.

FRIDAY.

Father, I will that they also whom Thou hast given me be with me where I am.—John 17, 24.

Lastly the Lord prayed for all those, too, of whom He knew that they would believe in Him through the Word preached by the Apostles. He prayed thus: "Neither pray I for these alone, but for them also that shall believe on Me through their Word, that they all may be one as Thou, Father, art in Me, and I in Thee, that they also may be one in us: that the world may believe that Thou hast sent Me. And the glory which Thou gavest Me I have given them, that they may be one, even as We are one: I in them, and Thou in Me, that they may be made perfect in one, and that the world may know that Thou hast sent Me, and hast loved them as Thou hast loved Me. Father, I will that they also whom Thou hast given Me be with Me where I am, that they behold my glory which Thou hast given Me; for Thou lovedst Me before the foundation of the world. O righteous Father, the world hath not known Thee, but I have known Thee, and these have known that Thou hast sent Me. And I have declared unto them Thy name, and will declare it, that the love wherewith Thou hast loved Me may be in them, and I in them." (John 17, 20-26.)

Those who believe in Jesus Christ, through the Word preached by the Apostles, and are sanctified unto God through such faith, must, by such faith, be one with the Apostles and with one another, one, as the Father and the Son are one, one in the Father and in the Son. And the Savior's glory must rest upon them: it must unite them. And they must be the Savior's witnesses to the world, so that children of the world may also come to faith in their Savior: those whom the Father, through faith kindled in them, has given to the Son. And the love with which the Father loveth the Son will rest upon them, for through faith the Savior is within them. And at last they shall be where Christ is; they shall be with Him and behold and enjoy the glory which the Father has given His eternally beloved Son.—What glorious Christian calling! What blessed Christian hope! —But, oh, for our sin! How little of this unity, of this glory on earth, do we see! How we do hinder the work of God! And yet—all those are one who truly are in Christ, and the Savior's glory nevertheless is gleaming on them, and God nevertheless does His work through them, and they shall nevertheless in the end come to Jesus. The Savior's prayer prevails. What blessed grace!

PRAYER.—Dear Father in heaven, for the sake of the prayer of Thy Son have mercy upon us and do not cast us, Thy Christians, away because of our sin and infirmity. Defend us against all that would seduce us, and ward off all self-conceit, every delusion, every false doctrine that opposes Thy truth and divides Thy dear Church. Let me, a poor sinner, continue steadfast in Thy truth; let Thy Son's saving glory be seen upon me; let many who are still afar off be brought to faith in Christ through me, and in the end graciously receive me into Thy heavenly glory. Have mercy, Thou gracious God, have mercy, for Christ's sake! Amen.

Hymn 239, 10. 11.

SATURDAY.

Awake, O sword, against my Shepherd and against the Man that is my Fellow, saith the Lord of hosts. Smite the Shepherd, and the sheep shall be scattered; and I will turn mine hand upon the little ones.—Zech. 13, 7.

When they had sung a hymn, Jesus and His disciples went out to the Mount of Olives. It was about midnight. And the Lord said: "Simon, Simon, behold, Satan hath desired to have you, that he may sift you as wheat; but I have prayed for thee, that thy faith fail not; and when thou art converted, strengthen thy brethren." Peter answered: "Lord, I am ready to go with Thee, both into prison and to death." And Jesus said unto all: "All ye shall be offended because of Me this night; for it is written, I will smite the Shepherd, and the sheep of the flock shall be scattered abroad.

But after I am risen again, I will go before you into Galilee." Peter answered: "Though all men shall be offended because of Thee, yet will I never be offended." Jesus said to him: "Verily I say unto thee, That this night, before the cock crow, thou shalt thrice deny that thou knowest Me." And Peter still said: "Though I should die with Thee, yet will I not deny Thee." Likewise also said all the disciples. On approaching their destination, the Lord said: "When I sent you without purse, or scrip, or shoes, lacked ye anything?" And they said: "Nothing." Then Jesus said unto them: "But now, he that hath a purse, let him take it, and likewise his scrip; and he that hath no sword, let him sell his garment and buy one. For I say unto you that this that is written must yet be accomplished in Me, And He was reckoned among the transgressors; for the things concerning Me have an end." They were to prepare spiritually for great trouble. But they put an altogether carnal interpretation upon this and said: "Lord, behold, here are two swords." Jesus did not wish to instruct them on this point any further, and so He said: "It is enough."—The disciples now faced the greatest temptation. And, poor men, they boasted of their strength, Peter especially. Thus they had to fall, Peter especially. And temptation will approach thee too, O Christian. In no wise depend upon thyself! Rely solely upon Jesus and on His Word, in which He promises to keep thee, and through which He gives thee of His power.

PRAYER.—Lord Jesus, I rely wholly upon Thee, Thou faithful Shepherd! Of myself I can do nothing. By Thy grace I will fight. But unless Thou provide strength and victory I am lost. Assist me in all temptation! And if I fall by reason of my conceited flesh, let not my faith cease. Comfort me again, raise me, receive me into Thy strong saving arms. I rely on Thee, my Savior! Amen.

Hymn 365, 5.

Week of the Third Sunday in Lent.

SUNDAY.

He hath made Him to be sin for us who knew no sin, that we might be made the righteousness of God in Him.—2 Cor. 5, 21.

Now they came to Gethsemane. Gethsemane was a place, a garden where olive trees were grown. It was at the foot of the Mount of Olives, toward Jerusalem. Upon arriving at the gate, Jesus said to His disciples: "Sit ye here while I go and pray yonder." And He took with Him Peter, and John and James, the two sons of Zebedee. And He began to be sorrowful and greatly amazed and sorely troubled. And He said: "My soul is exceeding sorrowful, even unto death." And He begged the three disciples: "Tarry ye here and watch with Me."—Oh, what is that? Why did the Fount of Joy sorrow? Why was the powerful Lord amazed? Why was He troubled who had entered the deadly fray so willingly, so exultantly confident of victory? Why did the sorrow of death, of eternal death, come over Him? Why did the Comforter now seek comfort and support with His poor disciples?—The hour was now at hand that the Lamb of God that taketh away the sin of the world was actually and truly sacrificed. Now He who knew no sin was made sin for us. Now God poured out on Him all the wrath and curse which the world had incurred. Now God withheld from Him all consolation. Now Satan attacked Him. Now the Savior was in His deepest humiliation. Canst thou comprehend this? No? But so it was. So it was in truth and reality. But do thou rejoice and thank God! For God hath made Him to be sin for us who knew no sin, that we might be made the righteousness of God in Him, and be rid of wrath and curse, of death and damnation, and be glad and rejoice, be of good cheer and exult, and be blessed forever. Avail thyself of Christ's suffering, O Christian, in firm faith.

PRAYER.—My sin, my curse, my condemnation, my sorrowing and trembling, yea, my eternal grief, didst Thou, O my Lord, take upon Thee. Therefore I rejoice and heartily give thanks unto Thee. Indeed, I am now righteous before God in Thee; God loves and blesses me for Thy sake; God grants me comfort and joy and eternal blessedness. O my Lord and Savior, grant me Thy Holy Spirit, that I may grasp and take and keep what God so graciously gives me for Thy sake. Amen.

Hymn 196, 1.

MONDAY.

Yet it pleased God to bruise Him.—Is. 53, 10.

Sorrowful unto death, under the burden of God's wrath and curse, Jesus withdrew from His disciples, and went about a stone's cast farther into the garden, and falling upon His face, He prayed that, if it were possible, the hour might pass from Him. He said: "Abba, Father, all things are possible unto Thee; take away this cup from Me. Nevertheless, not what I will, but what Thou wilt." But God did not turn to Him now. However, there appeared an angel unto Him from heaven and strengthened Him. A creature must strengthen its Creator! And being in agony, He prayed more earnestly. And His sweat was mingled with blood, and in great drops fell down to the ground. And He came to His disciples. And He found them sleeping. And He said to Peter: "Simon, sleepest thou? Couldst thou not watch with me one hour? Watch ye and pray, lest ye enter into temptation. The spirit, truly, is ready, but the flesh is weak." O my dear Savior!—And He left them again and prayed, saying: "O my Father, if this cup may not pass away from Me, except I drink it, Thy will be done." And He arose from prayer and returned to His disciples. And again He found them sleeping for sorrow; for their eyes were heavy, neither did they know what to answer Him.—And He left them, and prayed the same words for the third time. And He came to His disciples the third time and said: "Sleep on now and take your rest; it is enough." He was now fully resolved. And He added: "Behold, the hour is at hand, and the Son of Man is betrayed into the hands of sinners. Rise, let us be going. Behold, he is at hand that doth betray Me."

No pen can describe, no tongue can utter, no reason can comprehend what cup of suffering it was which our Savior drained in that hour. Unfathomable, inconceivable sufferings of the soul when forsaken by God! The torments of hell! But it was *for us* that the Savior drained that cup, in order that we must not drain it, but that the heavenly Father might most graciously turn to us poor sinners and embrace and comfort us in life and death.

PRAYER.—O Heavenly Father, who for my sake didst forsake Thy dear Son, and didst deliver Him into the utmost anguish and agony of soul, restore unto me the joy of Thy salvation and uphold me with Thy free Spirit. Hide Thy face from my sins and blot out all my iniquities, since Thy Son, my dear Lord, hath borne them for me. From Thy Word and through Thy Holy Spirit make me to hear joy and gladness, that my heart may rejoice. Nevermore forsake me, but comfort me with Thy mighty love in life and death. I ask this for Jesus' sake. Amen.

Hymn 209, 2. 4.

TUESDAY.

If, therefore, ye seek Me, let these go their way.—John 18, 8.

And immediately, while He yet spake, lo, Judas, one of the Twelve, came, and after him a multitude of Roman soldiers and officers from the chief priests and Pharisees, elders and scribes, with lanterns and torches and swords and staves. And he that betrayed Him had given them a token, saying: "Whomsoever I shall kiss, the same is He; take Him, and lead Him away safely." Jesus therefore, knowing all things that should come upon Him, went forth to the multitude and said unto them: "Whom seek ye?" They answered Him: "Jesus of Nazareth." Jesus saith unto them: "I am he." And Judas also, who betrayed Him, stood with them. As soon, then, as Jesus had said unto them: "I am he," they went backward and fell to the ground. This Jesus did to show that He surrendered Himself of His own free will. And then He asked again:

"Whom seek ye?" And they said: "Jesus of Nazareth." Jesus answered: "I have told you that I am he; if therefore ye seek Me, let these go their way." He referred to His disciples who now were unable to bear the affliction which capture would entail. And so those words of His last prayer were fulfilled: "Of those whom Thou gavest me have I lost none." For now they could not lay hands on the disciples. As for Him, He bade them to take Him.

Note, Christian! Thou believest in the Lord Jesus, dost thou not? The Father, who through His Word and the Holy Spirit has graciously wrought faith in thee, therewith gave thee to Jesus. And Jesus does not want to lose thee, nor will He do so. He will keep thee in true faith. Note again! He who delivered Himself into chains and death for thee now says to all hands that reach out for thee: If ye seek me, let these go their way. What hands? The hands of the Law, of divine retribution, of death, of judgment, of damnation. Because those hands took Him in thy stead, thou art free, thou art saved.

PRAYER.—My Lord and Savior! Thou, the Righteous, hast been taken for me, the unrighteous; hence I am free. This is most certainly true. Grant me grace to depend upon this blessed truth in life and death. This truth will save me. This day I commend myself into Thy hand: Thou wilt not lose me, for Thy heavenly Father hath given me to Thee, and Thy own beloved heart, O Savior, doth not mean to lose me. I love Thee, my Savior. Amen.

Hymn 198, 5.

WEDNESDAY.

All this was done that the Scriptures of the prophets might be fulfilled.—Matt. 26, 56.

Forthwith came Judas, and drew near unto Jesus, and said, "Hail, Master!" and kissed Him. Jesus, however, said to this thoroughly hardened and doomed man: "Friend, wherefore art thou come? Judas, betrayest thou the Son of Man with a kiss?" Then came the captors and laid hands on Jesus and took Him. When the disciples saw what would follow, they said unto Jesus: "Lord, shall we smite with the sword?" And Peter stretched out his hand and drew his sword, and struck a servant of the high priest, and struck off his right ear. The servant's name was Malchus. But the Lord Jesus stopped Peter and said: "Put up thy sword into the sheath; for all that take the sword shall perish with the sword. Thinkest thou that I cannot now pray to my Father, and He shall presently give Me more than twelve legions of angels? The cup which my Father hath given me, shall I not drink it? But how, then, shall the Scriptures be fulfilled, that thus it must be?" And He touched Malchus' ear and healed him. And to the chief priests and captains of the temple who were come along He said: "Are ye come out as against a robber, with swords and staves, to take me? I sat daily with you teaching in the temple, and ye laid no hold on me; but this is your hour and the power of darkness. But the Scriptures must be fulfilled. All this was done that the Scriptures of the prophets might be fulfilled." Then all the disciples forsook Him and fled. And among them there was a certain young man who had followed Him to Gethsemane, having a linen cloth cast about his naked body. And the bailiffs laid hold on him; and he left the linen cloth and fled from them naked.

Judas' satanic betrayal, the murderous hatred of the elders of the church, the dark power of hell, the pitiful flight of the disciples, the capture of the great Lord and Savior at the hands of sinners,—what awful things do we see here! Back of it all, however, there was, and in it all there prevailed the gracious counsel of God for our salvation as revealed in the prophecies of the Old Testament: all this was done, that the Scriptures of the prophets might be fulfilled. God be praised!

PRAYER.—Yea, praise and glory be unto Thee, O God, for so bridling and ruling and guiding the most accursed wickedness of Satan and of the ungodly that thereby Thy gracious counsel for the salvation of us poor sinners must prevail and be accomplished. Praise be unto Thee for giving Thy dear Son into the hands of sinners for the salvation of sinners. O gracious God, grant unto me, a sinner, that I may take comfort from this in true faith and obtain salvation. Amen.

Hymn 310, 5.

THURSDAY.
Took Jesus and bound Him.—John 18, 12.

And the band and the captain and the officers of the Jews took Jesus, and bound Him, and led Him away to Annas first. Annas was father-in-law to Caiaphas, who was the high priest that same year, and who gave counsel to the Jews that it was expedient that one man should die for the people. Annas had formerly been high priest, and still had great authority with the Jews. He, like Caiaphas, was a Sadducee and a bitter enemy of the Savior. Annas occupied a part of the palace of the high priest. To him, then, they led Jesus first, in the middle of the night, while Caiaphas was assembling the Chief Council. And Annas, no doubt in one of the porches toward the inner courts, ordered that Jesus be brought before him, and questioned Him regarding His disciples and His doctrine. Jesus answered: "I spake openly to the world. I ever taught in the Temple, whither the Jews always resort; and in secret have I said nothing. Why askest thou me? Ask them that heard me what I have said unto them; behold, they know what I said." When He had thus spoken to Annas, one of the officers that stood by struck Jesus with the palm of his hand, saying: "Answerest thou the high priest so?" Jesus answered: "If I have spoken evil, bear witness of the evil; but if well, why smitest thou me?" Now the Lord was held by Annas until everything was ready for trial before the Chief Council.

Here thou seest the Savior in chains and in disgrace. This He suffered that thou, the guilty, mightst have blessed liberty and the supreme honor of a child of God and the glory of heaven. All that the Savior suffered makes for thy salvation.

PRAYER.—I thank Thee, dear innocent Savior, that Thou wast bound for me, the guilty offender, that I might be free forever. I thank Thee, O Lord of Glory, that Thou

didst suffer Thy countenance to be struck for me, a base sinner, that I might be welcomed and highly honored by God and all the holy angels. Grant me, my Savior, I beseech Thee, that I may at all times in true faith own Thee the Author of salvation. Amen.
Hymn 196, 3.

FRIDAY.

By Him therefore let us offer the sacrifice of praise to God continually, that is, the fruit of our lips giving thanks to His name.—Hebr. 13, 15.

When Jesus was led from Gethsemane to Jerusalem, John and Peter followed afar off. When He was brought into the high priest's palace, John, who knew the high priest, also entered it. But Peter stood without. Then John went out and spoke to her that kept the door and brought Peter in. When the maid that kept the door saw Peter, she said: " Art not thou also one of this man's disciples?" But Peter passed her and went into the inner court, where the servants had made a fire of coals for themselves, for it was cold. And after standing there awhile, he sat down among them and warmed himself. He wanted to see what would happen to Jesus. Then the maid that kept the door followed him, and seeing him in the light of the fire, she looked sharply at him and said: "Thou also wast with Jesus of Galilee." And turning to the servants, she said: "This man was also with Him." But Peter denied before them all and said: " Woman, I am not; I know Him not, and I know not what thou sayest." And he went into the passageway. And the cock crew for the first time.—Meanwhile the things we heard yesterday transpired with Jesus. Peter saw it. He returned to the fire. And the first maid that kept the door also came back and said to them that were there: " This also is one of them." And another maid said: " This fellow also was with Jesus of Nazareth." And one of the servants said to Peter: " Thou art also of them." Then Peter denied for the second time, with an oath, and said: " Man, I am not! I do not know the man."—After a while, about an hour later, while the

Lord was detained before Annas, those who stood by came to Peter and said to him: "Surely, thou also art one of them; for thy speech betrayeth thee." They meant his Galilean dialect. And one of the servants of the high priest, being a kinsman of that Malchus whose ear Peter had cut off, said to him: "Did I not see thee in the garden with Him?" Then Peter began to curse and to swear, saying: "I know not this man of whom ye speak." And the cock crew for the second time. And the Lord turned and looked at Peter. And Peter called to mind the word of the Lord: "Before the cock crow twice, thou shalt deny Me thrice." And he went out and wept bitterly.

Since our dear Lord gave His life for our salvation and sacrificed Himself for us, we, who believe in Him, must offer the sacrifice of praise which consists in confessing His name freely, gladly, and fearlessly. Surely that is most certainly true.—Hast thou ever in any way denied thy Savior before the unbelievers and the wicked? But when Jesus most graciously turned to Thee, didst thou, like Peter, repent?

PRAYER.—Help me, O my Lord and Savior! Without Thy help I can do nothing. I cannot remain true to Thee unless Thou sustainest me. Let me never rely on my own ability; for then I shall fall. Did I not often fall, and in manifold ways? But Thou, dear, kind Savior, didst always raise me again. Lord, keep me, lest I fall into sin again! And if I should ever fall again, do not let me lie, my Savior, my Helper! Amen.

Hymn 1, 2, 3.

SATURDAY.

Then did they spit in His face.—Matt. 26, 67.

Now they arraigned the Lord before the Chief Council, the highest spiritual court of the Jews, which had assembled before Caiaphas. And the chief priests and the elders and the Council sought false witness against Jesus, that they might put Him to death, but found none; yea, though many false witnesses came, yet found they none, for their witnesses did not agree. At last there came two false witnesses. One of them testified that Jesus had said: "I will, and am able to, destroy this Temple of God which is made with hands, and within three days I will build another," while the other asserted that He had spoken of the temple that is not made with hands. Thus, very plainly, these, too, did not agree with each other. And Caiaphas arose and asked Jesus: "Answerest Thou nothing? What is it that these witness against Thee?" But Jesus held His peace. Then a thought occurred to the chief priest. He said to Jesus: "Art Thou the Christ? Tell us!" Jesus answered: "If I tell you, ye will not believe; and if I also ask you, ye will not answer me, nor let me go." Then the chief priest said: "I adjure Thee by the living God that Thou tell us whether Thou be the Christ, the Son of God, the Blessed!" Then Jesus said: "Thou hast said it, for I am. Nevertheless, I say unto you, Hereafter shall ye see the Son of Man sitting on the right hand of power, and coming in the clouds of heaven," namely, on Judgment Day. Then the chief priest rent his clothes, saying: "He hath spoken blasphemy! What further need have we of witnesses? Behold, now ye have heard His blasphemy. What think ye?" Then they all said: "Art Thou the Son of God?" And they all condemned Him and said: "He is guilty of death." Then they spat in His face, and the servants buffeted Him, and some covered His face, and struck Him on the face, saying: "Prophesy unto us, Thou Christ. Who is it that smote Thee?" And many other blasphemous things they spoke against Him, and in many other ways they treated Him most shamefully.

Thus the Savior was condemned to death by the elders of His people and of His Church, and was spit upon, because He had said under oath that He was the Messiah, the Christ. This is monstrous, extremely so. But His condemnation is our acquittal. When He was spit upon, we were received to the fatherly bosom of God. Praise be unto our Lord!

PRAYER.—I praise Thee, my Savior, Thou True and Righteous One, because Thou didst suffer Thyself to be condemned, in order that I, the faithless and unrighteous, might be acquitted. I praise Thee, Thou glorious Son of God, because Thou didst suffer Thyself to be disgraced and spit upon, that I, shameful child of sin, might be caressed by God and highly honored. O merciful Savior, let the saving power of Thy suffering be my chief knowledge and the sole foundation of my faith. Amen.

Hymn 196, 2.

Week of the Fourth Sunday in Lent.

SUNDAY.

Put on the whole armor of God, that ye may be able to stand against the wiles of the devil.—Eph. 6, 11.

About the dawn of Friday morning the Chief Council convened again to devise some concerted action in bringing this matter concerning Jesus before the Roman governor, Pontius Pilate; for their verdict had to be confirmed by him, and he must order the execution to take place. And then Jesus was bound and taken to Pontius Pilate, into the Hall of Judgment.—When Judas, who had betrayed his Master, saw that He was condemned, he repented of his evil deed, took the thirty pieces of silver to the chief priests and elders, from whom he had received them, and said: "I have sinned in that I have betrayed the innocent blood," whereupon they said: "What is that to us? See thou to that." And he cast the pieces of silver in the Temple and departed, and went and hanged himself.—And the chief priests took the silver pieces and said: "It is not lawful to put them into the treasury, because it is the price of blood." And they took counsel, and bought with them the potter's field to bury strangers in. Therefore that field was called, the Field of Blood. Then was fulfilled that which was spoken by the prophet, saying: "And they took the thirty pieces of silver, the price of Him that was valued, whom they of the children of Israel did value, and gave them for the potter's field, as the Lord appointed me," **Zech. 11, 12. 13.** Such was the frightful end of Christ's betrayer. In desperation he "went to his own place."

Guard thy soul, O Christian, against consenting to do any sin whatsoever. Put on the whole armor of God, that thou mayest be able to stand against the wiles of the devil. For how does the devil go about it? First he makes sin appear sweet, small, trifling, and easy. He then leads man from one sin into another, blinding him and hardening his conscience. And finally, when he has reached the utmost stage, he bawls at him: "You are lost!" and drives him to utter despair. Do withstand the first temptation, O Christian! Arm thyself with the Word of God! And if ever thou hast fallen, flee to Jesus at once. He receives thee and forgives thy iniquity and helps thee, according to the firm assurances of His Word.

PRAYER.—Keep me from the devil's wiles, O my Lord and Savior! I cannot keep myself. Put on me Thy whole armor. Arm me with Thy Word and the Holy Spirit, and give me Thy strength. When I have sinned, draw me to Thee in penitence and faith, and forgive my sin, and satisfy me with the comfort of Thy salvation. And when my last hour comes, grant me a blessed end. Amen.

Hymn 206, 4. 5.

MONDAY.

I am a King. To this end was I born, and for this end came I into the world, that I should bear witness of the truth. Every one that is of the truth heareth my voice.—John 18, 37.

It was very early in the morning when the councilors appeared with Jesus before the Hall of Judgment. But Pilate was there. The Jews themselves did not go into the Judgment Hall, lest they should be defiled, but might eat the passover, or the meals connected with the sacrifices at the Passover. Pilate then went out to them and said: "What accusation bring ye against this man?" They answered insolently: "If He were not a malefactor, we would not have delivered Him unto thee." Then Pilate said to them: "Take ye Him, and judge Him according to your law." The Jews said to him: "It is not lawful for us to put any man to death." For the saying of Jesus must needs be fulfilled that He would be delivered to the Gentiles and crucified. So the Jews began to accuse Him, saying: "We found this fellow perverting the nation, and forbidding to give tribute to Cæsar, saying that He Himself is Christ, a King." Then Pilate entered the Judgment Hall again, and called for Jesus, and said to Him: "Art Thou the King of the Jews?" Jesus answered him: "Sayest thou this thing of thyself, or did others tell it thee of me?" Pilate answered: "Am I a Jew? Thine own nation and the chief priests have delivered Thee unto me: what hast Thou done?" Jesus answered: "My kingdom is not of this world. If my kingdom were of this world, then would my servants fight that I should not be delivered to the Jews; but now is my kingdom not from hence." Pilate therefore said to Him: "Art Thou a King, then?" Jesus answered: "Thou sayest that I am a King. To this end was I born, and for this cause came I into the world, that I should bear witness of the truth. Every one that is of the truth heareth my voice." Pilate said, disdainfully: "What is truth?" And when he had said this, he went out again to the Jews and said to them: "I find no fault in this man." He took Jesus to be a religious fanatic, but not a rebel.

Forsooth, Jesus is a King. But His kingdom is not of this world, is not of the nature of the kingdoms of this world. He founds, sustains, and spreads His kingdom only through His Word, the Word of Truth, the truth of grace, which was conceived in God's eternal counsel, revealed and made manifest in Christ, and is proclaimed through His Word: the truth that He is the Lamb of God that taketh away the sins of the world. And every one that is of the truth, every one that is born of God, drawn by God to receive this Word of Truth, hears the voice and Word of Jesus with a spiritual ear, and enters His kingdom and remaineth therein, here in time and thereafter in eternity. Art *thou* of the truth?

PRAYER.—Most merciful God, I beseech Thee that Thou wouldst at all times make my ear and my heart quick to know and hear and receive the voice and gracious Word of my Savior as the only saving truth, that thus I may be and remain in His kingdom, believing here and blissfully beholding hereafter. This I ask, O God, for Jesus' sake. Amen.

Hymn 201, 5.

TUESDAY.

The same day Pilate and Herod were made friends together, for before they were at enmity between themselves. Luke 23, 12.

When Pilate declared Jesus innocent, the members of the Chief Council still persisted in bringing serious charges of sedition against Him. Pilate, it seems, had taken Jesus with him before the Jews. And when Jesus said nothing to all these accusations, Pilate asked Him: "Hearest Thou not how many things they witness against Thee? Answerest Thou nothing?" But Jesus answered to never a word, insomuch that the Governor marveled greatly. At last the Jews said: "He stirreth up the people, teaching throughout all Jewry, beginning from Galilee to this place." When Pilate heard of Galilee, he asked whether the man were a Galilean. And when he knew that Jesus was of Galilee, and that, therefore, he belonged to the jurisdiction of Herod Antipas, he sent Him to Herod, who was at Jerusalem at that time. And when Herod saw Jesus, he was exceeding glad; for he was desirous to see Him of a long season, because he had heard many things of Him: and he hoped to see some miracle done by Him. And he questioned Him in many words; but Jesus answered him nothing. And the chief priests and scribes stood and vehemently accused Him. And Herod with his men of war set Him at naught, and mocked Him, and arrayed Him in a gorgeous robe of white to show that he, too, considered Jesus harmless, and sent Him again to Pilate. And Herod and Pilate became friends with each other that very day; for before they were at enmity between themselves. For so it is with the unbelieving world: when Jesus is the target, the bitterest enemies become friends and join hands against Him. In a case like this they fully understand each other and fully agree with one another. Be thou on Jesus' side, O Christian, though all the world is against Him. For with Jesus there is eternal salvation.

PRAYER.—Alas, Lord Jesus, how the world does despise Thee! How do erstwhile enemies join hands against Thee! But as for me, my Lord and Savior, draw me unto Thee by Thy Word and the Holy Spirit, so that I may side with Thee against all the scorn and contempt of the world; for one day Thou wilt let me see, and partake of, Thy glory. Amen.

Hymn 201, 6.

WEDNESDAY.

*Away with this man, and release unto us Barabbas!—*Luke 23, 18.

Pilate now called together the chief priests and the rulers and the people, and said unto them: "Ye have brought this man unto me as one that perverteth the people: and, behold, I, having examined Him before you, have found no fault in this man touching those things whereof ye accuse Him; no, nor yet Herod; for I sent you unto him, and, lo, nothing worthy of death is done unto Him. I will therefore chastise Him, and release Him." But they would not be satisfied.— Then something happened. Pilate had the custom to release to the people at the Passover one prisoner, whomsoever they desired. And he had then a notable prisoner, a malefactor and a murderer, called Barabbas, who had committed a murder in an insurrection that had occurred in the city. And just now a deputation of the people appeared before him, asking Pilate to observe the usual custom. This was a welcome opportunity for Pilate, and he said unto the multitude: "Ye have a custom that I should release unto you one at the Passover: whom will ye that I release unto you, Barabbas, or Jesus, who is called Christ?" For he knew that for envy the high priests had delivered Jesus up, and he felt certain that the people would ask for Jesus. And as he was sitting on the judgment-seat, waiting for the answer of the people, there came a messenger delivering this message from his wife: "Have thou nothing to do with that righteous man; for I have suffered many things this day in a dream because of Him."—But the chief priests and elders persuaded and moved the multitude that they should ask that Barabbas should be released and Jesus be condemned to die.—And now Pilate asked: "Whether of the twain will ye that I release unto you?" Then they all cried out: "Away with this man, and release unto us Barabbas!" O the people, the blind, mad, fickle people! But—dost thou again see the ruling hand of God amidst all this sin? For Jesus was to be delivered unto death that we, the malefactors, might be released.

PRAYER.—At Thy Word, O merciful God, I seek salvation in this, that Thy dear Son, the Righteous, was delivered unto death, and that for His sake we, the malefactors, are acquitted. Let me remain steadfast in this faith, and nevermore be affrighted nor despair, for Thou, even Thou, dost promise to me, O God, that by faith in Thy beloved Son I shall be righteous in Thy sight and have life everlasting. Amen.

Hymn 202, 1. 4.

THURSDAY.

Behold the man!—John 19, 5.

When the people had cried in wild disorder: "Away with this man, and release unto us Barabbas!" Pilate, willing to release Jesus, asked them: "What shall I do, then, with Jesus who is called Christ?" They cried out again: "Crucify Him, crucify Him!" And he said unto them the third time: "Why, what evil hath He done? I have found no cause of death in Him; I will therefore chastise Him, and let Him go." But they cried out the more: "Crucify Him!" And they were instant with loud voices, requiring that He might be crucified. And the voices of them and of the chief priests prevailed. Then Pilate had Jesus scourged. And when Jesus was scourged, the soldiers of the Governor took Him into the common hall and gathered unto Him the whole band of soldiers. And they stripped Him, and put on Him a scarlet robe. And they plaited a crown of thorns and put it upon His head, and a reed in His right hand; and they bowed the knee before Him, and mocked Him, and began to salute Him, saying: "Hail, King of the Jews!" And they struck Him in the face, and spit upon Him, and took the reed, and smote Him on the head, and, bowing their knees, worshiped Him.—And Pilate went out again, and said to the Jews: "Behold, I bring Him forth unto you that ye may know that I find no fault in Him." Then Jesus came forth wearing the crown of thorns and the purple robe. And Pilate said to them: "Behold the man!"

Do thou, too, behold Jesus in His misery and in His shame! Do not, however, merely behold Him with feelings of human sympathy in your heart, but let deep and serious thoughts occupy thy mind. Consider that thy Savior, the eternal Son of God, had to suffer these things to redeem thee. Consider, furthermore, how holy, severe, firm, and unchanging is the righteousness of God which could not be satisfied in any other way. Consider what would be done to thee, a sinner, if thou wouldst not have Jesus. And when thus beholding Jesus, let also this saving truth take hold of thy heart that thou art redeemed, and that God will show thee naught but kindness and goodness in time and eternity.

PRAYER.—O Lord and Savior, Jesus Christ, I thank Thee that Thou didst offer up Thyself in order to satisfy the righteous God in my place. In my stead Thou didst suffer what I had deserved to suffer on account of my sin. Thou hast fully satisfied the righteousness of God. Thou hast merited for me the good will of my heavenly Father. Grant me grace, dear Savior, to take refuge in Thy bloody merit, to enwrap myself in it, as it were, and never to be found without it. Ah, let me always look upon Thee in faith, that Thy salvation may be my own. Amen.

Hymn 195, 5.

FRIDAY.

Crucify Him, crucify Him!—John 19, 6.

Pilate was sadly mistaken to think that scourging Jesus would satisfy the people. When the chief priests and officers saw Jesus, they cried out: "Crucify Him, crucify Him!" Pilate said to them: "Take ye Him and crucify Him; for I find no fault in Him." The Jews answered him: "We have a law, and by our law He ought to die, because He made Himself the Son of God." When Pilate heard that, he dreaded all the more to order the execution of Jesus. Again he took Jesus with Him into the Judgment-Hall, and asked Him: "Whence art Thou?" But Jesus gave him no answer. Then Pilate said to Him: "Speakest Thou not unto me? Knowest Thou not that I have power to crucify Thee, and have power to release Thee?" Jesus answered: "Thou couldst have no power at all against Me, except it were given thee from above; therefore, he that delivered Me unto thee hath the greater sin." Now Pilate most earnestly sought to release Jesus. But the Jews insisted on their demand that Jesus be crucified. And the counsel of God also remained unchanged. Jesus must be crucified. And Jesus' prediction must be fulfilled: He must be crucified. And what the prophets had foretold must be done: Jesus must be crucified. Pilate, though shamefully guilty, was but God's instrument in this matter. And the Jews who delivered Jesus, though they were more guilty than this blind heathen, also were but tools in the hand of God. And the mad and howling mob, though their sin was inexpressibly great, nevertheless but echoed the cry of God's great and unfathomable mercy: "Awake, O sword, against my Shepherd, and against the man that is my fellow: smite the Shepherd!" (Zech. 13, 7.) For God so willed to give up His only-begotten Son into the shameful death upon the cross for our salvation.

PRAYER.—I give thanks unto Thee, most merciful God and Father, that Thou didst not spare Thy own Son, but deliveredst Him up for us all to suffer the shameful death upon the cross in our stead and for our salvation. How merciful is Thy counsel, and how graciously hast Thou carried it into effect! How earnestly dost Thou desire my salvation and that of the whole world! Endow me, I beseech Thee, with the power of Thy Holy Spirit, that in true faith

I may comfort myself with Thy wonderful mercy and rejoice in the same in all eternity. Amen.

Hymn 198, 4.

SATURDAY.

His blood be on us and on our children!—Matt. 27, 25.

Pilate, indeed, sought to release Jesus. But the Jews finally cried out: "If thou let this man go, thou art not Caesar's friend: whosoever maketh himself a king speaketh against Caesar." When Pilate heard that, he brought Jesus forth, and sat down in the judgment-seat in a place that is called The Pavement; in Hebrew, Gabbatha. Now it was the Preparation of the Passover, the day before the great Passover-Sabbath, a little past six o'clock in the morning. And Pilate said to the Jews: "Behold your King!" But they cried out: "Away with Him, away with Him; crucify Him!" Pilate said to them: "Shall I crucify your King?" The chief priests answered: "We have no king but Caesar." But when Pilate saw that he prevailed nothing, but that rather a tumult was made, willing to content the people, he gave sentence that it should be as they required. And he took water and washed his hands before the multitude, saying: "I am innocent of the blood of this just person; see ye to it." Then answered all the people and said: "His blood be on us and on our children!" Then released he Barabbas unto them, who for sedition and murder was cast into prison, whom they desired; but Jesus, scourged and mocked, he delivered unto their will to be crucified.

A terrible thing to say: "His blood be on us and on our children!" It has come upon them. The days of God's vengeance did come. Jerusalem was destroyed, the Jews were dispersed among all nations, and they have ceased to be God's people, and bear upon their very countenances the mark of God's truth and earnestness. But faith gives a new interpretation to the blasphemy of the Jews and says: Ah yes, Lord Jesus, Thy blood, the blood of atonement, be on us, and on our children! And God says Amen.

PRAYER.—I thank Thee, my Lord and Savior, Jesus Christ, that by **Thy blood and death Thou** hast made amends for the sin of the world and likewise for mine, and that Thou hast brought about a full reconciliation with God, and thus didst present all the world righteous and good in the sight of God. I pray Thee, true man and God, my Lord and Savior, kindle true faith within me to the end that I may appropriate unto myself Thy blood and death, and thus be saved.—I, a poor sinner. Amen.

Hymn 326, 4. 5.

Week of the Fifth Sunday in Lent.

SUNDAY.

And they shall mourn for Him as one mourneth for His only son.—Zech. 12, 10.

Now the soldiers, under the command of a captain, took off the scarlet mock-robe from Jesus, and put His own raiment on Him, and led Him away to crucify Him. And He bore His cross. And it seems that He collapsed under the burden of His cross. For they met a man coming out of the country, Simon, of Cyrene in Africa, the father of Alexander and Rufus, well-known Christians of later days: him they compelled to bear Jesus' cross, and he bore it after Jesus. And there followed Him a great multitude of the people, and of women who bewailed and lamented Him. But Jesus, turning unto them, said: "Daughters of Jerusalem, weep not for Me, but weep for yourselves and for your children. For, behold, the days are coming in which they shall say, Blessed are the barren, and the wombs that never bare, and the paps that never gave suck. Then shall they begin to say to the mountains, Fall on us; and to the hills, Cover us. For if they do these things in a green tree, what shall be done in the dry?" Thus Jesus foretold the great and terrible doom that was to come upon the Jewish people, the dry tree, because it rejected the Savior, the green branch. And He desired not tears of human pity, but tears of repentance. Tears of **repentance are tears of the faith which** knows that Jesus bore our sin and our penalty for us, tears, therefore, of contrite sorrow and of a grateful believing heart. Such tears the prophet foretells, saying: "And they shall mourn for Him as one mourneth for his only son." God grant unto us the Spirit of grace and of prayer so to view and so to mourn Jesus.

PRAYER.—Alas, my Lord and Savior, of myself I am in no way sufficient or able to meditate properly and beneficially upon Thy holy Passion. Therefore I pray Thee to have mercy upon me, and to give me the Spirit of grace and of prayer that I may know that Thou didst suffer because of my sin, to redeem me therefrom, and to make me righteous before God and eternally blessed, to the end that I may truly mourn for my sin, and withal thank Thee with a joyful heart for having so graciously saved me. Amen.

Hymn 212.

MONDAY.

Father, forgive them; for they know not what they do.—Luke 23, 34.

Two malefactors were also led away with Jesus to be executed. And they brought Jesus to a place called Calvary, in Hebrew, Golgotha, which, being interpreted, is, The place of a skull. That was the place of execution, a hill near Jerusalem. And they gave Him vinegar to drink, or wine mingled with myrrh, mixed with gall, to partly benumb His senses. But when He tasted thereof He would not drink it. And they crucified Him, and the two malefactors with Him, one on the right hand and the other on the left, and Jesus in the midst. And the scripture was fulfilled which says: "And He was numbered with the transgressors." According to Jewish reckoning of time it was the third hour when they crucified Him, nine o'clock in the morning. Then said Jesus: "*Father, forgive them; for they know not what they do.*" This was Jesus' first thought, His first word, His prayer on the cross: "Father, forgive them!" For this was the reason why He so willingly died the death on the cross: He wanted to obtain the forgiveness of sins for us sinners and save us. This prayer refers to all of us. It referred also to His tormentors. And being the true Advocate with the Father, He kindly added: "For they know not what they do," The soldiers, blind heathen, knew Him not, and realized not what terrible sin they were committing. Likewise the multitude of the people, and even many of the elders, were not yet hardened, but did all this in ignorance, in the ignorance of unbelief. Ah, Father, forgive them; do not visit them with swift punishment; convert them; draw them to Me, that my death may give life to them too! Behold, they are blind; open their eyes unto saving knowledge! Such was Jesus' prayer.—But whosoever knowingly hardens himself against Jesus forfeits the grace of this intercessory prayer of Jesus, and will be eternally lost.

PRAYER.—O Lord and Savior Jesus Christ, I give thanks unto Thee for Thy suffering upon the cross, whereby I have been redeemed. I thank Thee for Thy intercession, by virtue of which I have been converted unto Thee. I thank Thee for the love wherewith Thou so dearly lovest me, a sinner, and drawest me unto Thee in faith. I thank Thee that Thou hast merited forgiveness of sin for me, and asked it to be granted to me, yea, hast actually given and appropriated it unto me. Continue to pray for me, my Savior, that I may continue in the faith and be saved. Amen, Thou wilt assuredly do this. Amen.

Hymn 203, 1.

TUESDAY.

If these should hold their peace, the stones would immediately cry out.—Luke 19, 40.

Pilate wrote a title, a superscription briefly telling what Jesus was accused of, and placed it on the cross above His head. It read thus: "JESUS OF NAZARETH THE KING OF THE JEWS." This title was read by many of the Jews; for the place where Jesus was crucified was nigh to the city; and it was written in Hebrew, Greek, and Latin. Then said the chief priests of the Jews to Pilate: "Write not:

'The King of the Jews,' but that He said: I am the King of the Jews." Pilate answered: "What I have written I have written."—Then the soldiers, when they had crucified Jesus, took His garments, and made four parts, to every soldier a part; and also His coat. Now the coat was without seam, woven from the top throughout. They said therefore among themselves: "Let us not rend it, but cast lots for it, whose it shall be," that the scripture might be fulfilled, which saith: "They parted my raiment among them, and for my vesture they did cast lots." (Ps. 22, 18.) And sitting down, they watched Him there. These things the soldiers did; and the people stood beholding.

Did not one among the people lift his voice to confess Jesus? None. Not one of His disciples? None; most of them had fled. Then the stones must cry out. The superscription of godless Pilate proclaimed in three languages that Jesus was the Savior. For "King of the Jews" was a familiar term applied to the Messiah, the Christ, the Savior. And the blind soldiers who divided His garments and cast lots for His coat visibly fulfilled the great and wonderful prophecy concerning the crucifixion of the Messiah which was and is still to be read in Psalm 22. Christian, open heart and lips to confess Christ the Crucified as thy Savior!

PRAYER.—Savior, O Savior, help me lest I shun the shame of Thy cross! Help me loudly, freely, and publicly to confess Thee to be my dear Savior and the only Savior of the world. Forsooth, Thou didst regard neither shame nor death to save me; Thou wilt confess me, a miserable sinner, to be Thine own in the presence of Thy Father and all the holy angels. Create, then, in me, O my Lord and Savior, that fruit of the lips which consists in giving thanks unto Thy name. Amen.

Hymn 91, 4-6.

WEDNESDAY.

The Lord hath been mindful of us.—Ps. 115, 12.

There stood by the cross of Jesus His mother. It is needless to say what sword now pierced her soul. And there

Week of the Fifth Sunday in Lent.

stood Mary, the wife of Cleophas, and Mary Magdalene. John also stood there. When Jesus saw His mother, and the disciple standing by whom He loved, He said to His mother: *"Woman, behold thy son!"* Then He said to the disciple: *"Behold thy mother!"* And from that hour the disciple took her unto his own home.—Even in the midst of His suffering and death the Savior did not forget His poor mother. He was mindful of her and provided for her. This is a lesson for children who have parents that are unprovided for. But what is it the Savior once said? He said: "Who is my mother or my brethren?" And He looked round about on them that sat about Him and said: "Behold my mother and my brethren! For whosoever shall do the will of God, the same is my brother and my sister and mother." (Mark 3, 33-35.) He calls us, who according to God's will believe in Him and are His own and follow Him, His brethren and sisters and mothers. And He is mindful of us. "The Lord hath been mindful of us." When we are in need, He is most lovingly mindful of us, and He provideth for us. "And as He was in humiliation, so is He still in exaltation." He is still the same kind Savior. Let every one comfort himself with this, and cast all his cares upon Him!

PRAYER.—Thy loving heart, O my Savior, is mindful also of me. This I know, in this I rejoice, herewith I comfort myself, and for this I give thanks unto Thee. Yea, Thou art mindful of us and wilt bless us, both small and great. Though we should lose all things, yet will we not lose Thee. Help me, Lord Jesus, to be and remain Thine own; then all will be well in time and eternity. And likewise grant me grace that I, who am Thine own, may consider all others who are Thine my brethren and sisters and fathers and mothers, and that to the best of my ability I may help them when in need, as Thou, dear Savior, wouldst have me do. Amen.

Hymn 198, 8. 9.

THURSDAY.

But I am a worm and no man, a reproach of men, and despised of the people. All they that see me laugh me to scorn; they shoot out the lip, they shake the head, saying, He trusted in the Lord that He would deliver Him; let Him deliver Him, seeing that He delighted in Him.—Ps. 22, 6-8.

Thus did the Savior, the Messiah, by the mouth of David, foretell His own suffering. See how it all was fulfilled! They that passed by the cross railed on Him, wagging their heads and saying: "Ah, Thou that destroyest the temple, and buildest it in three days, save Thyself! If Thou be the Son of God, come down from the cross." Likewise the chief priests, mocking among themselves with the scribes and elders, together with the people, said: "He saved others; Himself He cannot save! If He be Christ, the King of the Jews, the Chosen of God, let Him save Himself and descend now from the cross, that we may see and believe. He trusted in God; let Him deliver Him now if He will have Him; for He said, I am the Son of God." The thieves also who were crucified with Him cast the same thing in His teeth and reviled Him. And the soldiers also mocked Him, coming to Him, offering Him vinegar, and saying: "If Thou be the King of the Jews, save Thyself!"—Thus from every quarter scorn and derision was poured out upon the Righteous One in His bitter suffering. He suffered this for us. And now we sinners are to be hailed by God with none but kindest greetings, and be received with highest honors. But while we live here below, let us go forth unto our Savior, who still is continually reviled, and let us freely confess His name and bear His reproach. May He Himself help us to do so!

PRAYER.—Lord Jesus, the reproach which I, a miserable sinner, have deserved has fallen upon Thee, for Thou didst bear my sin. And the sublime honor and glory which belongeth unto Thee shall be my portion. I glorify Thee for such mercy! Grant that in faith I may grasp this and hold fast to it. Bestow upon me Thy Holy Spirit that unafraid I may take my stand with Thee, gladly bearing Thy reproach, O Lord, my only Salvation! Amen.

Hymn 87, 5.

FRIDAY.

Verily I say unto thee, To-day shalt thou be with Me in paradise.—Luke 23, 43.

One of the malefactors crucified with Jesus railed on Him persistently, saying: "If Thou be Christ, save Thyself and us!" But the other one had experienced a great change. He rebuked his companion and said: "Dost not thou fear God, seeing thou art in the same condemnation? And we indeed justly; for we receive the due reward of our deeds. But this man hath done nothing amiss." And he said unto Jesus: "Lord, remember me when Thou comest into Thy kingdom!" And Jesus said unto him: "*Verily I say unto thee, To-day shalt thou be with Me in paradise.*"—O precious word of our Redeemer! It shows that Jesus receives the very worst of sinners if they come to Him. It shows that Jesus receives them though they come to Him in the last hour, after a long life of sin. It shows that Jesus gives them the same blessedness which He gives to the greatest saint, and He gives it at once, without an intervening purgatory. Let every one comfort himself herewith!—And this whole delightful story shows how alone a man may come to true faith in the Savior: by seeing and hearing Christ Crucified, as we may do now in His Word. And it shows what fruits faith brings forth at once: true sorrow for sin, childlike trust in Jesus, a blessed hope in death, a bold and cheerful confession of Jesus, and penitent patience in cross and affliction. May all here take a lesson!—Christian, be like yon malefactor who repented in his last hour. And dost thou not believe that had his life been spared him a while longer, he would have renounced his former life of sin and followed Jesus? Most certainly. Then do thou do so! May God help thee!

PRAYER.—O Jesus, grant unto me the mercy which Thou didst grant the malefactor. Not that I am worthy of it, but grant it because Thou lovest to show mercy. Remember me for Thy saving mercy's sake. Forgive unto me my great and numerous sins. Let me belong to Thy Kingdom of Grace. When my last hour comes, receive me into paradise. Give me true knowledge of Thee through the preaching of Thy cross. Give unto me at all times repentance to salvation, firm confidence in Thee, sure hope of eternal life, a new heart and courage to cheerfully confess Thy name, to serve Thee, and to suffer patiently. Have mercy on me, O Jesus! Amen.

Hymn 200, 1. 2.

SATURDAY.

Eli, Eli, lama sabachthani?—Matt. 27, 46.

And when the sixth hour was come, at noon, the sun was darkened, and there was a darkness over all the land until the ninth hour, until three o'clock in the afternoon. This was no eclipse of the sun such as we know of, for it was the time of the full moon. And about the ninth hour Jesus cried with a loud voice: "*Eli, Eli, lama sabachthani?*" which is, being interpreted: "My God, my God, why hast Thou forsaken Me?" Some of those that stood there, when they heard that, said: "He calleth Elias."—That must have been a gruesome darkness in those three hours! What did Jesus all go through in those three hours? No one knows, nor does Scripture tell. So much, however, is certain that in those three hours Jesus was forsaken by God. We know this from the cry He uttered. To be forsaken by God—no living man can comprehend what that is. In body and soul was Jesus forsaken of God. That was the curse of hell and the pain of hell. He who was made to be sin for us was made also a curse for us. (Gal. 3, 13.) Then, just then, Satan must have seen his opportunity. He summoned all his forces for a last desperate attack upon Jesus, in order to get Him into his power and to ruin Him. More than this we cannot say. Terrible! Inconceivable! But the

Savior overcame it all. All the onslaughts against Him came to naught. And thus He redeemed us from the power of the devil and from eternal damnation. We who in faith are His own shall never experience what it means to be forsaken by God. No; God, for Jesus' sake, receives us into His full fatherly favor. And what that means we shall perceive and enjoy and experience in the blessed life to come.

PRAYER.—My Lord and Savior, I thank Thee that Thou wast forsaken by God in order that I might not be eternally forsaken by Him. My Heavenly Father, for the sake of Christ, whom Thou didst make a curse for me, Thou dost receive me and dost bless me with the infinite fullness of Thy blessings. God Holy Ghost, Thou Spirit of the Father and of the Son, let me apprehend these mercies in true faith, until in the regeneration of blissful eternity I shall fully comprehend all things and extol Thee for them eternally. Amen.

Hymn 207, 6.

Week of the Sixth Sunday in Lent.

SUNDAY.

I thirst.—John 19, 28.

Consider what the Savior had all suffered so far. And now He was in bodily anguish of death. In the prophecy He Himself relates this as follows: "I am poured out like water, and all my bones are out of joint; my heart is like wax; it is melted in the midst of my bowels. My strength is dried up like a potsherd, and my tongue cleaveth to my jaws; and Thou hast brought me into the dust of death." (Ps. 22, 14. 15.) But Jesus also knew that all things were now accomplished that were necessary for our salvation. And now, like a poor dying man, He said: "*I thirst.*" Does that not touch one's heart? Now there was a vessel full of vinegar; and straightway one of them that stood by ran, and took a sponge, and filled it with vinegar, and put it on a reed of hyssop, and put it to His mouth and gave Him to drink. But in doing it, he mockingly remarked, together with the others: "Let Him alone; let us see whether Elias will come to take Him down!" Thus also that word of Scripture was fulfilled which, again, He Himself had spoken through the mouth of David: "They gave Me also gall for my meat; and in my thirst they gave Me vinegar to drink." (Ps. 69, 21.)—When putting the two words together which came from the lips of Jesus in immediate succession, the words: "My God, my God, why hast Thou forsaken Me?" and: "I thirst," thou must perceive that the Savior tasted all the anguish of death which we sinners have deserved. Thereby He merited for us that God will tenderly care for us in the hour of death, more tenderly than a mother cares for her sick and restless child, and through His Holy Spirit will soothe us into a blessed sleep.

PRAYER.—Lord Jesus Christ, since Thou didst suffer all, yea, truly, all things for me and for my soul's welfare, I pray Thee: When the anguish of death shall come upon me, when my strength shall leave me, when my heart shall break with fear, when all human aid must vanish, do Thou come and help me, shorten the agony of death, drive the evil spirits from me, comfort me with the comfort of Thy salvation, and let me gently fall asleep in Thee. Amen.

Hymn 195, 6.

MONDAY.

It is finished. Father, into Thy hands I commend my spirit.—John 19, 30; Luke 23, 46.

When Jesus had received the vinegar, He said with a loud and cheerful voice: *"It is finished."* The sin of the world was atoned for. The penalty of the world's sin had been endured. The inexorable justice of God which demands the punishment of the transgressor had received full satisfaction; God was reconciled unto the world. The sin of the world was forgiven. The punishment all mankind deserved was abolished. God's grace now was ready to receive all sinners as His children and to give them eternal life. Our Savior, our Substitute, had accomplished all this. Every sinner may and should now say in faith: "It is finished; all that was necessary to save me has been accomplished. Just as the Savior is thy Savior and thy Substitute, so also this word shall be thy word: "It is finished." Thou hast not accomplished thy salvation, but He has accomplished it for thee, yes, for thee; hence thou too must say: "It is finished." This word of Jesus penetrated into the highest heaven. Let it penetrate into thy poor sinful heart. It saves thee.—And again Jesus cried aloud and cheerfully: *"Father, into Thy hands I commend my spirit."* Since He had finished all, there no longer lay upon Him the sin, penalty, and curse of the world; God's wrath, burning like fire, was turned into most fervent love; God no longer forsook Him, but held out His fatherly hands toward Him. And so Jesus said: "Father, into Thy hands I commend my spirit." In this, too, Jesus is thy Savior, thy Substitute. All that is His is thine. This word, too, thou mayest and must take from His lips. When thy last hour cometh, thou, too, shalt say right gladly and confidently: "Father, into Thy hands I commend my spirit."—And having said this, Jesus bowed His head, beckoned Death to come, and gave up the ghost. His human soul now was in the hands of the Father, while His human body hung dead upon the cross. And in soul and body His eternal Godhead had its being. And, Christian, when thou diest, the grace of God in Christ will keep thy soul and thy body. This is most certainly true.

PRAYER.—My dear Heavenly Father, who hast made Thy dear Son a Savior for me, a poor sinner, and didst set Him forth to be my Redeemer, give unto me, I beseech Thee, Thy grace and Holy Spirit, that when my last hour shall come, I may not look upon myself nor upon my unworthiness, but only upon my Lord and Savior Jesus Christ, who hath accomplished all things for me. And let me also with full confidence commend my soul into Thy hands. And then keep my body and soul unto eternal life. Amen.

Hymn 207, 8.

TUESDAY.

By his own blood He entered in once into the holy place, having obtained eternal redemption for us.—Hebr. 9, 12.

The innermost part of the Temple at Jerusalem, the Holy of Holies, contained the Ark of the Covenant with the tables of the Law. This Ark of the Covenant was covered with the mercy-seat and the cherubim, between whose extended wings the Shekinah appeared, the cloud which manifested the presence of the glory of the Lord. Into this Holy of Holies, which was shut off from view by a veil, or curtain, no man dared enter, save the high priest, and he only once a year, on the great Day of Atonement, when he bore the typifying blood of atonement. Thereby the Holy Spirit indicated that Christ, the true Atoner, had not yet come and finished His work of atonement. When Jesus died, this great, thick, heavy veil which hung before the Holy of Holies was rent in twain from top to bottom by unseen hands. And thereby the Holy Spirit plainly indicated that Christ had now come and had finished His work of atonement, and that *Jesus, the Crucified, is this Christ.* Yes, Jesus has reconciled us to God; by His own blood He entered in once into the holy place, that is to say, He appeared before God whom we had offended, having obtained eternal salvation for us. And now every sinner can come to God in Jesus' name and cheerfully say: " Abba, Father ! "—And something more happened when Jesus died. The earth quaked, the rocks rent, the graves about Jerusalem were opened, and many bodies of the saints of God that slept arose and came out of their graves; and after His resurrection they went into the Holy City, as Jerusalem was called, and appeared unto many. Thereby, too, the Holy Ghost plainly indicated that Christ had now come and had finished His work of atonement and eternal redemption, and that *Jesus, the Crucified, is this Christ.* The earth, this great burying-ground, shall no longer be able to retain us. We who believe in Jesus shall rise, and see one another, and be reunited with one another. And even this old earth, which God has cursed because of our sins, shall become new. The holy seer says: " I saw a new heaven and a new earth; for the first heaven and the first earth were passed away." (Rev. 21, 1.)

PRAYER.—My Lord and Savior Jesus Christ, Thou true High Priest, Thou Lamb of God that taketh away the sin of the world, I thank Thee that Thou hast come, and by Thine all-propitiating blood didst once appear before the face of God, and didst obtain eternal salvation for us. I thank Thee that Thou didst rend the veil of guilt which separated me from God. I thank Thee that in Thy name I may come unto God and may call Him Father. I thank Thee that Thou hast procured for me the resurrection from the dead and eternal bliss in heaven. Keep me in true faith, my Lord and Savior! Amen.

Hymn 314, 6.

WEDNESDAY.

The preaching of the cross is to them that perish foolishness; but unto us who are saved it is the power of God.— 1 Cor. 1, 18.

When the centurion who stood over against the cross of Jesus, and they that were with him and were watching Jesus, saw that He cried out so triumphantly just before giving up the ghost, and when they saw the earthquake, and those things that were done, they feared greatly and glorified God, saying: "Certainly, this was a righteous man! Truly, this was the Son of God!" These people were converted by the Savior's suffering and death. Thereby the Holy Ghost shows that the preaching of the cross, which to them that perish is foolishness, nevertheless is the only power of God to kindle faith in the sinner's heart and through faith to save him. Wilt thou note this well? And all the people that had gathered there, on beholding the things which were done, smote their breasts and returned. Were not these things the beginnings of faith in Jesus, the Crucified?—And afar off stood all the acquaintances of Jesus and many women that had followed Him from Galilee, and beheld these things. Among them were Mary Magdalene, and Mary, the mother of James the Less and of Joses, and Salome, the mother of

Zebedee's children (James and John), who had followed Jesus when He was in Galilee, and had ministered unto Him, and many other women that had come up with Him to Jerusalem. All these, with a longing and burning heart, beheld the cross of Jesus and could not turn their eyes away from it, though great temptation besetting them threatened to stifle their faith. Thereby the Holy Ghost would teach us that we who believe in Jesus should always abide with the preaching of the Cross, for this is the only power of God to preserve our faith against every temptation unto a blessed end. The eyes of our faith must be directed toward our Redeemer as He hung upon the accursed tree; otherwise it is an empty show.

PRAYER.—God Holy Ghost, let me abide with the preaching of the Cross, that my faith may be proved and found steadfast against every temptation. For within this Word is Thy divine power, by which alone saving faith can dwell within my heart. Grant me Thy grace, O precious Comforter, that my eyes may be ever fixed upon my crucified Redeemer, and that they may rest upon Him when my sight grows dim in my dying hour. Amen.

Hymn 201, 10.

MAUNDY THURSDAY.

This is He that came by water and blood, even Jesus Christ; not by water only, but by water and blood. And it is the Spirit that beareth witness, because the Spirit is truth. 1 John 5, 6.

Deut. 21, 22. 23 thou mayest read that it was forbidden to let the bodies of hanged criminals remain upon the tree over night, lest the land be defiled. And remember the day on which Christ died was the day preceding the great Easter Sabbath, called Preparation. Therefore the chief council sent to Pilate, and asked him to order the legs of the crucified to be broken and their bodies taken away. So the soldiers broke the legs of the two malefactors who were crucified with Christ. But when they came to Jesus and saw that He was dead already, they did not break His legs; but one of the soldiers pierced His side with a spear, and forthwith there came out blood and water. The Apostle John was an eye-witness of this. And in his Gospel, where he tells of this occurrence, he says: "And he that saw it bare record, and his record is true, and he knoweth that he saith true, that ye might believe. For these things were done, that the scripture should be fulfilled: 'A bone of Him shall not be broken.' And again another scripture saith: 'They shall look on Him whom they pierced.'" All the details of the death of Jesus proved that He is the Lamb of God that taketh away the sin of the world, prophesied and typified in the Old Testament, and that He is the Christ Jehovah, whom they were to pierce. (Exod. 12, 46; Zech. 12, 10.) Thus the blood and water that flowed from the cleft side of Jesus is the fountain opened for sin and uncleanness whereof Zechariah prophesies. (Zech. 13, 1.) And this fountain flows for us in Baptism and in the Lord's Supper. For when John says that Christ comes by water and blood, he means by water Baptism and by blood the Lord's Supper. And in the Word, too, which is spirit, the Savior comes to us and makes the fountain flow for us therein. And the Word, which is spirit, convinces us through the divine power of the Spirit dwelling within it that this Word is truth, and so kindles saving faith within us.

PRAYER.—Lord Jesus, who didst suffer Thine heart to be cleft that therefrom the fountain might flow which cleanseth us from all sin and uncleanness, to the end that we poor sinners may stand before God righteous and be saved. I give thanks unto Thee that Thou dost cause this fountain to flow freely in the Word, in Baptism and in Holy Communion. Grant me Thy Holy Ghost, dear Savior, that I may always eagerly seek Thy salvation in these means of grace, in order that I may inherit life eternal which Thou hast purchased for me at so great a price. Amen.

Hymn 436, 6.

GOOD FRIDAY.

Come, my people, enter thou into thy chambers and shut thy doors about thee; hide thyself, as it were, for a little moment, until the indignation be overpast.—Is. 26, 20.

Jesus had died upon the cross. What did they do with His body?—In Jerusalem there lived a member of the chief council named Joseph of Arimathea, a city of the Jews. He had not consented to the counsel and deed of them, for he was a good and just man, and waited for the kingdom of Christ; indeed, he was a disciple of Jesus, but secretly, for fear of the Jews. He went boldly to Pilate and besought him that he might take the body of Jesus from the cross. And Pilate marveled if He were already dead; and calling unto him the centurion, he asked him whether He had been any while dead. And when he knew it, he commanded the body of Jesus to be delivered unto Joseph. And Joseph bought fine linen for the burial of Jesus. And there came also Nicodemus, who at the first came to Jesus by night, and brought a mixture of myrrh and aloes, about a hundred pound weight. After they had taken the body of Jesus down, they wrapped it in a clean linen cloth, and wound it in linen clothes with the spices, as the manner of the Jews is to bury. Now, nigh to Golgotha there was a garden and in the garden a new sepulcher, a tomb that belonged to Joseph, which he had hewn out of a rock, wherein was never man yet laid. There then laid they Jesus because the Jews' Preparation Day drew to a close. Soon it was six o'clock, the great Paschal Sabbath was drawing nigh. This place, however, was near at hand. And they rolled a great stone to the door of the sepulcher and departed. Mary Magdalene and Mary, the mother of Joses, also were there, sitting over against the sepulcher; other women also who came with Jesus from Galilee beheld how and where His body was laid. Then they likewise departed, and prepared spices and ointments to anoint the body of Jesus. And they rested the Sabbath day according to the law.

Thus the Savior was also laid in the grave for us, and hence the grave has lost its terrors for us. For us Christians it is to be a chamber where we are to sleep, and where no man will be able to wake us. There we shall be hidden, as it were, for a little moment; there we shall rest in peace until the wrath of God against the wicked world will be overpast.

PRAYER.—Merciful and kind Heavenly Father, who didst cause Thy Son to die and be buried for my sin, grant that in true faith I may be united with my Savior, and ever remain so, that by virtue of His death my death may become a blessed sleep, that by His grave my grave may be sanctified, and that, lastly, I may rise again unto everlasting joy, through the same, Thy dear Son, Jesus Christ, my Lord. Amen.

Hymn 216, 2. 4. 5.

SATURDAY.

Neither wilt Thou suffer Thine Holy One to see corruption.—Ps. 16, 10.

On the day that followed the day of Preparation, hence on **Easter Sabbath**, the chief priests and Pharisees came together to Pilate, saying: " Sir, we remember that that deceiver said while He was yet alive: After three days I will rise again. Command therefore that the sepulcher be made sure until the third day, lest His disciples come by night, and steal Him away, and say unto the people: He is risen from the dead, so the last error shall be worse than the first." Pilate said to them: " Ye have a watch; go your way, make it as sure as you can." So they went and made the sepulcher sure, setting a watch and sealing the stone with the seal of the Chief Council. Troubled by secret unrest, they wanted to make altogether sure of keeping Jesus, whom they hated so bitterly, in death, grave, decay, and corruption, and relegate Him to utter oblivion. But here is God's prophecy concerning Christ: " Neither wilt Thou suffer Thine Holy One to see corruption." God kept Christ's body in the grave without corruption. Death and the grave had not swallowed up and overpowered Christ, but Christ had conquered death and the grave. Soon this became evident. It shall become fully evident to all the world on the Day of Judgment. Also the present-day pharisaical and sadducean enemies of Christ, who fill so many pulpits and chairs of learning and seats of church-government, and would keep Christ in the grave, shall be utterly confounded: God will make them His footstool, and they shall wail and confess that the Holy One of God did not see corruption. But thou, O Christian and child of God, do thou look upon the buried Savior with altogether different eyes: confess that He is Thy Substitute who bears thy sin and suffers thy death and thy burial, and conquers it all for thee, that thou mayest live in righteousness and blessedness forever.

PRAYER.—Lord Jesus, I thank Thee that Thou didst take my sin upon Thyself and into the grave, and didst bury it there, and didst procure for me eternal rest. Thou Conqueror of sin and death and grave, grant that henceforth I may not stand in dread of my grave, but that in the knowledge of Thee I may gladly enter my chamber, knowing that I am a partaker of Thy victory,—O Thou who hast abolished the terrors of the grave. Amen.

Hymn 215, 8.

Week of Easter Sunday.

EASTER SUNDAY.

He is risen.—Matt. 28, 6.

When it began to dawn on Easter Sunday morning, Mary Magdalene and Mary, the mother of James, and Salome, and Joanna, and a small company of other women that came with Jesus from Galilee, went toward the sepulcher of Jesus, bearing spices to anoint His holy body.—At the same time there was a great earthquake; for the angel of the Lord descended from heaven, and came to the sepulcher, and rolled back the stone from the door, and sat upon it. His countenance was like lightning, and his raiment white as snow; and for fear of him the keepers did shake and became as dead men.—And the women said among themselves: "Who shall roll us away the stone from the door of the sepulcher?" Mary Magdalene outran the others and was the first one to come to the grave. The others followed more slowly. And when they looked toward the sepulcher, they saw that the stone was rolled away. That was easy to see as it was a very big stone. When Mary Magdalene saw the open sepulcher, she straightway ran back to Jerusalem to tell the disciples of it. But some of the women entered the tomb. And they did not find the body of the Lord. But they saw there a young man sitting on the right hand clothed in a long white garment. It was the above-mentioned angel of the Lord. And they were affrighted. But the angel said to them: "Fear not; for I know that ye seek Jesus, who has been crucified. He is not here; for *He is risen,* even as He said. Come, see the place where the Lord lay. And go quickly, and tell His disciples and Peter that He is risen from the dead. And, behold, He goeth before you into Galilee; there shall ye see Him: lo, I have told you." Meanwhile the other women also came into the tomb, and they were much perplexed because they did not find the body of Jesus. And, behold, two men stood by them in shining garments. And they were afraid, and bowed down their faces to the earth. Then the angels said: "Why seek ye the living among the dead? He is not here, but *is risen.* Remember how He spake unto you when He was yet in Galilee, saying: The Son of Man must be delivered into the hands of sinful men, and be crucified, and the third day rise again." And they remembered His words. And all the women departed quickly from the grave with fear and great joy. They fled from the sepulcher; for they trembled and were amazed; neither said they anything to any man there; for they were afraid.— This was the first news of Jesus' resurrection. *"He is risen!"* So much of the glad tidings for to-day.

PRAYER.—Almighty God, who by the death of Thy Son hast abolished sin and death, and through His resurrection hast restored innocence and life immortal, that we, being delivered from the power of the devil, might live in Thy kingdom: grant that I may believe this with all my heart, and that, remaining steadfast in such faith, I may glorify and thank Thee always, through the same, Thy Son, Jesus Christ, our Lord. Amen.

Hymn 224, 1-3.

EASTER MONDAY.

Be not deceived: evil communications corrupt good manners.—1 Cor. 15, 33.

Is this a fitting text for Eastertide? It seems not. But learn what happened on Easter Day.—Some of the guards, on recovering from their faint and fright, hurried into the city and told the chief priests all the things that had come to pass. These then assembled with the elders and took counsel. And as a result of their deliberations they gave a large sum of money to the soldiers, saying: "Say ye: His disciples came by night, and stole Him away while we slept. And if this come to the governor's ears, we will persuade him, and secure you." The soldiers took the money and did as they were taught. This, then, became the common report among the Jews. And this or a similar report has been adopted by unbelievers of all times. In our day, too, there are such unbelievers. Even numberless pastors and professors and high officers of the Church preach, teach, and stoutly maintain that Jesus has *not* risen from the dead. And they gloss their Jewish, antichristian, and Scripture-profaning teaching with many a specious tale. And the superficial masses flock after them. But be thou not deceived, my dear Christian! Scripture says: "Evil communications corrupt good manners," or morals. If thou lendest thy ear to such communications, thy faith will be corrupted, thy faith in the Word of God and in thy Savior, Jesus Christ. For a dead Savior cannot save. In this Eastertide thou wilt hear much of what the Scriptures have recorded of the resurrection, the bodily resurrection, of Jesus. Lend thy ear to these precious truths. There strengthen and quicken thy faith.

PRAYER.—My Lord and Savior Jesus Christ, Thou didst take my sin and death upon Thee, and didst completely overcome and destroy it, and didst rise from the dead a Conqueror and the Prince of Life, and didst give unto me righteousness and eternal life: I pray Thee so to strengthen and to steel my poor soul by Thy Word and Holy Ghost that all evil communications will rebound from it, and that I may firmly believe in Thee who didst rise and livest, a true Savior. Amen.

Hymn 229, 1. 2.

TUESDAY.

For as yet they knew not the Scripture, that He must rise from the dead.—John 20, 9.

Mary Magdalene found Peter and the other disciple, whom Jesus loved (John), and said to them: "They have taken away the Lord out of the sepulcher, and we know not where they have laid Him." Peter therefore went forth, and that other disciple, and they came to the sepulcher. And both ran; and the other disciple outran Peter, and came first to the sepulcher. And stooping and looking in, he saw the linen cloths lying; yet went he not in. Then cometh Simon Peter, following him, and went into the sepulcher, and seeth the linen cloths lie, and the napkin that was about His head, not lying with the linen cloths, but wrapped together in a place by itself. Then went in also that other disciple who came first to the sepulcher, and saw, and believed. What did he believe? "That He was taken away, as Mary Magdalene had told them," says Dr. Luther. "For as yet they knew not the Scripture, that He must rise again from the dead." Then the disciples went away again unto their own home.—God kindles and preserves true faith through His Word. If this is lost sight of, the cheerless appearance of things overpowers one. So it was with the disciples. Indeed, they knew the Scripture that Christ must rise from the dead; Christ had told them that repeatedly. But this very Word had never become a living knowledge with them. Hence the terrors of the cross and the horrors of the grave and of death so clouded their vision that from the vacant tomb they learned only that the body was gone, and not that

Jesus was risen. Christian, let the Scripture illumine thee, or thou wilt see naught but darkness!

PRAYER.—O God the Holy Ghost, Thou Spirit of Christ, our Savior, who through the Word dost illumine the hearts of Thy believers to know the divine truth and to comfort themselves with it, illumine my heart also, that I may comfort myself abundantly with the resurrection of our Savior, and that I may have the full assurance that He has completely overpowered sin, death, and the grave for my benefit, and has procured for me righteousness, life, and eternal salvation, until I shall reach those blessed abodes where believing will be changed to seeing. Amen.

Hymn 224, 4.

WEDNESDAY.

Rabboni.—John 20, 16.

And Mary Magdalene stood without at the sepulcher weeping; and as she wept, she stooped down and looked into the sepulcher, and saw two angels in white sitting, the one at the head and the other at the feet, where the body of Jesus had lain. And they said to her: "Woman, why weepest thou?" She said to them: "Because they have taken away my Lord, and I know not where they have laid Him." And when she had said this, she turned back, and saw Jesus standing, and knew not that it was Jesus. Jesus said to her: "Woman, why weepest thou? Whom seekest thou?" She, supposing Him to be the gardener, said to Him: "Sir, if thou have borne Him hence, tell me where thou hast laid Him, and I will take Him away." Jesus said to her: "Mary!" She turned and said unto Him: "Rabboni!" which is to say: "Master!" Jesus said unto her: "Touch Me not; for I am not yet ascended to my Father; but go to my brethren and say unto them: I ascend unto my Father and your Father, and to my God and your God." —Thus did the Savior, when He had risen early the first day of Easter-week, appear first to Mary Magdalene, from whom He had cast out seven devils. And highly enraptured, she said: "Rabboni!"—But He refused to be detained, to continue with His own as before, visibly and in humiliation. No, He wanted to ascend to His Father. But just then and thus would He be with His disciples, better, more intimately, and more closely united; and by His Holy Spirit He would enlighten them truly to know the blessed union with Him, and through Him with God the Father. And this grace we all possess. Knowing the risen and ascended Lord through His Word, and knowing Him to be present, rich in mercy, we, too, may say in rapture: "*Rabboni!*"

PRAYER.—Rabboni! Lord Jesus, Thou livest and art with me, full of grace. Thou hast procured salvation for me. Thy Father is my Father, Thy God is my God. I am blessed. Grant me grace, O Lord, to love Thee and to rejoice in Thee. With Thy kind saving hand lead me through death to where I may see Thee bodily, and where in never-ending rapture I may exclaim: "Rabboni!"

Hymn 229, 3. 4. 7.

THURSDAY.

And their words seemed to them as idle tales, and they believed them not.—Luke 24, 11.

What became of the other women who had fled from the grave? As trembling they went their way, behold, Jesus met them, after He had appeared to Mary Magdalene, and said to them: "All hail!" And they came and held Him by the feet and worshiped Him. Then He said to them: "Be not afraid; go tell my brethren that they go into Galilee, and there they shall see Me." And they went and told all these things to the eleven Apostles, and to all the rest of them that had been with Jesus, as they mourned and wept. And lo, Mary Magdalene came and told the disciples that she had seen the Lord, and that He had spoken this to her. But the Apostles and the other disciples, when they heard that Jesus lived, and had been seen of the women, did not believe. "And their words seemed to them as idle tales, and they believed them not." Their hearts were too badly crushed beneath the temptation of the cross. They could not comprehend these things. But soon the Savior came to them to cheer them, and to rescue them from the fatal sadness, and to grant them grace to know Him and His salvation. After all, they were His own.—O Christian, thou, too, wilt live to see times of sore trial and great sadness, and it will seem to thee that thou hast lost thy Savior, and Satan will insinuate to flesh and blood that the Gospel truths are idle tales. But hold fast to the Word, and wait on the Lord. He will deliver thee, and make thee rejoice in the knowledge of Him. Be not terrified when afflictions come. Must they not come because thy flesh is evil and Satan is waylaying thee?

PRAYER.—Deliver me, my Lord and Savior, for in Thee do I hope! Let me not be ashamed, for I put my trust in Thee, my almighty and faithful Shepherd. My flesh is evil, and Satan is too powerful for me. How will I be able to keep my faith? O risen Lord, let me, a miserable worm, feel the almighty power of Thy life in me, and preserve me in true faith unto a blessed end. Amen, even so, Thou wilt perform it. Amen.

Hymn 224, 6.

FRIDAY.

And their eyes were opened, and they knew Him.—Luke 24, 31.

In the afternoon of Easter Day two of the larger circle of disciples went from Jerusalem to a village called Emmaus, about three hours' walk. And they talked together of all these things which had happened. And it came to pass that, while they communed together and reasoned, Jesus Himself drew near and went with them. But their eyes were holden that they should not know Him. And He said to them: "What manner of communications are these that ye have one with another as ye walk, and are sad?" And one of them, whose name was Cleopas, answering, said to Him: "Art Thou only a stranger in Jerusalem, and hast not known the things which are come to pass there in these days?"

And He said to them: "What things?" And they said to Him: "Concerning Jesus of Nazareth, who was a prophet mighty in deed and word before God and all the people; and how the chief priests and our rulers delivered Him to be condemned to death, and have crucified Him. But we trusted that it had been He who should have redeemed Israel. And besides all this, to-day is the third day since these things were done. Yea, and certain women also of our company made us astonished, who were early at the sepulcher; and when they found not His body, they came, saying that they had also seen a vision of angels, who said that He was alive. And certain of them that were with us went to the sepulcher, and found it even so as the women had said; but Him they saw not." Then He said to them: "O fools, and slow of heart to believe all that the prophets have spoken! Ought not Christ to have suffered these things, and to enter into His glory?" And beginning at Moses and all the prophets, He expounded unto them in all the Scriptures the things concerning Himself. And they drew nigh unto the village whither they went; and He made as though He would have gone further. But they constrained Him, saying: "Abide with us; for it is toward evening, and the day is far spent." And He went in to tarry with them. And it came to pass, as He sat at meat with them, He took bread, and blessed it, and brake, and gave to them. And their eyes were opened, and they knew Him. And he vanished out of their sight. And they said one to another: "Did not our heart burn within us while He talked with us by the way, and while He opened to us the Scriptures?"

How? Should anything be added to this beautiful story, which is ever new? No, indeed! Do but always seek thy living Savior in His *Word;* then will thy eyes be opened ever more, and ever better and ever more clearly wilt thou know Him, and ever more firmly wilt thou believe in Him.

PRAYER.—Lord God, Heavenly Father, who didst reveal Thy Son Jesus Christ to the two disciples of Emmaus, I pray Thee also to illumine my heart by Thy Word and Holy Spirit that I may grow strong and firm in faith, continuing faithfully, steadfastly in Thy Word, gladly speaking of it, and diligently seeking its companionship to the end that here on earth I may have true comfort through Thy Word, until, after this life, through Thy Son I may be raised to enjoy eternal bliss. Amen.

Hymn 40, 1. 3. 8.

SATURDAY.

The Lord is risen indeed.—Luke 24, 34.

When the disciples of Emmaus had recognized the Risen One, they rose up that same hour, and returned to Jerusalem with haste, and found the eleven gathered together, and them that were with them. And immediately they were met with the cry: "The Lord is risen indeed, and hath appeared to Simon!" And they told those assembled there what things were done in the way, and how He was known of them in the breaking of the bread. But even so they did not all believe that the Lord had actually risen. And while they spoke, and the doors being shut for fear of the Jews, lo, Jesus Himself stood in the midst of them and said: "Peace be unto you!" But they were terrified and affrighted, and supposed that they beheld a spirit. And He said to them: "Why are ye troubled, and why do thoughts arise in your hearts? Behold my hands and my feet that it is I myself; handle Me and see; for a spirit hath not flesh and bones, as ye see Me have." And when He had thus spoken, He showed them His hands and His feet and His side with the prints of His wounds. And while they yet believed not for joy and wondered, He said to them: "Have ye here any meat?" And they gave Him a piece of a broiled fish and of a honeycomb. And He took it and ate before them. Then, finally, were the disciples glad when they saw the Lord. Now they all knew that He had risen indeed.

Such knowledge is peace. For since Christ is risen, we know that He is the Savior indeed, and has truly saved us, so that now we are children of God, reconciled through Him, and heirs of eternal life. Such knowledge is peace. Dost thou possess this knowledge, this peace?

PRAYER.—O Jesus, grant to me, too, at all times, through Thy Word and the Holy Spirit, the living knowledge that Thou art the true and risen Savior, to the end that I may take comfort in Thee, and firmly believe that through Thee I have been redeemed and am a child of God and an heir of eternal life. Give me Thy peace, O Jesus! Amen.

Hymn 221, 1. 2. 6.

Week of the First Sunday After Easter.

SUNDAY.

As my Father hath sent Me, even so send I you.—John 20, 21.

When the disciples came to rejoice at seeing the Lord in their midst, He repeated the words of greeting: "Peace be unto you!" And then He said: "As my Father hath sent Me, even so send I you." And when He had said this, He breathed on them and said to them: "Receive ye the Holy Ghost; whosesoever sins ye remit, they are remitted unto them; and whosesoever sins ye retain, they are retained."— The Father had sent the Son to procure peace for mankind. This was accomplished now. The Father had also sent the Son to communicate this peace to mankind, to bestow peace upon us through the knowledge of Him, the Savior. He had just done this for the frightened company of disciples. But He means to do this for all of us. Therefore He said to His disciples: *"As my Father hath sent Me, even so send I you."* Through the Word of Christ, the Crucified and Risen One, the disciples were to convey to their fellow-men the knowledge of Christ, and peace by this knowledge. To this end He breathed on them and gave them the Holy Ghost. For the Holy Ghost is the eternal personal breath of the Father and of the Son. And He is with the Word of Christ. Through the Word He kindles faith in Christ in the heart, and gives peace through this faith. This peace, however, is rooted in the forgiveness of sins. Therefore the disciples, by the Word of the Gospel, were to deliver to mankind the forgiveness of sins procured by Christ. And faith, wrought through this Word by the Holy Spirit, was to have and possess this forgiveness. For whatsoever the disciples give by means of the Word, God Himself gives through it. But whoever would reject their gift, his sins the disciples were to retain. And whatsoever thus they would retain, God Himself would retain.—This office and command the Savior gave to His assembled disciples on Easter evening, not to the Apostles only, but to all the disciples there assembled, both men and women. This office and command the Savior gives to His disciples of all times, not only to the called and ordained teachers and preachers, but to all disciples, both men and women. This office and command He also gives to thee, Christian. Note this well!

PRAYER.—I thank Thee, my Lord and Savior Jesus Christ, Thou sole Bringer of peace, that through Thy Word, which is preached by the Church, Thou hast bestowed peace upon me also. Grant that I may know Thy gracious will and my calling, and be most eagerly intent upon conveying this peace and the forgiveness of sins to others, too. Hereunto grant me Thy Holy Spirit and abundance of grace. Amen.

Hymn 426, 2-4.

MONDAY.

Blessed are they that have not seen, and yet have believed. John 20, 29.

But Thomas, one of the Twelve, called Didymus, was not with the disciples when Jesus came. O Thomas!—The other disciples therefore said to him: "We have seen the Lord." But he said to them: "Except I shall see in His hands the print of the nails, and put my finger into the print of the nails, and thrust my hand into His side, I will not believe." O Thomas!—And after eight days again His disciples were within. And Thomas was with them. Then came Jesus, the doors being shut, and stood in the midst and said: "Peace be unto you!" O Thomas!—Then saith He to Thomas: "Reach hither thy finger and behold my hands; and reach hither thy hand and thrust it into my side, and be not faithless, but believing." And Thomas answered and said to Him: *"My Lord and my God!"* Jesus saith unto him: "Thomas, because thou hast seen Me, thou hast believed. *Blessed are they that have not seen, and yet have believed."*

So mercifully did the Savior deal with Thomas, and bring him back to faith. But he also permitted him to see Him, for Thomas was an Apostle, and was to be a witness of Christ's resurrection, an eye-witness. But we must not see, and yet believe. We must believe the Word of the Apostles, the eye-witnesses. We must believe the Scripture both of the Old and the New Testament—of the Old Testament, where the resurrection of Christ is foretold, and of the New Testament, where the resurrection of Christ is attested. We must believe the Holy Spirit, who has given the Scripture, the Old and the New Testament, by inspiration, and who moves and is active therein, and mightily and convincingly witnesses that it is the truth. In heaven we too shall see.

PRAYER.—Deal mercifully with me, Lord Jesus, and do not altogether quench the smoking flax of my faith, but fan it into a flame through Thy Word and the Holy Spirit, by Thy great mercy. I call upon Thee, Lord Jesus—hear me! I trust in Thee, firmly believing that Thou wilt not permit me to be bereft of the comfort of true faith, but wilt preserve my faith until I shall come to Thee in heaven. Amen.

Hymn 243, 4-6.

TUESDAY.

This is now the third time that Jesus showed Himself to His disciples after that He was risen from the dead.—John 21, 14.

After these things Jesus showed Himself again to the disciples at the Sea of Tiberias, hence, in Galilee. And on this wise showed He Himself. There were together Simon

Peter, and Thomas, and Nathanael, and the brothers James and John, and two other of His disciples. Simon Peter said to them: "I go a-fishing." They said to him: "We also go with thee." They went forth, and entered into a boat immediately; and that night they caught nothing. But when the morning was come, Jesus stood on the shore; howbeit the disciples knew not that it was Jesus. Then Jesus said to them: "Children, have ye any meat?" They answered Him: "No." And He said to them: "Cast the net on the right side of the boat, and ye shall find." They cast therefore, and now they were not able to draw it for the multitude of fishes. Therefore John, the disciple whom Jesus loved, said to Peter: "It is the Lord!" Now when Simon Peter heard that it was the Lord, he girt his fisher's coat about him, (for he was naked,) and cast himself into the sea. But the other disciples came in the little boat, (for they were not far from the land, but about 200 cubits off,) dragging the net with fishes. As soon as they were come to land, they saw a fire of coals there, and fish laid thereon and bread. Jesus said to them: "Bring of the fish which ye have now caught." Simon Peter went up, and drew the net to land, full of great fishes, 153; and though there were so many, yet the net was not broken. Jesus said to them: "Come and dine." And none of the disciples durst ask Him: Who art thou? knowing that it was the Lord. Jesus then came, and took bread, and gave it to them, and fish likewise. —This is the third time that Jesus showed Himself to His Apostles after He had risen from the dead. And these are the men who testify the resurrection of Jesus in their writings, that we might believe. They testify what they themselves have seen. And the Holy Spirit attests the truth of their testimony.

PRAYER.—I thank Thee, Lord Jesus, that Thou so plainly, unmistakably, and often didst manifest Thyself to Thy Apostles as the risen Conqueror of sin, death, and the devil, so that their testimony of Thy resurrection is true beyond all doubt. Grant me, I beseech Thee, Thy Holy Spirit, that by such testimony He may make me so certain of Thy salutary resurrection that in life and death I may firmly found my faith thereon. Amen.

Hymn 226, 1.

WEDNESDAY.
Lovest thou Me?—John 21, 17.

When the disciples had dined with the risen Lord, as we heard yesterday, Jesus said to Simon Peter: "Simon, son of Jonas, lovest thou Me more than these?" He said to Him: "Yea, Lord; Thou knowest that I love Thee." He said to him: "Feed my lambs."—Jesus now said to him the second time: "Simon, son of Jonas, lovest thou Me?" He said to Him: "Yea, Lord; Thou knowest that I love Thee." He said to him: "Feed my sheep."—He said to him the third time: "Simon, son of Jonas, lovest thou Me?" Peter was grieved because He said to him the third time: "Lovest thou Me?" And he said unto Him: "Lord, Thou knowest all things; Thou knowest that I love Thee." Jesus said to him: "Feed my sheep."—So mercifully did the Lord remind Peter of his former haughtiness and contempt of the other disciples, as well as of his subsequent threefold denial, and at once reinstated him in his apostolic office.

Though we have fallen ever so low, yea, and ever so often, Jesus receives us again, and is gracious, gentle, and kind toward us, and permits us to be His own. And we? We love Him. And He knows it. But if we love Him, we must also serve Him. And the service He most desires of us is, that we take care that His lambs and sheep are fed, that is, that His believers, small and great, are properly and abundantly nourished with the Word of God, so that they, too, may rightly know their Savior, love Him, and be saved. —Dost thou love thy Savior, and dost thou serve Him diligently and faithfully in His Church?

PRAYER.—Lord Jesus, I love Thee. Thou knowest it. I am a great sinner. But Thou hast done everything for me, and again and again dost Thou reveal to me Thy kind heart. Therefore I love Thee; indeed, I cannot but love Thee. Help me, O help me, Lord Jesus, to lovingly serve Thee by serving those who, together with me, are Thine, both the small and the great in the Church, in order that they may have the Word of Thy grace plentifully, and remain with Thee, and be eternally saved. Amen.

Hymn 349, 7. 8.

THURSDAY.

What is that to thee? Follow thou Me.—John 21, 22.

The risen Lord addressed also these words to Peter: "Verily, verily, I say unto thee, When thou wast young, thou girdedst thyself, and walkedst whither thou wouldst; but when thou shalt be old, thou shalt stretch forth thy hands, and another shall gird thee, and carry thee whither thou wouldst not." This He said to indicate to him by what death he would glorify God, namely, by the death of a martyr. And when He had spoken this, He said to him: "Follow me." Peter was to follow His Lord unswervingly unto death; and Peter now was most willing to do so, in the strength of Jesus.—But Peter turned about, perhaps because he heard some one walking, and seeing John, the disciple whom Jesus loved, who also had leaned on Jesus' breast at the Paschal Supper, and had said: "Lord, who is it that betrayeth Thee?" he said to Jesus: "Lord, and what shall this man do?" He meant to say: By what death shall this man glorify God? Jesus said to him: "If I will that he tarry till I come, what is that to thee? Follow thou Me." Here take a lesson, my dear Christian! Thou must follow Jesus lovingly, and Jesus will love thee and guide thee as He wills, perchance along rugged paths, but to eternal salvation. And thou must not turn about and look at others and say: If I am led so, how will these be led? Or: If I must suffer so much, why not these, too? It is none of thy concern how Jesus shall lead each one. That is His concern, and not thine. He will not have anyone interfere with His government. Do thou follow Jesus fearlessly, and He will lead thee a blessed way. But refrain from interfering with His government!—Then the saying went abroad among the brethren that that disciple should not die; yet Jesus had not

Week of the First Sunday After Easter.   181

said to him: He shall not die; but: "If I will that he tarry till I come, what is that to thee?"

PRAYER.—Lord Jesus, my dear Savior, crucified and risen for me, thanks to whose great mercy I, a miserable sinner, have become Thy disciple, grant me the Spirit of faith and of love and of power and of humility, that cheerfully and gladly I may follow Thy guidance, whither Thou wilt, without presumptuously questioning why Thou doest this or that; for I know, O Lord, that Thou leadest me to the realms of eternal bliss. Amen.

Hymn 331, 1. 4.

FRIDAY.

All power is given unto me in heaven and in earth. Go ye, therefore, and teach all nations, baptizing them in the name of the Father and of the Son and of the Holy Ghost; teaching them to observe all things whatsoever I have commanded you. And, lo, I am with you alway, even unto the end of the world.—Matt. 28, 18-20.

Chiefly in Galilee did the Lord, by many infallible proofs, as He had promised them, show His disciples that He was risen and alive. There He finally appointed a certain mountain where they should witness a great manifestation of Himself. And when they had assembled there, and probably above 500 disciples with them, they saw Jesus. And they worshiped Him; but some doubted. And Jesus spoke to them the royal words found at the head of this lesson.— Christ the Crucified has been raised and thus exalted by the Father, so that He, the Son of Man, has all divine power in heaven and on earth. But it is the will of Him who has redeemed all men with His blood to bring all men to salvation through faith in Him. Therefore He commands His believers of all times to carry the Gospel to all men, and to make disciples of all who believe in Him, through Baptism. Through Baptism we are brought into the gracious communion of the Holy Trinity, in whose midst is Jesus, for He is the Son. And the disciples of Jesus were to hear, learn, and observe every word which He had commanded His Apostles, and which they have expounded to us in their writings by inspiration of the Holy Ghost. And Jesus is with His own alway, even unto the end of the world. He is with our testimony of Him, to strengthen it; with our faith in Him, to keep us steadfast; He is with us in life and death.—This is the royal decree of the risen Lord to His disciples of all times and all places. Whoever disregards this cannot be His disciple.

PRAYER.—Omnipotent Lord and Savior, true God with the Father and the Holy Ghost, King and Lord of Thy beloved congregation which Thou hast purchased with Thy blood and sanctified with Thy Spirit: I give thanks unto Thee that Thou hast made me, unworthy though I am, Thy disciple. Grant that, obedient to Thy command, I may use all diligence, so far as in me lies, to proclaim Thy Word and Gospel to all mankind. And always be with me, according to Thy promise, until, finally, I shall come to Thee in Thy heavenly kingdom. Amen.

Hymn 110, 1. 3.

SATURDAY.

Then opened He their understanding, that they might understand the Scriptures.—Luke 24, 45.

The forty days in which the risen Lord was seen by His disciples were drawing to a close. The feast of Pentecost was near at hand. The Lord had again assembled His disciples, especially the Apostles, in Jerusalem. And one day, when He appeared to them, He said to them: "These are the words which I spake unto you while I was yet with you, that all things must be fulfilled which were written in the law of Moses, and in the prophets, and in the psalms, concerning Me." Formerly the disciples had never been able to understand when the Lord Jesus spoke to them of His suffering and death and His resurrection on the third day; and the Scriptures which had foretold these things had been just as obscure to them as Jesus' words. But now they saw the fulfillment, now they saw the Crucified before them alive, now all was different, now they understood it all. So now

He went through all the Scriptures with them; He showed them how everywhere they prophesied concerning Him, and opened their understanding, that they might understand the Scriptures. It must have been a long and precious sermon: the risen Lord the Preacher, and the disciples, now so glad, the hearers. He closed this sermon with the words: "Thus it is written, and thus it behooved Christ to suffer, and to rise from the dead the third day; and that repentance and remission of sins should be preached in His name among all nations, beginning at Jerusalem. And ye are witnesses of these things."—Note well, Christian: not the New Testament only, but the Old Testament as well everywhere testifies of Christ, and is a Christ-book. Unless thou understandest this, thou dost not understand the Old Testament at all. And Jesus, crucified and risen, of whom the New Testament witnesses, is the Messiah foretold and prefigured in the Old Testament, the Savior of the world. Thus at all times there was but one true faith: the faith of the Christians. And all who ever were saved, from the days of Adam, were saved in no other way than by faith in Christ, the crucified and risen Lord. And there never will be any other saving faith. Let this be *thy* faith, O Christian!

PRAYER.—Lord Jesus, Thou true Messiah and Christ, the Son of God the Father, Thou only Savior of the world, help me at all times and with all my heart to believe the eternal and unchanging, old and ever new Gospel concerning Thee, which tells that it behooved Thee to suffer and to die for my sins and the sins of the whole world, and to rise again the third day for my justification and eternal blessedness and for the justification and blessedness of the whole world. Help me, lest I, as so many do, turn away from this Gospel. Grant me grace to cling firmly to it and be saved by it. Amen.

Hymn 225, 1. 2.

Week of the Second Sunday After Easter.

SUNDAY.

Go ye into all the world, and preach the Gospel to every creature. He that believeth and is baptized shall be saved, but he that believeth not shall be damned.—Mark 16, 15. 16.

The fortieth day after the resurrection of our Lord was at hand. The eleven Apostles were at Jerusalem. They were just sitting at meat when Jesus came to them. And now that they were able rightly to understand it, He upbraided them for their unbelief and hardness of heart, because they had not believed them that had seen Him after He was risen. It is well for us to know the perverseness of our heart; and we never know it more fully than just when we are certain of our sonship with God through faith. Thus we are then impelled always to trust in Jesus only, and never in ourselves.—Then the Lord repeated the command concerning the conduct of their apostolic office which He had previously entrusted to them by saying: "Go ye into all the world, and preach the Gospel to every creature." And the Lord invested this office with supreme authority: "He that believeth and is baptized shall be saved, but he that believeth not shall be damned." Nor can it be otherwise. Only in Christ there is salvation. He that believeth in Him is saved; he that rejecteth Him is damned.—And then the Lord equipped His Apostles and their fellow-disciples with the power to perform miracles, in order to confirm their preaching: "And these signs shall follow them that believe: In my name shall they cast out devils; they shall speak with new tongues; they shall take up serpents; and if they drink any deadly thing, it shall not hurt them; they shall lay hands on the sick, and they shall recover." And then—but that we shall hear on the festival of the Ascension.—O Christian, dear Christian, abide in the faith in Thy Savior, who has died and is risen for thy sake. But do not rely on thy own strength or constancy. For thy heart is a frail heart. Seek the strength and help of Jesus. He gives it to thee through His Word.

Week of the Second Sunday After Easter. 185

PRAYER.—Almighty God and Lord, by Thy grace I believe that Thy dear Son Jesus Christ, the Crucified and Risen, is the only Savior, besides whom there is no salvation, and that He is my dear Savior and Redeemer. But since I know the fickleness and inconstancy of my heart, and perceive that without Thy grace I cannot persevere in faith, O Lord, therefore at all times bestow upon me Thy grace, and keep me in Thy Word and faith unto life everlasting. Amen.

Hymn 225, 5-7.

MONDAY.

Destroy this temple, and in three days I will build it up. John 2, 19.

Thus Jesus said to the Jews when they desired of Him a sign showing that He was the promised Christ. He spoke of the temple of His body. Kill me, and in three days I shall rise again; that was the meaning of His words. The resurrection of Jesus, who had been put to death, is the great sign which shows that He is the Christ promised in Scripture, the Son of God, the Savior of the world, and that His doctrine is right and true. If Jesus had not been the Christ, but—the pen fairly refuses to write it—a false prophet, then He surely would not have risen, but would have remained in the grave, like all false prophets. But since He is risen, He has proved beyond all controversy that He is the Son of God, and the Savior promised in the Scripture, the ever truthful, whose words shall not pass away. When, therefore, He was risen from the dead, His disciples remembered that He had said to them the words that thou readest above, and they believed, they believed in Him, they believed the Scripture, and the word which Jesus had said. Everything, the truth of all the Scripture, the whole Christian faith, yea, everything depends upon the resurrection of Jesus. If His resurrection did not take place, then all is vain, but since it has, all is sustained. Christian, thou must be altogether certain of Jesus' resurrection, or thou canst not believe in Him as thy Savior. And thou mayest be altogether certain of it. The eye-witnesses testify to it with one accord. These eye-witnesses testify to it in writings which radiate naught but holiness. The same is true of the Old Testament prophecies. And the Holy Ghost bears witness, divine and powerful witness, that the Scripture of the Prophets and of the Apostles and Evangelists is truth. Nothing on earth is so strongly attested as the resurrection of Jesus. And so thy faith in Jesus Christ, Thy Savior, is well founded. Thou art redeemed.

PRAYER.—Lord Jesus, Thou heavenly Sun, Thou didst set before the eyes of the world and even of Thy disciples, when Thou diedst on the cross. Soon, however, Thou didst rise again, when Thou camest forth alive from the grave, and in rapture did Thy disciples behold Thee. And in their Spirit-testimony Thou dost shine unto me also, O true Light of mercy, full of life, salvation, and never-ending bliss. O my Lord and Savior, let my eyes always be fixed on Thee, that in Thee I may know my salvation. Amen.

Hymn 226, 4.

TUESDAY.

Who was delivered for our offenses, and was raised again for our justification.—Rom. 4, 25.

Christ was delivered for our offenses, delivered into death. He atoned for our sins by His death. And He was raised again for our justification. By the resurrection of Christ, God has made us righteous, declared us righteous, has justified us. Even as Christ's surrender into death is our atonement, so His resurrection is our justification. I wonder if thou dost understand this, kind reader. Christ is our Substitute. By atoning for our sins with His death as our Substitute, He has reconciled God unto us. And then God raised Him from the dead. Thereby God declared in very fact that nothing has remained for Christ to do for our reconciliation, towards the atonement for our sins. By the resurrection of our Substitute, God declared that our sins have been atoned for, that in His sight we are righteous—in Christ. Christ's resurrection is Christ's justification of our sins, and hence it is *our* justification; for Christ is justified for *our* sins, as our Substitute, in our stead, for us. If Christ had not been raised from the dead, we would not know whether our sins were really atoned for, whether God had actually accepted His sacrifice for our sins, whether we were actually reconciled to God, whether we were actually righteous before God in Christ. But now that God has raised Christ, we know that He has actually atoned for our sins, that God has actually accepted the sacrifice of Christ for our sins, that we are actually reconciled to God, that we are actually righteous in the sight of God. And so we must look upon Christ's resurrection from the dead as upon the declaration of our righteousness, our justification, and fully trust in it. What was said yesterday may be said again to-day: Everything, the truth of all the Scripture, the whole Christian faith, ya, everything depends upon Christ's resurrection. If this did not take place, then all is vain. Since this did take place, all is sustained. My dear Christian, thou must be altogether certain of the resurrection of Jesus, or thou canst not really believe Him to be thy Savior.

PRAYER.—Lord and Savior Jesus Christ, Thou Risen One, Thou art my Righteousness; Thou art made righteousness unto me by God; when God raised Thee, after Thou hadst died for me, He justified me in Thee. Grant that my faith hold fast to Thee, Lord, my Righteousness. This is the name whereby I will know Thee, O Lord, and cling to Thee: Jehovah Zidkenu, The Lord, Our Righteousness. Amen.

Hymn 324, 3. 4.

WEDNESDAY.

But now is Christ risen from the dead, and become the first-fruits of them that slept.—1 Cor. 15, 20.

Death is dreadful! It takes all away from us. We return to dust. But that does not make an end of us. After the darkness of death there is the darkness of death: judgment and eternal damnation. Death is the wages of sin. The bands of death are as strong as God, who has subjected us to it. But Christ has taken our sin upon Himself and atoned for it. He entered into our death and arose from the dead.

Week of the Second Sunday After Easter.

He arose from the dead to give us resurrection. He has destroyed *our* death. He has riven the bands of *our* death. He is become the first-fruits of them that sleep. We who are His own in faith do but sleep when we die, and in this sleep naught shall disturb us. And then we shall follow Him, the first-fruits, and shall likewise rise from the dead, full of eternal life, full of inexpressible joy, unto eternal bliss. Dost thou rejoice when now, in springtime, thou beholdest the first little flower lift its head. Ah, yes, for thou knowest that more shall follow, a rich profusion of spring and summer grandeur. So Christ, our first-fruits, has lifted up His head from the great burying-ground, but many will follow, all those who believe in Him. If Christ were not risen, we would all be lost in death. But now that Christ is risen, we all shall rise. Once more we say: Everything, the truth of all the Scripture, the whole Christian faith, yea, everything depends upon the resurrection of Jesus. If this did not take place, then all is vain. Since, however, it did take place, all is sustained. Christian, thou must be altogether certain of the resurrection of Jesus, or thou canst not believe Him to be Thy Savior.

PRAYER.—Grant, O faithful God, that I may live in true faith which rests on my Savior, die in Thy grace, sleep in peace, rise by Thy power, and thereupon inherit the blessed hope of eternal life, for the sake of Thy Son Jesus Christ, who has destroyed all the terrors and bands of death for me. Amen.

Hymn 226, 2. 5.

THURSDAY.

He shall redeem Israel from all his iniquities.—Ps. 130, 8.

Christ has redeemed us from all our *sins.* Scripture says so. This is our faith. And this is most certainly true. —But how is this? We still have sin, we are sinners, we sin. How, then, are we to understand that Christ has redeemed, rid, freed us from all our sins?—We sin against the Law of God. Hence we are guilty and liable to penalty. Because of our sins we are under the curse of the Law. From the *guilt* and *penalty* of sin, or from the curse of the

Law, which is the same thing, Christ has redeemed, rid, and freed us. "Christ hath redeemed us from the curse of the Law, being made a curse for us," says the holy Apostle, Gal. 3, 13. And from the *dominion* of sin Christ has redeemed us. Sin, which indeed still dwells within us, can no longer own, dominate, enslave, rule, govern us, and shape our lives. We can laugh and mock at sin, resist it, be disobedient to it, and act contrary to it. Christ has rid and freed us from our former vain conversation under the authority of sin, received by tradition from our fathers from the beginning. The Apostle Peter writes: "Ye know that ye were not redeemed with corruptible things, as silver and gold, from your vain conversation received by tradition from your fathers, but with the precious blood of Christ, as of a Lamb without blemish and without spot," 1 Pet. 1, 18. 19. And the time will come when we shall be freed altogether from every sin that still clings to us, for the sake of the sacrifice which Christ made for us. And all this has been brought to light and vouched for by the resurrection of Christ, when Christ, our Substitute, having finished the work of our salvation, entered into a new life, which no longer was subject to our sin.

PRAYER.—Risen Savior! Now art Thou rid of the sins of the world; Thou hast atoned for it and vanquished it. And in Thee I am rid of my sin; it can neither damn nor rule me. For this I give thanks unto Thee with all my redeemed heart. O grant that I may enjoy the knowledge of this my blessed freedom, and, being rid entirely of an evil conscience, of anxiety and fear, may serve Thee with a cheerful heart, until I shall awake from the sleep of death with Thy likeness. Amen.

Hymn 224, 5.

FRIDAY.

And deliver them who through fear of death were all their lifetime subject to bondage.—Hebr. 2, 15.

Christ has redeemed us from *death*. Scripture says so, and such is our firm belief. And it is most certainly true;

—But how about this? We must die, and the germ of death grows and is rank within us. How, then, are we to understand that Christ has redeemed, rid, and freed us from death? —Our dying in this present time is in reality the entrance to eternal death, eternal damnation. But this eternal death, eternal damnation, has been done away with entirely for us through Christ, who has redeemed us from the guilt and penalty of our sins. We who are in Christ need in no wise fear it. And for this reason we also need not fear temporal death. For if, in departing this life, we do not enter eternal death, why need we afraid to die? What, then, do we enter through temporal death? Eternal life. Knowest thou not what the Savior said to the dying robber who believed in Him? He said to Him: "Verily, I say unto thee, To-day shalt thou be with me in paradise." This He also says to us when we die. Should we, then, be afraid? And even our body He will raise from the grave, and fashion it like unto His glorious body. Fear? No, we need not fear temporal death. Quite the reverse! When, according to the will of our Lord, the hour of our death approaches, then we must join aged Simeon in exclaiming: "Lord, now lettest Thou Thy servant depart in peace, according to Thy word; for mine eyes have seen Thy salvation." All this has been brought to light and vouched for by the resurrection of Christ, when Christ, our Substitute, having accomplished the work of our salvation, entered into a new life, which was free from our death.

PRAYER.—Risen Savior! Now art Thou free from the death of the world; Thou hast borne and vanquished it. And in Thee I am free from death; it can no longer devour and keep me. For this I give thanks unto Thee with all my redeemed heart. O grant that I may enjoy the knowledge of this my blessed freedom, and, being rid of every anxiety and fear of death, may commit my soul into Thy hands in the hour of death, until Thou wilt also quicken my body unto eternal life. Amen.

Hymn 221, 5.

SATURDAY.

That through death He might destroy him that had the power of death, that is, the devil.—Hebr. 2, 14.

For this purpose Christ came. And He really accomplished it. He has delivered us from the *power of the devil.* Scripture says so, and such is our firm belief. And it is most certainly true.—But how about this? Are we not still on earth where "the prince of this world" rules with "great might and deep guile?" And what are we in comparison with him? How, then, are we to understand that Christ has redeemed us from the power of the devil?—First, and above all, Christ has taken from the devil the power to accuse us and to demand our death, at the bar of God's unalterable righteousness because of our sins. For Christ, by His death, has atoned for our sins, has made full satisfaction to the righteous God, and reconciled God unto us. Thus our accuser has been cast down once for all. Furthermore, Christ, as our Substitute, in His great struggle with the devil, so completely conquered and vanquished him that through Him we are able to withstand all the temptations of the devil, and to gain the victory over him at all times, by means of the Word of Christ. "One little Word can fell him," him, the Evil Foe. And lastly, as a result of Christ's victory over the devil, he can do nothing to us unless Christ permits it for our good—dost thou hear? for our good. Ah, yes, Christ has redeemed us from the power of the devil. Trusting in Christ, we may and dare and must deride and scorn the devil. This will sorely vex that proud spirit, and make him flee from us. Thus did Christ destroy the power of the devil. And this has been brought to light and vouched for by the resurrection of Christ, whereby Christ, our Substitute, triumphed over the devil.

PRAYER.—Risen Savior! Thou hast bruised the devil's head, and taken all his power from him. And now I am redeemed from the power of the devil. The devil can no longer accuse me, can no longer seduce me, no longer harm me. I may deride and scorn him. For this I give thanks unto Thee with all my redeemed heart. O grant that I may rejoice in the knowledge of this my blessed freedom, and at all times boldly resist the devil and firmly cling to Thee, until Thou shalt free me from every temptation, and take me into Thy Kingdom of Glory. Amen.

Hymn 218, 5.

Week of the Third Sunday After Easter.

SUNDAY.

Ye know that ye were not redeemed with corruptible things, as silver and gold, from your vain conversation received by tradition from your fathers, but with the precious blood of Christ, as of a Lamb without blemish and without spot.—1 Pet. 1, 18. 19.

We have been redeemed, yea, redeemed by Christ from all sins, from death, and from the power of the devil. Hallelujah! But *wherewith* has Christ redeemed us? Not with gold and silver, but with His holy, precious blood and with His innocent suffering and death. How are we to understand this? Thus: With His holy, precious blood and with His innocent suffering and death Christ has rendered satisfaction for us, has paid the penalty of our guilt, has suffered our punishment required by God's righteousness. Hence we are free from the guilt of sin, and God declares us guiltless. Hence we are free from death, the penalty of sin, and God gives us life. Hence we are free from the power of the devil, and God receives us as His children. We are redeemed. What does Scripture say? It says: "He (God) hath made Him to be sin for us who knew no sin, that we might be made the righteousness of God in Him." And it says: "Surely, He hath borne our griefs and carried our sorrows; yet we did esteem Him stricken, smitten of God, and afflicted. But He was wounded for our transgressions, He was bruised for our iniquities; the chastisement of our peace was upon Him, and with His stripes we are healed." (2 Cor. 5, 21; Is. 53, 4. 5.) And in raising Christ, God declared before heaven and earth and hell that Christ has in reality and truly redeemed us from all sins, from death, and from the power of the devil, with His holy, precious blood and with His innocent suffering and death.

PRAYER.—O my Lord and Savior, let me never forget how dearly it cost Thee to redeem me. But God has accepted the purchase-price and has considered it sufficient, and has raised Thee from the dead, O my Savior. Thanks, thanks be unto Thee, Lord Jesus, for Thy holy, precious blood and for Thy innocent suffering and death. Give unto me the spirit of faith, that I may rejoice in the knowledge that Thy resurrection is my salvation. Amen.

Hymn 223.

MONDAY.

To this end Christ both died, and rose, and revived, that He might be Lord both of the dead and living.—Rom. 14, 9.

To what end has Christ redeemed us? To this end, that we might be His own, and live under Him in His kingdom, and serve Him in everlasting righteousness, innocence, and blessedness. Yes, that we might live in blessedness, to this end Christ has redeemed us. For this is blessedness, that we are His own and live under Him in His kingdom, and serve Him in everlasting righteousness, innocence, and— well, there it is: blessedness. His great love for us who were lost moved Him to redeem us at so great a price, and to deliver us from all sins, from death, and from the power of the devil, that we might be His own again, and live under Him in His kingdom, and serve Him in everlasting righteousness, innocence, and blessedness. Perhaps thou art thinking of all the dead who hoped in Christ, and now for years and centuries, yea, thousands of years have been lying in their graves; and thou wouldst ask how the merciful purpose of Christ was accomplished in them? O my friend, death there makes no difference at all. All the dead who have died believing in Him He has in His bosom, and He even keeps their dust; they are all His own; they shall all rise and live under Him in His kingdom, and serve Him in everlasting righteousness, innocence, and blessedness, even as He is risen from the dead, lives and reigns to all eternity. This is most certainly true. For to this end Christ both died, and rose, and revived, that He might be Lord both of the dead and living.—O Christian, lift up Thy heart to the risen Savior, who by His death has redeemed thee at so great a price, and say to Him: Lord Jesus, I am Thine, and Thou art my Lord. Give me Thy blessedness!

PRAYER.—Indeed, Lord Jesus, I am Thine, and Thou art my Lord! With Thy God's blood Thou hast bought me from all sins, from death, and from the power of the devil. I want to belong to Thee, and to none other. I want to live in Thy kingdom, and nowhere else. I want to serve Thee, and no one else. I am Thine in life and death. I will be Thy own in life everlasting. Amen.

Hymn 218, 7. 9.

TUESDAY.

He is the propitiation for our sins; and not for ours only, but also for the sins of the whole world.—1 John 2, 2.

Whom has Christ redeemed? The very best answer for thee to give to this question is: Me and all lost and condemned mankind. By answering thus, thou appropriatest the salvation of Christ to thy own self; thou seizest upon it and comfortest thyself with it as firmly and confidently as if Christ had redeemed thee only. And this is what thou mayest and shouldst do; God wants thee to do this. For Christ has redeemed all lost and condemned mankind, and hence thee also. No man is excepted from the salvation of Christ, hence neither thou. If it were not so, if the cheerless doctrine of Calvin, the father of the Reformed Church, were true, that Christ had only redeemed the believers, how, then, wouldst thou be altogether certain that Christ had redeemed thee, even thee? For, in the first place, faith is often assailed and obscured; and moreover, faith must have a foundation to rest upon. But the foundation faith has is just this, that Christ has redeemed all lost and condemned mankind, and hence, thee and me too. And this is most positive Bible doctrine. Dost thou note the text above? So all Christians must believe. And thou knowest that other Word of God: "Behold the Lamb of God, that taketh away the sin of the world," John 1, 29; and this: "The Son of Man is come to save that which was lost," Matt. 18, 11. Even the unbelievers, the godless, who deny, reject, despise, and scorn Christ, have nevertheless been redeemed by Christ. But just because they deny Christ, and for this reason only, they are lost. Peter writes concerning such: "They deny the Lord that *bought them,* and bring upon themselves swift destruction," 2 Pet. 2, 1. My dear Christian, the risen Savior has redeemed *thee,* for He has redeemed *all* lost and condemned mankind. Mayest thou believe this gladly and most assuredly, thou poor sinner! This faith will not deceive thee.

PRAYER.—Risen Savior, in Thy victory over sin, death, and the devil I behold the victory over my sin, my death, my evil accuser and foe. Yea, Thou, O Lord, hast redeemed all lost and condemned mankind, and hence also me, a lost and condemned sinner. Thanks, thanks be unto Thee, my Lord and Savior! Give me Thy Holy Spirit, that I may firmly cling to this blessed truth, and nevermore fear nor faint in such faith. Me, even me, Thou hast redeemed, O Lord! I, even I, am redeemed. Amen.

Hymn 106, 7. 9.

WEDNESDAY.

Moreover, brethren, I declare unto you the Gospel which I preached unto you.—1 Cor. 15, 1.

Let me put thee in mind, my dear Christian, of the Gospel which has been proclaimed to thee in this book from Holy Scriptures. Thou hast embraced this Gospel in true faith, and thy faith firmly rests on it. And by this Gospel, just as it has been taught thee, thou art saved, if thou holdest fast to it, unless thou renderest thy faith useless through subsequent unbelief. Now, what is it that thou hast been taught? First of all, that Christ died for our sins according to the prophecy of Holy Writ, and that He was buried; but that, furthermore, also according to the prophecy of Holy

Writ, *He rose again the third day*. And thou hast been told how He was seen alive by Mary Magdalene; by her companions; by Peter; by those two disciples going to Emmaus; by the whole company of disciples assembled in Jerusalem, twice; by the seven Apostles at the Sea of Gennesaret; by all the Apostles and over 500 brethren with them on a mount in Galilee; again, twice, by the Apostles in Jerusalem. And last of all He was also seen alive by Paul, the great Apostle of the heathen, who for so long had been His enemy, and a persecutor of those who believed in Him. And thou hast been told that He was seen alive after His resurrection by the Apostles on many more occasions than those enumerated in Scripture. And these eye-witnesses have declared unto us the above-mentioned Gospel, the glad tidings that Christ, true God and man, according to the prophecy of the Old Testament, died for our sins and was buried and triumphantly rose again the third day. This is the Gospel that saves thee. Abide with that! Hold fast to that! Let nothing turn thee from it!

PRAYER.—Lord God, Heavenly Father, I thank Thee for Thy holy Gospel, that divine power to save, which tells me that Thy dear Son Jesus Christ died also for my sins, but that, conquering sin, death, and the devil, and all that opposes me, He rose and became my true Redeemer. Give me, I beseech Thee, Thy Holy Ghost, that unto my end I may firmly believe these glad tidings and find abiding comfort in them, and die a blessed death. Amen.

Hymn 224, 1.

THURSDAY.

Now if Christ be preached that He rose from the dead, how say some among you that there is no resurrection of the dead?—1 Cor. 15, 12.

If, as was shown yesterday, this is the saving Gospel that Christ the Crucified rose from the dead, how dare any one say that there is no resurrection from the dead, even such as profess to be Christians, yea, preachers and teachers of the Christian Church? Do they know that thereby they overthrow the entire Gospel? For if there be no resurrection of the dead, then Christ is not risen. And if Christ be not risen, then the preaching of the Apostles is vain, and all preaching that conforms to theirs; and then also thy faith, dear Christian, is vain. Yea, then the Apostles are found to be false witnesses of God, because they have testified of God that He raised up Christ whom He raised not up, if so be that the dead rise not. For let it be said once more: if there is no resurrection from the dead, then Christ is not raised; and if Christ be not raised, then He is not the true Savior sent by God on whom thou buildest thy hope, O Christian; and thy faith, therefore, is vain. Then thou art yet in thy sins; then all they also who are fallen asleep in Christ are perished. If there is no resurrection from the dead, then we Christians would only in this life have hope in Christ, and even that were a vain and futile hope, and we would of all men be most miserable.—Ah, Christian, look at the matter squarely, and let not the great and universal delusion of the present day beguile thee!—But now is Christ truly risen from the dead, and become the first-fruits of them that slept. All who fall asleep in Christ follow Him in the resurrection unto life everlasting. This is most certainly true.

PRAYER.—God Holy Ghost, Thou Spirit of truth and Spirit of Christ, who by the mouth of the Apostles didst cause the salutary death and triumphant resurrection of my Savior to be preached, I pray Thee to steel and strengthen my heart against all the specious seduction of false prophets, who withal clothe themselves with the name of Christ. Grant that I may cling fast and immovably to Thy Gospel, which proclaims unto me a blessed resurrection and eternal life pledged me by the resurrection of my Savior. Amen.

Hymn 228, 1. 4. 6.

FRIDAY.

For as in Adam all die, even so in Christ shall all be made alive.—1 Cor. 15, 22.

Christ is risen from the dead, and become the first-fruits of them that slept. For by one man came death, and by one man comes the resurrection of the dead. The one man by whom death came is the first man, Adam. Through his sin death, the wages of sin, first entered into the world. And death passed upon all men, for in Adam, the progenitor of the human race, all have sinned. And death rules with dread power, extending its power into eternal death, eternal damnation. And the one man by whom comes the resurrection of the dead is the second man, Christ. Through His substitutional righteousness the free gift came upon all men unto the justification of life. Righteousness and resurrection from the dead and eternal life are at hand for all men because Christ is the Substitute for all mankind. Eternal blessedness now beckons invitingly from beyond the grave. This is how it is: Christ, our Savior and Substitute, has risen from the dead and become the first-fruits of them that sleep in the bowels of the earth. Christ died for us, and conquered death for us, and as the first-fruits He rose from the dead and entered into eternal life—as the first-fruits. All that are His own through faith must and shall follow Him in the resurrection to come and enter life eternal with Him. For as in Adam all die, even so in Christ shall all be made alive. O thou child of Adam and heir of death by nature, watch and pray that thou mayest abide in Christ; then shalt thou most assuredly arise to inherit eternal life.

PRAYER.—My Lord and Savior, who like the first sweet little flower of spring didst lift Thy head from the icy pall of winter, grant that to my dying day I may be among those who through faith are rooted in Thee and grown together with Thee, that I, too, may rise from the dead, and bloom in eternal life with all that are Thine. Amen. Lord Jesus, keep me from the gloomy, deadly deceit of unbelief. Amen.

Hymn 547, 6.

SATURDAY.

Every man in his own order.—1 Cor. 15, 23.

In the resurrection of the dead every one and everything shall come in the order appointed by God. The first-fruits in the resurrection is Christ, as has been abundantly shown.

Then they shall rise unto eternal life who are Christ's at His coming to Judgment. Then, immediately after this resurrection and the Judgment, cometh the end of the world. Then, having done all things well, Christ will deliver up to the Father the Kingdom of Grace, the King and Mediator of which He has been hitherto. Then He will also abolish all worldly rule and authority and power, and, in particular, all power hostile to His own. But Christ must reign as King of His Kingdom of Grace and as our Mediator until, at the end of the world, He will have made all His enemies His footstool and utterly have made an end of them. The last enemy of His own that shall be destroyed, is death: they who have risen unto eternal life shall see nothing more of it. For the Father has put all things under Christ's feet. He has told us so in His Word. But when He says that all things are put under Christ, it is manifest that He is excepted who did put all things under Him, that is, the Father. But when at last, and right manifestly, all things shall have been subdued unto Christ, then shall also the Son, Christ, the King and Mediator, Himself be subject unto Him that put all things under Him, that is, to the Father; then shall He appear before the Father with His entire congregation of the redeemed of all times and say: I have finished the work which Thou hast commanded me to do; then shall He deliver up the Kingdom of Grace and His mediatorship unto the Father who gave it to Him. And then shall the Triune God, Father, Son, and Holy Ghost, be all in all; then shall the riches of blessedness and of glory pour forth upon us from the Triune God.

PRAYER.—O God the Father, what riches of bliss dost Thou vouchsafe me to see! O God the Son, Lord Jesus Christ, my King and Mediator, how well wilt Thou accomplish all, even unto my eternal glory! O God the Holy Ghost, by Thy holy Word Thou wilt confirm me in faith unto the end, that I may live to see it all. O Triune God, indeed, I shall live to see it, for Thou wilt quicken me from the dead by Thy divine power and grace, and bring me to the eternal consummation, where Thou shalt be all in all. Amen.

Hymn 222, 1.

Week of the Fourth Sunday After Easter.

SUNDAY.

Awake to righteousness!—1 Cor. 15, 34.

"In confirmation of the resurrection, Christians were baptized standing on the graves of the dead, to indicate that they would rise again," says Dr. Luther. And St. Paul writes: "Else what shall they do who are baptized for the dead, if the dead rise not at all? Why are they, then, baptized for the dead?" And concerning himself and his companions he writes: "And why stand we in jeopardy every hour? I protest by your rejoicing which I have in Christ Jesus, our Lord, I die daily. If after the manner of men I have fought with beasts at Ephesus, what advantageth it me if the dead rise not?" Then one might say as the worldlings do: "Let us eat and drink, for to-morrow we die." See how firmly the first Christians and the Apostles held to the certain hope of the resurrection of the dead! Wilt thou be misled from the positive doctrine of Holy Writ by the mouthings of those preachers and writers who have fallen from the faith, and of their satellites, who say that there is no resurrection of the dead? Be not deceived! Turn thy ears from such talk. "Evil communications corrupt good manners," says the proverb. And such communications will destroy thy faith and thy conversation in the faith. "Awake to righteousness!" so does the Apostle exhort the Christians. He calls them to awaken to the soberness of righteousness, lest they be intoxicated and misled by the arguments of carnal reason, and with singleness of heart to abide with the Word of Scripture, which teaches a resurrection of the dead in Christ, and a Christian life in the hope thereof. "Awake to righteousness, and sin not!" cries the Apostle. And to those Christians who are infatuated with above-mentioned evil communications he says: "Some have not the knowledge of God: I speak this to your shame." Those who deny the resurrection of the dead know neither the Scriptures nor the power of the omnipotent God.

Week of the Fourth Sunday After Easter. 201

PRAYER.—Lord God, dear Heavenly Father, bestow upon me, Thy child, I beseech Thee, through Jesus Christ, my Savior, the power of Thy Holy Spirit, that in all things I may believe Thy Word with singleness of heart, not being misled by evil communications, but firmly and gladly hoping for the resurrection of the dead in this uncertain life, and in such hope having my conversation here with a view to gain heaven, and lastly, when my end will be at hand, sinking into Thy fatherly hands, which shall keep my soul and body securely unto that great Easterday. Amen.
Hymn 230, 1. 4.

MONDAY.

How are the dead raised up? and with what body do they come?—1 Cor. 15, 35.

But some doubting man will say: "How are the dead raised up? and with what body do they come?" Are they not dust and ashes?—Thou fool, if God in His Word promises anything, wouldst thou then doubt His ability to perform it? And that which thou sowest into thy field, must it not first die and decompose before it germinates and is quickened and sprouts? Thou sayest: Yes, but this germinates in the midst of decomposition, and I see no germination in corpses. No, thou seest nothing of that in corpses; but notwithstanding God will bring about life and resurrection. What is the limit to God's omnipotence? And as to thy question, with what manner of body the dead shall come forth from the grave, let me refer thee again to the seed which thou sowest into thy field. Is the seed which thou sowest the body which shall be and rise from that seed? Will the seed come forth just as thou castest it into the ground? Certainly not! This is but a bare grain, say, of wheat or some other grain. But God giveth unto the seed, when it sprouts, a body as it hath pleased Him, as He hath determined; to every seed He giveth his own body. Do but look at the seed thou sowest. Thou droppest it into the ground. Now it sprouts. How? First there is the young green blade. Then it grows into an ear. After that there is the full grain in the ear. How different is the grain when it shoots up from the grain that is laid into the ground! How much more glorious is the body it receives when it comes forth! And yet that quickened body is the very body of the grain that has been laid into the ground. Is it not? Likewise our body will not rise just as it has been laid into the ground. Far from it! It will rise infinitely more glorious. And yet it will be the same body that was laid into the ground. And hark! In the resurrection we shall know full well that we are ourselves again. For we are human beings, not the fruit of the field. And our dear ones will know us, and we shall know them. Did not Peter, James, and John on the Mount of Transfiguration know Moses and Elias who appeared to Jesus with glorified bodies?

PRAYER.—Lord God Almighty, I am waiting for the great miraculous salvation which Thou wilt manifest in me. Most mightily and miraculously and gloriously wilt Thou raise me up from the earth and lead me into life everlasting. So I will gladly and rejoicingly be laid into the ground as Thy seed-corn, Thou heavenly and omnipotent Sower. Grant that through Thy Holy Spirit I may belong to Jesus, the first-fruits of resurrection, that I may follow Him, and likewise rise when the great springtime cometh. Amen.

Hymn 220, 1. 4.

TUESDAY.

So also is the resurrection of the dead.—1 Cor. 15, 42.

God giveth to every grain its own body when it comes forth, and not another. A blade of barley never grows from a grain of wheat. And more than this: from each and every seed-corn the body of just this one seed-corn grows, and not that of another. And yet the glory of the growing seed-corn is far and immeasurably greater than that of the seed which was laid into the ground. So also is the resurrection of the dead. Every man will rise with a human body, not with a body of an altogether different nature. Moreover, every man will rise with his own body, not with a wholly new and strange one. Thou wilt be thyself again, and not another. But the glory of our resurrection body will be so immeasur-

Week of the Fourth Sunday After Easter.

ably great that the difference between it and our present body will be as great as between heaven and earth.—Let me illustrate this, citing words of Scripture. All flesh is not the same flesh; but there is one kind of flesh of men, another flesh of beasts, another of fishes, and another of birds. There are also celestial bodies and bodies terrestrial. In the resurrection thou wilt not receive a different flesh, a different body, but thy human flesh, thy own human body. And now as regards the glory. The glory of the celestial is one, and the glory of the terrestrial is another. There is one glory of the sun, and another glory of the moon, and another glory of the stars; for one star differeth from another star in glory. So also, as respects the glory, will be the resurrection of the dead. There thy body will far, far excel thy present body in glory and splendor and celestial properties, though it will still be the same body.

To-day thou hast heard nothing essentially different from yesterday's devotion. But this matter is worth being understood fully. To-morrow thou shalt hear in what manner thy resurrection body will excel thy present body in glory, though it will still be the same body.

PRAYER.—Lord, my God, I am dust and ashes, and do not know how long I shall tarry here below. Soon, even to-day, death may overtake me. And yet I shall live forever. Lord, through Thy Word Thou givest me a glimpse of eternity and dost permit me to see a great and everlasting glory, unto which I shall awake and arise. Lord, I am Thine own through Jesus Christ, my Savior, the Conqueror of death. Do unto me according to Thy word. Amen.

Hymn 220, 6.

WEDNESDAY.

It is sown in corruption; it is raised in incorruption: it is sown in dishonor; it is raised in glory: it is sown in weakness; it is raised in power: it is sown a natural body; it is raised a spiritual body.—1 Cor. 15, 42-44.

This is what the Holy Ghost says concerning the glory which thy body will have when it rises from the grave. Now thy body is corruptible, of a corruptible nature; the fire of corruption glows within it and comes to the surface now and then, and it will decay altogether in the bowels of the earth; but on the day of resurrection it will come forth with life incorruptible. Now thy body, God's own creation, is dishonored, and it will lie in the earth in a most horrible and despicable state; but on the day of resurrection it will be all glory and splendor. Now thy body is in weakness; any accident may destroy it, a little disease germ may kill it. But on the day of resurrection it will be endued with eternal power. And still more. Now thy body is a *natural* body, "eating, drinking, sleeping, digesting, begetting children, etc.," as Dr. Luther puts it, but on the day of resurrection it will be a *spiritual* body, "requiring," to quote Luther again, "none of these things, and yet being a true body, alive with the spirit." As surely as thou now hast a natural body, so surely shalt thou then have a spiritual body. For consider, the first man, Adam, from whom thou art descended, was made a living soul, as thou mayest read in the Scripture, made for natural life; but the last Adam, Christ, with whom thou art united through faith, through His resurrection entered upon a spiritual life: His human body is pervaded and made spiritual by His divine nature and Spirit. Here thou beholdest a twofold condition of the human body: the natural and the spiritual. Howbeit, that was not first which is spiritual, but that which is natural; afterward that which is spiritual. The first man, Adam, as St. Paul teaches, is of the earth, earthy, for this terrestrial life; the second man, Christ, is the Lord from heaven, and hence, forsooth, for the heavenly life. As is the earthy, Adam, such are also we that are earthy: while we live on this earth we have a natural body like Adam. And as is the heavenly, Christ, such also shall we, the heavenly, be: when we rise and enter heaven, we shall have a spiritual body like Christ. As we have borne the image of the earthy, Adam, so we shall also bear the image of the heavenly, Christ.—So, then, on the day of resurrection our body will be incorruptible, all glory, all strength, entirely spiritual, yea, spiritual: no longer subject to the laws of this natural life, but qualified for the heavenly life, glorified, pervaded by our spirit which has been made heavenly, like unto Christ's glorious body. O wonderful hope!

PRAYER.—O my Lord and God, I cannot comprehend it now, but I shall most certainly live to see and experience and enjoy it. Thy Word, which fails not, nor passes away, assures me of it. O what glory! O my Lord and Savior, let me be and remain Thy own unto my end, that I may obtain and behold what now I long for in faith, until I shall be satisfied, when I awake, with Thy likeness. Amen.

Hymn 220, 7.

THURSDAY.

Now this I say, brethren, that flesh and blood cannot inherit the kingdom of God; neither doth corruption inherit incorruption.—1 Cor. 15, 50.

Surely, this now is plain to thee, O Christian, that our present flesh and blood, our body, which has become so miserable through sin, and which from the beginning was made and fashioned for this natural and earthly life, cannot in this condition and disposition inherit and enjoy the heavenly, eternal kingdom of God; our body, which now is subject to corruption, cannot dwell where incorruption dwelleth. Hence on the day of resurrection it will be changed, altered, made new and glorious, spiritual and incorruptible. But let us show thee a divine mystery. We Christians will not all be sleeping in death, but a number of us will be living on earth when Christ comes to establish the heavenly and eternal kingdom of God. But we shall all be changed, all without exception. The bodies of the Christians living on the last day will be changed to be like the bodies of those who are sleeping in their graves and will then be wakened. And all this change and alteration shall take place in a moment, in the twinkling of an eye, at the last trump. For the trumpet of God will sound, and the dead will rise incorruptible, and those of us who are then yet alive will be changed unto the same likeness. Indeed, this corruptible must put on incorruption, and this mortal must put on immortality to be fit for eternal life and the Kingdom of Glory.

PRAYER.—O Thou almighty Creator, how wilt Thou make all things new! O Thou Lord and Savior, plenteous in mercy, how wilt Thou glorify us! O Thou Spirit of the Father and of the Son, who dost offer me such hope in Thy Word, and dost excite in me a great and mighty yearning, steadfastly grant me grace to cling to my Savior in true faith, that through Thy sanctification I may be worthy to partake of such glory. Amen.

Hymn 220, 10.

FRIDAY.

Death is swallowed up in victory.—1 Cor. 15, 54.

When the dead will rise, and those will have been changed who will be living when Christ will appear unto Judgment, when this corruptible will put on incorruption, and this mortal put on immortality, then will be brought to pass that saying which is written: "Death is swallowed up in victory." "That is to say," writes Dr. Luther, "death will lie prostrate and have no more power; and life will be on top, as it were, and say: The combat has been won! Where art thou, death?" Then shall we shout in glee and sing: "O death, where is thy sting? O grave, where is thy victory?" The sting of death, that which brought death into the world and gave it the power it has over us to destroy and devour us and to drag us down to hell, is sin; and the strength of sin, that which makes sin so deserving of death, is the Law, the divine Law, which we have transgressed. "But thanks be to God, who giveth us the victory through our Lord Jesus Christ." Our Lord Jesus Christ bore our sins for us, in our stead, as our Substitute, and rendered full satisfaction to the Law of God; He entered into combat with death, our death, conquered it, arose triumphantly, brought eternal life to light for us, calls us unto Himself, gives us His victory, His righteousness, His life, His blessedness, and glory. Indeed, death is swallowed up in victory! "O death, where is thy victory? O grave, where is thy sting? But thanks be unto God, who giveth us the victory through our Lord Jesus Christ!" Through faith in Christ Jesus, our Savior, we are God's dear children. Sin is forgiven. Eternal life is

Week of the Fourth Sunday After Easter.   207

our inheritance. We shall take possession of that when we awaken with the body glorified. Hallelujah!

PRAYER.—Yea, Amen, hallelujah, Lord Jesus Christ! I see Thee and have Thee, my Savior. And so I see and have light in the darkness of sin and death. Sin is forgiven, death has lost all its terrors. In my last hour I shall say unto Thee: Lord Jesus, receive my spirit! And Thou shalt also quicken my body and make it all heavenly and glorious. Yea, Amen, Lord Jesus, Thou wilt surely do this, and give me eternal glory. Keep me in true faith in Thee, Lord Jesus! This also wilt Thou do. Hallelujah, Lord Jesus. Amen.

Hymn 221, 5.

SATURDAY.

Therefore, my beloved brethren, be ye steadfast, unmovable, always abounding in the work of the Lord, forasmuch as ye know that your labor is not in vain in the Lord.—1 Cor. 15, 58.

What a hope have we! What a blessedness is ours! Death may come at any moment. We laugh at it. We commend our spirit into Jesus' hands, and He receives it. We commend our body into Jesus' hands, and He keeps it; He will wake it on that great day of His, and clothe it with heavenly glory. Then we shall be in eternal glory, within and without. What a hope we have! What a blessedness is ours! Therefore, my beloved Christians, let us be steadfast in the faith in our Savior who is so rich in mercy; let us not be moved from the hope of eternal life; let us always abound in the work of the Lord; let us fight valiantly against sin with the mighty weapons of the Spirit, which our great Lord and Hero furnishes us; let us strive after everything that is good, which our Lord desires; let us hold fast to His Word and to prayer; let us be patient in cross and tribulation; let us be charitable toward our neighbor; let us confess and spread the name of Jesus; let us do good to all men, especially to them that are of the household of faith, and not grow weary. To be sure, our labor will not be in vain in the Lord. What, then, will the end be, the goal? Thou knowest it.

Our Lord has given us everything, yea, everything; and brightly, invitingly, sweetly, even ravishingly does the light of eternal life shine upon us through His promises. O Christian, let us belong to Jesus; let us live unto Him, serve Him, love Him, honor and praise Him. He gives us eternal and inestimable blessedness.

PRAYER.—O Lord Jesus, who hast given me all things necessary unto my salvation, and who wilt most assuredly give unto me an eternal and exceeding weight of glory, grant unto me, I beseech Thee, a firm faith, make me immovable with respect to the hope of eternal life, and grant that I may do the work Thou desirest me to do, and always abound in it. Do Thou, O Lord, perform all these things in me. What am I? I am weak and miserable. But in Thee do I hope; work effectually in me, O Lord, even as Thou hast been and art still and always wilt be effectual for me. Amen.

Hymn 230, 4.

Week of the Fifth Sunday After Easter.

SUNDAY.

Our conversation is in heaven, from whence also we look for the Savior, the Lord Jesus Christ, who shall change our vile body, that it may be fashioned like unto His glorious body, according to the working whereby He is able even to subdue all things unto Himself.—Phil. 3, 20. 21.

The whole life, all the imaginations, all the thoughts and aspirations, the wishes and desires, and the entire conversation of those pitiable people who neither know nor want to know Jesus and His Word, is determined by this perishable earth and—by sin. It is quite different, however, with such of us as are true Christians, who by faith know Christ and His Word. Our whole life, our imaginations, **our thoughts and aspirations**, wishes and desires, and **our conversation,** are in heaven; all is ruled and determined by that which is **in heaven,** where we have obtained citizenship through our

Week of the Fifth Sunday After Easter.

Savior, the Lord Jesus Christ. This is not saying that our conversation is perfect. Ah, no; the old sin still clings to us and makes us sluggish and earthly-minded. And yet, this ever and again asserts itself: our conversation is in heaven. How could it be otherwise? For from thence, from heaven, we look for the Savior, the Lord Jesus Christ, who will come and change our vile body, which has been degraded and humiliated through sin, that it may be fashioned like unto His glorious body. Surely our Lord will do this for us, as thou hast abundantly seen on the previous pages of this book; He will do this according to the working whereby He is able even to subdue all things unto Himself; He will do this by His unlimited divine power. This, then, is our hope, our aim, the blessed end of our earthly conversation: the resurrection from the dead, the transfiguration of our body, eternal and blissful life in heaven. Shall not our conversation be in heaven, directed toward heaven, and determined by our hope of heaven? Most certainly.

PRAYER.—O my God, what mercies dost Thou shower upon me through Jesus Christ, my dear Savior! Thou hast made me, a poor sinner, a citizen of heaven. And Thou, dear Lord Jesus, wilt come and raise me up from the grave, and wilt change my poor body that it may be fashioned like unto Thy glorious body, and wilt give me the eternal bliss of heaven. God Holy Ghost, Thou gracious Lord, who workest all good things within me, give me a heavenly mind, and direct my course toward heaven. Amen.

Hymn 195, 2. 3. 14.

MONDAY.

Every man that hath this hope in him purifieth himself.
1 John 3, 3.

O Christian, do behold what manner of love the Father hath bestowed upon us through our Lord Jesus Christ: we poor sinners are called the sons of God! Children of God, can there be anything more exalted? Therefore God has also given us His Holy Spirit, that we should be like unto Him in mind and disposition, in action and performance.

True, this divine newness within us is still much hidden by sin, suffering, and death, here below. Therefore the unbelieving world does not recognize us for what we are in fact; and what it does perceive of our new godlike being it heaps with scorn and hatred, for it does not know God. But all this must not trouble us. We are the children of God, though it does not now clearly and resplendently appear what we are. But it will appear; it will most certainly appear. It will appear, when Christ shall appear on His great day to wake us from death and to change our bodies. Then it will be apparent before the eyes of all the world what we are. And we know that then we shall be like Him. Like whom? **Like Christ.** Then we shall be holy, pure, and righteous altogether, without sin; then we shall be altogether perfect and glorious within and without, rid of the misery of death; then our divine disposition, which even now we have, will pervade and shine through our body and soul, and we shall shine in grandeur as the children of God, which even now we are. For then we shall see God as He is, from face to face. Such perfection excludes all the former misery of body and soul. Thus to behold Him changes us into the likeness of God. What a hope we have in Him! In whom? In Christ, who will bring His work of salvation to full perfection in **us.** And every man that hath this hope in Him *purifieth himself,* even as He is pure. This our hope which we have in **Him** does not suffer us to longer serve sin, and, through sin, **the** devil. In such hope we purify ourselves: we mortify the **old** Adam in us with all sins and evil lusts through daily contrition and repentance; and the new man daily comes forth and **arises,** who lives before God in righteousness and purity, and shall live forever. Mark this well, my dear Christian! **Purify** thyself, knowing that thou hast such a blessed hope!

PRAYER.—Purify Thou me, Father of our Lord Jesus Christ, of whose body, by Thy grace, I am a living member. Purify Thou me, my heavenly Father, who hast adopted me as Thy child through Jesus Christ, our Savior. Purify Thou me, most kind God, who wilt soon give me eternal and heavenly purity and glory. Purify Thou me, who hast given me Thy Holy Spirit, the Spirit of purity and of blessed hope, for I delight not in sin, nor do I want to serve it. I am Thine, my God, in time and eternity. Amen.

Hymn 380, 1. 2. 5. 6.

TUESDAY.

For I reckon that the sufferings of this present time are not worthy to be compared with the glory which shall be revealed in us.—Rom. 8, 18.

The children of God in this world do not suffer less, but more than unbelievers. For the devil and the wicked world are against them; they are also harassed by their own flesh and blood, which it is their duty and which it is also their desire to crucify; and God chastises them in fatherly mercy, it is true; but it smarts for all that. The narrow way which leads to heaven is beset with afflictions. *Whither* does it lead? To heaven. Ah! so it is. That comforts and quickens. The narrow way leads to heaven and to eternal life. The broad way, so agreeable to flesh and blood, leads not to life, but to damnation. Therefore we all surely want to walk the narrow way. And the heavenly glory which has been promised us, which awaits us at the end of the narrow way, which follows upon the sufferings of this present time, this glory is so exceedingly great—and everlasting!—that the sufferings of this present time are not worthy to be compared with them, are not to be taken into account against them, are as naught against them. In consideration of this glory we must gladly bear the sufferings which the trusty hand of God appoints for us on our pilgrimage thither. Why, shall we be put to shame by men of the world who, to acquire some earthly treasure, some temporal good, often undergo grievous hardships and misery without minding these at all? And how often are they disappointed in their expectations! Scarce acquired, their fortune vanishes again. But we shall not be deceived. We shall most surely obtain the glory which shall be revealed in us; for God is true, who promiseth it. And it shall not vanish from us. All other treasures vanish, but we shall remain in possession of our inheritance in all eternity. Therefore willingly suffer, O Christian, whatever falls to thy lot. God will give thee strength. And He will moderate thy suffering and graciously apportion to thee a fixed measure. And He will, furthermore, give thee courage and a cheerful spirit. Do but lift up thy head and fix thy eyes upon the inviting goal before thee!

PRAYER.—Lord, my God, right well do I know that the sufferings of this present time are not worthy to be compared with the glory which is to be revealed in me, yea, in me. But Thou knowest how weak and faint-hearted I am, and how easily depressed. Have mercy upon me, Thou faithful, gracious God, and cure me of my diffidence by the almighty power of Thy Holy Spirit, and let Thy word of promise concerning the eternal and exceedingly great glory which is in store for me evermore sparkle within my heart and greatly comfort me, that I may by no means draw back, but cheerfully overcome all suffering. This I pray for Jesus' sake. Amen.

Hymn 526, 14.

WEDNESDAY.

And He led them out as far as to Bethany.—Luke 24, 50.

This brief text takes us back to the Biblical stories relating to our Savior. On the fortieth day after His resurrection He appeared to His Apostles, who were assembled in Jerusalem. And after He had conversed with them, He led them out of the city up to the Mount of Olives as far as Bethany. And there He commanded them not to depart from Jerusalem, but to wait for the promise of the Father, " which," He said, " ye have heard of me. For John truly baptized with water; but ye shall be baptized with the Holy Ghost not many days hence." Then the Apostles asked Him: " Lord, wilt Thou at this time restore again the kingdom of Israel?" They meant the Kingdom of Glory, concerning which their conceptions were still quite worldly. And He said to them: " It is not for you to know the times or the seasons which the Father hath put in His own power. But ye shall receive power, after that the Holy Ghost is come upon you; and ye shall be witnesses unto me both in Jerusalem, and in all Judea, and in Samaria, and unto the uttermost parts of the earth." These were Jesus' very last words on earth to His disciples. While the earth remains, until the last day will come, and with it the Kingdom of Glory and the consummation of all things, we Christians, we disciples of Jesus, endued with the power of the Holy Ghost, are to be *witnesses of Jesus* by word and deed, each in his own sphere. The Lord demands this of us. It is for this purpose that He still leaves us in this world. This is our true calling. Christian, dear Christian, do not forget that! Think not that thou needst only work out thy own salvation, and otherwise needst merely perform the works of thy calling without concerning thyself about others. No, no! Though thou be no apostle, nor an ordained preacher, thou must, nevertheless, be a witness for Christ.

PRAYER.—O my Lord and Savior, grant me grace to testify to the world of Thee, the Crucified and Risen, and tell them what Thou hast procured for all mankind and hast given unto me. Endue me for this purpose with the power of Thy Holy Spirit, the Spirit of faith and of love and of obedience. And make my testimony concerning Thee effective through Thy Holy Spirit. O Lord, help me to do what Thou dost bid me do. Amen.

Hymn 426, 2.

ASCENSION DAY.

And it came to pass, while He blessed them, He was parted from them, and carried up into heaven.—Luke 24, 51.

When our Lord had told His Apostles what we heard yesterday, He lifted up His hands and blessed them. And it came to pass, while He blessed them, He was parted from them, and taken up into heaven. He was taken up visibly, while they were looking on. And a cloud received Him out of their sight. This cloud, again, was the Shekinah, the cloud in which, during the Old Covenant, the Lord had revealed His presence. It was full of the multitude of heavenly hosts. "God is gone up with a shout, the Lord with the sound of a trumpet." (Ps. 47, 5.) And while the disciples looked steadfastly toward heaven as He went up, behold, two men stood by them in white apparel. And they said: "Ye men of Galilee, why stand ye gazing up into heaven? This same Jesus which is taken up from you into heaven shall so come in like manner as ye have seen Him go into heaven." —This is Christ's ascension. So did the Son of God, our Savior, end His visible sojourn on earth. In blessing them, He parted from His disciples. He blesses all His disciples, all His Christians. This is the blessing which He purchased on the cross and brought with Him from the grave. Whenever thou thinkest of thy Savior, remember that He blesses thee. And when He will come again in the Shekinah, He will bless thee. He will then say unto thee and to all that are His own: "Come, ye blessed of my Father, inherit the kingdom prepared for you from the foundation of the world." (Matt. 25, 34.) Do but make sure that thou art and remainest His disciple!

PRAYER.—Omnipotent God, grant unto us who believe that Thine own Son, our Savior, this day ascended into heaven, that we also may live unto Him in newness of spirit and continue in the spirit, comforting ourselves with His blessing, and, when in the end He shall come again, inheriting the eternal blessing: through the same, Thy Son Jesus Christ, our Lord. Amen.

Hymn 233, 1. 7.

FRIDAY.

And sat on the right hand of God.—Mark 16, 19.

Our Lord Jesus Christ, the crucified and risen Savior, has ascended into heaven and sitteth on the right hand of God the Father. This is the highest exaltation possible. Our Lord Jesus Christ now without reserve partakes of all divine majesty. God has "set Him at His own right hand in the heavenly places, far above all principality, and power, and might, and dominion, and every name that is named, not only in this world, but also in that which is to come: and hath put all things under His feet, and gave Him to be head over all things to the Church." (Eph. 1, 20-22.) Christ Jesus, who is the Head over all things, unto whom is given all power in heaven and in earth, He is in particular the Head of His beloved Church. Upon this His beloved Church He bestows His grace. And this His grace is wedded with His divine power. And so He gathers, keeps, governs, and protects us, His beloved Christians. He makes all things work together for our good. He governs all things so that they must work together for our good. Sin, world, devil, joy, sorrow, death, all things work together for our good. For He sitteth at the right hand of God and is the Head over all things, and in particular the Head of His beloved Christian Church. Indeed, what shall we lack if we are His own? With strong compassionate hands, and with divinely gracious providence He leadeth us through this world into the world to come, over which He is set as well as over this world. Us and our life, and all things that may in any way concern our life, He holds as with thousand reins in His mighty divine hands, and guides all things unto our salvation. Christian, Christian, in true faith commit thyself altogether into the hands of this thy Savior.

PRAYER.—I commit myself into Thy hands, Thou exalted, omnipotent Lord and Savior Jesus Christ. Thou art the Head, I am a member of Thy body. Keep, govern, protect, guide, lead, direct me through all things unto eternal life, according to the command and the office which Thy heavenly Father, at whose right hand Thou sittest, hath given Thee even now. I commit myself into Thy hands, my Lord and Savior! Amen.

Hymn 239, 5. 7.

SATURDAY.

He ascended up far above all heavens, that He might fill all things.—Eph. 4, 10.

Thinkest thou that God is encompassed by any heaven? Certainly not. On the contrary, God encompasses all heavens and all things, and God fills all things with His presence. So it is also with Jesus, our brother, our flesh and blood, our Savior. Jesus is not encompassed by any heaven, but He encompasses all heavens and all things, and fills all things with His presence. He ascended far above all heavens, that He might fill all things. He sitteth at the right hand of God. So just by reason of His ascension He is right near to us. "Lo, I am with you alway, even unto the end of the world." "He is not far from every one of us; for in Him we live, and move, and have our being." This is true of Jesus also. With grace and love and tender mercy He is with us. We Christians are encompassed by Him and His compassion. He is our Rock, and our Fortress, and our Deliverer, our God, our Strength, in whom we will trust; our buckler, and the horn of our salvation, and our high tower. Being so encompassed, who can harm us? Wherever we may be, in this place or that, in life or in death: He is with us, and we are in Him. He is now much nearer to us, much more intimately so, than He was with His own at the time of His visible sojourn on earth. Therefore, when Mary Magdalene had found Him, the Risen One, and wanted to hold Him, He consoled her, saying: "I ascend unto my Father and your Father, and to my God and your God." As if to say: Then, then will my communion with you be most intimate, then will ye truly possess and hold me. Christian, let thy eyes be anointed by the Word and Spirit of God, and see how near Thy Savior is to thee.

PRAYER.—Lord Jesus, I thank Thee for the assurance Thou givest me that Thou art with me and with all that are Thine, and dost encompass us like a firm fortress which no one can storm. Let me be Thine own and remain in Thee; then will I be secure forever. Let me always rest assured that Thou art with me, and that I am in Thee, that in Thee I may be confident, cheerful, bold, and of a strong heart, in life and death. Amen.

Hymn 239, 2. 3.

Week of the Sixth Sunday After Easter.

SUNDAY.

Where I am, there shall also my servant be.—John 12, 26.

When Jesus became man and dwelt on earth, and suffered and died, and even when He rose and ascended into heaven, His aim ever was to prepare a place for us in His Father's house, in the realms of eternal bliss. May I now speak after the manner of men, and very plainly, of a heavenly and mysterious matter? When, having finished His work, Christ ascended into heaven and came to the gates of heaven, they opened unto Him wide, and all the cherubim and seraphim rapturously welcomed Him. But Jesus said He did not come to desire admittance for Himself, but for us whom He had redeemed; He came as our Savior, our Substitute, to take possession of heaven for us, and to prepare a place for us where we might be forever. I speak after the manner of men. Yes, and then the gates of heaven were not barred, then all the heavenly hosts, moved by the Holy Ghost, shouted with joy to welcome our Savior in the name of God the Father—*for us.* Thus did our Atoner at His ascension take possession of heaven for us, and prepare a place there for us; and now in great loving-kindness He says: "Where I am, there shall also my servant be." Whoever does not reject Him, the Atoner and Opener of heaven, but embraces Him in true faith, and serves Him, and is His disciple and servant,—for him heaven is opened, for him the place is prepared where in everlasting bliss he will be with the Savior. The cherub has lowered his flaming sword which turns every way, the cherub no longer stands forbiddingly at the gate of Paradise.

PRAYER.—My Lord and Savior, by Thy substitutional suffering and death Thou hast fully and completely reconciled me, a lost and condemned sinner, unto God, hast opened the gates of heaven for me, and prepared a place for me where I may abide in all eternity. For this I thank Thee as heartily as ever I can. Grant me, I beseech Thee, Thy

Holy Spirit, that with the eyes of faith I may firmly and steadfastly gaze upon Thee, and trust in what Thou hast merited for me. And then let me cling to Thee gratefully, and serve Thee, until in heaven I shall thank and serve Thee better. Amen.

Hymn 233, 4.

MONDAY.

He ascended up on high; He led captivity captive.— Eph. 4, 8.

This text evidently speaks of a triumph, a triumphal procession. Christ's ascension is represented as a triumphal procession. Christ ascended up on high and triumphantly led captivity captive. What was our captivity? Surely, sin, death, damnation, the power of the devil. Was not this the prison that held us with fetters we could not tear, with lock and bolt we could not break? But our Savior bore, and atoned for our sins, suffered our death and conquered it for us, tasted and destroyed our damnation, and bruised the head of the devil, in whose power we were. In fact, in the early morning of Easter Sunday He descended into hell as the living and risen Conqueror, and preached of His victory and of their vanquishment to the spirits in prison. (1 Pet. 3, 19.) That was a triumph in itself. And now He ascended into heaven, and in triumphal procession He carried with Him our sins atoned, our death vanquished, our damnation destroyed, our evil foe trampled under foot. Verily, He despoiled our prison and all the hostile powers that were arrayed against us, stripped them of their power, and made a show of them openly, triumphing over them in Himself, in His glorious exaltation. Wilt thou not sing and say: "This is a sight that gladdens"? In the name of Jesus, hearest thou? trusting in Him, thou mayest deride sin, laugh at death, defy damnation, and tauntingly fly in the face of Satan. No prison can hold thee, no foe can harm thee. He, thy Savior, has ascended up on high, He led captivity captive.

PRAYER.—O Jesus, Thou wondrous conquering Hero, I trust in Thee, in the work Thou hast accomplished for me, and in Thy Word, Thy blessed Gospel. My captivity is ended and led captive. Thou hast triumphed over it. I am free, wholly free. I am in bliss. Give unto me, O Jesus, the bold assurance of victory in Thy name. Amen.

Hymn 239, 6. 8.

TUESDAY.

And gave gifts unto men.—Eph. 4, 8.

The ascended Conqueror gave *gifts* unto us. What gifts? We will mention but one, in which all other gifts are comprised. He gave us the *Holy Ghost.* Because Jesus reconciled us unto God, the Holy Ghost again comes to us. The Holy Ghost is the Spirit of the Father and of the Son, true personal God together with the Father and the Son. Him the Father, being reconciled, sends; Him the Savior gives unto us; He comes to us with an abundance of grace. He comes to us through the Word of Christ, the Gospel, the Author and real and first Preacher of which He is. He comes to us through the Word now found in Scriptures. He comes to us through the Word that is preached, taught, heard, and studied. Hence He comes to us through the ministr. of the Apostles and of all true and faithful preachers and teachers whom He gives us. He comes to us and, through His Word works faith in us, true faith; and through and by faith He leads us to Jesus, our Savior; and He makes us members of His body, of Jesus' body, so that in Jesus we have all things: forgiveness of sins, righteousness in the sight of God, life and salvation, the adoption of sons, peace, joy, comfort, courage, strength, victory, resurrection, eternal glory. Without the Holy Ghost we have nothing; through Him we have all things. If we lose the Holy Ghost, we lose all things; if we keep the Holy Ghost, we keep all things. The Holy Ghost is willing to abide with us forever. Here on earth He will abide with us through His *Word.* Christian, abide by the Word, that thou mayest keep the Holy Ghost and all things that are given thee through Jesus and in Jesus. In heaven the Holy Ghost will fully change thee into the image of God.

PRAYER.—I thank Thee, Lord and Savior Jesus Christ, my Atoner and conquering Hero, for the gift of the Holy Ghost which Thou hast given me. O Lord, by nature I am dead in sin, and unable to believe in Thee, and to obtain the blessings which Thou hast procured. But through Thy Word Thou hast given me Thy Holy Spirit and faith in Thee through Him. So now I have Thee, and in Thee I have all things that save me. Help me, my Shepherd, that I may always abide by Thy Word and keep Thy precious Holy Spirit. Amen.

Hymn 254, 1. 3.

WEDNESDAY.

But this man, after He had offered one sacrifice for sins forever, sat on the right hand of God.—Hebr. 10, 12.

The Jews of the Old Testament worshiped God aright. Their worship throughout was a Christ-worship. There is no other true worship, and never has been, but the worship made in the name of Christ. But the worship of the Old Testament consisted in types that foreshadowed Christ and pointed to Christ. The sacrifices of the Old Testament were types of the sacrifice of Christ, foreshadowing the sacrifice of Christ, and pointing to it. Hence these sacrifices had to be continually repeated, since in themselves they could not take away sins. But Christ had offered one single sacrifice, the sacrifice of Himself. That is valid forever. It has taken away all sins of all men and of all times. In proof and public confirmation thereof Christ now sitteth at the right hand of God. So thou seest that God made public acknowledgment to the fact that the sacrifice of Christ truly took away all sins and is valid forever in that He set Christ, who in our stead and in the stead of all the world was to atone for all the sins of the world, and really did atone for them, at His right hand. All the world has been redeemed and reconciled to God through that one sacrifice of Christ, which is valid forever. If thou wouldst be altogether certain of thy redemption, of the atonement for thy sins, of thy salvation, of the forgiveness of thy sins, of life and eternal happiness, then look neither here nor there, but look upon Christ, who sitteth at the right hand of God, for He offered *one* sacrifice for sins which is valid forever. Behold, there is thy redemption, thy atonement, thy salvation, the forgiveness of thy sins, thy life and thy eternal happiness: at the right hand of God, fully acknowledged, confirmed, sealed, and ratified by the divine Amen. Look thither! This look, this look alone, will kindle the right, true, certain, unconquerable, living, mighty, strong, all-, all-conquering faith in thee.

PRAYER.—Lord Jesus, who didst offer the *one* sacrifice for sins forever, and in proof thereof dost sit at the right hand of God, grant me grace to look upon Thee, and in unwavering faith to recognize in Thee my salvation, and henceforth to look for no other sacrifice for sins, and to offer naught but sacrifices of thanks, the fruit of my lips, giving thanks and singing praises unto Thy name. Amen.

Hymn 233, 5.

THURSDAY.

Who is even at the right hand of God, who also maketh intercession for us.—Rom. 8, 34.

Our Savior makes intercession for us, He intercedes for us, He pleads our cause, He prays for us, He always implores grace for us, He is our Advocate with the Father, the almighty God. Could we be better represented? Surely not. He is the eternal Son of the Father, God born of God. When He had become man, God the Father spoke these words from heaven: "This is my beloved Son, in whom I am well pleased." He gave His life for us and reconciled God with us. And God exalted Him unto His right hand in heaven. We could not be better represented. We may rely upon Him fully, we may safely and confidently let Him plead our cause. We may rely upon His love and faithfulness. We may depend upon it that His representation is efficacious with the Father. Our Savior firmly stands by us. And the Father does what the Savior asks Him to do for us. And praying for us, our Savior pleads His death for us, as well as the fact that by raising Him and setting Him at His right hand God ratified the full satisfaction which He rendered. And the Father cannot deny Him anything. Being represented by Him, we are altogether safe. How much we poor sinners do need a representative with the Father! And we have Him; He, the Savior, represents us. Let me repeat it—being represented by Him, we are altogether safe. And with our Savior Himself we have and need no representative. For He is our dearest Friend and Lover. Compared with His love and friendship, all other love and friendship in heaven and in earth is as nothing. Wilt thou rely entirely upon thy Savior, my dear Christian? Do so. Most assuredly, thou wilt not be deceived.

PRAYER.—If Thou, O Jesus Christ, dost represent me before God, and pleadest my cause, I am altogether safe. For Thou dost plead for me, a poor sinner, Thine all-sufficient merit, which Thou hast procured for me and given unto me, and which God, Thine eternal Father, has fully acknowledged. Lord Jesus, I rely upon Thee. Do Thou plead my cause. I know Thou dost plead it. I would have no other mediator, no other intercessor, but Thee only. Amen.

Hymn 348, 6.

FRIDAY.

Draw me, we will run after Thee.—Song of Solomon, 1, 4.

Oh, all is accomplished, all is glorious. We are saved. Heaven is ours.—But we—what are we? Has our soul decked itself with festive and resplendent joy in faith, in conformity with, and in honor of, the salvation which has been given us, and the glory we are so firmly assured of? Has it divested itself of its love for sin? Has it put on the garments of light, and of the new day which has dawned for it, and does it display their beauty? Woe unto us! We must confess that we are beyond measure indifferent and prone to sin, and that many unseemly things of the night and of darkness that are a shame and a disgrace unto us are still to be found with us.—"Draw me, we will run after Thee!" There is no other remedy but that Jesus, the crucified, risen, and ascended Lord, draw us mightily away from it all and unto Himself. If Jesus, through His Word and the Holy Spirit, always assures us of His grace and of the forgiveness of sins; if Jesus, through His Word and the Holy Spirit, always makes us eager for His salvation and of the glory that awaits us; if Jesus, through His Word and the Holy Spirit, so captivates our hearts that with all our might we hate sin and dearly love Him; in short, if, through His Word and the Holy Spirit, Jesus takes hold of us with the almighty power of His grace, and draws us unto Him, and if with the great patience of a Savior He does this again and again: then will we run, then will we run after Him with heart and soul and mind, heavenward. And, Christian, He will do it, He does it. Call upon Him, thou poor, weak, weary child of God! He draws thee unto Himself, heavenward.

PRAYER.—Yea, Amen, my Lord and Savior, do so, I pray Thee. Without Thee I can do nothing. Unless Thou draw me, I shall certainly be left lying by the wayside. Take hold of me, sweet Jesus, and draw me after Thee on the road that we must wander unto heaven. Do unto me in Thy own Savior-love what an earthly mother does unto her tired and reluctant child. Draw me after Thee, that I may run the way to heaven. Amen.

Hymn 234, 1.

SATURDAY.

I am black, but comely.—Song of Solomon 1, 5.

Come, dear Christian, let us show thee how to move the Savior to draw thee after Him to heaven. True, His own compassionate heart moves Him thereto. But does He not also want to be asked?—Thou redeemed Christian, beloved of thy Savior, look into the mirror, the mirror of God's holy Law, and thou wilt see that of thyself thou art black, black with sin. And if thou considerest all that He did for thee, what grace He bestowed upon thee, and how He gave thee His Holy Spirit, and then lookest upon thyself, then thou wilt be constrained to admit, with a heart full of shame, that even yet thou art black beyond measure. But now look into the light of His Gospel. What thou seest there will move thee to say:

>   Thou, O Christ, art all I want;
>   More than all in Thee I find;
>   Raise the fallen, cheer the faint,
>   Heal the sick, and lead the blind.
>   Just and holy is Thy name;
>   I am all unrighteousness:
>   False and full of sin I am;
>   Thou art full of truth and grace.
>
>   Plenteous grace with Thee is found,
>   Grace to cover all my sin;
>   Let the healing streams abound;
>   Make and keep me pure within.
>   Thou of life the Fountain art,
>   Freely let me take of Thee:
>   Spring Thou up within my heart,
>   Rise to all eternity.

Yes, Christian, thy Lord and Savior has clothed thee with His own righteousness, so dearly purchased, and has given thee the Spirit of faith, for thee to wrap thyself therein and therein to appear before Him. And so, so He loves thee, and cannot leave thee, and draws thee after Him to heaven. And the blacker thou seemest unto thyself, and the more firmly thou drawest about thee the folds of His righteousness, purchased for thee and given unto thee, the more He loves thee, all the more thou mayest be assured that He cannot leave thee, the more lovingly does He draw thee after Him. And when thou sayest unto Him that in thyself, indeed, thou art black, but that in His righteousness, imputed unto thee, and in His beauty thou art comely, then does His heart yearn for thee, and He holds out His arms unto thee, and He draws thee, body and soul, after Him to heaven.— See, so thou mayest move Jesus to draw thee after Him.

PRAYER.—My Lord and Savior, I am altogether black with sin, and Thou canst have no pleasure in me. But in

Thee, in Thy righteousness, in Thy bloody merit, wherewith Thou hast clothed me, I am comely and beautiful; for there Thy righteousness is without a flaw, Thy merits without the least blemish. Arrayed with them I am sure to please Thee, O Lord; arrayed with them, Thou lovest me and must love me. Come now, and draw me unto Thee and after Thee, until I shall be with Thee as Thine own. Amen.

Hymn 107, 2. 3.

Week of Whitsunday.

FIRST DAY OF PENTECOST.

And they were all filled with the Holy Ghost.—Acts 2, 4.

When the day of Pentecost, the fiftieth day after Easter, was fully come, ten days after the ascension of Jesus Christ, at nine o'clock in the morning, the disciples were all, one hundred and twenty of them, both men and women, assembled with one accord in an upper room of a house. And suddenly there came a sound from heaven as of a rushing mighty wind, and it filled all the house where they were sitting. And there appeared unto them cloven tongues like as of fire. And the Holy Ghost sat upon each of them. And they were all filled with the Holy Ghost, and began to speak with other tongues, other languages, as the Spirit gave them utterance. And there were dwelling at Jerusalem Jews, devout men, out of every nation under heaven, who had come to the feast. Now when this was noised abroad, the multitude came together at this house, and were confounded, because that every man heard the disciples speak in his own language. And they were all amazed and marveled, saying one to another: "Behold, are not all these which speak Galileans? And how hear we every man in our own tongue wherein we were born? Parthians, and Medes, and Elamites, and the dwellers in Mesopotamia, and in Judea, and Cappadocia, in Pontus, and Asia, Phrygia, and Pamphylia, in Egypt, and in the parts of Lybia about Cyrene, and strangers of Rome,

Jews and proselytes, Cretes and Arabians,—we do hear them speak in our tongues the wonderful works of God." And they were all amazed, and were in doubt, saying one to another: "What meaneth this?" Others, mocking, said: "These men are full of new wine."

This outpouring of the Holy Ghost upon the disciples of Jesus had been prophesied in the Old Testament, and repeatedly promised by Jesus, both before His suffering and death and after His resurrection. And it was attended by great and miraculous signs and wonders, so that all might observe it. The Holy Ghost wanted to equip the first witnesses of Jesus with power from on high unto their great calling of preaching the Gospel to all the world. And He always wants to glorify Christ through the Word of the Evangelists and Apostles in the hearts of those whom He brings to faith in Christ. He also wants to glorify Christ in thy heart, O Christian!

PRAYER.—God Holy Ghost, I beseech Thee, glorify Christ also in my heart, that I may firmly rely on Him and on His gracious Gospel over against sin, temptation, affliction, death, judgment, and eternal damnation, and finally obtain eternal salvation: who livest and reignest with the Father and with the Son, true God, world without end. Amen.

Hymn 260, 1. 2.

SECOND DAY OF PENTECOST.

Therefore let all the house of Israel know assuredly that God hath made that same Jesus whom ye have crucified both Lord and Christ.—Acts 2, 36.

While the devout men marveled at the miraculous outpouring of the Holy Ghost, and the scoffers were scoffing, Peter arose with the eleven. And the fire of the Holy Ghost burned in their hearts and on their lips, as well as visibly on their heads. And Peter said: "Ye men of Judea, and all ye that dwell at Jerusalem, be this known unto you, and hearken unto my words; for these are not drunken, as ye suppose, seeing it is but the third hour of the day." And then he delivered a powerful sermon, which thou mayest read in the second chapter of the Acts. First he showed that this outpouring of the Holy Ghost had been foretold by the Prophet Joel, who said that it would occur in the last days, that is, *after the Messiah had come.* (Joel 3.) And then, yes, then he showed that *Jesus of Nazareth,* approved of God among them by miracles and wonders and signs, but crucified and slain by them according to the counsel of God, had *risen* from the dead, as the Scriptures (Ps. 16) had likewise foretold of the Messiah. "Whereof we all are witnesses," said Peter. And then he showed them that the risen Lord, after He had been exalted to the right hand of God, according to the prophecy of Scripture concerning Christ, the Messiah (Ps. 110), *had shed forth this* which they now saw and heard, that is, the Holy Ghost, attended by wonders and great signs, as again foretold by Joel for the time of the Messiah. And most impressively he said, in closing: "Therefore let all the house of Israel know assuredly that God hath made that same Jesus whom ye have crucified both Lord and Christ." And immediately the Holy Ghost proved His power upon the hearts of the hearers: when they heard this, they were pricked in their hearts.—To-morrow we shall see what followed. But for to-day note that this outpouring of the Holy Ghost after Jesus' ascension proves that Jesus is the Christ promised in the Old Testament, for it was to happen in the days of Christ. And note also that the Holy Ghost works and sustains saving faith in us through the Word of Christ, and not otherwise.

PRAYER.—Lord God, Heavenly Father, who out of fatherly love toward us poor sinners didst give us Thy Son, that we should believe in Him and through faith be saved, I pray Thee, let Thy Holy Spirit enter also my heart, that I may remain steadfast in such faith unto my end, and obtain everlasting life, through Jesus Christ, our dear Lord. Amen.

Hymn 262, 3. 4.

Week of Whitsunday.

TUESDAY.

And they continued steadfastly in the Apostles' doctrine and fellowship, and in breaking of bread, and in prayers.—Acts 2, 42.

Those whose hearts were moved by the Holy Ghost through Peter's sermon now said to Peter and to the rest of the Apostles: "Men and brethren, what shall we do?" Then Peter said to them: "Repent, and be baptized, every one of you, in the name of Jesus Christ for the remission of sins, and ye shall receive the gift of the Holy Ghost," (like as we). "For the promise is unto you, and to your children, and to all that are afar off, even as many as the Lord, our God, shall call." And with many other words did he testify and exhort, saying: "Save yourselves from this untoward generation" (the scoffers). Then they that gladly received his word were baptized; and the same day there were added unto them about three thousand souls. And they continued steadfastly in the Apostles' doctrine, and fellowship, and in breaking of bread, and in prayers. And fear came upon every soul. And many wonders and signs were done by the Apostles. And all that believed were together, and had all things common; and sold their possessions and goods, and parted them to all men as every man had need. And they, continuing daily with one **accord** in the Temple, and breaking bread from house to **house,** eat their meat with gladness and singleness of heart, praising God, and having favor with all the people. And the Lord added to the Church daily such as should be saved.

What a pentecostal festival! What powerful grace of the Holy Ghost by means of Peter's sermon! Three thousand repented and believed in the Savior and were baptized! And they continued steadfastly in the Apostles' doctrine, in order to ground and strengthen themselves more fully. They loved one another; and it was a true, self-denying, and most active love. And they came together daily in larger and smaller assemblies to hear the Word and receive the Sacraments, to offer prayer, praise, and thanksgiving. Their light shone. Even more souls that embraced Christ in faith were added to the congregation.—Are we living in a time in which faith is rare? Indeed! Do our congregations resemble that first congregation? Alas, no! But we have the Word of the Apostles, the same saving grace of the Holy Ghost. The fault lies with us. God help us!

PRAYER.—My God, I am ashamed of the poor use I make of Thy Word and of the power of the Holy Spirit given me therein. Forgive me this sin for Jesus' sake! O grant that in true and heartfelt repentance I may be renewed by Thy Holy Spirit to become a true Christian, thus being saved myself, and also becoming a light unto others, pointing them to Jesus and salvation in Him. Perform this miracle of grace in me, O God! Amen.

Hymn 257, 1.

WEDNESDAY.

The Holy Ghost, whom the Father will send you in my name, He shall teach you all things.—John 14, 26.

What is this Holy Ghost who was poured out so miraculously upon the disciples of Jesus, and who gathered so glorious a congregation from among the Jews? Is this Holy Ghost some spiritual state and power of the human mind, wrought and effected by God? When it is said that the Holy Ghost was poured out, and that He did these wonderful things, does this merely mean that God wrought and effected such marvelous things? No. The Holy Ghost is God, the living and personal God Himself. Scripture says that they in whom the Spirit of God, the Holy Ghost, dwells, are the temple of God. (1 Cor. 3, 16.) Hence the Holy Ghost is *God*. But again, Jesus said to His disciples in the night before His death: "The Holy Ghost, whom the Father will send you in my name, He shall teach you all things." If the Father *sends* the Holy Ghost in the name of the Son, then, evidently, the Holy Ghost, who is God, is *not the same person* as the Father and the Son. And are we not baptized "in the name of the Father and of the Son and of the Holy Ghost"? The Holy Ghost is the third person of the Holy Trinity, true God with the Father and the Son. He is the gracious and merciful God who through the Gospel calls us poor miserable sinners to Christ, and enlightens us, so that we believe in our Savior and come to Him, and are saved; and with great longsuffering He sanctifies and keeps us in the true faith unto our end. To this end the Father sends Him in the name of the Son, who has reconciled us unto Him and re-established the communion between God and us. The Holy Ghost teaches us to believe in Christ, our Savior, and so to become God's dear children, whom God will take to heaven. O Christian, know, honor, praise, and love the Holy Ghost, and abide with His Word, by means of which He keeps thee in true faith and brings thee to heaven.

PRAYER.—God Holy Ghost, who art true God with the Father and the Son, and who dost show me like compassion with the Father and the Son, forsake me not, but give me of Thy strength, that I may steadfastly cling to my Savior in true faith, and overcome all temptations of the devil, the world, and my flesh, and obtain life everlasting. Amen.

Hymn 251.

THURSDAY.

No man can say that Jesus is the Lord but by the Holy Ghost.—1 Cor. 12, 3.

To say that Jesus is the Lord is to believe in Him and to come to Him in true faith. No man can do this by his own reason or strength; we can only do this through the gracious working of the Holy Ghost. By nature, by virtue of our own reason and strength, we can do various and many things, always, of course, under God. But not this. Of ourselves we cannot do a particle, not the least little thing towards inclining our heart to believe in Jesus, nor in any way adapt or prepare ourselves thereto. For by nature we are spiritually dead. Unto all things that concern Jesus, and which the Gospel and Spirit of God convey to us, we are dead. This is due to our sinful state. We are by nature "dead in trespasses and sins." (Eph. 2, 1.) "The natural man receiveth not the things of the Spirit of God; for they are foolishness unto him; neither can he know them, because they are spiritually discerned." (1 Cor. 2, 14.) And we are not spiritual by nature, but carnal, only carnal, controlled and actuated by sin, carnal-minded. And this carnal mind not only considers the Gospel of God foolishness, but even hates it. By nature we do not want to come to God through Jesus Christ, because we love sin and hate the life with God and in God. We do not like to be subject to the Law of God, neither indeed can we. Hence we have a slavish fear of God, and hate Him, and wish there were no God. "The carnal mind is enmity against God." (Rom. 8, 7.) So no man can say that Jesus is the Lord but by the Holy Ghost. Faith is the work of the Holy Ghost, and of Him only. Faith is kindled in man's heart entirely without his co-operation; there is as little co-operation as in creation—even less; for in creation there is no hostile resistance. O how completely dependent we are upon the grace of the faithful Lord, the Holy Ghost!

PRAYER.—God Holy Ghost, Thou merciful Lord, I thank Thee with all my heart that Thou hast freed me, a poor sinner, spiritually dead, from the bonds of blindness and of hostile resistance, and in faith hast brought me to my only Savior, Jesus Christ, that I might be saved. I pray Thee, do not by any means leave me, but through Thy gracious almighty power keep me in true faith unto my end. Amen.

Hymn 246, 1.

FRIDAY.

God hath saved us, and called us with an holy calling, not according to our works, but according to His own purpose and grace, which was given us in Christ Jesus before the world began.—2 Tim. 1, 9.

Get a clear notion from Scripture, Christian, of the way in which the Holy Ghost has kindled faith in Christ in thy heart.—God has saved thee, that is, He has worked saving faith in thee. How did He do it? He has *called* thee, through the Gospel He called thee to Christ. Through this very call He has saved thee, kindled saving faith in Christ in thee. By so calling thee, He at once *enlightened* thee with His gifts, He caused the light of faith to shine in Thy dark heart (2 Cor. 4, 6); He mightily, powerfully, and effectively called thee out of darkness into His marvelous light (1 Pet. 2, 9); He regenerated and *converted* thee. As Christ called Lazarus back from the grave into the life of this body, so the Holy Ghost, in a spiritual manner, called thee from spiritual death into spiritual life with His holy calling, with an unparalleled, divine, divinely powerful calling, with a calling that is in full accord with His divine holiness, and in itself is holy, without spot or blemish. For He has called thee, and converted thee, and kindled faith in thee, not according to thy works, not because thou hast been willing and even desiring to be called, nor because of thy better conduct. That would be teaching contrary to His Word, which says that by nature thou art spiritually dead, contrary to the plain words of Scriptures which attribute all to grace, to grace alone. It would not be holy, not in accord with His divine holiness. No, He has called thee according—well, according to what?—He has called and converted thee according to His own purpose and grace, according to His gracious purpose, according to His purpose, which rests alone on His grace, which was given thee in Christ Jesus and for His sake before the world began, from eternity. It is due to grace, and to grace only, that the Holy Ghost has kindled saving faith in Christ in thee, grace within and without, grace in time and eternity, grace in Christ Jesus. Now thank Him for it.

PRAYER.—O Lord, I did not approach Thee, but Thou hast lovingly approached me. I did not seek Thee, but Thou hast sought me. I did not choose Thee, but Thou hast chosen me. It is owing to Thy grace alone that Thou hast called me in Christ and brought me to faith in Him. O holy God, how shall I thank Thee? Keep me in true faith and give unto me eternal life which Thou hast given me in faith. **In heaven I will thank Thee fully and in all eternity. Amen.**

Hymn 349, 4. 5.

Week of Whitsunday.

SATURDAY.

We are His workmanship, created in Christ Jesus unto good works, which God hath before ordained that we should walk in them.—Eph. 2, 10.

Dear Christian, the Holy Spirit has performed a creative act in kindling faith in Christ within thee. He infused life into thy spiritual death, light into thy darkness. In thy present condition thou art His workmanship, created in Christ Jesus. Thou art a new man in Christ Jesus, with whom thou art united through faith. Thou possessest new life, a new mind, new powers. Now thou must also do new *works*, must walk in new works, in the works of faith, of the new life, the new mind, the new strength which thou hast received. The Holy Spirit has before ordained that thou shouldst walk in them. When according to His purpose and grace in Christ Jesus He created thee anew, He thereby endowed thee with the ability and will to do good works. He *sanctified* thee in the faith. And now it is His will that thou shouldst lead a sanctified life. "This is the will of God, even your sanctification." (1 Thess. 4, 3.) Remember this! But also remember that faith, once kindled within thee, is *sustained* in thee only by the constant and powerful operation of the Holy Ghost within thee. "Ye are kept by the power of God through faith unto salvation." (1 Pet. 1, 5.) And so all new things that are given thee together with faith, hence also thy sanctification, are sustained in thee only by the power of the Holy Ghost constantly operating within thee. And He does this by the *Gospel,* not otherwise. As iron can remain hot only by constant union with fire, so thou canst remain in faith and sanctification only through constant union with the Holy Ghost. And this union with the Holy Ghost and with His divine power by which He creates and sustains true sanctification within thee is established solely through the Gospel. Therefore, Christian, abide by the Gospel, or thou canst not but die spiritually.

PRAYER.—God Holy Ghost, I thank Thee that through Thy Gospel Thou hast created me anew in Christ Jesus. I thank Thee that Thou hast given me a new mind and new strength. Help me, Lord, to perform new works, those works which Thou hast before ordained that I should walk in them. And grant me grace to continue steadfastly in the Gospel all my life, and let Thy power abide in me, for without it I can do nothing. Let me depart this life in faith and enter eternal life. Amen.

Hymn 271, 3.

Week of Trinity Sunday.

SUNDAY.

To whom will ye liken Me, and make Me equal, and compare Me, that I may be like?—Is. 46, 5.

It is an extremely foolish and idolatrous undertaking when men want to fashion or measure God according to human standards, as if He could be compared with man, or were like man, He, the Most High. No, God is as He is. And thou must know, believe, and worship Him according as He reveals Himself in His Word. And do not allow thy faith to suffer shipwreck when thou findest that this exceeds thy faculties of comprehension and understanding. God were small and inconsiderable indeed if He could be comprehended and understood by thee or any man.—And now listen. There is but *one God,* but one Divine Being. "Hear, O Israel: the Lord, our God, is *one* Lord." (Deut. 6, 4.) But in this one God, in this one Divine Being, there are *three distinct Persons*: FATHER, SON, HOLY GHOST. God is the Triune God. God is three persons in one and the same divine being or essence. These three Persons are not three Gods and Lords, but only *one* God and Lord. These three Persons are not parts and particles of the Divine Being, but each Person is and possesses the whole and undivided Divine Being. The Father is the Lord, the Son is the Lord, the Holy Ghost is the Lord. Father and Son and Holy Ghost are alike great, alike eternal, altogether alike, *one* in every way; for they are the *one* God. So thou hast been baptized "in the name of the Father and of the Son and of the Holy Ghost." God is the *one* God in three Persons, three Persons in *one* God. This is the testimony of Scripture. True, one man is but *one* person. And it is utterly beyond our comprehension how *one* God can be three Persons. But "to whom will ye liken Me, and make Me equal, and compare Me, that I may be like?" says God. God is as He is, and as He reveals Himself to us in Scripture.

PRAYER.—Almighty, eternal God, who hast taught us to know and confess in true faith that Thou art one eternal God in three Persons, all three alike in power and majesty, and to worship Thee as such, I pray Thee, keep Thy Christendom steadfast in such faith at all times against all adversities: Thou who livest and reignest from everlasting to everlasting. Amen.

Hymn 266.

MONDAY.

Thou art my Son; this day have I begotten Thee.—The Spirit of Truth that proceedeth from the Father.—The Spirit of His Son.—Ps. 2, 7. John 15, 26. Gal. 4, 6.

Shall we feebly lisp a little more about the unsearchable mystery of the Trinity as revealed to us in the Scriptures? —The Father has from eternity begotten the Son from His essence. The Father saith to the Son: "Thou art my Son; this day have I begotten Thee." "This day"—here is the incomprehensible divine eternity, where there is neither *before* nor *after,* but an everlasting *now* and *to-day.* Hence the Son has been begotten or born of the Father, out of His essence, from eternity. The Son is "the brightness of His glory and the express image of His Person." (Hebr. 1, 3.) But He is the living and personal Brightness of His glory and the living and personal Image of His Person. From everlasting to everlasting the Father is imaged and reflected in the Son. And the Holy Ghost is the living and personal breath which from eternity "proceedeth from the Father," and from the Son as well, for He is also the Breath, the "Spirit of the Son." What more shall we say? The mystery is too profound. There is a great and complete unity in the divine Trinity. From everlasting to everlasting, in an eternal *to-day,* the Father begets the Son from His being; from everlasting to everlasting, in an eternal to-day, the Son is the living and personal Brightness of the Father, begotten of Him, and the express Image of His Person; from everlasting to everlasting, in an eternal to-day, the Holy Ghost proceeds from the Father and the Son, personal and living, completing the perfect unity of the Holy Trinity. This is the true God as He reveals Himself: Father, Son, and Holy Ghost, three distinct Persons in one and the same eternal divine essence.—And now we will be still and worship. But knowest thou the Son? It is Jesus Christ.

PRAYER.—O almighty and eternal God, who hast given us, Thy servants, grace to know and to confess in true faith the glory of the eternal Trinity and to worship the unity of equal power and majesty: grant, I beseech Thee, that Thy Church may at all times be fortified against the attacks of all adversaries by steadfastly adhering to such faith, through Jesus Christ, our Lord, who liveth and reigneth with Thee, the Father, in unity with the Holy Ghost, true God, world without end. Amen.

Hymn 264, 3.

TUESDAY.

In the beginning God created the heaven and the earth. And the earth was without form and void; and darkness was upon the face of the deep. And the Spirit of God moved upon the face of the waters. And God said: Let there be light!— Gen. 1, 1-3.

These are the very first words in the Bible, the revealed Word of God. They treat of the very first things that happened. And these words contain the very first revelation of the Holy Trinity.—" In the beginning God created the heaven and the earth." This is the *Father.* "And the Spirit of God moved upon the face of the waters," upon the dark, watery, and still unformed mass of the earth. This is the *Holy Ghost.* "And God said." This is the *Son.* This is not a mere speaking of God, but a Speaker distinct from the Father, the Son. This is not a mere word of God, but the essential, personal Word, the Son. He spake. Does this seem to thee a forced interpretation of Scripture? thrusting as it were, a foreign sense into it? Take the first words of the Gospel of St. John: " In the beginning was the Word, and the Word was with God, and the Word was God. The same was in the beginning with God. All things were made by Him." (John 1, 1-3.) Dost thou see? The Word by which in the beginning all things were made, is not merely a word of the almighty God, but it was in the beginning, and was with God, and was God. This Word that was *God* was *with* God. Seest thou here two persons in God? And thou hast already seen the third Person. Who was this personal Word that was God? John writes: " And the Word was made flesh, and dwelt among us, (and we beheld His glory, the glory as of the Only-begotten of the Father,) full of grace and truth." (John 1, 14.) This Word which was in the beginning, and was with God, and was God, through whom all things were made, is the Son, the only-begotten Son of the Father, who in the fullness of time became man and our Savior. He is called the " Word," because God in Him reveals Himself outwardly, to usward, just as through Him He also created the world.—O yes, Scripture, from the beginning and everywhere, teaches the mystery of the Holy Trinity. Do but open thy eyes and see.

PRAYER.—Almighty, eternal God, Father, Son, and Holy Ghost, I thank Thee from my inmost heart that through Jesus Christ Thou hast, as a loving Father, revealed Thy being and Thy will. Bestow Thy grace upon me, I beseech Thee, that with all Christendom I may know, honor, and praise Thee as my Creator, Redeemer, and Savior: who livest and reignest from everlasting to everlasting. Amen.

Hymn 579.

WEDNESDAY.

Building up yourselves upon your most holy faith.— Jude 20.

The First Article of the holy Christian Creed reads thus: "*I believe in God the Father Almighty, Maker of heaven and earth.*" But woe is me! What a gulf yawns between me and God! I am a sinner, a lost and damned sinner! God is the Father of His only-begotten Son, but not my Father! —The Second Article reads thus: "*And in Jesus Christ, His only Son, our Lord, who was conceived by the Holy Ghost, born of the Virgin Mary, suffered under Pontius Pilate, was crucified, dead, and buried; He descended into hell; the third day He rose again from the dead; He ascended into heaven, and sitteth at the right hand of God the Father Almighty, from thence He shall come to judge the quick and the dead.*" Jesus Christ, the only Son of the Father, has bridged the chasm. Blessed be His name! He has reconciled me and all the world with God, has conquered hell, and opened heaven. Only he that rejects Him shall be judged. He that believeth in Him shall be saved. Praise God!— The Third Article reads thus: "*I believe in the Holy Ghost; the holy Christian Church, the communion of saints; the forgiveness of sins; the resurrection of the body; and the life everlasting. Amen.*" The Holy Ghost, eternal God with the Father and the Son, has through the Gospel brought me, dead in sin, to faith in Christ and to the blessed communion, the blessed multitude of those who are sanctified through the blood of Christ. There I daily have forgiveness of sins, and with the entire multitude of believers I shall rise from the dead and live forever. This is most certainly true.—This is the holy Christian faith. Upon this faith we want to build ourselves up. Then with new lips we, every one of us, will be able to say: "I believe in God the Father Almighty, Maker of heaven and earth." In Jesus' name, through the gracious working of the Holy Ghost, we believe with a confidence that is invincible that the almighty God, Creator of heaven and earth, the Father of our Lord Jesus Christ, is also *our* Father. Thus Christ said after He had finished the work of redemption: "I ascend unto my Father and your Father." (John 20, 17.)

PRAYER.—Praise, glory, blessing, and thanks be unto Thee, Almighty God and Father of our Lord Jesus Christ, that Thou so mercifully didst take compassion on us, and didst not spare Thine own Son, but didst deliver Him up for us all. Praise, glory, blessing, and thanks be also unto Thee, Lord Jesus Christ, Thou eternal Son of the Father, that with Thy blood Thou didst fully redeem us and reconcile us unto God. And praise, glory, blessing, and thanks be unto Thee, God the Holy Ghost, that Thou didst adorn Thy Christendom with faith, and didst make them a family of God's beloved children. Triune God, bestow upon me, too, the greatness of Thy mercy in time and eternity. Amen.

Hymn 264, 4.

THURSDAY.

Grace be unto you and peace.—Rev. 1, 4.

This is a salutation of our God, written in the Holy Book by inspiration of the Holy Spirit. This greeting is sent to the churches, to the multitudes of those on earth who believe in Christ, to the Christians,—to thee, O Christian! A truly valid, mighty, blessed salutation of God! This nullifies every curse. It brings thee God's grace and the peace of God in time and eternity. So doth He greet thee "who is, and who was, and who is to come," Jehovah, the most high, the eternal God, God the Father, almighty Creator of heaven and earth. This salutation cometh to thee "from the seven Spirits that are before His throne," from God the Holy Ghost, who with gifts manifold proceedeth from the Father and descendeth upon the Christians. And this salutation cometh "from Jesus Christ, who is the faithful Witness, and the First-begotten of the dead, and the Prince of the kings of the earth. Unto Him that loved us, and washed us from our sins in His own blood, and hath made us kings and priests unto God and His Father: to Him be glory and dominion forever and ever. Amen." For He, Jesus Christ, is equal with the Father. He saith: "I am Alpha and Omega, the **Beginning** and the Ending, who is, and who was, and who is to come, the Almighty," just as the Father. "Grace be unto you and peace!" So doth the Holy Trinity greet us—thee. So doth the eternal Father greet thee. His heart burns for thee. This greeting the eternal Spirit bringeth thee through His Word as it is recorded in the Bible, and implanteth it in thy heart. With this salutation doth the eternal Son, our Lord Jesus Christ, greet thee, who at so great a price procured grace and peace for thee, and who exalteth thee into the most sublime heights, unto His heart and into His glory. How wilt thou respond to this salutation of God?

PRAYER.—Thus will I respond, most good and gracious God: Give, O give unto me Thy grace and Thy peace! Shall I stand back when Thou dost meet me so kindly? Full well dost Thou know my most miserable condition, and still Thou dost greet me thus. Yea, give me Thy grace, give my Thy peace, Thou triune, Thou eternal God! I will bask in Thy grace, in Thy peace will I exult in all eternity. Amen.

Hymn 261, 1.

FRIDAY.

Great is the Lord, and greatly to be praised; and His greatness is unsearchable.—Ps. 145, 3.

"God is a *Spirit.*" (John 4, 24.) He is not bound by any limits as is a material body. But let no one be given to foolish and childish notions. God is not a spirit in the sense of a phantom or "spirit," or "ghost," such as the disciples imagined to behold. (Luke 24, 37; Matt. 14, 26.) Nor is He a spirit like the created spirits, the angels. God is a Spirit who is actively and powerfully immanent in all creation, and is infinitely above and beyond every creature. And God is a living and personal Spirit having intelligence and will, and He has created whatever there is of life, of personality, of intelligence, of will in all creation. God is a Spirit *" from everlasting to everlasting"* (Ps. 90, 2), without beginning and without end, and immutable. And so God is *omnipresent, omnipotent, omniscient.* (Jer. 23, 23. 24; Luke 1, 37; Ps. 139, 1-13.) And God is *holy.* (Is. 6, 3.) He is

Holiness itself. His is a spotless holiness, yea, it is impossible that any blemish should be found in it. And therefore He is *just*. (Dan. 9, 7.) Everything that He does is good and right—everything. And He is *faithful*. (Ps. 33, 4.) His Word does not fail, His faithfulness is immovable. And He is *benevolent, merciful, gracious*. (Ps. 145, 9; Exod. 34, 6. 7.) "*God is Love.*" (1 John 4, 8.) He delights in doing good to His creatures, in showing mercy and grace; He is Love, Love itself, that Love whereof all love in heaven and in earth is but an emanation, a reflection, a faint shadow. Yes, great is the Lord, and greatly to be praised; and His greatness is unsearchable!—And this God, this Lord, this Spirit, this eternal Spirit, this omnipresent, omnipotent, omniscient, holy, just, faithful, benevolent, merciful, gracious God, who is Love, He, from everlasting to everlasting, subsists *in three Persons*. The Father, the Son, the Holy Ghost, these three distinct Persons, are in one and the same eternal, altogether indivisible and undivided divine essence. So God is sufficient in Himself, and surely has need of no creature. But He has made creatures. And He is Love. Such is our God. Great is the Lord, and greatly to be praised; and His greatness is unsearchable!

PRAYER.—O Thou great, Thou ineffably great God, help me to know Thee and to worship Thee in spirit and in truth! God, who art Love, and who in Thy love bestowest grace upon me in Christ Jesus, my Savior, grant unto me Thy Holy Spirit, that through Jesus Christ I may rest my soul in Thy love and grace revealed unto me in Thy Word, and thus unfailingly obtain salvation. Amen.

Hymn 264, 5.

SATURDAY.

I saw also the Lord.—Is. 6, 1.

In the year that King Uzziah died, the Prophet Isaiah, in a vision in the Temple, saw the Lord sitting upon a throne, high and lifted up, and His train filled the temple. Above Him stood the seraphim: each one had six wings; with twain he covered his face, and with twain he covered his feet, and with twain he did fly. And one cried unto another and said: "Holy, holy, holy, is the Lord of hosts: the whole earth is full of His glory." And the posts of the door moved at the voice of him that cried, and the house was filled with smoke.—The Lord, the invisible Spirit, in this vision assumed a human form. He likewise gave form and voice to the seraphim, the exalted spirits, the angels. With God, who worketh all things, this is not wonderful.—But what does the Apostle John say through the Holy Spirit? John says that Isaiah "saw His glory and spake of Him." (John 12, 41.) Whose glory did Isaiah see, and of whom did he speak? Isaiah saw *Jesus'* glory and spoke of Jesus, the eternal Son of the Father, who at that time had not yet become man. Learn here, O Christian, that Jesus, the Son of the Father, came forth from out of the Holy Trinity to "declare" that God to thee. In Jesus God reveals Himself to thee. In Jesus thou must know God. Thou must form no thoughts about the will of God toward thee beyond what thou seest in Jesus and hearest from Him. If thou knowest Jesus aright from His Word, thou knowest God aright. On this blessed knowledge thou mayest rest thy faith in life and in the hour of death. The knowledge of Jesus, and hence the knowledge of God in Jesus, is a saving knowledge. Jesus, God, is thy Savior. So shalt thou behold the Lord!

PRAYER.—Lord, Thou great and unsearchable God, with all my heart I thank Thee that in Jesus Thou didst reveal Thyself to me, and wouldst have us know and embrace Thee in Jesus, and firmly believe that Thou art like Jesus. Jesus is my dear, merciful Redeemer and Savior, in whom I have placed all my confidence. And so I trust in Thee, O Thou great and most gracious God, Thou Savior, Thou Redeemer! Keep me in such faith and trust! Amen.

Hymn 263, 1. 2.

SECOND PART.

CATECHISM LESSONS.

Week of the First Sunday After Trinity.

SUNDAY.

Blessed are they that hear the Word of God and keep it. Luke 11, 28.

So saith Christ. But where have we the Word of God? In Holy Scripture, or the Bible. What is the Bible? It is the Word of God. It is a collection of books written by the Prophets of God in the Old Testament and by the Apostles and Evangelists in the New Testament, by inspiration of the Holy Ghost. Thus the Bible is the Word of God. "All Scripture is given by inspiration of God," says the Apostle Paul concerning the writings of the Old Testament. (2 Tim. 3, 16.) "Holy men of God spake as they were moved by the Holy Ghost," says the Apostle Peter concerning the same writings. (2 Pet. 1, 21.) Every word in these writings is the Word of God. When referring to one particular word, the Lord Jesus says: "And the Scripture cannot be broken." (John 10, 35.) Just so it is with the writings of the New Testament. The Apostle Paul says: "Which things also we speak, not in the words which man's wisdom teacheth, but which the Holy Ghost teacheth." (1 Cor. 2, 13.) So the whole Bible is the Word of God. It does not merely claim this for itself, but it proves itself to be such by its great holiness, which cannot be man-made, but must be of God; and by the Holy Ghost, who witnesses and operates through it. "It is the Spirit that beareth witness, because the Spirit is truth." (1 John 5, 6.) And for what purpose did God in the Old and the New Testament give His Word? Thereby to "make thee wise unto salvation through faith which is in Christ Jesus." (2 Tim. 3, 16.) Jesus Christ is the nucleus, the pith and marrow, not only of the

New Testament, but also of the Old. "Search the Scriptures," says Christ, speaking of the Old Testament; "and they are they which testify of Me." (John 5, 39.) Yea, blessed are they that hear the Word of God and keep it. Hear it and keep it, my dear Christian!

PRAYER.—Almighty and most gracious God, I thank Thee that unto all the world and to me Thou hast given Thy Word, which maketh me wise unto salvation through faith which is in Christ Jesus. Give me Thy Holy Spirit, that I may gladly hear and learn Thy Word, read and study it daily, and keep it in an honest and good heart, and obtain eternal salvation. Amen.

Hymn 111.

MONDAY.

The letter killeth, but the spirit giveth life.—2 Cor. 3, 16.

In Holy Scriptures we have two chief doctrines. Both are of God. And yet they differ as widely as death and life. And unless thou clearly perceivest the difference between these two doctrines, thou wilt not know what to make of it all or what to believe.—These two doctrines are the *Law* and the *Gospel.*—In His *Law* God tells us how we ought to be, and what we should do and not do. In His *Gospel* God tells us that He lovingly desires to save us by grace for Christ's sake. Every word of the Bible that tells us how we ought to be, and what we should do and not do, is Law. Every word of the Bible that tells us that it is God's will to save us by grace for Christ's sake, is Gospel. Take thy Bible and try to become adept in discerning what therein is Law and what is Gospel.—The *Law* ("the letter") killeth, damneth us. How so? Why? Because we have not kept it and cannot keep it, because we have transgressed it and still transgress it, we poor sinners. The *Gospel* ("the spirit"), however, giveth life, salvation. How so? Why? Because it demands nothing of us, but merely gives freely, so that we need but take, and rely upon it, and believe. Thus saith the Law: "Cursed be he that confirmeth not all the words of this Law to do them." (Deut. 27, 26.) Thus saith the

Gospel: "God so loved the world that He gave His only-begotten Son, that whosoever believeth in Him should not perish, but have everlasting life." (John 3, 16.)—The *Law* shows thee thy sin and ruin. The *Gospel,* however, shows thee the deliverance, salvation. Learn to know thy sin and thy utter spiritual ruin from the Law, but learn to know the deliverance, thy salvation, from the Gospel. From the killing Law flee into the life-giving Gospel. Then the Law will cease to curse thee, then thou wilt have eternal salvation given thee by the Gospel. Dear Christian, let the Law be thy schoolmaster, to drive thee to Christ, whom the Gospel preaches to thee.

PRAYER.—Enlighten me, O God, that I may rightly understand Thy Word. From Thy holy Law let me learn to know my boundless spiritual ruin. But from Thy holy Gospel let me learn to know Thy grace, which doth much more abound, the grace which is in Christ Jesus, my Lord and Savior, and which saves me from my utter ruin and gives me eternal salvation. And, O merciful Lord, let me abide in true faith in Thy Gospel, the secure place of refuge against every curse. Amen.

Hymn 314, 9.

TUESDAY.

He hath showed thee, O man, what is good; and what doth the Lord require of thee.—Micah 6, 8.

God has given His Law to every man. To every man these words apply: "He hath showed thee, O man, what is good; and what doth the Lord require of thee." In creation God wrote His Law into man's heart: man knew by nature how he ought to be and what God wanted him to do and not to do. By sin this writing was blurred, but not totally effaced. Because it was blurred, God afterwards laid down His Law in Ten Commandments written on two tables of stone, published it through Moses and the Prophets of Israel, and expounded and explained it through Christ and His Apostles. But that the natural knowledge of the Law of God has not been lost entirely is proved by the heathen.

The heathen have neither the Ten Commandments nor their exposition. And yet, by nature they do various works of the Law, as is evidenced by their moral teachings and their laws. Since they have not the Law that is revealed in Scripture, they are a law unto themselves. And so they show that something of the Law is still within their hearts. Have not also the heathen a conscience? Do not their thoughts accuse or else excuse one another? (Rom. 2, 14. 15.) So every man knows the Law of God. No man can plead ignorance of the divine Law to excuse his sin. Least of all canst *thou* plead this. He hath shown thee what is good, and what the Lord doth require of thee, not only by the writing within thy heart, but much more so by the writings of the Prophets and Apostles. Sinner, flee to Christ, thy Savior, that thy guilt be taken from thee!

PRAYER.—Yea, Lord, I am a sinner, and my sin is inexcusable. I know Thy Law, and still I transgressed it. I sin daily. I flee unto Thee, Lord Jesus Christ! Wash me of my sin, and I shall be whiter than snow! Forgive my sins unto me, since Thou didst bear them for me and didst expiate them. Give me Thy free Spirit, that henceforth I may strive against sin and serve Thee according to Thy commandment. Amen.

Hymn 109, 3.

WEDNESDAY.

Thou shalt love the Lord, thy God, with all thy heart, and with all thy soul, and with all thy mind. Thou shalt love thy neighbor as thyself.—Matt. 22, 37. 39.

This is the sum, the chief contents, the real and true meaning of all commandments, each commandment being but an application of this to particular requirements; this must be the living heart of the fulfillment of all commandments; each separate commandment marks but the pulsebeatings that should and must come from this heart. "Thou shalt love the Lord, thy God, with all thy heart, and with all thy soul, and with all thy mind; thou shalt love thy neighbor as thyself." Thus Christ said, thus says the entire

Scripture. And thou canst see that it is so, my dear Christian. In a measure every man can see this, especially when he hears it. Since God is the Most High, since He is Goodness itself and worthy of being loved more than anything else, thou must love Him with all thy heart, with all thy soul, and with all thy mind. If thou dost this not, thou art sinful and dost what is wrong. Since God regards thy neighbor just as highly as thyself, thou must love thy neighbor as thyself. If thou dost not do this, thou art sinful and dost what is wrong. God desires no outward, unwilling, slavish, loveless fulfillment of His commandments. Love must impel thee to fulfill all commandments. If thou hast this love, as God demands it of you, then thou wilt gladly and properly fulfill all commandments. Thou wilt serve God in perfection, thou wilt do no evil to thy neighbor, but only good. "Therefore love is the fulfilling of the Law." (Rom. 13, 10.) If thou hast not this love, thou lackest the heart, thou art dead, spiritually dead, sinful beyond measure, then thou canst not keep any of the commandments of God. Hast thou this love, O Christian? Since thou art a regenerated child of God, thou beginnest, it is true, to love God and thy neighbor. But oh, how much does thy love still lack the true quality and strength! How sinful art thou, how sinful am I! Is it not so? Self-love grows rank within us. And the love toward God and toward the neighbor is but a poor and pitiable seedling standing in the shadow and among the weeds of many sins.

PRAYER.—O God, Thou Most High, Thou Fountain of goodness, and most worthy to be loved, whose love toward me and my fellow-sinners on earth knows neither bound nor measure, who didst not spare Thine own Son, but didst deliver Him up for us all that in Him we might live forever: continue to have mercy upon me, a poor sinner, and for Christ's sake forgive me for loving Thee so little and keeping Thy commandments so poorly. And through Thy Holy Spirit, O Lord, kindle love toward Thee and toward my neighbor in my heart, and grant that in eternal life this small flame of God will become a perfect and a holy fire. Amen.   Hymn 413, 3.

THURSDAY.

Thou shalt have no other gods before me.—Exod. 20, 3.

This is God's First Commandment. God forbids us to have other gods besides Him. There are no other gods besides God, it is true; but if we fear, love, and trust in any creature in heaven or in earth more than in God, then with a madly sinful heart we make a god, an idol, of such a creature, and commit idolatry. How enormously sinful the world is! Since the Fall it is, on the one hand, steeped in gross idolatry and worships images, the concoctions of its own impure thoughts,—and Satan knows that in reality it is he that is worshiped; and on the other hand, it is steeped in fine idolatry,—if such a thing may be called fine,—inasmuch as it exalts itself above God, and serves its own belly, and fears the creature, loves the creature, trusts in the creature. We must know God aright, and fear, love, and trust in Him above all things. And the fear of God must keep us aloof from every wicked thing that is opposed to God; the love of God must make us zealous unto every good thing desired of God; the trust in God which we should have must make us bold and glad to run into the outstretched arms of God. Alas, while it is true that in us who have learned to know Christ and God in Christ such new life is budding, planted, and nursed by God,—how sinful we are nevertheless! How frail is our fear of God, our love of God, our trust in God! How wild does that hateful idolatry still grow in our mortal body! "O wretched man that I am! Who shall deliver me from the body of this death? I thank God through Jesus Christ, our Lord." In Christ we have the forgiveness of sins, and that righteousness which God imputes to us for Christ's sake, the righteousness wherein we can stand before God, He also gives us His Holy Spirit, and He renews us. And so, while sin still cleaves to us heavily, yet with a freed spirit we serve God, fear Him, love Him, trust in Him.

PRAYER.—O my God, I am a poor, miserable sinner. I am devoid of the fear, love, and trust in Thee which I should have. Forgive me my sins, impute unto me the righteousness of my Savior. Thou surely dost do so. Thy Word assures me of it. And behold, Thou hast given me Thy Holy Spirit, who beginneth the new and right life within me. Let Him abide with me, O God! And on the day of resurrection let me awake from the sleep of death with Thy likeness, in perfect holiness, for Jesus Christ's sake. Amen.

Hymn 391, 2.

FRIDAY.

Thou shalt not take the name of the Lord, thy God, in vain.—Exod. 20, 7.

This is God's Second Commandment. God forbids us to take His name in vain. God's name is everything by which He reveals Himself to us, particularly His precious Word. If we take this divine name in vain, if we profane it, we commit a grievous sin and profane the Divine Majesty itself. We should not use the various appellations of God for frivolous exclamations. It is shameful impudence and blasphemy to do so. We should not curse by the name of God, that is, neither blaspheme, nor invoke upon ourselves or others the wrath and punishment of God. We should not swear by the name of God, not utter unnecessary, frivolous, sinful, or even false oaths. We should not use witchcraft nor incantations, not have our fortune told, nor tell fortune ourselves, not consult the dead, nor practice similar satanic arts by the name of God. We should not lie nor deceive by God's name, not adorn nor cover up false doctrine or an ungodly life by making use of the Word and name of God. No, since God has so graciously revealed Himself to us by making known to us His name and giving us His Word, we should hold fast to Him by making proper use of His name and His Word, for this is what He would have us do; and in childlike fear and love we should call upon Him in every trouble of body and soul; and we should confidently believe that He will surely hear us, and be good and kind to us, and shower His blessings upon us; and at all times we should pray to Him, praise Him, and give thanks to Him. What poor sinners we are! How graciously does God tender Himself to us through His name and Word! But what poor use do we make of that, how unwillingly do we take what He so lovingly offers!

PRAYER.—God, Thou great God, Thou makest Thyself known unto me—oh, so graciously!—by revealing us Thy name and Thy Word. And Thou willst that there I should seek and find Thee, and let my heart's delight be in Thee, and honor, praise, and magnify Thee. But oh! how sinful, how weak of faith, how tardy, and cold I am! Forgive me this sin for Christ's sake. Grant unto me, I beseech Thee, Thy Holy Spirit that He may draw me, heart, soul, and mind, into Thy name and Word, that I may have my being wholly in Thee. Amen.

Hymn 391, 3.

SATURDAY.

Remember the Sabbath day to keep it holy.—Exod. 20, 8.

This is God's Third Commandment as it was written on the table of stone, that is to say, the first words. The Sabbath day, the day of rest, was the seventh day, Saturday. God commanded His people, the children of Israel, to keep this particular day holy. But this requirement was expressly abrogated in the New Testament. The Holy Ghost says through the Apostle: "Let no man therefore judge you in . . . respect of an holy-day, or . . . of the Sabbath days." (Col. 2, 16.) The Apostle then teaches that Christ has brought the true day of rest; by the grace of God we may now rest from sin. The day of rest of the Old Testament was but a type and shadow of this. Now that the body has come in Christ, the shadow has been done away with. The specific Sabbath day is no more. Nor has another specific holy-day been instituted in its place, not even Sunday. The whole life of a Christian is to be a Sabbath. But "let the Word of Christ dwell in you richly," so God commands. (Col. 3, 16.) In the Christian congregation the Word of Christ is to be taught and preached publicly. This is most necessary and most salutary. For this purpose a day and a certain time of the day must be appointed when the Christian congregation meets for public worship.

Since the earliest times the Church has appointed Sunday for this purpose. We still observe this custom. He that will not take time to hear the Word of Christ despises the Word of Christ. And we are not to despise the Word of Christ, but to keep it holy, and gladly hear and learn it. Behold the mercy of God in having His saving Word preached to us. We must heartily thank Him for this, and do our utmost to retain this spiritual boon, regularly attend divine worship, and eagerly listen to the Word preached to us. But knowest thou not the sinful disinclination of thy heart to hear the Word of God, even though thou art a Christian?

PRAYER.—Lord God, Heavenly Father, I pray Thee so to rule and guide me by Thy Holy Spirit that with all my heart I may hear and receive Thy Word and truly sanctify the Sabbath day, that by Thy Word I, too, may be sanctified, place all my trust and hope in Jesus Christ, Thy Son, and then also correct my life in conformity with Thy Word, guarding against every offense, until by Thy grace in Christ I shall obtain eternal life. Amen.

Hymn 391, 4.

Week of the Second Sunday After Trinity.

SUNDAY.

Honor thy father and thy mother.—Exod. 20, 12.

This is God's Fourth Commandment. By father and mother our own parents are meant first and above all, but also all those who, according to God's ordinance, are our superiors in home, state, school, and church. We must not disregard this divine order. We must not despise our parents and masters, nor provoke them to anger, but give them honor, serve and obey them, and hold them in love and esteem. Certainly, "we ought to obey God rather than men." (Acts 5, 29.) If our parents and masters demand anything of us that is against the Word of God, we must not obey them. But otherwise we must give them the honor with which God has invested them, and do so with a willing heart, for God's sake. Young children must obey their parents in all things. (Col. 3, 20.) Adult children must show their parents love and kindness. To other masters we must give that honor which they can claim by virtue of their office and their station. This commandment "is the first commandment with promise: that it may be well with thee, and thou mayest live long on the earth," says the Apostle. (Eph. 6, 2. 3.) You may judge what is meant thereby from what is threatened to those who ruthlessly disregard this commandment. If children blankly refuse to obey their parents, employees their employers, subjects their government, pupils their teachers, church-members the preachers of God's Word, —just imagine what that means,—can there be any prosperity then, indeed, would life be tolerable? But if the Fourth Commandment is respected, then things will be well. Alas! many sins could be recorded here. Examine thy own conduct.

PRAYER.—My God, I know that from a child I am evil and full of sin. Wash me of all my sins by the blood which Thy dear Son has shed for me, and grant me Thy good Spirit, that He may teach me, while I sojourn here on earth, to live according to Thy holy will in my own sphere and calling. Amen.

Hymn 391, 5.

MONDAY.

Thou shalt not kill.—Exod. 20, 13.

This is God's Fifth Commandment. But they err greatly who think they have kept this commandment as long as they have not murdered any one, or done their fellow-man any other hurt or harm in his body. Anger proceeding from hate, gnashing of the teeth, and abusive language is murder in the sight of God. (Matt. 5, 21. 22.) "Whosoever hateth his brother is a murderer; and ye know that no murderer hath eternal life abiding in him," the Spirit of God teaches us. (1 John 3, 15.) The civil authorities, according to God's ordinance, are to punish murderers and evil-doers. (Gen.

9, 6; Rom. 13, 4.) But we must not harbor thoughts of revenge against those who have harmed us. Wrath and revenge we must leave to the holy God. The Holy Ghost says to us by the mouth of the Apostle: "Dearly beloved, avenge not yourselves, but rather give place to (the) wrath (of God); for it is written: Vengeance is mine; I will repay, saith the Lord. Therefore, if thine enemy hunger, feed him; if he thirst, give him drink; for in so doing thou shalt heap coals of fire on his head. Be not overcome of evil, but overcome evil with good." (Rom. 12, 19-21.) Where are we most prone to transgress the supreme commandment of love to our neighbor? Over against our enemies and those who do us harm. Hence it is there, too, that we must be most careful to observe its precepts.—We are most miserable sinners. Just because the wicked love of self dwells within us, the still feeble sprig of all-conquering love of our neighbor, which has been implanted in us Christians, has but a miserable existence. "Out of the heart proceed evil thoughts, murders." (Matt. 15, 19.) And how often the thoughts develop into something worse! If we desire to remain children of God, we must live in daily repentance and pray for the Holy Spirit, the Spirit of Love.

PRAYER.—Lord God, dear Heavenly Father, am I not Thy dear child? But I am a very weak and miserable child, easily led into wrong paths and seduced to wickedness. Have patience with me for Jesus' sake. Forgive me my sin. I pray Thee that by Thy Holy Ghost Thou wouldst daily check and change the virulent evil, until in the end Thou wilt deliver me from the body of this death and renew me to blessed perfection. Amen.

Hymn 391, 6.

TUESDAY.

Thou shalt not commit adultery.—Exod. 20, 14.

This is God's Sixth Commandment. Matrimony is instituted by God. Therefore we must not profane it nor commit adultery. Neither by fornication, nor by willful desertion, nor by divorce obtained in the civil courts must we dissolve the bands of holy wedlock. Only when the one party has thus severed the matrimonial ties is the other party free. Christ says: "What therefore God hath joined together, let no man put asunder." "Whosoever shall put away his wife, except it be for fornication, and shall marry another, committeth adultery." (Matt. 19, 6. 9.) But not only the gross adultery just mentioned is adultery in the sight of God. Christ says: "Whosoever looketh on a woman to lust after her hath committed adultery with her already in his heart." (Matt. 5, 28.) Each should love and honor his spouse. Each should be true to his spouse in heart, mind, inclination, word, and deed. And all, including, of course, the unmarried, must be chaste and decent in word and deed. "Fornication and all uncleanness, or covetousness, let it not be once named among you, as becometh saints; neither filthiness, nor foolish talking, nor jesting, which are not convenient; but rather giving of thanks," says the Holy Ghost. (Eph. 5, 3. 4.) We must take this commandment most seriously. For that reason we must avoid all opportunities where our heart, so unclean by nature, is further inflamed with evil desires. We must rather quench the evil desires with God's Word and prayer, by working industriously and exercising due temperance in eating and drinking. Oh, our heart is very unclean! "Out of the heart proceed evil thoughts, murders, adulteries, fornications." (Matt. 15, 19.) Only in the righteousness of Christ, imputed unto us, can we stand before God; only the Holy Ghost can guard us against suffocating our faith by uncleanness.

PRAYER.—It grieveth me, O my Lord and Savior, that I am so unclean. Cover my impurity with Thy purity in the sight of Thy Father, who through Thee is also my Father. And graciously grant me Thy Holy Spirit, that by His almighty help and power I may control the evil desires within me, until the light of Thy countenance shall completely dispel all darkness within me. Amen.

Hymn 391, 7.

WEDNESDAY.

Thou shalt not steal.—Exod. 20, 15.

This is God's Seventh Commandment. But not only pickpockets and burglars transgress this commandment. Whoever defrauds his neighbor in business, or craftily wrests trade and profit from him, or takes advantage of his neighbor's ignorance or distress to get his money or goods, or borrows without returning what he has borrowed, or is in secret partnership with thieves, and so seeks to profit by the dishonesty of others, or enriches himself by means of usury, wringing his neighbor's sweat and blood from him, or refuses to work, depending on others to support him,—such a one steals. The world is full of thievery. Civil laws are not able to stop all thievery. And men refuse to be restrained by the Law of God. Trade and commerce are very corrupt.— We must be honest in the sight of God. One day God will judge. He keeps account of every deed of men. We should fear and love Him, that we do not take our neighbor's money or goods, nor get them by false ware or dealing; on the contrary, we should love our neighbor as ourselves, and in word and deed help him to improve and protect his property and business. By word and deed we should seek to keep him from harm. We should lend him money, if by doing so we may help him, without seeking advantage for ourselves. We should take pity on the poor.—Alas! we stand condemned before this Seventh Commandment: our hand has taken where it should not have taken; it has not given where it should have given. And our heart! How full of thievery it is, how void of pity!

PRAYER.—O my God, grant me Thy Holy Spirit, that I may learn to know my sin, seek forgiveness depending on Thy grace in Christ, and thereupon amend my ways, keep myself unspotted from the world and its sinful ways, love my neighbor and deal with him faithfully and honestly and according to the standards of love, diligently attend to my calling, and expect the blessing from Thee alone; for Thou blessest those that walk in Thy ways. Hear me for Jesus Christ's sake! Amen.

Hymn 391, 8.

Week of the Second Sunday After Trinity.

THURSDAY.

Thou shalt not bear false witness against thy neighbor.— Exod. 20, 16.

This is God's Eighth Commandment. God forbids us to bear witness against our neighbor with a deceitful heart, give testimony against him to harm him. " Let none of you imagine evil in your hearts against his neighbor." (Zech. 8, 17.) The most obvious tale-bearers are those who spread vile lies about their neighbor. But those, too, are tale-bearers who withhold from the neighbor the truth which would benefit him. Tale-bearers are those who reveal the secret sin and shame of their neighbor. " A tale-bearer revealeth secrets; but he that is of a faithful spirit concealeth the matter." (Prov. 11, 13.) Those are tale-bearers who speak evil of their neighbor in his absence. Why not tell him to his face if thou knowest any evil of him, and tell him with a true and loving heart? " If thy brother shall trespass against thee, go and tell him his fault between thee and him alone," says Christ. (Matt. 18, 15.) Those are tale-bearers who injure or destroy their neighbor's good reputation. An evil word spoken of the neighbor, how quickly does it spread! God earnestly forbids this, and He enjoins us to speak whatever is to our neighbor's advantage. We must defend him against false accusations. " Open thy mouth, judge righteously, and plead the cause of the poor and needy!" (Prov. 31, 9.) We should speak well of our neighbor as far as it is in keeping with the truth. Lovingly we should cover up our neighbor's faults and failings, emphasizing his good qualities and being quiet about his faults and shortcomings. Remember we must love our neighbor as ourselves. Oh, miserable sinners that we are! Scarcely another commandment shows as plainly as this does how sinful we are.

PRAYER.—Each one of Thy commandments, O God, seriously accuses me. How often and manifold have I sinned against my brother with heart and mouth, through speech, but also by keeping silence. I cast myself into the dust, before Thee, O holy God! Be gracious unto me for Christ's sake. Graciously let Thy Word and the Holy Spirit effect a change in me, and incline my heart and tongue unto true love for my neighbor. Amen.

Hymn 391, 9.

FRIDAY.

Thou shalt not covet thy neighbor's house.—Thou shalt not covet thy neighbor's wife, nor his man-servant, nor his maid-servant, nor his ox, nor his ass, nor anything that is thy neighbor's.—Exod. 20, 17.

This is God's Ninth and Tenth Commandment. These two commandments are alike as to their meaning. And yet they are two distinct commandments, as indicated by the hyphen in the Hebrew text. God would impress upon us that He regards not only the outward deed, but also the desire of the heart. "Thou shalt not covet." (Rom. 13, 9.) This is what God wants us to understand. And it is so hard for us to understand. We refuse to consider evil lust as sin. We think that as long as we refrain from the outward act, all is well. But God does not want an unclean heart. "Ye shall be holy," says He. (Lev. 19, 2.) We are not to desire anything, not to covet anything greedily, not to hanker after anything nor endeavor to get into our possession, even though it be with a show of right, whatever is our neighbor's. To do so is against the divine law of love. Just as God enjoins love, so He forbids evil lust. Both dwell within the heart. God wants our heart to be holy. Instead of coveting what is our neighbor's, we should heartily desire that he may keep what is his, and also assist him in this. "Look not every man on his own things, but every man also on the things of others," in kind and thoughtful consideration. (Phil. 2, 4.) "The love of money is the root of all evil." (1 Tim. 6, 10.) "Envy is the rottenness of the bones." (Prov. 14, 30.) Greed and envy are an abomination unto the Lord, and roots of sin, and vicious and prolific seeds of evil. Read James 1, 14. 15. Who can stand before these commandments?

PRAYER.—My God, I am full of evil lust and most unclean. Evil roots of sin sprout up within my heart, unholy desires are as rottenness in my bones. Be gracious unto me, O God, be gracious unto me for Jesus' sake! Hide Thy face from my sins; impute unto me the righteousness of Thy dear Son! Give unto me the divine power of Thy Holy Spirit; create and sustain a new spirit within me, that I may serve Thee in the new mind according to Thy commandment. Amen.

Hymn 391, 10.

SATURDAY.

I, the Lord, thy God, am a jealous God, visiting the iniquity of the fathers upon the children unto the third and fourth generation of them that hate me, and showing mercy unto thousands of them that love me, and keep my commandments.—Exod. 20, 5. 6.

With these words God threatens to punish all that transgress His commandments. In proof of His earnestness and holy jealousy He points to His acts recorded in Bible history, which tells us that He punished the iniquity of the fathers even upon the children unto the third and fourth generation when the children hated Him as their fathers had done. But He promises mercy unto all that keep His commandments. And here, too, He points to Bible history, which shows that He has done good unto thousands of pious Israelites. Because of His threat we should fear His wrath, and not act contrary to His commandments. And because of His promise we should love and trust in Him, and willingly do according to His commandments. But tell me, Christian, have the threats God utters the power to keep us from sin, so that we do not act contrary to His commandments? By no means! And can we obtain His mercy by keeping His commandments? By no means. Sin has too largely, too firmly and completely, taken possession of us. Driven and drawn by the Holy Ghost, through the Gospel, we must flee to Christ, and daily lay hold upon the grace of God for the forgiveness of sins. And then, then, moved by the Holy Ghost in faith, we must fear and love God, that we may shun sin and do according to His commandments. Then,

then God looks upon us in Christ with eyes of mercy as upon His dear children, hiding His face from the many sins that still cling to us, and seeing only our keeping of His commandments being pleased with it, although it is so imperfect, and showing mercy unto us. And this is naught but grace, pure grace, grace only.

PRAYER.—My Lord and Savior, here am I, a poor sinner, who has deserved naught but wrath and punishment. But bestow upon me that grace which Thou hast procured for me and promised unto me. Forgive me my sins. Let me be a child of God. Teach me by Thy Holy Spirit to walk, though ever so feebly, in the paths of God's commandments. And be pleased with it according to Thy tender mercy, and bless me, and do good unto me, O Jesus! Amen.

Hymn 424.

Week of the Third Sunday After Trinity.

SUNDAY.

The wages of sin is death, but the gift of God is eternal life through Jesus Christ, our Lord.—Rom. 6, 23.

The real and adequate punishment with which God threatens those who hate Him and transgress His commandments is *death*. "The wages of sin is death." "In the day that thou eatest thereof thou shalt surely die," God said to Adam in Paradise, when He forbade him to eat of the tree of the knowledge of good and evil. (Gen. 2, 17.) What is death? Let us add another Word of God to show us what death really is: "Cursed be he that confirmeth not all the words of this Law to do them." (Deut. 27, 26; Gal. 3, 10.) The curse of God and death go together. So death is God's wrath and disfavor, temporal death, and eternal damnation. The curse of God is upon the transgressors of His commandments, His wrath and disfavor; and through temporal death they enter eternal death, eternal damnation. It is a terrible thing to hate that God who is Holiness and Righteousness itself, and to transgress His commandments. No creature can do that and go unpunished.—But there is a great and gracious deliverance. "The gift of God is eternal life through Jesus Christ, our Lord." In Jesus Christ, our Savior and Atoner, there is grace for us sinners and blessing and eternal life. In Jesus Christ the love of God embraces us in time and eternity, and abolishes death. But this is a gift, a free gift of God; we cannot merit that with works as we have merited death. God gives us eternal life in Christ, freely and without price, by grace only. And He offers us this gift through His Word and His Spirit. And we, we Christians, who believe in Jesus Christ and accept this gift of God, have eternal life.

PRAYER.—Holy and righteous God, merciful Father! By my sin and transgression of Thy commandments I have deserved death. Thou sayest it. Thou truthful God, and I know it. But, O God, Thou also sayest that Thou givest me eternal life through Jesus Christ, my Lord. And it is grace alone that moved Thee to draw me to my Savior, and thus to make me an heir of eternal life. Now complete Thy grace in me, Thou God of mercy, and help me to continue with my Savior in true faith and so to obtain life everlasting. Amen.

Hymn 418, 1. 2.

MONDAY.

Enter not into judgment with Thy servant; for in Thy sight shall no man living be justified.—Ps. 143. 2.

Is it true that all men, without exception, have deserved death by their transgression of the divine Law? And is it true that all men without exception can receive eternal life only through the free grace and gift of God? Can no man keep God's commandments as He would have us keep them? Can no man stand before the judgment-seat of God?—Inspired by the Holy Ghost, David says to God: "Enter not into judgment with Thy servant; for in Thy sight shall no man living be justified." And he furthermore says: "The Lord looked down from heaven upon the children of men to see if there were any that did understand and seek God.

They are all gone aside, they are all together become filthy: there is none that doeth good, no, not one." (Ps. 14, 2. 3.) No, "there is not a just man upon earth that doeth good and sinneth not." (Eccl. 7, 20.) "We are all as an unclean thing, and all our righteousnesses are as filthy rags." (Is. 64, 6.) Natural man, man as he is by nature since the Fall, cannot keep the Law of God, no, not in the least; for in all that he does the heart is lacking: the love of God; his best works are not done to please God, they are as an empty shell without the kernel. And the regenerate Christian, who possesses the Holy Ghost, can fulfill the Law of God but imperfectly, because sin still clings to him. Regenerate Paul says by inspiration of the Holy Ghost: "Not as though I had already attained, either were already perfect; but I follow after, if that I may apprehend that for which also I am apprehended of Christ Jesus." (Phil. 3, 12.) And he says: "I know that in me (that is, in my flesh), dwelleth no good thing; for to will is present with me, but how to perform that which is good I find not." (Rom. 7, 18.) It is certain: every man deserves death because of his sin, and can only receive eternal life through the free grace of God in Christ Jesus, only as a gift, as a present.

PRAYER.—My God, I accuse myself, and I humbly confess that by sinning against Thee I have deserved death, and daily deserve it. But I rely upon Thy grace promised me in the Gospel in which Thou hast pledged forgiveness of sins, life, and salvation to me for Jesus' sake. And I confidently pray as Thou hast taught me to pray: "Enter not into judgment with Thy servant; for in Thy sight shall no man be justified." Amen.

Hymn 421, 3.

TUESDAY.

By the Law is the knowledge of sin.—Rom. 3, 20.

God knows, of course, that we cannot keep His Law as He would have us keep it. But we also should know it. Now because of that faint knowledge of the Law which man still has by nature man naturally also knows something about his transgression of the Law, hence of his sin. But God wants to deepen this knowledge, make it more thorough. We must know our total depravity. Such knowledge is wrought by His Law, His Law revealed in the Bible. There we behold as in a mirror how unholy we are; for there we see how holy we ought to be. The Law reveals to us the inmost crevices of our hearts, and lays bare the evil lust, which hates God, and which nestles there like a venomous sin-vermin. This evil lust is the very basic sin within us, from which all the various sins are born. Of this fact we have no true knowledge without the Law. And so without the Law we do not know the full force and awfulness of our sin, its depth and enormity. This is what St. Paul refers to when he writes: "Nay, I had not known sin but by the Law; for I had not known lust except the Law had said: Thou shalt not covet." (Rom. 7, 7.) By the Law is the knowledge of sin. Why does God want us to thus learn to know our sin through the Law? That we might cling all the closer to Jesus in true faith and to the righteousness which He has purchased for us and given to us. True, the Law, and the knowledge of sin which we gain through it, does not work faith, not in the least. The Gospel and the knowledge of the grace of God in Christ alone does this. But the Gospel makes use of the Law and thereby shows us how hopelessly lost we are without Christ, and impels us all the more to seek refuge in the loving arms of our Savior.

PRAYER.—My God, I, Thy child, give thanks unto Thee that by Thy Law Thou revealest unto me my total depravity, and that by Thy Gospel Thou revealest unto me Thy grace, which heals all our diseases. O Lord, give me Thy Holy Spirit, that, the more fully I learn to know my sin, the more firmly I may hold to Thy grace which is in Christ Jesus, my Lord. Amen.

Hymn 314, 9.

WEDNESDAY.

This book of the Law shall not depart out of thy mouth, but thou shalt meditate therein day and night, that thou

Week of the Third Sunday After Trinity.

mayest observe to do according to all that is written therein; for then thou shalt make thy way prosperous, and then thou shalt have good success.—Joshua 1, 8.

Regenerate Christians, children of God, in whom the Holy Ghost dwells, are desirous, yea, anxious to lead a life that is well pleasing to God. They wish to do good works that are acceptable unto God. But in this they must not be guided by their own would-be pious opinion, much less by the commandments of men, but by the Law of God. The Law of God must be the rule guiding their every action. The Law of God should never depart out of their mouths, but they should meditate therein day and night, and seek to follow all its precepts. Then they will be sure of doing what is right, and will always act wisely. Thus, notwithstanding God knows that man cannot fulfill His Law, He nevertheless has made it a rule for us, His children, which we should follow, and which tells us with what and what kind of works we should serve Him. It is acting presumptuously if we ourselves choose the works with which we want to serve God. God has told us in His Law how we should be, and what we must do and must not do, and these precepts alone we must follow. Forsooth, that will give us enough to do as long as we live. The more earnestly we strive to keep God's commandments, the more we shall become aware of how much we still lack, how poorly we have kept the Law, are still keeping it, and, in fact, how little we can keep it.

PRAYER.—O Lord, give me Thy Holy Spirit, that I may run the way of Thy commandments! And be Thou with me on this way, Thou gracious God, and richly and daily forgive all sins unto me for Jesus' sake, and comfort and strengthen me by the Spirit of grace, that I may ever and again lift up the hands which hang down, and the feeble knees, and make straight paths for my feet to run in the ways of Thy commandments. Amen.

Hymn 341, 1-3.

THURSDAY.

Sin is the transgression of the Law.—1 John 3, 4.

What, properly speaking, is *sin?* "Sin is the transgression of the Law," says our text. The divine Law tells us what is right. Sin is every transgression of the divine Law, every departure from its rules and precepts, each and every failure to do whatsoever it demands of us, each and everything that is done contrary or in opposition to it. Mark that well, Christian: sin is every departure from the rule of the divine Law. Since God, the holy God, has told us in His Law how we should be, and what we must do and must not do, every transgression of that Law must be wrong, wickedness, error, sin. Men often speak of great and of trifling sins, and are not so punctilious as regards the latter. This is wrong. Everything, without exception, that is against God's Law is wrong, is sin, ungodly, impious. But if any one claims something to be a sin which is not forbidden in the Law of God, do not listen to him. Only that is sin which is contrary to God's Law, and nothing else. No one has a right to bind our conscience with man-made laws. But thou wilt find plenty of sin, many departures from the rule of the divine Law if thou wilt but examine thyself. Take these sins to Christ, that He may forgive them unto thee. Strive against them valiantly in the power of the Holy Ghost.

PRAYER.—Lord Jesus Christ, I know that I cannot stand before Thy divine Law. I am not as I should be; I fail to do what I should; I do not refrain from those things which Thou hast forbidden in Thy Law. Free and rid me, I beseech Thee, from the load of my sin, and declare unto Thy Father that Thou hast rendered satisfaction for me. But also grant me holy courage and endue me with strength of Thy Spirit, that I may earnestly and successfully resist sin and serve Thee in accordance with Thy Law. Amen.

Hymn 322, 1. 4.

FRIDAY.

He that committeth sin is of the devil; for the devil sinneth from the beginning.—1 John 3, 8.

How did sin enter the world? This is a question which human reason cannot answer. Our Catechism is right in answering from the Word of God: "By the devil, who first departed from God, and by man, who of his own free will suffered himself to be misled by Satan into sin." So the very first originator of sin is the devil. "The devil sinneth from the beginning," that is to say, he was the first one to sin; with him sin originated. *How* it came about that a great many of the angels whom God created good fell into sin we know nothing of, nor can we comprehend it. God has not revealed it to us in Scripture. He only says that it was done, and Satan, the prince of the fallen angels, has seduced the first man, and the first man of his own free will suffered himself to be misled. So it came about that also "by one man sin entered into the world," into the world where man dwells. (Rom. 5, 12.) But, as stated above, the devil is the originator of sin. And he that committeth sin is of the devil; he is not of God, he is of the devil, begotten of the devil, is the devil's child, like the devil, of the same nature as the devil. This is a hard saying. But it is true, fully true. So says St. John, "the Apostle of love," inspired by the Holy Ghost. Our dear and loving Savior said the same thing to the unbelieving Jews: "Ye are of your father, the devil." (John 8, 44.) Since the fall of Adam all men, by nature, are of the devil. There is no difference. Awful! But thanks be unto God: "for this purpose the Son of God was manifested that He might destroy the works of the devil." (1 John 3, 8.) Thou knowest this. Through faith in the Son of God thou poor sinner art a child of God, His beloved child, to whom God forgives all sins, and whom God purifies ever more by His Holy Ghost, and finally, in eternal life, will make like unto Himself, perfectly holy, without sin.

PRAYER.—My Lord and Savior Jesus Christ, Thou Son of God, Thou strong and merciful Helper and Savior, I thank Thee that Thou hast made me, a child of the devil, a child of God, and from direst bondage didst exalt me unto the most blessed liberty, from deepest degradation unto highest honors. Help, O help me, that through faith I may retain this grace and precious gift of Thine, and thus obtain eternal salvation. Amen.

Hymn 92, 2. 3.

SATURDAY.

That which is born of the flesh is flesh; and that which is born of the Spirit is Spirit.—John 3, 6.

By "flesh" is meant the sinful depravity of human nature. And, indeed, human nature is totally and entirely depraved, it is deprived of the righteousness it had when God first created it, and is inclined to all that is evil. "In my flesh dwelleth no good thing," says the Apostle Paul. (Rom. 7, 18.) "The imagination of man's heart is evil from his youth," says God Himself. (Gen. 8, 21.) So human nature is subject to the wrath of God and to damnation. "We were by nature the children of wrath, even as others," says St. Paul. (Eph. 2, 3.) Such total depravity of the hole human nature is not acquired by education or habit or implanted into us in some other way, but is *inherited*. We have inherited it from Adam by virtue of our conception and birth from sinful progenitors. "That which is born of the flesh is flesh," says Christ, our Lord. And David writes by inspiration of the Holy Spirit: "Behold, I was shapen in iniquity, and in sin did my mother conceive me." (Ps. 51, 5.) So sin is most deeply and most firmly connected with our nature. By nature we are flesh. No human power can change that. No human power can bring us into the kingdom of God. This is called *original sin.*—But "that which is born of the Spirit is spirit," says Christ. God can change it. God can bring us into the kingdom of God. He does it through His Holy Spirit, who operates in us through His Word, through the Word of Christ. He creates a new thing within us. He implants faith in Christ within us, and so He brings us into the kingdom of God. And He creates and brings about within us a new life. And He regenerates us, makes us "spirit," spiritual. In consequence of this there is a constant warfare in this life between flesh and spirit. But the spirit is mightier than the flesh. In heaven we shall be all spirit.

PRAYER.—I thank Thee, my God, that Thou hast regenerated me, who by nature am flesh, through Thy Word and Holy Spirit, and hast made me spirit, so that now I believe in my Savior and find true comfort in Him, but also serve Him with the new powers Thou hast given me, and confidently hope to obtain eternal life. Thou hast brought me into Thy kingdom, Thou God of mercy. Keep me therein, here in time and thereafter in eternity. Amen.

Hymn 310, 2. 4.

Week of the Fourth Sunday After Trinity.

SUNDAY.

Out of the heart proceed evil thoughts, murders, adulteries, fornications, thefts, false witness, blasphemies.—Matt. 15, 19.

From original sin, from the depravity of our nature, there result what are called *actual sins,* that is to say, sins that are acted, done, carried into effect. By these actual sins are meant all transgressions of the divine Law, not only such as may be observed by our fellow-men, sinful words and deeds, but also all sinful thoughts, which are known to God and ourselves only, yea, also the sinful desires slumbering within us which we ourselves do not notice, which only the eye of God can detect. Consider the text at the head of this lesson, and see what abominations arise from our heart. And indeed, it cannot be otherwise. From a bad fountain only foul water will issue forth, and a corrupt tree will bring forth nothing but evil fruit. And not only do we do the wicked things forbidden in the Law of God, but we also fail to do the good things which we are commanded to do. We are totally depraved; within us there is a countless brood of sin. The more we are enlightened by the Holy Spirit, the more we realize this. Where there is nothing but darkness, the various shades of darkness, so to speak, are not distinguishable; but the brighter the light, the more pronounced the shadows will be. What an awful delusion, then, to think that by the works of the Law, by the fulfillment of the Law, man might become righteous before God and obtain salvation! No, it is solely through faith in Christ, who fulfilled the Law in our stead and bore its curse for us, that we become free from sin, righteous before God, and obtain life everlasting.

PRAYER.—Lord, most holy God, I confess that not only am I conceived and born in sin and therefore sinful from the very beginning of my existence, but that also knowingly and unknowingly I have daily and in manifold ways transgressed Thy commandments, and therewith surely have deserved Thy wrath and punishment in time and eternity. Nor can I help myself in the least or find ways or means thereto. But since Thou, O gracious God, hast revealed to me in the Gospel that Thy beloved Son, Jesus Christ, is the propitiation for our sin and our Righteousness, in short, our Savior, I rely upon this Thy Word and pray Thee to forgive me all my sins, and to give me eternal life through grace in Him. O dear Father in heaven, also grant me, I beseech Thee, Thy Holy Spirit, that henceforth I may resist the sinful desires, and be earnestly and sincerely intent upon serving Thee according to Thy Law. Amen.

Hymn 413, 2.

MONDAY.

In the beginning God created the heaven and the earth.— Gen. 1, 1.

Every child in Christendom knows these very first words of the Bible. And the truth they contain, namely, that there is a great, eternal, omnipotent God, who has created heaven and earth, and all that in them is, is a knowledge which every man has by nature. Of all, I repeat it, of all men, St. Paul says: "That which may be known of God is manifest in them; for God hath showed it unto them. For the invisible things of Him from the creation of the world are clearly seen, being understood by the things that are made, even His eternal power and Godhead, so that they are without excuse." (Rom. 1, 19. 20.) And still brazen fools and scoffers, willfully hardening their hearts, deny the existence of this almighty Maker of heaven and earth, and speak of an eternal matter which of itself, by eternal revolutions, developed and formed itself into what now is. They have no excuse for their ungodly foolishness. To "create" means to produce something out of nothing by a mere word. This God did in the beginning. (Hebr. 11, 3.) How immeasurably great is God! We confess in unison with all Christendom of all times: "I believe in God the Father Almighty, Maker of heaven and earth." Yes, and we believe and may and should believe that through Jesus Christ this almighty God and Creator is our Father, and that we are His dear children. O faith, faith, how highly dost thou exalt us! And how small we make our faith through our own fault! If the almighty God is our Father and we are His dear children, should we not then exult and sing, and always be full of courage, and joyful, and undismayed, and boldly glory in Him though the world and even hell assail us? And should we not then adorn ourselves with holiness and righteousness well pleasing unto our God and Father, and befitting us, His children? But—oh, how weak in faith we are!

PRAYER.—O Lord God, whose greatness and might are incomprehensible, who by Thy Word didst create heaven and earth out of nothing, what a diminutive grain of dust am I in Thy sight, and what is more, ruined by sin and death. And still I am to be Thy dear child through Jesus Christ. O Lord, give me Thy Spirit, that He may lift me up unto Thee! Amen.

Hymn 62, 3.

TUESDAY.

He shall give His angels charge over thee.—Ps. 91, 11.

It is not to be marveled at that besides man God has also created other rational and personal beings who do not dwell on earth. Scripture tells us that God has created angels. They are spirits. (Hebr. 1, 14.) Although we are all familiar with the word "spirits," we do not understand the meaning of it. God created these spirits in the beginning, countless numbers of them, and all of them at one time. They sang together and shouted for joy when He layed the foundations of the earth. And God calls them His sons. (Job 38, 7.) They are holy. (Matt. 25, 31.) To-morrow we shall hear that, though created holy, not all of them remained thus. To-day we shall hear only of the holy angels. These are now confirmed in their bliss, and do always behold the face of God in heaven. (Matt. 18, 10.) They excel in strength, and praise God, and as ministers of His they do His pleasure and His commandments. (Ps. 103, 20. 21.) And, O yes, God has given them charge over us, God's children, to keep us in all our ways. "The angel of the Lord encampeth round about them that fear Him, and delivereth them." (Ps. 34, 7.) What grand and beautiful stories does Holy Writ tell about angels who assumed visible shape and form, and did God's commandments on earth, and served men and guarded them. Wilt thou read 2 Kings 6, 8-17? The last service that they render us on earth is when they bear our souls up to heaven. (Luke 16, 22.) But on the last day they will have much to do with men. And then we shall be in their blessed communion eternally, we, who are God's children. How gracious God is toward us!

PRAYER.—Almighty, eternal, merciful God, who out of wondrous mercy didst ordain the angels to be ministers unto us, grant me grace, I beseech Thee, that my life may also be guarded and protected here on earth by those who unceasingly attend Thy divine majesty, through Jesus Christ, Thy Son, our Lord. Amen.

Hymn 23, 7.

WEDNESDAY.

Be sober, be vigilant; because your adversary, the devil, as a roaring lion, walketh about, seeking whom he may devour: whom resist steadfast in the faith.—1 Pet. 5, 8. 9.

There are also evil angels. They are the spirits who fell from God, though in the beginning they were created good and holy. They are ruled by a prince, and, as a rule, Scripture usually mentions him alone when speaking of the evil angels. He, as thou knowest, was the first one to sin. (1 John 3, 8.) These evil angels did not abide in the truth. (John 8, 44.) They kept not their first glorious estate, but left their own habitation of blessedness. And God has rejected them forever; He has reserved them in everlasting chains under darkness unto the judgment of the great day. (Jude 6.) Therefore they are God's declared enemies. They endeavor to destroy and to ruin the works of God. And they are also our, man's, declared enemies. Remember the temptation and the fall in Paradise! Until Judgment Day, God in His holy counsel permits the devil and his evil spirits to roam about on earth and practice their evil designs. The devil has a kingdom here, a kingdom constituted of deep guile and great might. He is the prince of this world. He is the ruler of the darkness of this world. (Eph. 6, 12.) With this evil foe, with all these evil foes, we Christians must wrestle, as the Apostle writes. See how the Holy Ghost, in the text at the head of our devotion, warns us against our adversary, and admonishes us to be sober and vigilant, and steadfastly to resist him in faith. But with might of ours can naught be done, soon were our loss effected. Christ, Christ, the Valiant One, whom the devil knows, and who has bruised the devil's head, helps His own, those who abide in His Word and arm themselves with His Word. With them all the power of the devil can avail nothing. My dear Christian, be Christ's own!

PRAYER.—My Lord and Savior, Thou great Conqueror, who hast overcome devil and hell, guard me against carnal security, and grant me grace that I may at all times watch the evil eye of the devil which is fixed upon me with the intention of destroying me. But also help me to call upon Thee, and to arm myself with Thy Word, and so in Thy power successfully to withstand Satan, and having done all, to stand. Amen.

Hymn 9, 1. 5.

THURSDAY.

Let us make man in our image, after our likeness; and let them have dominion over . . . all the earth.—Gen. 1, 26.

Such was the counsel and deliberation of the Holy Trinity in creation. Great are the works of the Lord that we see, and most marvelous. But the foremost among the visible creatures is man. For he was made the lord of the earth; he is to have dominion over everything that is on earth; even the sun, moon, and stars are at his service. As thou mayest read in Genesis 2, God Himself has prepared the body of man with particular love and care, has given him a rational soul, has endowed him with the greatest perfection of body and soul, and, above all, has made him in His image, in the likeness of God. This last point is seen from our text. And the image of God consisted in this that man was created in righteousness and holiness like that of God, and that he possessed the greatest knowledge possible, the knowledge of God, a knowledge of exalting and glorifying purity. (Eph. 4, 24; Col. 3, 10.) Thus man is the foremost of the visible creatures of God.—But woe is us! How shamefully disfigured in body and soul are we through sin! The image of God has been changed in us into the image—the pen will scarce write it—into the image of the devil. But in the regenerate Christians the beginnings, the lineaments of the divine image, though faintly and imperfectly, reappear. In eternal life the image of God shall be restored in us fully, in heavenly perfection. "I will behold Thy face in righteousness: I shall be satisfied, when I awake, with Thy likeness." (Ps. 17, 15.)

PRAYER.—Lord, my God, Thou hast highly exalted me, and I have fallen very low. And Thou didst bend down to me in Jesus Christ, my Savior, and didst draw me again unto Thee, and Thou wilt draw me into heaven, into supreme exaltation and perfection. Praise and glory be unto Thee, my God! Finish Thy work in me, and leave me not, Thou faithful Lord! Amen.

Hymn 348, 1.

FRIDAY.

Though He be not far from every one of us; for in Him we live, and move, and have our being.—Acts 17, 27. 28.

Having in the beginning created the earth (to make mention of that only) and, above all, man, God does not withdraw His hand from creation, but continues to create and to work. He does this according to laws which He has made and laid down in nature, but always in absolutely free exercise of His will. He does this according to laws for our sake, for we are to cultivate the soil and make the earth, with all it contains, serve our purposes; and how could we do this if there were no laws of nature? He does this always according to His free and sovereign will, for, being the Lord, He is not subject to these laws, but superior to them. He says: "Let the earth bring forth grass, the herb *yielding seed,* and the fruit-tree *yielding fruit* after his kind, whose seed is in itself." And when He created the beasts, He said: "*Be fruitful and multiply*"; and the very same words He spoke when He created man. Sun, moon, and stars are to divide the day from the night, and to be for signs, and for seasons, and for days, and years. (Gen. 1.) These are laws of nature given by God. But it is always the great and sovereign Lord who in and through them continues to create and to work and to sustain. So it behooved not only Adam and Eve, but thee and me to-day as well, to say: "I believe that God has made me and all creatures; that He has given me my body and soul, eyes, ears, and all my members, my reason and all my senses, and still preserves them." God is not far from every one of us; for in Him we live, and move, and have our being. To God we owe our life and being; in God, by virtue of His almighty power it is that we exist; each breath we draw, every motion of the body we make, is to be attributed to this almighty power of His.—What an abomination it must be unto God if we abuse the power He thus gives us to sin! And oh, the patience of God to sustain us notwithstanding!

PRAYER.—Thou great God, in whose all-sustaining power I, as well as every creature, live, and move, and have my being, for Jesus Christ's sake forgive me my sins which so grievously offend Thee! And give me Thy Holy Spirit, that not bodily only, but spiritually as well, I may live, and move, and have my being in Thee. And be patient with Thy frail child, until Thou shalt bring me to the state of eternal perfection. Amen.

Hymn 35, 2. 5. 8.

SATURDAY.

Cast all your care upon Him; for He careth for you.— 1 Pet. 5, 7.

God sustains His creatures here below as long as it pleases Him. He who is present within His entire creation "upholds all things by the word of His power." This text speaks of the Son, our Savior, and proves His eternal Godhead. (Hebr. 1, 3.) The Son does this together with the Father and the Holy Ghost. God's omnipotence and wisdom are needed to preserve all things thus, and to provide for so great a household. He keeps also thee, provides for thee. To this end He gives thee clothing and shoes, meat and drink, house and home, wife and children, fields, cattle, and all goods,—according as thou art in need of each of these things within thy station and calling. He richly and daily provides thee with all that thou needest to support this body and life. God does this, God alone. Certainly, thou must labor, as long as thou art able to do so; for "if any would not work, neither should he eat." (1 Thess. 3, 10.) Ordinarily God wants to keep thee by means of thy labor. And thou must also make use of thy understanding. But thou must trust, rely, and build, neither upon thy labor nor upon thy understanding. With these thou canst accomplish nothing, unless God deigns to bless thy doing and thy planning. Much less must thy labor and thy understanding be made to serve the purposes of sinful greed. And do not *worry.* Take no thought, saying, What will I eat? or, What will I drink? or, Wherewithal shall I be clothed? For God keepeth thee and provideth for thee, not thou. And God is thy Father in Christ Jesus. How sinful, then, is care and worry! O Christian, child of God, poor sinner, take thy care and cast it upon God; for He careth for thee. This is most certainly true. So says the Holy Spirit.

PRAYER.—O God, my Father, I thank Thee that Thou assurest me of Thy care and providence! I thank Thee that Thou so kindly exhortest me to cast all my care upon Thee! Forgive the sinful weakness of my faith. Grant unto me Thy Holy Spirit through Thy Word, that I may cheerfully and wholly rely upon Thee. Hear my prayer for Jesus Christ's sake. Amen.

Hymn 292, 14. 15.

Week of the Fifth Sunday After Trinity.

SUNDAY.

There shall no evil befall thee, neither shall any plague come nigh thy dwelling.—Ps. 91, 10.

Thus does God put thee at ease, thou child of God. And Dr. Luther, in his Small Catechism, in accordance with this promise, teacheth thee to believe that God defends thee against all danger, and guards and protects thee against all evil.—But how is this? Does not, in reality, manifold evil and does not a plague befall us? Does not dire experience teach this a thousand times? Does not also Scripture teach the very same thing? Think of the story of Joseph! But, listen, what does this very story of Joseph show? It shows that God makes all things that seem to be evil, and that actually taste bitter enough, to work together for good to them that love Him. Even Joseph finally said to his brothers who had steeped his soul in bitter grief: " Ye thought evil against me; but God meant it unto good, to bring to pass as it is this day, to save much people alive." (Gen. 50, 20.) Just so does God deal with thee if thou art His child. Everything that befalls thee, though it seem ever so evil, must contribute to thy welfare, thy soul's eternal welfare. And hence it cannot actually be an evil. Nor must thou consider it a plague. My dear Christian, this life is as nothing compared with the blessed life hereafter. There all will be glorious beyond comprehension. Thy heavenly Father, who dearly loves thee, sometimes, it is true, permits something to befall thee which seems very hard to bear. But in each and every instance it is merely a well-planned and foreordained station on the way to eternal life to which He is taking thee under His guidance. And thus He, in loving kindness, eases and tempers everything, and being full of compassion and love against thee, He comforts thee. Put thy trust in the promise He gives thee in the above Scripture text. And "commit thy way unto the Lord; trust also in him, and He shall bring it to pass." (Ps. 37, 5.)

PRAYER.—My dear Heavenly Father, give me, I beseech Thee, a childlike mind to trust in Thee implicitly, and firmly to believe that Thou dost safely guide me and dost deal well with me. And when I needs must cry and weep, help me to lift up my eyes unto Thee, and to seek consolation and help with Thee, for Thou art my dearly beloved Father in Christ Jesus. Amen.

Hymn 109, 4.

MONDAY.

I am not worthy of the least of all the mercies and of all the truth which thou hast showed unto Thy servant.—Gen. 32, 10.

Thus spake Jacob, the patriarch. And so every Christian should say. We are not worthy of the blessings which the

Week of the Fifth Sunday After Trinity.

Lord showers upon us. He confers nothing but fatherly, divine goodness and mercy upon us, though He finds no merit or worthiness in us. O let us search and examine our lives and our ways! Have we deserved it that God provides for us and watches over us, that He governs and protects us, yea, that He punishes and chastises us as a faithful father does his children, and that He makes all things work together for our good in such a manner that in the end we reach the goal which His grace in Christ sets before us? Have we deserved this? Certainly not. We have deserved something altogether different. "Like as a father pitieth his children, so the Lord pitieth them that fear Him." (Ps. 103, 13.) That we fear Him, that we live in childlike fear of God, this, too, is His mercy. But that this fear of God is such a struggling and miserable little plant in the garden of our heart, that is our fault. But God continues to show us His mercy. What do we owe Him for all this? "What shall I render unto the Lord for all His benefits toward me?" (Ps. 116, 12.) Ah, indeed, I cannot render Him anything as a recompense. But it is my duty to thank Him, to praise Him, to serve and to obey Him. Is it not so? Surely we owe this to God. Our thanks and our praise, our service and obedience, will be poor and paltry enough in comparison with the benefits of God. But our Heavenly Father will notwithstanding accept the feeble beating of our hearts toward Him, our feeble stammering of praise and thanks, our feeble and childish efforts. He makes the fullness of Christ replace our deficiency. His Spirit makes intercession for us. God be praised!

PRAYER.—O Lord God, Heavenly Father, from whom we receive all good gifts unceasingly and in abundant measure, and who daily, out of pure grace, guardest us against all evil: grant me, I beseech Thee, Thy Holy Spirit, that, acknowledging in true faith all this Thy goodness, I may now and evermore thank and praise Thy loving-kindness and tender mercy; through Jesus Christ, Thy beloved Son, our Lord. Amen.

Hymn 62, 15.

TUESDAY.

Neither is there salvation in any other; for there is none other name under heaven given among men whereby we must be saved.—Acts 4, 12.

This name is JESUS CHRIST. There is salvation in none other. Except through Jesus Christ no man can be saved. O the lie, the lie, the soul-destroying lie, that is now preached from so many pulpits and proclaimed by so many "ministers of the Gospel" who deny that Christ is the only Savior, claiming that He is merely one among many, and that the Christian religion is not the only true religion, but only more perfect, possibly, than others. Let us here loudly and firmly testify with Scripture that there is salvation in none other; for there is no other name under heaven given among men whereby we must be saved than the name of JESUS CHRIST alone. "Jesus" means Savior. And this name was given to Him of whom we speak because He is the only Savior of all mankind. (Matt. 1, 21.) And "Christ," or "Messiah," means The Anointed. Anointment was customary in the Old Testament when kings and high priests, and perhaps also the prophets of Israel, were installed in their office. This name was given to Him of whom we speak because He was ordained by God to be our only Savior, our true Prophet, High Priest, and King. (Ps. 2, 6.) And He is anointed with the Holy Ghost without measure. (Ps. 45, 7; Acts 10, 38.) Always seek Jesus Christ, always and ever better learn to know Jesus Christ, always believe in Jesus Christ, always follow Jesus Christ, always bear witness of Jesus Christ before all men. There is salvation in none other; for there is no other name under heaven given among men whereby we must be saved.

PRAYER.—Lord Jesus, Thou art the only Savior of all mankind, and beside Thee there is no salvation. Help, O help me to believe in Thee, and to cling to Thee, and not to be torn from Thee by the great and powerful lie which Thy adversary and mine disseminates on earth. Thou only Savior, save me through faith in Thee. Amen.

Hymn 83, 2.

WEDNESDAY.

This is the true God.—1 John 5, 20.

Who is this Jesus Christ of whom we speak? Scripture says: "This is the true God." It says that He is "over all, God blessed forever. Amen." (Rom. 9, 5.) It says that He is "The Lord, our Righteousness." (Jer. 23, 6.) Therefore Thomas said to the Risen One: "My Lord and my God." (John 20, 28.) Scripture says that He is the only-begotten Son of the Father, the second person of the Holy Trinity. The Father says to Him: "Thou art my Son; this day have I begotten Thee." (Ps. 2, 7.) He Himself testifieth and says: "God so loved the world that He gave His only-begotten Son." (John 3, 16.) The Holy Ghost says: "God spared not His own Son." (Rom. 8, 32.) Jesus Christ is the "Word" which was in the beginning and was with God and was God, and through whom all things were made. (John 1, 1-3.) He is the Omnipotent, the Omniscient, the Omnipresent. (Matt. 28, 18; John 21, 17; Matt. 28, 20.) "He upholds all things by the word of His power." (Hebr. 1, 3.) He forgives sins, He will execute Judgment. (Matt. 9, 6; John 5, 27.) "Let all the angels of God worship Him." (Hebr. 1, 6.) "All men should honor the Son even as they honor the Father." (John 5, 23.)—Here is the parting of the ways. Whosoever does not believe the clear doctrine of Scripture that Jesus Christ is the true God begotten of the Father from eternity, cannot believe in Him. This is wonderful and miraculous beyond everything: God has become man, Jesus Christ. Flesh and blood will not accept this. How do we get such faith? How may we retain such faith? We must see the glory of Jesus Christ, see it ever again, the glory of the only-begotten Son of the Father, full of grace and truth—*in Holy Scripture.* Through it the Holy Ghost works faith.

PRAYER.—Lord Jesus, true God and man, Thou Son of the Father and Mary's Son, grant me Thy Holy Spirit to the end that I may behold Thy glory in Thy Word, even as Thy disciples beheld it with enlightened eyes, and that I may believe in Thee, as Thy disciples believed in Thee, in order that I may belong to the blessed company of those who obtain eternal life through faith in Thee. Amen.

Hymn 155.

THURSDAY.

And the Word was made flesh.—John 1, 14.

The Word, the eternal Word, has become flesh. The only-begotten Son of the Father became Mary's son. God became man. This is Jesus Christ. Jesus Christ is true God, begotten of the Father from eternity, and also true man, born of the Virgin Mary. He is true man. It was not a phantom body that people saw, nor did He assume a human body only temporarily as when He invested Himself with a body whenever He appeared to the saints of Old Testament times. No, He became a true man. Very frequently He called Himself "the Son of Man." (John 3, 14.) The Holy Spirit, in Scripture, calls Him the "Man Christ Jesus." (1 Tim. 2, 5.) He has a true human body. After His resurrection He said to His disciples: "Behold my hands and my feet that it is I myself: handle me and see; for a spirit hath not flesh and bones, as ye see me have." (Luke 24, 39.) He has a true human soul. In Gethsemane He said: "My soul is exceeding sorrowful, even unto death." (Matt. 26, 38.) He walked about and stood, He slept and waked, He hungered and thirsted, He grieved and He rejoiced, yea, He died and became alive again. On the last day He, the Son of Man, will come in His glory. (Matt. 25, 31.) He was, He is, and He will remain a true man. He, the Man Christ Jesus, who, however, also is God and the Lord of heaven, is the last Adam, the second man, who restores all things that we lost in the first Adam, the first man: righteousness, life, and eternal salvation. Both according to His person and to His office He is the Mediator, the only Mediator between God and man. (1 Tim. 2, 5.) And thou must firmly believe Him to be such.

PRAYER.—O Thou great God, eternal Son of the eternal Father, I praise Thy incomprehensible compassion, which Thou hast shown in becoming true man and our Mediator, in order that, as the second Adam of the human race, Thou mightst reconcile us unto God and give us righteousness and salvation. Grant me grace to believe that Thou becamest true man to redeem the human race, and thus be assured that God is gracious unto me and will give me eternal life. Amen.

Hymn 141, 4. 5.

FRIDAY.

And they, being afraid, wondered, saying one to another: What manner of man is this!—Luke 8, 25.

We must be filled with holy fear and wonder when we behold Jesus as Scripture pictures Him to us. We must say as the disciples did: "What manner of man is this!" We observe in the Lord Jesus two natures very distinct from one another: the uncreated eternal, divine nature, and the created temporal, human nature. The eternal Son of God in the fullness of time received the human nature into His person: *the true God WAS MADE true man.* The human nature now is the own nature of the Son of God. Jesus Christ is God and is man in *one* person. And so each of the two natures, though always distinct as to the essence of each, partakes of the properties of the other. Thus, because of this union of the two natures in one person, *the eternal Son of God* was born nineteen centuries ago (Gal. 4, 4. 5): He, the true God, the Lord of Glory, the Prince of Life, shed His blood for us, was crucified, put to death. (1 John 1, 7: Acts 20, 28; 1 Cor. 2, 8; Acts 3, 15.) And He, the Son of Man, possesses all divine majesty: omnipotence, omniscience, omnipresence, power to give life, power to forgive sins and to execute Judgment, the honor of worship. (Matt. 28, 18; John 21, 17; Matt. 28, 20; John 5, 26. 27; Hebr. 1, 6; John 5, 23.) And it was necessary that Jesus Christ should be true God and man in *one* person, because He was to be our Redeemer. It was necessary that He should be *man,* that He might be capable of fulfilling the Law, of suffering and dying, as all men's Substitute; it was necessary that He should be *God,* that He might be able to appease the wrath of God and to overcome sin, death, and the devil.—Meditate upon this, Christian, and worship Him whose name is "Wonderful."

PRAYER.—Indeed, Lord Jesus Christ, Thou art wonderful, Thou art "The Wonderful" foretold by the Prophet. No man's reason can comprehend Thee. But do Thou shine in my heart by means of Thy Word; by means of Thy Gospel cast Thy image into my soul, glorify Thyself within my heart and soul through Thy Holy Spirit, that I may believe in Thee, true God and man and my only and dearly beloved Savior, blessed forever! Amen.

Hymn 151, 1. 4.

SATURDAY.

The Lord, thy God, will raise up unto thee a Prophet from the midst of thee, of thy brethren, like unto me; unto Him ye shall hearken.—Deut. 18, 15.

The office of our Lord Jesus is to redeem and save us. For this purpose He was sent into the world by the Father. Into this office He was installed by the Father; for this reason He is the Anointed, the Messiah, the Christ. As such He is, first of all, our *Prophet,* our Preacher. He is the great Prophet whose coming Moses foretold to the people of Israel in the words of Scripture quoted above. He is the only Prophet who reveals, proclaims, preaches unto us the counsel and will of God respecting our redemption and salvation. There is no other prophet that could do this. For "no man hath seen God at any time; the only-begotten Son, who is in the bosom of the Father, He hath declared Him." (John 1, 18.) Of Him the Father says: "This is my beloved Son, in whom I am well pleased; hear ye Him." (Matt. 17, 5.) And how does He fulfill the duties of His prophetic office? When He sojourned on earth, He testified Himself both by word and deed, that is to say, by great signs and wonders, that He is the Son of God and the Savior and Redeemer of the world. Then He ordered His disciples and Apostles to preach His Word and by inspiration of the Holy Ghost to put it down in writing. And what has thus been written, His Word, is to be proclaimed on earth to the end of days. And to His servants who proclaim this His Word He says: "He that heareth you heareth me; and he that despiseth you despiseth me; and he that despiseth me despiseth Him that sent me." (Luke 10, 16.) So at all times He, He alone, is the Prophet, the Preacher. Even in the Old Testament He was the Prophet, He, the Son of God, who was to become man. For the prophets who prophesied of the grace that should come did this by the "Spirit of Christ that was in them." (1 Pet. 1, 11.) My dear Christian, Jesus Christ is thy only Prophet or Preacher. Listen to no other one! Accept no one besides Him! Hear His Word only, His Word, I say, and nothing else!

PRAYER.—Lord Jesus, help me, a poor sinner, to listen to no one, no matter who he is or whence he comes, in everything pertaining to my salvation, but to Thee only. Thou art the one Prophet come from heaven. Thy Word is the infallible Truth. To this Word let me cling, O Jesus, let me trust in it, let me depend on it in life and death. Amen.

Hymn 110, 5. 8.

Week of the Sixth Sunday After Trinity.

SUNDAY.

Such an high priest became us who is holy, harmless, undefiled, separate from sinners, and made higher than the heavens.—Hebr. 7, 26.

The high priest of the Church of God in the Old Testament had three duties to perform. In the first place, he had to see that the people kept the Law of God. Secondly, he had to sacrifice for the sins of the people. Thirdly, he had to pray for the people. All this was imperfect. For, in the first place, the high priest could not keep the Law of God himself. So, secondly, he had to sacrifice for himself also. And what did he sacrifice? Beasts. And thirdly, he himself was in need of intercession. The high priests of the Old

Testament were but shadows and types of the true High Priest. " Such an high priest became us who is holy, harmless, undefiled, separate from sinners, and made higher than the heavens." And Him we have. Christ is our true and only *High Priest*. In the first place, seeing that we cannot keep the Law of God, He keeps it for us. " When the fullness of the time was come, God sent forth His Son, made of a woman, made under the Law, to redeem them that were under the Law, that we might receive the adoption of sons." (Gal. 4, 4. 5.) Secondly, He sacrificed for our sins—what? —Himself. " Christ His own self bare our sins in His own body on the tree." (1 Pet. 2, 24.) " Behold the Lamb of God, which taketh away the sin of the world." (John 1, 29.) " This He did once." (Hebr. 7, 27.) In doing so, all was accomplished. Thirdly, He continually intercedes for us before His heavenly Father, pleading the atonement which He has wrought. " If any man sin, we have an Advocate with the Father, Jesus Christ, the Righteous: and He is the propitiation for our sins, and not for ours only, but also for the sins of the whole world." (1 John 2, 1. 2.) Dear Christian, put thy trust wholly and solely in this High Priest.

PRAYER.—My Lord and Savior, my only High Priest, how merciful art Thou! Thou hast fulfilled the burdensome Law for me. Thou hast sacrificed Thyself for me. Thou dost at all times intercede for me. In Thee, in Thee alone, will I trust. Thou wilt do it, Thou wilt save me. Amen.

Hymn 244.

MONDAY.

I am a King.—John 18, 37.

Thus the Lord said to Pilate. And verily, He is a *King*. He is a King whom no king can equal. All majesty on earth is but a faint, paltry, insignificant shadow of His majesty. His majesty is the divine majesty. For " in Him dwelleth all the fullness of the Godhead bodily," in a human body. (Col. 2, 9.) So according both to His divine and His human nature He is King over all. His kingdom and His power extend over heaven, earth, and hell. Heaven is

His throne, earth is His footstool, hell is the prison-house of His kingdom. "By Him were all things created that are in heaven, and that are in earth, visible and invisible, whether they be thrones, or dominions, or principalities, or powers: all things were created by Him and for Him. And He is before all things, and by Him all things consist." (Col. 1, 16. 17.) "He upholds all things by the word of His power." (Hebr. 1, 3.) He rules and reigns over all. All things are subject to Him. Great and small, things present and things to come, death and life: He holds all things in His hand, and guides them according to His counsel with divine omnipotence and omniscience. What a King! We do not now see that all things are subject to Him; He still suffers Himself to be despised and derided. But what is this present time? A brief moment. Soon and everlastingly it will appear that He is the King.—O Christian, this King is thy Savior, thy dear, faithful, merciful Savior, who loves thee with unutterable and inestimable love. How safe, how blessed art thou in His keeping!—This was speaking of His *Kingdom of Power.*

PRAYER.—Almighty Lord and Savior, Thou King and Lord over all, who wilt prove Thyself to be strong and terrible to Thy enemies: I thank Thee that Thou art my Jesus, my dear Savior! Behold, I commend myself into Thy strong hands for time and eternity. And I know that these Thy hands will receive me and keep me. Amen.

Hymn 93, 1. 6.

TUESDAY.

Behold, thy King cometh unto thee meek.—Matt. 21, 5.

Jesus Christ, the great King, whose kingdom has neither bound nor limit, who will be a terror to His enemies, cometh unto thee meek. To "thee"? To whom? To thee who receivest Him as thy Savior, and desirest to be saved through Him.—Let us tell thee something. Jesus Christ has a kingdom here on earth, a peculiar kingdom, which ever was a small and insignificant-looking kingdom. To this kingdom all poor sinners belong who believe in Him as their Savior and put their trust in Him. All these taken together constitute His kingdom. This kingdom is called His *Kingdom of Grace*. There He holds sway with His grace, yes, indeed, with His great, pure, immeasurable grace. He embraces each one who belongs to this kingdom with His wondrous grace, yes, He, the great, omnipotent King. In this kingdom He daily and richly forgives all sins. The members of this kingdom He protects, and guides, and directs, and leads, and governs, so that, despite all the temptations of the devil, the world, and the flesh, they remain His own and obtain eternal bliss. But how, by what perceptible means, does He govern this Kingdom of Grace? By His *Word* alone—nothing else. But in this Word His, mark! His Holy Spirit is present, and through it He is operative and effective. Let no one attempt to rule the members of this kingdom by any other means than by the Word of Christ. Let no one attempt to rule at all in this kingdom. Christ alone is the King of this kingdom. He is a meek King, meek toward poor miserable sinners. But these He will draw away from sin through His Word and Holy Spirit, and rule them inwardly, that they may serve Him. My dear Christian, rejoice and thank God for having brought thee into this kingdom!

PRAYER.—Meek King, Lord Jesus Christ, I thank Thee that Thou hast brought me too, a poor sinner, into Thy Kingdom of Grace, into this Thy most precious kingdom, where Thou embracest Thine own with great compassion, and leadest them to salvation. Dearly beloved Lord Jesus, let me remain in this kingdom until my eyelids shall close in death. Amen.

Hymn 138, 4. 5.

WEDNESDAY.

The Lord shall deliver me from every evil work, and will preserve me unto His heavenly kingdom.—1 Tim. 4, 18.

Jesus Christ, the King of the Kingdom of Power and the King of the Kingdom of Grace, also has a heavenly kingdom, a kingdom prepared for us who here on earth are His own, a kingdom into which all those shall enter who here on earth have been in the Kingdom of Grace; when they leave the earth they shall enter this heavenly kingdom. This is called the *Kingdom of Glory;* for there is naught but honor and glory. There we shall be wholly free of everything that here we call evil. There our prayer, "Deliver us from evil," will in fullest measure be granted. There shall forever be fullness of honor and glory such as we cannot even conceive of now. There our souls shall ever be abundantly satisfied, rejoicing over all the gifts of heaven; and we shall never once grow weary of them, but shall ever desire them anew, and there shall be ever new abundance. And so it shall be in all eternity. That will be our true home, purchased for us by the Savior with His precious blood. There we shall enjoy real life graciously merited for us by Christ. Thither let thy heart and mind be directed! Who would continue to bemoan the hardships of the journey since this is the goal? And the Savior has promised, the King has assured us that He will bring us there. Doubt not! Say: "The Lord shall deliver me from every evil work, and will preserve me unto His heavenly kingdom." Ah, thy Savior does not treat thee parsimoniously. Here He showers upon thee the fullness of His grace, and there He will give thee the fullness of His glory. Abide with Him, remain His own!

PRAYER.—Ah yes, Thou great, rich, gracious, lavishly bountiful King, my Lord and Savior Jesus Christ, give me all, yea, all Thy grace and glory. I cannot comprehend it. But Thou hast promised it. Oh, therefore give it unto me, O Lord, my dear Savior! Amen.

Hymn 238, 4. 5.

THURSDAY.

He humbled Himself.—Phil. 2, 8.

Jesus Christ was "in the form of God." His human nature, being personally united with His divinity, possessed all divine majesty. And still "He thought it not robbery to be equal with God." The use of this majesty communicated to His human nature the Lord Jesus did not hold so fast as one does a spoil. "But He made Himself of no reputation."

He made no show of His divine majesty, He waived the constant and full use of it. He "took upon Him the form of a servant, and was made in the likeness of men, and was found in fashion as a man." Thou seest this in the Bible stories of the evangelists. He was born a little, frail infant. He grew up, was obedient to His parents, learned, toiled, ate, drank, waked, slept, was fatigued, became sad, while at another time He was glad. He also walked from one place to another. To the will of His Father, who had foreordained this, He "became obedient unto death, even the death of the cross." (Phil. 2, 5-8.) Thus He humbled Himself. This is called the *State of Humiliation* in which He remained from His conception to His burial. In this state He did not, according to His human nature, make use of the divine majesty which was communicated to it. Only when He performed divine works, miracles, or when He spoke words of divine majesty, did He suffer His divine majesty to shine forth. Why did Jesus Christ humble Himself so? Having become our Substitute, He wanted to redeem us by His obedience to the divine Law and by His bitter suffering and death. How could He have done this if He had used His divine glory always and fully? See Him in His deep humiliation, my dear Christian, and thank Him for it with all thy heart!

PRAYER.—Lord Jesus Christ, Thou divinely glorious Savior, I thank Thee that also for my sake Thou didst so exceedingly humble Thyself as to become like unto me poor lost and damned sinner in all things, sin alone excepted. Kindle faith in Thee in my heart and true love toward Thee through this blessed Gospel truth, and finally let me see Thy glory in the realms of eternal glory. Amen.

Hymn 157, 3, 7.

FRIDAY.

Wherefore God also hath highly exalted Him.—Phil. 2, 9.

God has raised Christ from the state of obedient humiliation, and has exalted Him to the very highest height and sublimity. Now Christ, according to His human nature, uses the divine majesty communicated unto it continually and fully, unrestrictedly. God has given to the Son of Man, Jesus Christ, a name which is above every name. At the name of *Jesus* every knee should bow, of things in heaven, and things in earth, and things under the earth, and every tongue should confess that Jesus Christ is the Lord, to the glory of God the Father. (Phil. 2, 9-11.) Blessed is he who gladly does this, believing here, beholding there in eternal bliss! Woe unto him who, in unbelief, refuses to do this here! One day he will be compelled to do it trembling and wailing dreadfully.—This is called Jesus Christ's *State of Exaltation.* Our Lord entered this state when He was quickened in the grave and, having triumphantly descended into hell, showed Himself to His disciples as the Risen One, and when he ascended into heaven and sat at the right hand of God the Father Almighty. In this State of Exaltation all the world shall see Him when He will come again to judge the quick and the dead. And in this state He will remain forever. My dear Christian, know thy Savior, thy beloved Savior, who so dearly loves thee in His exaltation. And then rejoice exceedingly! Who or what can harm thee, who or what can rob thee of salvation, since thy Savior is exalted above all things and encompasses thee, and guards and protects thee with His great divine power?

PRAYER.—Lord Jesus, my Savior, gladly do I bow my knee at Thy name; with great rejoicing do I confess that Thou art the Lord, to the glory of Thy Father, who hath both humbled and exalted Thee for my salvation. I commit myself into Thy hands, which were affixed to the cross for me, and which now have all divine power. O Lord Jesus, my glorious Savior, I wait for, and hope in, Thee alone; save me! Amen.

Hymn 235.

SATURDAY.

Christ was put to death in the flesh, but quickened by the Spirit; by which also He went and preached unto the spirits in prison which sometime were disobedient.—1 Pet. 3, 18-20.

"Christ was put to death in the flesh." As concerns His flesh, His human nature, His life on this earth, He was put to death. "But quickened by the Spirit." As concerns His spirit, His divine nature, His life as it was controlled by this spirit, He was quickened. Hence the man Jesus, put to death, was quickened on the third day, so that now He is in divine glory. In this divine glory the Man Jesus Christ, put to death, but quickened, went and preached unto the spirits in prison which sometime were disobedient. This prison is hell. There are the spirits of unbelievers, the disobedient. To them Jesus Christ preached, living in divine glory. What did He preach to them? His victory. To the devils, too, He preached this. "He spoiled principalities and powers; He made a show of them openly, triumphing over them in it." (Col. 2, 15.) Christ's descension into hell was a triumphal procession, His preaching in hell a cry of victory. Hell must know that He has conquered, and that, on the contrary, it has lost. This was the first act of the Exalted. If there are spirits in hell to whom Jesus preached His victory, then there are also spirits in heaven who were informed of His victory. The former wailed, and the latter rejoiced. Let us here on earth rejoice over the victory and the exaltation of our Savior, that we may belong "to the spirits of just men made perfect" (Hebr. 12, 23), joining them in their songs of praise when our earthly pilgrimage will have been ended.

PRAYER.—Lord Jesus, Thou exalted Savior, who dost declare Thyself to the living and the dead, let us who are living in this time of grace receive Thy testimony in true faith, that when our last hour cometh we may depart this life, not passing into howling unrest, but into jubilant peace. Hear me, O my blessed Lord, who wast dead and wilt live in all eternity. Amen.

Hymn 225, 4.

Week of the Seventh Sunday After Trinity.

SUNDAY.

Ye are a chosen generation, a royal priesthood, an holy nation, a peculiar people, that ye should show forth the praises of Him who hath called you out of darkness into His marvelous light.—1 Pet. 2, 9.

Here on earth there is a generation, a people, that is gathered from among all nations. It is God's chosen generation. All its members are spiritual kings and priests, who rule over devil, world, and flesh, and offer themselves a sacrifice unto God. It is a holy nation, because it has the righteousness of God, and serves God with holy works. It is a peculiar people, a people purchased by God to be His own forever. It shows forth and proclaims by word and deed the excellencies of God, and spreads abroad the glory of His name. This is the generation, the people, which God has called, which by His almighty call of grace He has called out of the darkness of sin and unbelief into His marvelous light, the light of His grace which is in Christ Jesus, the light of faith in Christ Jesus. This generation, this people, is *the whole Christian Church on earth,* the true Christian Church, which the Holy Ghost continually calls by the Gospel, gathers, enlightens, sanctifies, and keeps with Jesus Christ in the one true faith. This is the *one Holy Christian Church* on earth, the *communion of saints,* the communion of those who are sanctified through faith in Christ. This is the generation, the people, which makes a joyful noise, and is glad, and sings: "Know ye that the Lord He is God: it is He that hath made us, and not we ourselves; we are His people and the sheep of His pasture." (Ps. 100, 3.) This generation, this people, is born through grace alone, and lives by, of, and unto grace alone. It can tell and sing of nothing but grace. And what wondrous grace has been bestowed upon this people! What a blessed people this is! And thou, O Christian, belongest to this people!

PRAYER.—Thanks be unto Thee, Heavenly Father and

Week of the Seventh Sunday After Trinity.

eternal God, that by Thy precious Holy Spirit Thou hast also called me to Christ, my Savior, and hast made me a partaker of His salvation in faith, so that I belong to that chosen generation which is Thy holy nation and peculiar people in time and eternity. I pray Thee, Lord, to graciously bestow upon me the gifts of Thy Spirit, that before all the world I may show forth the praises of Thee who so graciously hast called me out of darkness into Thy marvelous light. Amen.

Hymn 249, 1. 4.

MONDAY.

Ye stiff-necked and uncircumcised in heart and ears, ye do always resist the Holy Ghost.—Acts 7, 51.

When through the Word and Spirit of God one has come out of darkness into light, and so belongs to God's chosen people, this is in no respect and in no manner due to one's merits or conduct, but only and solely to God's pure grace. We now ask: Is God willing to do all this with every one who hears the Gospel? Yes; most assuredly! "As I live, saith the Lord God, I have no pleasure in the death of the wicked, but that the wicked turn from his way and live." (Ezek. 33, 11.) "God will have all men to be saved, and to come to the knowledge of the truth." (1 Tim. 2, 4.) "The Lord is not willing that any should perish, but that all should come to repentance." (2 Pet. 3, 9.) Why, then, are most men not converted? Because they obstinately resist the Word and Spirit of God, because they refuse to be converted. Jesus said: "O Jerusalem, Jerusalem, thou that killest the prophets, and stonest them that are sent unto thee, how often would I have gathered thy children together, even as a hen gathereth her chickens under her wings, and ye would not!" (Matt. 23, 37.) And Stephen, being full of the Holy Ghost, said to the Chief Council of the Jews: "Ye stiff-necked and uncircumcised in heart and ears, ye do always resist the Holy Ghost." Forsooth, whosoever does not come to God's people, and therefore is lost, is lost solely by his own fault. And so many are lost who are called Christians and are hearing the Word of God! But for the fact that thou be-

Week of the Seventh Sunday After Trinity. 293

longest to God's people through faith, thou must thank the gracious God alone.

PRAYER.—Merciful God, who am I that through faith in Christ Thou hast made me a member of Thy people which Thou wilt save? It is not because I desired it, but because it was Thy gracious will that I should be Thy own. It is due, not to my choosing, but to Thy choosing, Thou Fount of Grace! Continue to give me Thy grace; complete Thy work within me; keep me in the noble order of those who are Thy own, and take me to the mansions of eternal bliss! Amen.

Hymn 344, 3.

TUESDAY.

Christ also loved the Church and gave Himself for it, that He might sanctify it.—Eph. 5, 25. 26.

The one "Holy Christian Church" of which we speak in the Third Article of the holy Christian Creed is the "communion of saints," that is to say, all Christendom on earth, or the sum total of those who truly believe in Jesus Christ, and in such faith are sanctified unto God. Hence only believers truly belong to the Church, but all believers without distinction. They are the Church which Christ has loved, for which He gave Himself, which He sanctified by the Gospel and through the Holy Ghost in faith. This Church is not a visible congregation or organization, whose names and full membership might be given, but an invisible, spiritual congregation, which the Lord only knows, names, and counts, since only the Lord can tell with certainty who believes in Christ and therefore belongs to Him. "The Lord knoweth them that are His." (2 Tim. 2, 19.) The Church is the kingdom of God, Christ's Kingdom of Grace. And "the kingdom of God cometh not with observation; neither shall they say, Lo, here! or, Lo, there! for, behold, the kingdom of God is within you." (Luke 17, 20. 21.) Faith, which makes us members of the Church, the kingdom of God, is within us and is known to the Lord alone. And so the Church is but *one.* There is but *one* kingdom of God. It is "*one* body and *one* Spirit." (Eph. 4, 4.) The Church is holy. Christ has sanctified it through His righteousness given unto it, and through His Spirit, who incorporates it with Him. So it is "holy and without blemish" before God Through grace. (Eph. 5, 27.) It, furthermore, is a Christian Church. It is "built upon the foundation of the apostles and prophets, Jesus Christ Himself being the chief cornerstone." (Eph. 2, 20.) And this Church and congregation—listen, dear Christian!—is the beloved bride of Christ, to whom, to whom alone, all eternal promises are given. Now examine thyself, whether thou be in the faith, and if, therefore, thou belongest to this Church. Prove thine own self! (2 Cor. 13, 5.)

PRAYER.—I believe in Thee, my dear Lord and Savior Jesus Christ! I am Thine; I belong to those who are Thine, to Thy Church. But I cry unto Thee: Help Thou mine unbelief! O Thou great Shepherd and Bishop of my soul, keep me, and let me be and remain Thy own unto my dying breath, and then take me home, yes, home unto Thee, into Thy secure dwellings. Amen.

Hymn 274, 2.

WEDNESDAY.

For as the rain cometh down, and the snow from heaven, and returneth not thither, but watereth the earth, and maketh it bring forth and bud, that it may give seed to the sower and bread to the eater, so shall my Word be that goeth forth out of my mouth: it shall not return unto me void, but it shall accomplish that which I please, and it shall prosper in the thing whereto I sent it.—Is. 55, 10. 11.

Where on earth is this one holy Christian Church, this congregation and people of God, to be found? Wherever and only where the Gospel of Christ is proclaimed; for according to God's promise His Word never fails to bring forth fruit. See God's own promise at the head of this lesson. If thou knowest of any place where the Word of God is preached, where people gather to hear the Gospel of Christ, then thou mayest and shouldst be altogether certain:

here is the Church, here are believers, here is a part of Christendom, here are some who belong to God's people. For though many among those who hear and read the Word of God be hypocrites and ungodly, yet the Word of God never returns void to God; there must be at least a few who believe the Gospel, a few who are converted, and who will be kept steadfast in their faith by means of this Word. God has promised it, and thou must believe it. So if thou belongest to a congregation in which the true Gospel is proclaimed, thou shouldst say: I am among people in whose midst there are children of God, in whose midst God begets children and nourishes them unto eternal life. And though thou observest much weakness and many abuses there, and though conditions be such as to make thee think that there are but very few true believers in that place, thou must believe God's promise and say: There surely are children of God in this place. And instead of complaining and grumbling, or even withdrawing and fleeing, thou shouldst rather be active, and do thy utmost to cure the weakness and to correct every abuse.

PRAYER.—I thank Thee, O Lord, that Thou hast brought me where Thy Word is proclaimed pure and unadulterated, and the Sacraments are rightly administered, hence, where there is a communion of such as are Thy children through faith in Jesus Christ. Let me always remain Thy dear child. Grant me grace to be watchful on my part, and strengthen those who are on the point of losing their faith. Amen.

Hymn 475, 1. 2.

THURSDAY.

Again, the kingdom of heaven is like unto a net that was cast into the sea and gathered of every kind.—Matt. 13, 47.

Not only is the Gospel preached, but there are also those who profess the Christian faith, and come together to hear the Gospel. Of course, one can see these people, and count them, and draw up a list of their names. The whole number of those who profess the Christian faith and go to hear the Gospel is called the *visible* Church. The whole number of those who at one place and in an organized body profess the Christian faith and are gathered about the Gospel, is called a local Christian congregation. But in this visible Church, and within the local congregations, there are also hypocrites and ungodly people besides the true Christians. Only the Lord knoweth them that are His. If it becomes manifest that one who professes to be a Christian is a hypocrite and ungodly, then, according to Christ's precept and established order, he must be put away from among the Christian congregation and declared a heathen man and a publican. Such is God's will. But beyond this we cannot distinguish between believers and hypocrites, and consequently cannot excommunicate. It is because we do not know the state of any man's heart. The Kingdom of Heaven, the Kingdom of God, the Church of Christ on earth, is like unto a net that was cast into the sea and gathered of every kind, both good and bad fish. And when the net is full, they draw it to shore, and sit down, and gather the good into vessels, but cast the bad away. This sorting in the Kingdom of God shall be done on the last day, not now. At the end of the world the angels shall come forth at God's behest, and sever the wicked from among the just. And then the wicked shall be cast where there shall be wailing and gnashing of teeth. He that hath ears to hear, let him hear!

PRAYER.—Lord Jesus, I thank Thee that through Thy Word and Holy Spirit Thou hast given me the true faith, and hast made me a true member of Thy Church. Keep me, I beseech Thee, in true faith unto my end, that at the great sorting on the last day I may not be cast into hell, but be received into heaven. Amen.

Hymn 552, 5.

FRIDAY.

If ye continue in my Word, then are ye my disciples indeed; and ye shall know the truth, and the truth shall make you free.—John 8, 31. 32.

There are so many denominations on earth, with various doctrines and various creeds! To which of these denominations is a Christian to belong? To the one which has, teaches, and confesses the entire doctrine of the Word of God in all its purity, and in which the Sacraments are administered as instituted by Christ. It is quite clear that such is the Lord's will. The Lord said to His disciples, and He says it to all Christians: "If ye continue in my Word, then are ye my disciples indeed." True disciples of Jesus should have, and desire to have, nothing but Jesus' Word, Jesus' doctrine, and no other. Then, and then only, do they know the truth, the truth which Christ has brought from heaven for the salvation of poor sinners. And this truth shall make them free of the darkness of error and unbelief in which they are by nature, and give them the true knowledge of all that they possess in Jesus, and make them partakers of all this through faith. When, therefore, our Lord gave His disciples that great royal command to go and make disciples of all nations by teaching and baptizing them, He said: "Teach them to observe all things whatsoever I have commanded you." (Matt. 28, 20.) Always, unto the end of the world, the disciples of Jesus are to keep, and to adhere to, what Jesus commanded His first disciples, what He taught them. Be very careful, my dear Christian, to belong and adhere to a denomination which has, teaches, and confesses all the doctrines of the Word of Christ in unalloyed purity. Then thou hast the truth, which saves and makes thee free.

PRAYER.—My Lord and Savior Jesus Christ, I desire to be Thy true disciple. I desire to have and to hear Thy Word only, no word or doctrine of man. O Lord, I beseech Thee, let me always find a place where Thy Word is taught and preached in its truth and purity. Let the fullness of Thy truth shine forth on earth, that the darkness of error may not prevail. Amen.

Hymn 110, 2.

SATURDAY.

Now I beseech you, brethren, mark them that cause divisions and offenses contrary to the doctrine which ye have learned, and avoid them.—Rom. 16, 17.

The denomination which has, teaches, and confesses all the doctrines of God's Word in unalloyed purity, is called an *orthodox* church. To this we must adhere, and contribute toward its maintenance and propagation according to our ability. Any denomination, on the other hand, that does not have, teach, and confess all the doctrines of the Word of God as we find them in the Bible, is called *heterodox*. Such denominations cause divisions and offenses among Christ's people by departing from the doctrine which we learn from the Word of God. These the disciples of Jesus must *avoid;* for so the Holy Spirit teaches us to do. Listen, Christian, how this is! Thou must curse false doctrine. (Gal. 1, 8. 9.) Hence thou must carefully beware of false teachers as destroyers of thy soul, and must not believe them, but must try, or prove, them by the standard of God's Word, and thou wilt find them to be liars. (Matt. 7, 15; 1 John 4, 1; Rev. 2, 2.) Heterodox churches, where false teachers hold sway, thou must avoid; thou must come out from such a church if hitherto thou hast belonged to it; thou must be separate; thou must avoid it. (2 Cor. 6, 14-18.) Heterodox Christians, however, thou must not judge or condemn, but in charity thou must believe that they are merely deficient in this or that point of Christian knowledge. For consider, if some of the saving doctrines are still taught in a heterodox denomination, then there may be, in fact, then there still must be, some children of God among them. And thou must rejoice that it is even so. But as far as thou art concerned, if thou wouldst be a true disciple, thou must continue in His Word and in the church which has, teaches, and confesses His Word in all its purity.

PRAYER.—Lord Jesus, grant me Thy Holy Spirit, that I may become sure of what is the true doctrine of Thy Word, that I may prove every doctrine offered me by teachers and preachers by the standard of Thy Word, guard against being seduced to believe false doctrines, continue in Thy Word, always confess it by word and deed, and may thus be a helpful and useful instrument for the propagation of Thy kingdom here on earth, until Thou shalt take me home, into the realms of eternal joy and bliss. Amen.

Hymn 110, 1. 6. 7.

Week of the Eighth Sunday After Trinity.

SUNDAY.

Bless the Lord, O my soul, and forget not all His benefits: who forgiveth all thine iniquities.—Ps. 103, 2. 3.

Christendom, the one holy Christian Church, the communion of saints, God's chosen people, those who through true faith in Jesus Christ have become His dear children,— this Christendom, and each and every member of it, possesses something daily in rich abundance that is better than anything there is, and which cannot be procured or purchased with any deed man may do, or any treasure in the world: *forgiveness of sins.* Dr. Luther says in his Small Catechism: "In which Christian Church He daily and richly forgives all sins to me and all believers." And the Holy Ghost prompts every Christian to say these words, these words of praise and rejoicing: "Bless the Lord, O my soul, and forget not all His benefits: who forgiveth all thine iniquities." Forsooth, this forgiveness of sins is better than all the treasures of the world. If God would not forgive us our sins, we should be lost. If but one single sin were not forgiven us by God, we should be lost. But God forgives us, us Christians, all our sins, and He does this daily and richly. Daily He takes us to His fatherly bosom and forgives us all our sins in an overabundance of grace. And hence we also have life and salvation. For where there is forgiveness of sins, there is also life and salvation. Since we have received forgiveness of sins, yea, because our sins are being forgiven every day, every curse and every punishment is far removed from us, and blissfully and peacefully do we rest in the bosom of God and await eternal life, which He will surely give us. " Bless the Lord, O my soul, and forget not all His benefits: who forgiveth all thine iniquities." This is most certainly true.

PRAYER.—O Thou gracious God and Father, how shall I duly thank and praise Thee? That is more than I can do. But, O Lord, I rejoice that by Thy Word and the Holy Spirit Thou hast made me a member of the noble and blessed order of those to whom Thou daily and richly forgives all sins for Christ's sake. Now I, a poor sinner, have peace and shall be saved. Abba, Father, let me at all times, and wherever I may be, belong to this Christian Church. Amen.

Hymn 415, 2.

MONDAY.

In whom (Christ) we have the redemption through His blood, the forgiveness of sins, according to the riches of His grace.—Eph. 1, 7.

My dear Christian, dost thou know how the matter really stands concerning that most precious gift of God, the forgiveness of sins?—It is given us by the *grace* of God; for, surely, we have no claim or title whatever to the forgiveness of sins; and, to be sure, it is given us out of the great and inexhaustible riches of the grace of God, for we are very grievous transgressors. And it is given us *for Christ's sake.* Not merely from a gracious impulse does God forgive sins; that would be against His righteousness and against His holiness, which is a flaming fire, as well as against His truthfulness, the truthfulness of His Word, in which He threatens to punish transgressors. But in Christ, our Savior, who bore our sin and our punishment as our Substitute, we have the redemption through His blood; and this redemption consists in this that God forgives us our sins. And by the *Gospel* of the grace of God in Christ the forgiveness of sins is made known unto us, yea, and offered unto us. And through *faith,* through faith in this gracious Word of God concerning Christ and concerning the redemption and the forgiveness of sins in Him, we receive and accept the forgiveness of sins. And thus we have it.—This is how the matter stands concerning the forgiveness of sins, and not otherwise. And now, Christian, take freely! The grace of God is rich unto thee also. Christ is also thy Savior. The Gospel is meant also for thee. God wants thee, too, to say rejoicingly: "I believe the forgiveness of sins."

PRAYER.—I thank Thee, most merciful God, that of Thy pure grace for Christ's sake Thou dost at all times through the Gospel offer me forgiveness of sins, that treasure which alone can save me. I have but to take freely, only to believe. Now, then, my God, I pray Thee, give unto me Thy Holy Spirit, that I may not fear nor doubt, but believingly and rejoicingly take the salvation which Thou dost give unto me freely and without price: the forgiveness of my sins. Amen.

Hymn 59, 2.

TUESDAY.

Therefore we conclude that a man is justified by faith, without the deeds of the Law.—Rom. 3, 28.

If a man is not found righteous before the judgment-seat of God, he is damned. But no man can be found righteous before God by the deeds of the Law. For no man can perform even a single deed of the Law that is perfect in the sight of God; much less can he be fully justified before God by the deeds of the Law. So what is to be done? Now God comes and proclaims that man is justified before Him without the deeds of the Law, without merit, yea, in spite of and regardless of all sin and guilt. But this is quite beyond all human conception. How shall a man become righteous before God without the deeds of the Law, without merit, yea, in spite of and regardless of his sins and guilt? God says: "by faith." But how so by faith? by what faith? By that faith which rests on the blessed fact that God forgives sins out of His great mercy, for Christ's sake. Thou knowest that God does this. And now ponder and consider what is meant by the words: God forgives sin. It means: God does not impute sin. If God does not impute sin unto us, then, of course, He declares us—righteous. And it is just this that God does say to us lost and condemned sinners: He forgives us our sins, and thus declares and makes us righteous in His sight, justifies us. And now we must not reject this, but accept it in true faith as a most gracious deliverance. Thus we are righteous in the sight of God by faith, without the deeds of the Law.—This is the true, genuine Christian banner, our standard, following which we shall conquer everything and obtain eternal salvation: "Therefore we conclude that a man is justified by faith, without the deeds of the Law." Let this also be thy faith.

PRAYER.—Lord, my God, because Thou sayest it unto me, therefore will I believe it, and cling to it in life and death, that I am justified in Thy sight by faith, without the deeds of the Law. Trusting in this, will I depart, and lifting up my head before Thy judgment-throne, I shall say: Thou, O God, hast forgiven my sins unto me and thereby declared me righteous. I pray Thee, my God, keep me in this faith which alone will save me. Amen.

Hymn 415, 3.

WEDNESDAY.

Who of God is made unto us . . . Righteousness.—1 Cor. 1, 30.

In ourselves we have no righteousness whereby we might stand before God. But Christ is made Righteousness unto us by God. We must say: Considering myself, I confess that I am all unrighteousness; but Christ is my Righteousness. God has made Christ our Righteousness. How are we to understand this? Christ is *for us;* He is our Substitute. Christ has fulfilled the Law of God perfectly—for us. Christ, though He knew no sin, nevertheless was made sin by God—for us. (2 Cor. 5, 21.) On Christ lay all the chastisement for sin—for us. (Is. 53, 5.) Christ did all that the Law of God demands of us—for us. Christ suffered all with which the Law of God threatens us—for us. Christ fulfilled all the righteousness demanded by the Law of God—for us. God did this in His great mercy. So Christ was made Righteousness unto us by God. So Christ is our Righteousness. A blessed exchange was made: Christ was made sin for us, we are made the righteousness of God in Him. (2 Cor. 5, 21.) Surely, the righteousness of Christ is valid before God, and the righteousness of Christ belongs to us. Thou must firmly believe, my dear Christian, that the righteousness wherewith thou mayest stand in the sight of God is not thy own, but that of another—the righteousness of Christ. This God gives to thee; it belongs to thee; thou must apprehend it in true faith. Thus thou mayest stand before God. Thus all thy sins are taken away from thee and gone; they are forgiven thee for Christ's sake, and pure righteousness, spotless, blameless, perfect righteousness, envelopes thee, as it were,— the righteousness of Christ. If thou firmly apprehendest this in true faith, thou wilt nevermore fear nor despair. Then thou at all times possessest that perfect righteousness wherewith thou mayest stand before God.

PRAYER.—O God, how graciously didst Thou help me: Thou didst make Christ Righteousness unto me. Christ is my jewel, Christ is my glorious dress, Christ is the robe of my righteousness. Grant that through the gracious operation of Thy Holy Spirit I may put on Christ, by believing in Him, and wrap myself in Christ, and hide myself in Him. And for Christ's sake, O righteous God, declare me, a sinner, righteous! Amen.

Hymn 83, 6.

THURSDAY.

God was in Christ, reconciling the world unto Himself, not imputing their trespasses unto them; and hath committed unto us the word of reconciliation.—2 Cor. 5, 19.

"*God was in Christ*"; for Christ was and is God, who became man. "*And reconciled the world unto Himself.*" God has reconciled the world unto Himself through Christ. As far as God is concerned, the old relations of love that obtained before the fall are reestablished. The righteous wrath of God, which had been kindled against sinful and ungodly mankind, was appeased. All punishment is done away with. God is reconciled. *"Not imputing their trespasses unto them."* Since God is reconciled unto the world, He, self-evidently, no longer imputes their trespasses unto them. How could He be reconciled and still impute sin? *"And hath committed unto us the word of reconciliation."* Through His Word, which He has committed unto us, God now informs us that He was in Christ, reconciling the world unto Himself, not imputing their trespasses unto them. And God not merely informs us of such reconciliation, but He also offers it to us, and actually presents it to us, chartered and sealed, through His Word. And now we must be reconciled to God; we must accept this reconciliation. Yes, and God most kindly invites and with a loving heart and powerfully persuades us by means of His Word, and the Holy Spirit graciously operating through this Word, to accept this reconciliation. He that accepts it has it, and in time and eternity he enjoys its blessed fruits. He that rejects it remains under the wrath of God by his own fault and is lost forever.

PRAYER.—Great God, what wondrous compassion Thou hast bestowed upon me! Me, the sinner and Thy enemy, Thou hast reconciled unto Thyself, and hast not imputed my sins unto me, but unto Christ. And unto this reconciliation Thou dost invite me through Thy Word and Holy Spirit. Help me, O Lord, that I may always follow this gracious invitation, and through faith rest in Thy fatherly bosom. Amen.

Hymn 311, 4.

FRIDAY.

But to him that worketh not, but believeth on Him that justifieth the ungodly, his faith is counted for righteousness. Rom. 4, 5.

He that worketh, he that in any way worketh, in order thus to stand righteous in the sight of God, he—note this well!—renounces the grace of God and lays claim to salva-

Week of the Eighth Sunday After Trinity.

tion not as a gift of grace, but as a gift which God is in duty bound to give him in remuneration for his works. He that is so blinded as to work in this way, in defiance and derision of the entire Word of God, shall receive wages very different from salvation. "For as many as are of the works of the Law are under the curse." (Gal. 3, 10.) "But to him that worketh not, but believeth on Him that justifieth the ungodly"— Stop! What does this mean: "that justifieth the ungodly"? This means that God was in Christ, reconciling the world, the ungodly world, unto Himself, thus not imputing their trespasses unto them. Now, then: "To him that worketh not, but believeth on Him that justifieth the ungodly, his faith is counted for righteousness." What does this mean: "to him his faith is counted for righteousness"? It means this: To him this is counted for righteousness what the Word of Reconciliation proclaims and communicates unto him, namely, that God in Christ reconciled all the world unto Himself and therefore no longer imputed their trespasses unto them:—this gracious deed of God, which he accepts in faith, on the strength of the Word of God, is counted unto him for righteousness. The believer accepts for himself what God in Christ did for the whole ungodly world, namely, that God in Christ justified them in His sight. Thus, through such faith, he has the righteousness of God, and now in fact he is the beloved child of God and is saved. Therefore, do not thou work, but believe in Him that justifieth the ungodly. Then shall thy faith be counted unto thee for righteousness. And thou shalt obtain salvation.

PRAYER.—My Lord and God, grant grace unto me, Thy child, to be diligent, indeed, in good works, but nevermore to presume that by such miserable works of mine I might become righteous before Thee. Help me to live and to die in the right faith which alone justifies me, in the firm assurance that in Christ Thou hast justified the ungodly, and hence also me. Amen.

Hymn 307, 3.

SATURDAY.

By grace are ye saved, through faith; and that not of yourselves: it is the gift of God; not of works, lest any man should boast.—Eph. 2, 8. 9.

We Christians are saved. We are rescued from damnation, and salvation is given us, the fullness of which we shall soon enjoy. But we are saved by grace, yes, indeed, by grace, through faith, through faith in Christ. And this is in no wise of ourselves; there was nothing whatsoever in us, nor did we do anything for the sake of which God would have been moved to save us. It is wholly and solely the gift of God, a gracious gift of God. Not because of our works were we saved. None of us can boast of any work for the sake of which God would have been moved to save him. Hence also our faith is not a work of which we might boast. No, faith is but the spiritual hand given and even opened by God, into which He has put the righteousness and salvation which He so mercifully gave us for Christ's sake, that we might have, hold, and enjoy it. In the very moment indeed in which faith receives these free gifts of grace and is conscious of their possession, it begins to be the fruitful mother of all good works; for love, which is the fulfilling of the Law, is at once conceived in it. But though we become righteous before God and are saved by faith, it nevertheless is in no wise a work which might have moved God to give us righteousness and salvation. No one should say: I believe, and *therefore* God justifies and saves me, but this is what all should say: God gives me righteousness and salvation solely by grace, and therefore I believe. "For by grace are ye saved, through faith; and that not of yourselves: it is the gift of God; not of works, lest any man should boast."

PRAYER.—O Lord, my God, I rest assured of Thy grace, and depend upon it to save me. I depend upon Thy grace in Christ Jesus, my Lord, which Thou givest unto me through Thy Word. I depend upon nothing in or of myself. Even my faith is frail and miserable through my own fault. Do not let the spark of faith within my heart be extinguished, O

Lord, but preserve and strengthen my faith. Let it be a vessel that holds Thy grace. Amen.

Hymn 311, 5.

Week of the Ninth Sunday After Trinity.

SUNDAY.

I know whom I have believed, and am persuaded that He is able to keep that which I have committed unto Him against that day.—2 Tim. 1, 12.

We have heard so much about believing. What is meant by *believing?*—In order to believe in God through Christ Jesus, our Lord, it is necessary, first, to have a *knowledge* of the Gospel. One must be able to say: "I know whom I have believed." For "how shall they believe in Him of whom they have not heard?" (Rom. 10, 14.) And then one must *accept* the Gospel *as true.* He that imagines the Gospel to be a lie naturally cannot believe. "He that believeth not the Son shall not see life, but the wrath of God abideth on him." (John 3, 36.) But, Christian, the devils surely have a knowledge of the Gospel, and they also hold it to be true; and still they do not, in the true sense of the word, believe. "The devils also believe, and tremble." (James 2, 19.) Therefore the third and foremost, the most essential part of faith is *confidence,* trusting with firm confidence in that God whom the blessed Gospel has taught us to know. If thou canst say: "I know in whom I have believed, and am persuaded that He is able to keep that which I have committed unto Him against that day"; if thou canst say: I know God from the Gospel; I know His grace which is in Christ Jesus, my Lord; I know what by grace, through Christ, He has committed unto me, and am persuaded that through it He shall on that great day save me, a poor sinner,—then thou truly believest. May God give thee such faith and keep thee in such faith by grace, through His Word and the Holy Spirit!

PRAYER.—I thank Thee, O Lord, that through Thy Word Thou hast plainly revealed Thy divine majesty and Thy gracious will toward me, a sinner, as well as what Thy great mercy has prompted Thee to do toward my salvation and that of the whole world. Enlighten me, I pray Thee, with Thy Holy Spirit, that I may firmly trust in Thy bountiful grace, relying and depending upon it in life and death,— through Jesus Christ, Thy dear Son, my only Savior. Amen.

Hymn 120, 4.

MONDAY.

I am persuaded that neither death, nor life, nor angels, nor principalities, nor powers, nor things present, nor things to come, nor height, nor depth, nor any other creature, shall be able to separate us from the love of God which is in Christ Jesus, our Lord.—Rom. 8, 38. 39.

Mark well how confident the Apostle Paul was of possessing the grace and love of God and of obtaining eternal salvation! His was a confidence that excluded all doubt whatsoever. So unshakable was his confidence that many expositors of Scripture think he must have had a special revelation. But just see what he said! Does he speak only of himself? Does he not say "us"? Does he, therefore, not speak of all Christians? Certainly, he does. Every Christian may and must be just as sure of the forgiveness of his sins and of eternal salvation as St. Paul was. Every *Christian,* I say. I am not speaking of unbelievers. And what must such confidence be founded on? *On God's Word and promise.* God says that for Christ's sake He daily and richly forgives all thy sins unto thee. Thou knowest that God says so. Does God lie? That is impossible. Hence thou mayest and must be altogether sure of the forgiveness of thy sins. And where there is forgiveness of sins, there is also life and salvation. Hence thou mayest and must be altogether sure of thy salvation. But, sayest thou, what if I fall from faith? Indeed, if thou fallest from faith, thou art lost. But God has promised and assured thee that He will keep thee in true faith. "Ye are kept by the power of God through faith unto salvation," says the Holy Ghost. (1 Pet. 1, 5.) Read once more what the Holy Spirit has inspired Paul to write in the text above. So thou must be altogether sure, my dear Christian, that God will preserve thy faith. Such confidence, alas! is often clouded within us by the diffidence of our flesh. But always consider again the Word and promise of God. Then this confidence will ever again burst forth like a light; thou wilt always regain the assurance of the forgiveness of thy sins and of thy salvation.

PRAYER.—My God! It is certain that for Christ's sake Thou dost forgive my sins and dost save me. For Thou sayest it and promisest it. Therefore, give unto me, I beseech Thee, Thy Holy Spirit, that I may have full assurance of the same. Help me to have regard to nothing else than solely to Thy sure Word and promise. And comfort me and fill my soul with joy over this blessed assurance, so that I may gladly walk in newness of life. Amen.

Hymn 356.

TUESDAY.

I will run the way of Thy commandments when Thou shalt enlarge my heart.—Ps. 119, 32.

No man as he is by nature delights in doing according to God's commandments; neither, indeed, can he; for sin has taken possession of him. But it is quite different with one who is justified through faith in Christ. Such a one knows that he is loved by God. And knowing that God loves him, he realizes his sinfulness all the more. In the light of the loving grace of God his sinfulness appears so much darker unto him. And that pains him. And notwithstanding all this, he knows that God loves him, and that He sees and desires to see nothing upon him but the righteousness of Christ. And his heart becomes enlarged in view of this great and wonderful grace of God. His heart is filled with consolation, and being comforted, it opens wide toward God and the love of God towards him; and in a heart thus comforted and opened the love to God is born, the love towards Him who loved him first. And then, yes, then man begins to run the way of God's commandments. "I will run the way of Thy commandments when Thou shalt enlarge my heart." Then there is no need of the rod of the Law, no need of an oppressor, of any compulsion. Within the justified sinner there is a new law, the law of love to God; he is mightily impelled by the Spirit of Christ. And the love of Christ constraineth him—it is a sweet compulsion—to do what is well pleasing to Christ, to God. The Law of God no longer needs come to him from without, as a stranger, with insistent demands; no, it is written in his very heart and mind: he wants to, he really, truly, wants to do it. Justification through faith in Christ is the means, the only means, and the strong and sure means, through which man becomes desirous of doing according to God's commandments. My dear Christian, dost thou know this from experience? Dost thou know what this means: "I will run the way of Thy commandments when Thou shalt enlarge my heart"?

PRAYER.—O Lord, this is my life and my only consolation, that Thou daily and richly forgivest all my sins and thus justifiest me, a poor sinner, for Jesus Christ's sake. How great, O God, is Thy love and Thy compassion, which Thou hast vouchsafed me to know through Thy Word and Holy Ghost. My poor heart can hardly realize it. But, O Lord, I love Thee and delight in Thy commandments after the inward man. O that I might love and serve Thee better! Help Thy poor child, Thou faithful God, help me! Amen.

Hymn 348, 5.

WEDNESDAY.

The just shall live by faith.—Rom. 1, 17.

Man is justified before God and saved, not through any *work, action, or conduct, but alone through faith in Jesus Christ.* This is what our text teaches. This article of justification and salvation through faith is the chief article, the very heart of Christian doctrine. This is the only saving faith. This, therefore, is the faith of all the children of God, both before and after Christ's incarnation. This is what Adam believed, and Abraham, and David, and many thousands. This the robber on the cross believed, and Peter, and Luther, and many thousands. This is the doctrine of the Prophets and of the Apostles. By this article of faith the Christian Church distinguishes itself from all false religions. By this faith all true Christians distinguish themselves from false Christians. If thou wouldst be a Christian and be righteous in the sight of God, and obtain eternal salvation, thou must hold fast to this article. If, as a Christian, thou wouldst be a useful member of God's kingdom, thou must do thy utmost to have this article retained and preached in the Church in all its purity. As thy eye cannot bear to harbor a grain of dust, just so impossible must it be for thee to suffer this article to be darkened, obscured, attacked, or injured in the slightest degree. By this article alone all true glory is given to God. By this article alone true and enduring comfort is afforded poor sinners who long for salvation. It is awful how furiously Satan rages against this article through his servants, the false teachers. It is awful how people, both young and old (pity on them!) are led away from this faith. Hold fast, hold fast to this blessed truth, that thou art justified before God, and wilt be saved, not through any work, action, or conduct of thine, but solely through faith in Jesus Christ. " The just shall live by faith."

PRAYER.—Lord, this is Thy word of grace for all sinners from the beginning until the end of the world: " The just shall live by faith." This I will wrap about me, as it were; I will hold fast to it; I will die trusting in it, yea, and appear before Thy judgment-seat and obtain life everlasting. So help me, O faithful God! Let this Word be proclaimed to the end of days, Thou merciful God! Amen.

Hymn 311, 2.

THURSDAY.

Many of them that sleep in the dust of the earth shall awake, some to everlasting life and some to shame and to everlasting contempt.—Dan. 12, 2.

Everything, yea, everything, and for all eternity, depends upon the forgiveness of sins, upon justification. Think of the great day of resurrection, of which thou hast heard so much particularly in the Easter season. Then shall the many, the innumerable many that sleep in the dust of the earth, awake. Some to everlasting life; those, namely, who have been justified through faith in Christ. Some to shame and to everlasting contempt; those who died with their sins unforgiven, in unbelief. God-fearing Lazarus was carried by the angels into Abraham's bosom. The ungodly rich man was cast into hell and torment. The justified shall rise with glorified bodies. (Phil. 3, 21.) Those whose sins were retained shall be an abhorring unto all flesh. (Is. 66, 24.) The justified shall awake unto everlasting life. The unjustified shall awake unto everlasting shame and contempt; and "their worm shall not die, neither shall their fire be quenched." (Is. 66, 24; Mark 9, 44.) O Christian, always think of the awakening on the day of resurrection! At any moment thou mayest fall asleep in death. Then the awaking! How unutterably awful it must be when one awakes unto shame and everlasting contempt! How glorious beyond measure it shall be when thou awakest unto everlasting life! Christian, every evening let forgiveness of sins cover thee; every morning wrap the robe of salvation about thee, the righteousness of Christ. Then, then, shalt thou awaken unto life everlasting.

PRAYER.—My Lord and Savior, Thou dost offer me the forgiveness of sins: I accept it; Thou dost give me the robe of Thy righteousness: I put it on. So will I go to sleep when my last hour cometh; so will I awaken when Thy hour cometh. So will I enter eternal life. Lord, let me never fall away from true faith and the comfort it gives. Amen.

Hymn 326, 1. 6.

FRIDAY.

I give unto them eternal life.—John 10, 28.

Thus says Jesus concerning His sheep, the believers. And what do the Scriptures teach concerning eternal life? They teach that the souls of all believers are with Christ the moment they leave the body in death, that body and soul shall be reunited on the day of resurrection, and that the believers shall thus live with Christ in everlasting joy and glory. To the dying thief the Savior said: "Verily I say unto thee, To-day shalt thou be with Me in paradise." (Luke 23, 43.) Dying Stephen said to the Savior: "Lord Jesus, receive my spirit!" (Acts 7, 59.) And the voice from heaven said: "Blessed are the dead that die in the Lord from henceforth." (Rev. 14, 13.) And concerning the eternal consummation which the last day shall usher in, when all the dead shall rise, the Apostle says by inspiration of the Holy Ghost: "Beloved, now are we the sons of God, and it doth not yet appear what we shall be; but we know that, when He shall appear, we shall be like Him; for we shall see Him as He is." (1 John 3, 2.) In the night in which He entered upon His suffering, the Savior prayed: "Father, I will that they also whom Thou hast given Me be with Me where I am, that they may behold my glory which Thou hast given Me." (John 17, 24.) And through David the Holy Ghost prophesies concerning eternal life: "In Thy presence is fullness of joy; at Thy right hand there are pleasures forevermore." (Ps. 16, 11.)—Ah, my dear Christian, let us always cling to these words of life, and trust in them, "though the night of death be fraught still with many an anxious thought." May these and similar words of life awaken in us a fervent longing for the life everlasting! Let us hold fast to the forgiveness of sins through faith in Jesus Christ, through which alone, but most assuredly so, we shall inherit eternal life. Ah, yes, let us hold fast to the forgiveness of sins; then we need not be anxiously concerned about obtaining everlasting life.

PRAYER.—Lord, my God, forgive my sins unto me for Christ's sake; forgive my sins unto me until I shall depart this life. Amen. I know Thou wilt do it. And then give unto me eternal life! Amen. I know Thou wilt do it. O Lord, Thou beckonest me, Thou callest me through Thy Word unto life everlasting. And Thou wilt not disappoint me. O no, Lord, Thou abidest by Thy promise. Amen.

Hymn 556, 3.

SATURDAY.

Blessed be the God and Father of our Lord Jesus Christ, who hath blessed us with all spiritual blessings in heavenly places in Christ: according as He hath chosen us in Him before the foundation of the world, that we should be holy and without blame before Him in love: having predestinated us into the adoption of children by Jesus Christ to Himself, according to the good pleasure of His will, to the praise of the glory of His grace, wherein He has made us accepted in the Beloved.—Eph. 1, 3-6.

We know of a certainty that God, in great mercy, with great earnestness, and with great power, through the Gospel and His Holy Spirit seeks to convert and to save every one who hears the Gospel. Hence we know of a certainty that it is man's own fault exclusively if he is not converted and saved. And with like certainty we know that when man is converted and saved, this is exclusively by the grace and working of God, without any merit or coworking on the part of man. "For by grace are ye saved, through faith; and that not of yourselves: it is the gift of God; not of works, lest any man should boast. For we are His workmanship, created in Christ Jesus unto good works, which God hath before ordained that we should walk in them." (Eph. 2, 8-10.) And from the text at the head of our lesson we learn that we Christians, whom in this present time He has through the Gospel, by grace, made His believing children, and whom He will bring to salvation, have from eternity been chosen and predestinated by God unto such adoption of children, and that by grace alone, for Christ's sake, according to the good pleasure of His will. Yes, indeed, when a sinner is converted and saved, it is due exclusively to the grace and working of God, and not to any merit or coworking whatsoever on the part of man. What God in this present time works and effects in us by grace alone, He has determined to do from eternity, moved thereto solely by His grace. How sure we may and should be of our salvation! God has chosen and predestinated us thereto from eternity. And since Thou dost now experience the gracious working of God in thee, my dear Christian, thou must also be confident that from eternity God has chosen and predestinated thee unto salvation.

PRAYER.—Lord, my God, it is all Thy grace. By Thy grace Thou hast drawn me unto Thee and made me Thy child. By Thy grace, according to Thy promise, Thou wilt keep me in the faith and give me eternal bliss. By Thy grace Thou hast from eternity chosen and unalterably predestinated me, a poor sinner, unto the adoption of children and unto salvation. Complete Thy gracious work in me, O Lord, and keep me in true faith, and let me inherit eternal life for Jesus Christ's sake. Amen, Thou wilt do it. Amen.

Hymn 348, 2.

Week of the Tenth Sunday After Trinity.

SUNDAY.

Lord, teach us to pray.—Luke 11, 1.

We want to learn to pray. And God will teach us in His Word.—Prayer is an act of worship performed by the children of God. When God's children pray, they approach their heavenly Father, and speak to Him, talk with Him, and bring their petitions before Him, and offer up praise and thanks to Him. Prayer is offered both with our hearts and our lips. Prayer is the word of the mouth and the meditation of the heart. (Ps. 19, 14.) To speak with the mouth only, while being unheedful of the words spoken, is babbling, and not prayer.—God hears prayer. He hears even the faintest sigh of the heart. "Lord, Thou hast heard the desire of the humble; Thou wilt prepare their heart; Thou wilt cause Thine ear to hear." (Ps. 10, 17.) Indeed, what does God say? He says: "It shall come to pass that before they call, I will answer and while they are yet speaking, I will hear." (Is. 65, 24.) God hears and answers our prayer in advance. And never think, my dear Christian, that God desires thee to make many words and to use a very fine language. The Savior says: "When ye pray, use not vain repetitions, as the heathen do; for they think that they shall be heard for their much speaking. Be not ye therefore like unto them; for your Father knoweth what things ye have need of before ye ask Him." (Matt. 6, 7. 8.) We are God's children, and we are merely little children, however old we may be. So let us speak to our Father just as little children do. The simpler, the more childlike we address Him, the better He likes it. Every Christian can pray, may be he ever so unlettered a person; and the learned must forget his learning when he prays.

PRAYER.—Dear Heavenly Father, Thou great God, I thank Thee that through Jesus Christ I am Thy child, and dare pray unto Thee, and tell Thee all, take all my plaints and my petitions to Thee in prayer. And Thou wilt most graciously hear me, being as kind to me as a father to his child. Dear Father in heaven, grant me Thy Holy Spirit, that He may open my lips and my heart, so that at all times I may come to Thee and pray to Thee, Thou great Fount of all grace. Amen.

Hymn 67, 3.

MONDAY.

Call upon Me in the day of trouble: I will deliver thee, and thou shalt glorify Me.—Ps. 50, 15.

What should induce us to pray? What should encourage us poor, miserable sinners, but who, at the same time, are the children of God, to pray, yea, what should give us even a most earnest desire to do so? In the first place, God's command. God demands it of us. He says: "Call upon Me!" This is not a hard and harsh command, however, but a most kind and gracious one. And we should be glad that God thus commands us to pray, and we should say to Him: "When Thou saidst, Seek ye my face, my heart said unto Thee, Thy face, Lord, will I seek." (Ps. 27, 8.) Secondly, God's promise should induce us to pray. He says: "I will deliver thee." And Jesus says: "Ask, and it shall be

given you; seek, and ye shall find; knock, and it shall be
opened unto you." (Matt. 7, 7.) Could He have given a
kinder and more assuring promise? Ought we, therefore,
not to pray? St. James is right in saying: "Ye have not
because ye ask not." (James 4, 2.) Thirdly, our need
should induce us to pray. "Call upon Me in the day of
trouble," says God. Our need is so great and manifold.
We are in greater need than we know or even faintly imagine. We are in need of divine help over against the devil,
the world, and our own flesh. Our body and soul both are
in need. We are in need respecting both this present time
and eternity. There can be no greater need than that in
which we are every day. And we are entirely unable to
help ourselves. Therefore God says: "Call upon Me in
the day of trouble: I will deliver thee, and thou shalt glorify
Me." Should that not induce us to pray?

PRAYER.—I thank and praise Thee, O gracious God,
that Thou commandest me to call upon Thee in my need and
helplessness. And Thou dost promise to deliver me. O
God, let me not stand afar off, neither in dread of Thee nor
in self-reliance, but through Thy Holy Spirit grant me
grace to flee to Thee, seeking help alone with Thee, who
art not only almighty, but art also my gracious Father
through Jesus Christ, my Savior. Amen.

Hymn 515, 1. 2. 7.

TUESDAY.

*Thou shalt worship the Lord, thy God, and Him alone
shalt thou serve.*—Matt. 4, 10.

To whom should we pray? Surely, thou art not in doubt
about this. We should pray only to the true God, Father,
Son, and Holy Ghost. He, the Triune God, is the only true
God. And we have learned to know Him from His Word.
Everything that is called God beside Him is an idol, an imaginary, a man-made god. Wherever such an idol is worshiped, as among the Jews, the Unitarians, and the lodges,
thou must not take part in such sinful worship. "Nonsense!" some say, "why, there is but one God." They mean

to say that one may also pray to the so-called god of the people just mentioned. 'Tis true, there is but one God. But this one God is the Triune God. Whatever else is held to be a god is an idol. Is it right for thee to pray to idols, to take part in idol worship? Nor must thou call upon the holy angels. Though they are highly exalted, they are but ministering spirits who carry out God's will and command. They cannot hear and grant prayer. David by the Holy Spirit says unto God: "O Thou that hearest prayer, unto Thee shall all flesh come." (Ps. 65, 2.) And what are we to think of the invocation of saints as practiced in the Roman-Catholic Church? Listen to what the prophet says to God: "Doubtless Thou art our Father, though Abraham be ignorant of us, and Israel acknowledge us not. Thou, O Lord, art our Father, our Redeemer; Thy name is from everlasting." (Is. 63, 16.) The saints in heaven, the real saints, are ignorant of us and acknowledge us not and hear us not. And the saints of the Pope's making are nothing. We should pray to God alone, who is our Father and our Redeemer and our Comforter: He hears and grants our prayer; He is almighty and most gracious unto us.

PRAYER.—O Thou true, gracious, and loving God, Father, Son, and Holy Ghost, who hast revealed Thyself to me so graciously unto my salvation, and who so kindly invitest me to call upon Thee: why should I address my prayer to any one but to Thee alone? Far be it from me to do so! Do but grant me grace to address Thee with full confidence, and unceasingly seek Thy grace and help, firmly believing that Thou wilt surely hear my prayer. Amen.

Hymn 20, 4.

WEDNESDAY.

Be careful for nothing, but in everything, by prayer and supplication, with thanksgiving, let your request be made known unto God.—Phil. 4, 6.

What should we ask for in our prayers?—Dear Christian, dost thou not see what God says? Instead of caring and fretting and worrying, make thy request known unto God in everything by prayer and supplication, thanking Him with all thy heart for being thy gracious God, who desires thy prayer. Ask God for everything in prayer. Nothing is excepted. Thou mayest ask God for the very greatest of things. Nothing is too great for Him to give. And thou mayest ask God for the most trifling things. Nothing is too small or trifling for thy dear, loving heavenly Father to consider. Above all things, however, ask God for the great and glorious spiritual blessings which are necessary for thy spiritual welfare, for thy eternal salvation. Every Christian knows that this is of prime importance. And also ask God for the temporal blessings which are necessary for the preservation of this life. But thou must act as a loving child of God should, and not in presumptuous ignorance, perchance, ask God for things that conflict with the glory of God and with thy temporal and spiritual welfare. Jesus said: " What things soever ye desire, when ye pray, believe that ye receive them, and ye shall have them." (Mark 11, 24.) But canst thou truly believe that God will give thee something that would not promote His divine glory nor thy temporal and spiritual welfare? God's glory is advanced only when He gives us really good gifts. O Christian, be careful for nothing, but in everything, by prayer and supplication, with thanksgiving, let thy request be made known unto God. But always retain a childlike mind, which firmly believes that God knows best what is truly good and wholesome for thee. —We shall hear more of this to-morrow.

PRAYER.—I thank Thee, my dear Heavenly Father, that through the gracious promise Thou hast given Thou dost rid me of each and every care, and dost tell me to call upon Thee, and to trust that Thou wilt give me what is best for me in time and eternity. Give unto me, O kind Father, the Spirit of adoption, that I may confidently and joyfully entrust my fate entirely to Thee, always looking up to Thee, always calling upon Thee; for Thou art my most gracious God through Jesus Christ, my Savior. Amen.

Hymn 395, 1. 2.

THURSDAY.

Father, if Thou be willing, remove this cup from me; nevertheless, not my will, but Thine, be done.—Luke 22, 42.

We must observe a distinction in offering up our prayers. When asking for things that are necessary for our salvation, we must simply ask without affixing any condition to our prayer. And God will surely grant our prayer, for He has promised to do so. Our Lord and Savior says: "If ye, then, being evil, know how to give good gifts unto your children, how much more shall your heavenly Father give the Holy Spirit to them that ask Him?" (Luke 11, 13.) And "this is the confidence that we have in Him, that, if we ask anything according to His will, He heareth us." (1 John 5, 14.) It is otherwise when we ask for something that is not absolutely necessary for our salvation, and something that God has not expressly promised us. Faith of such high degree as Paul, for instance, or even Luther possessed, and particular gifts of the Holy Ghost, are precious spiritual gifts indeed, but not absolutely necessary for our salvation, and the Holy Spirit "divides unto every man severally as He will." (1 Cor. 12, 11.) The same thing holds true with regard to immediate deliverance from spiritual temptation or bodily affliction. Is this necessary for our salvation? On the contrary, is not such temptation and affliction wholesome for us? And thinkest thou that the constant enjoyment of good health, good fortune, and an abundance of this world's goods is always wholesome for us and our loved ones, or even necessary for our salvation? When asking for such things,—and surely thou mayest do so,—then learn of Jesus, the very best of teachers. When in the Garden of Gethsemane He had to drink that cup of bitterest soul-agony, He prayed most fervently, indeed, that this cup might be removed from Him, but He added: "Father, if Thou be willing, remove this cup from me; nevertheless, not my will, but Thine, be done." Thus thou, too, must pray in all matters not necessary for thy salvation. Leave it to the will of thy heavenly Father, who dearly loves thee, and who surely desires thy salvation, whether, and when, and how many of these things He wishes to give thee.

PRAYER.—My dear Heavenly Father, Thou faithful God, I know of a certainty that Thou dearly lovest me and desirest my salvation, and profusely and abundantly givest unto me all things necessary for my salvation. For this I thank Thee with all my heart. Give unto me, dear Father, Thy Holy Spirit, that I may be willing to leave everything else to Thy loving-kindness and Thy divine wisdom, firmly believing that with tender love and faithfulness Thou wilt keep me and lovingly take care of me, until Thou wilt gather me unto the community of Thy elect in heaven, who praise and glorify Thee in all eternity. Amen.

Hymn 383, 1.

FRIDAY.

Because ye are sons, God hath sent forth the Spirit of His Son into your hearts, crying, Abba, Father!—Gal. 4, 6.

Those who do not believe in our dear Savior Jesus Christ cannot truly pray, nor in a manner well pleasing unto God. For they neither know nor accept the grace and love of God which is to be found only in Jesus Christ, and embraced only through faith in Him. They are subject to the wrath of God. How can they truly pray? How can they have the childlike confidence in God necessary for a true prayer? How can their prayer be acceptable and well pleasing unto God?—No, unbelievers cannot pray. But we poor sinners who believe in our Savior Jesus Christ are God's dear children. And God hath sent forth the Spirit of His Son into our hearts, who cries from within us and together with us: "Abba, Father!" We can truly pray, and in a manner well pleasing unto God. We have the grace of God, we are holy and beloved. We always pray *in the name of Jesus Christ.* In all our prayer and supplication we make this plea, that through Jesus Christ we have been reconciled unto God. And from within us and together with us the Holy Spirit always prays and supplicates, the Spirit of our Savior, whom the Savior has sent into our hearts. Thus do we pray with a confidence acceptable unto God. We rely upon, we plead the word of our Savior: "Verily, verily, I say unto you, Whatsoever ye shall ask the Father in my name, He will give it you." (John 16, 23.) We are led by the Spirit of Christ, who is also the Spirit of the Father, to tell our heavenly Father everything, like little children, all our troubles, and always to trust that He will graciously grant our prayer and give us the best and most salutary gifts. Behold, dear Christian, this is true prayer.

PRAYER.—Ah, my Heavenly Father, at all times give me the right teacher to teach me how to pray, Thy Holy Spirit, the Spirit of Thy dear Son, my Savior, that in the name of this my Atoner I may pray unto Thee, and that in true faith and with joyful confidence I may commit myself into Thy outstretched almighty arms. And then hear my prayer, O Father, and richly, abundantly give me all that is good, wholesome, and salutary for me, and fill my poor heart with peace and joy. Amen.

Hymn 67, 6.

SATURDAY.

Pray one for another.—James 5, 16.

Thou must not only pray for thyself, my dear Christian, but also for others. Christians should pray for one another. Since thou shouldst love thy neighbor as thyself, thou shouldst also pray for thy neighbor as for thyself. Pray for thy loved ones, whom God has united with thee by ties of kinship. Pray for thy friends; this is the greatest possible favor thou canst bestow upon them. Pray for thy fellow-Christians, that the grace of God may always abide with them. Pray for him whom thou seest erring. Pray for thy enemy. The Savior says: "Pray for them that despitefully use you and persecute you." (Matt. 5, 44.) If thou prayest for thy enemy, thou wilt surely love him; for thou canst not hate him for whom thou prayest. Do not forget thy preacher, thy pastor, when thou prayest. The Apostle Paul asked for such intercession. (Eph. 6, 19; Col. 4, 3.) And the same Apostle admonishes us to pray "for all men." (1 Tim. 2, 1.)

This is in accord with the gracious will of God that all men be saved and come to the knowledge of truth. There are Christians who make a list of those for whom they wish to pray particularly, and who daily put this list before them when they pray in private. That is a very good thing to do. —But thou must *not* pray for the dead. "It is appointed unto men once to die, but after this the Judgment." (Hebr. 9, 27.) God has judged the dead. Their souls are either with the blessed in heaven or with the damned in hell. It is a violation of the honor of God to pray for the dead. God judges righteously. But pray, *pray,* PRAY for those who are still living, for they still live in the day of salvation.

PRAYER.—Lord, merciful God, who desirest that we, Thy children, pray for one another, pour out upon me, I beseech Thee, the Spirit of love and of prayer, that I may gladly and willingly, diligently and fervently do according to this Thy will, and that I may firmly believe that my intercession is not in vain, but moves Thee most mercifully to have compassion upon my neighbor, for Thou gladly helpest us through Jesus Christ, the world's Savior. Amen.

Hymn 38, 4.

Week of the Eleventh Sunday After Trinity.

SUNDAY.

Pray everywhere.—1 Tim. 2, 8.

Yes, thou mayest pray everywhere. Isaac had gone out to pray in the field at the eventide. (Gen. 24, 63.) To publicly profess his faith, Daniel prayed at the open window of his house three times a day. (Dan. 6, 10.) Jonah prayed to the Lord, his God, from out the fish's belly. (Jonah 2, 1.) Our Savior went up into a mountain apart to pray. (Matt. 14, 23.) The first hundred and twenty disciples of Jesus continued with one accord in prayer and supplication. (Acts 1, 14.) Paul and Silas prayed in prison at midnight. (Acts

16, 25.) Thou mayest pray everywhere. Only, "when thou prayest, thou shalt not be as the hypocrites are; for they love to pray standing in the synagogues and in the corners of the streets, that they may be seen of men. Verily I say unto you," says the Savior, "they have their reward. But thou. when thou prayest, enter into thy closet, and when thou hast shut thy door, pray to thy Father who is in secret; and thy Father who seeth in secret shall reward thee openly." (Matt. 6, 5. 6.) Hence, thy chamber is a good, a very good place for thee to offer your daily prayer. And when prayer is said in public worship or at family devotion, do not be inattentive or listless, but with all thy heart join in the prayer, supplication, thanksgiving, and praise. There is a special promise attached to joint prayer. For Jesus says: "If two of you shall agree on earth as touching anything that they shall ask, it shall be done for them of my Father who is in heaven. For where two or three are gathered together in my name, there am I in the midst of them." (Matt. 18, 19. 20.)

PRAYER.—Gracious God and Father, wherever I may be, Thou art with me, and Thine eye, O Father, seeth me, and Thine ear is inclined to hear what Thy child desireth of Thee. Should I then be mute, and should my heart be closed against Thee? Should I not speak to Thee and call upon Thee as a little child speaks to its mother, asking her for this thing and for that? O Thou Heavenly Father, who dost kindly bow down to me, give me Thy Holy Spirit, that in true childlike fashion I may lift up my heart to Thee through Jesus Christ. Amen.

Hymn 42, 3.

MONDAY.

Pray without ceasing.—1 Thess. 5, 17.

Scoffers would have this text say that Christians should do nothing but pray all the time. But let us tell thee what is meant. When a little child is with its mother, and plays or learns its lesson, or does this or that, does it not always speak with its mother at the same time? Is its little mouth ever long silent? And are there not many things it asks

Week of the Eleventh Sunday After Trinity. 325

for? Dost thou now understand what it means to "pray without ceasing"? Wherever a Christian, a child of God, may be, and whatever he may do, he always knows that he is with his God, and that his God is with him. And so his heart is ever with God, and he has something to say to God all the time or some complaint or some petition to bring before Him, or to give thanks for something. And so our kind and loving God would have us do. "Pray without ceasing." —But a Christian must also have stated hours of the day for his daily prayers. He should say his morning and his evening prayer. He should say grace before and after meal. And once a day, at the very least, he should have private devotions, that is to say, he should read the Bible with devout attention, adding a prayer, or, perchance, a hymn. For should a Christian merely desire to partake of bodily food and not of spiritual food as well, every day? In every Christian household the father or the mother should see to it that family devotions are held every day. These devotions should be short and good, lest, on account of our sinful flesh, we be filled with tedium and disgust. But especially, my dear Christian, when cross and tribulation afflict thee, remember the text: "Lord, in trouble have they visited Thee; they have poured out a prayer when Thy chastening was upon them."—Is. 26, 16.

PRAYER.—Lord God, who art my dearly beloved Father through Jesus Christ, my Savior, give unto me, I beseech Thee, Thy Holy Spirit, that I may pray unto Thee without ceasing as it becometh me, Thy beloved child. Grant me grace to nourish my poor, weak, and sinful soul with Thy Word every day, that it may be kept unto eternal life, and that in this present life it may grow and wax strong in the fear and love of Thee. Amen.

Hymn 40, 6. 7.

TUESDAY.

Our Father who art in heaven.—Matt. 6, 9.

The Lord's Prayer is the best prayer there is, for it has been taught us by Jesus Himself. And Christ instructs us to address God by the name "Father": "Our Father who art in heaven." And what Jesus teaches God teaches. And God would by these words tenderly invite us to believe that He is our true Father, and that we are His true children, so that we may with all boldness and confidence ask Him as dear children ask their dear father. "Behold, what manner of love the Father hath bestowed upon us that we should be called the sons of God!" (1 John 3, 1.) The Father did this through Jesus Christ and for the sake of Jesus Christ, who **is our** Atoner. And He has given us poor sinners His Holy Spirit, who draws us unto Him. And we have not received the spirit of bondage again to fear, as though we were still under the Law that damns us, but we have received the Spirit of adoption whereby we cry: "Abba, Father!" (Rom. 8, 15.) Now what more dost thou want, or what more dost thou wait for, seeing that the most holy God Himself, the entire blessed Trinity, is so lovingly condescending to thee, inviting and entreating thee to pray? God desires to be Thy dear Father, and thou art to be His dear child, **and thou must rely upon Him and ask Him for all things. Now,** do not hesitate! Fall to! Take freely! Be not timid! God knows that thou art a sinner. And still He would have thee call Him Father. So, then, be His child! And if thou lackest many a thing that a child of God ought to have, then do not stand back shyly on that account, but hasten to thy heavenly Father, and ask Him to give it to thee. With thy own power, to be sure, thou canst never acquire it. God must give it, and He will give it.

PRAYER.—O God, how gracious art Thou! Thou wilt be my dear Father, and I am to be Thy dear child. And with all boldness and confidence I am to ask Thee for everything. So, here I am, O Lord! But do Thou always encourage me again, dear Lord, that I may ask Thee for every truly good thing in the name of Jesus Christ. Always draw me into Thy fatherly embrace through Thy Holy Ghost! Amen.

Hymn 396, 1.

WEDNESDAY.

Hallowed be Thy name.—Matt. 6, 9.

This is the first petition which we are to make. We should pray that God's name be hallowed among us. What name of God? Why, the name "Father." We should beseech God to grant us grace to prize it as a sacred and as the very greatest boon there can be that God desires to be our loving Father, and that we may so address Him. We should pray God to write this name Father into our hearts with the fire of His Holy Ghost, so that this blessed truth may ever burn and glow in our hearts: God is my Father! God does this through His Word, His Word of Grace. Therefore we should pray that the Word of God may be taught among us in its truth and purity. We should furthermore pray God to grant us His Holy Spirit, that we may be sincerely glad and rejoice and be grateful for the fact that we are His children, and that as the children of God we may also lead a holy life according to His Word. May God preserve us from false doctrine, which keeps us from learning to truly know God in His great mercy, and, consequently, from having childlike confidence in God! May God preserve us from leading an ungodly life, from leading a life unbecoming a child of God! By false doctrine and an ungodly life the name of God is profaned. "Hallowed be Thy name!" This is and must be the First Petition. God comes to meet us poor sinners in Christ Jesus through His Word and Holy Spirit, and says: I wish to be, and desire to be called, your Father. Then each of us should answer above all things and pray: "Hallowed be Thy name!" Ah, yes, Lord, let me learn to know this, let me comprehend it, let me live and die trusting in this saving truth, that Thou art my Father, and that I am Thy child!

PRAYER.—Lord God, our Father in heaven, we, Thy children, who still are so weak and diffident, beseech Thee to grant us Thy grace, that Thy ineffably sweet name may be hallowed among us not only with our hearts, but in all that we say or do. Grant us Thy Word in its truth and purity, that the light of Thy great mercy may shine ever brighter unto us. Graciously guard us against every false doctrine whereby Thy name is profaned and desecrated, and all ungodly life, whereby Thy name is disgraced. Amen.

Hymn 396, 2.

THURSDAY.

Thy kingdom come!—Matt. 6, 10.

Not the Kingdom of Power is meant, for that comprises all creatures in heaven, earth, and hell. The Kingdom of Grace is meant, and the Kingdom of Glory. That the confines of the Kingdom of Grace may include us, too, that the glory of the Kingdom of Glory may adorn and bless us also, this is what we pray in this Second Petition. This should be our greatest concern and our most earnest prayer, that, while we live in this world, we may belong to the Zion of God, to the flock of Christ, to the one holy Christian Church, the communion of saints, to the true Christendom which He who once was crowned with thorns, but now is crowned with glory, rules with His grace and with His Word of Grace, and the citizens of which are made most willing by the Holy Ghost to kiss His scepter; and we pray that when our earthly life is ended, the angels may carry us where we shall see our Savior's glory and partake of it, and where we shall bask in continuous and unending glory. This will be done when our heavenly Father will give us His Holy Spirit, so that by His grace we believe His holy Word, and lead a godly life, here in time and hereafter in eternity. We also pray that the Holy Ghost may dwell within us constantly, that we may abide steadfast in the true faith and in a holy life, in the fear and love of God, until we shall reach the goal where all the blessed perfections of eternity will adorn and surround us, and be our portion and possession within and without. But we also pray that the Kingdom of Grace may be spread more and more here on earth, and that ever more souls may partake of the blessings of the Kingdom of Glory, and that it may appear soon, yes, soon.

PRAYER.—Lord God, dear Heavenly Father, I beseech Thee, keep me in the Kingdom of Grace of Thy dear Son, our Savior Jesus Christ, through faith in Him, and finally receive me into His blessed Kingdom of Glory. Bring also the wayward and the benighted, and the captives of Satan unto the knowledge of true faith in Christ, complete the number of Thine elect, and let the Kingdom of Glory dawn soon. Amen.

Hymn 396, 3.

FRIDAY.

Thy will be done on earth as it is in heaven.—Matt. 6, 10.

God's will toward us is a good and gracious will. God wants us to be His dear children and to obtain life everlasting. He wants us to live in His kingdom here in time and thereafter in eternity, and therefore to embrace Christ in true faith. Against this good and gracious will the evil counsel and will of the devil, the world, and our flesh rises in revolt. This evil counsel and will does not want us to hallow God's name, nor does it want to let God's kingdom come. We should therefore cry and pray: *Thy* will be done on earth, O Lord, as it is in heaven! In heaven no evil will revolts against God's good will. Hence we pray in this petition that God would break and hinder every evil counsel and will, and strengthen us and preserve us steadfast in His Word and in true faith unto our end. We beseech the almighty and faithful God and Father to come to our aid and oppose the devil, the world, and our flesh for us, so that despite their enmity we may remain His children and obtain eternal salvation. How necessary is this petition! And God will grant it, most assuredly. He has promised to strengthen and preserve us steadfast in His Word and in true faith unto our end. He has said unto us: "Ye are kept by the power of God through faith unto salvation." (1 Pet. 1, 5.) And what is more, He has Himself commanded us to pray thus.—My dear Christian, when viewing the matter rightly, thou must realize that thy most dangerous enemy is thy own depraved flesh. And when God breaks and hinders its evil counsel and will, it will hurt thee, and thou wilt be in tribulation. But be joyful then and patient, knowing that God is fulfilling His good and gracious will in thee; and say: "Thy will be done."

PRAYER.—Dear Heavenly Father, Thou faithful God, I pray Thee, by all means accomplish Thy good and gracious will in me, and break and hinder the evil and contrary will of the devil, the world, and my own flesh. And give me, O Father, Thy Holy Spirit, that at all times I may resign myself to this Thy will, that in all eternity I may praise and glorify Thee, O Father, for Thy great faithfulness. Amen.

Hymn 396, 4.

SATURDAY.

Give us this day our daily bread.—Matt. 6, 11.

How tenderly mindful our heavenly Father is even of our poor body and its wants and needs! His Son, our dear Savior, bids us pray: "Give us this day our daily bread." By "daily bread" everything is meant that belongs to the support and wants of the body. Hence God will give us this if we ask Him in the name of Jesus. Therefore we should not worry, as, alas! we are very prone to do, but we should pray. And we should pray for what we need each day, "this day"; we should not be uneasy about to-morrow. We should become as little children. Do little children worry about their food and raiment? Do they not rather ask their parents for what they need? And hast thou ever heard a child say: Mother, give me something to eat to-morrow? Does a child trouble itself about to-morrow? O let us be artless children of God! But remember, my dear Christian, that thy Savior does not bid thee ask for great abundance or for dainties, but for plain daily bread. This He promises to give thee. And if the thought occurs to thee that even to the wicked, who never pray, God gives, not daily bread alone, but even riches and abundance, then note two things. In the first place, as a child of God, thou surely wishest to receive thy daily bread from the hand of God with prayer and thanksgiving. And besides, may the wicked depend upon it that God will at all times give them their daily bread? By no means. But thou mayest. Hence pray with a childlike heart: "Give us this day our daily bread." And share thy bread with thy needy neighbor.

PRAYER.—Dear Heavenly Father, give me Thy Holy Spirit, that it may be my sole concern to **be and remain** Thy dear child. Then let me diligently perform **my duty** as required by my calling and station, wherein **Thou** hast placed me, and let me always look for my daily bread from Thy fatherly goodness, in no wise burdening my heart with heathenish cares; for Thou art my dear Father, through Jesus Christ, my Savior. Amen.

Hymn 396, 5.

Week of the Twelfth Sunday After Trinity.

SUNDAY.

And forgive us our debts as we forgive our debtors.— Matt. 6, 12.

We daily sin much. This, forsooth, is certain. And we deserve nothing but punishment. And we do not deserve that God should accept and hear our prayers and petitions. But the Son of God, our merciful High Priest, who has atoned for our sin and guilt, bids us, after the manner of children, to go to our heavenly Father every day and pray: "Forgive us our trespasses." And our heavenly Father most assuredly forgives us, and does so with great loving-kindness. And He does not regard our sins, and does not charge them to us, and does not on their account deny our prayer, but graciously gives us all manner of good things. And then our Savior teaches us to promise and to vow that we will also forgive those who trespass against us. If our heavenly Father daily and richly forgives us all our sins, and bestows all manner of blessings upon us, then, surely, we should also heartily forgive and readily do good to those who sin against us. The knowledge of, and faith in, the grace of God, which makes new creatures of us, naturally effects this in us. He that will not forgive his neighbor does not truly know and trust in the grace of God, or has wasted it, as it were, and forgotten it. Such a one cannot obtain forgiveness of God. And if, nevertheless, he prays the Fifth Petition of the Lord's Prayer, he thereby invokes upon himself the wrath of God. For the Fifth Petition reads: "Forgive us our trespasses, as we forgive those who trespass against us."

PRAYER.—Dear Heavenly Father, I pray Thee for Jesus Christ's sake and at His bidding that Thou wouldst not look upon my sins, nor on their account deny my prayer which I offer unto Thee. To be sure, I am worthy of none of the things for which I pray, nor have I deserved them; for I daily sin much, and indeed deserve nothing but punishment. But graciously grant them all to me nevertheless. So will I also heartily forgive and readily do good to those who sin against me, a poor sinner. So help me by the grace of Thy Holy Spirit. Amen.

Hymn 396, 6.

MONDAY.

And lead us not into temptation.—Matt. 6, 13.

There are two kinds of temptation, temptation for good and temptation for evil. Temptation for good is sent by God; temptation for evil comes from the devil, the world, and our flesh. Temptation for good consists in this, that God tries His children in order to purify and strengthen their faith. Thus God tempted Abraham (Gen. 22, 1-19), and thus Jesus tempted the Syrophenician woman (Mark 7, 25-30). Temptation for evil consists in this, that the devil, the world, and our flesh would deceive or seduce us into misbelief, despair, and other great shame and vice. Thus the devil tempted Adam and Eve (Gen. 3, 1-6), our Savior (Matt. 4, 1-11), and Judas Iscariot (John 13, 2). Through such temptation Cain and Judas fell into despair (Gen. 4, 13; Matt. 27, 4. 5), and Peter into the grievous sin of denying his Lord (Luke 22, 54-60). What, now, should be our meaning when we say to our heavenly Father: "Lead us not into temptation"? We should then mean and pray that God would so guard and keep us that the devil, the world, and our flesh may not deceive us, nor seduce us into false faith, or into despair, or into great shame and vice, and that, though we be sorely tempted, we may finally overcome and obtain the victory. And if we pray thus, we shall surely be heard. Hence this petition is for us a powerful and victorious shield and weapon in this poor life, which is so full of temptation.

PRAYER.—Dear Heavenly Father, I cannot in any way, by any power of mine, withstand the temptations with which I am assailed by the devil, the world, and my own depraved flesh. Very soon I am lost. But in the name of Thy dear Son, my Savior, I cry unto Thee, that Thou wouldst guard and keep me in all temptation. And thus, by Thy grace, I am confident that I shall finally overcome, obtain the victory, and through true faith enter eternal life. Amen.
Hymn 396, 7.

TUESDAY.

But deliver us from evil.—Matt. 6, 13.

Dost thou find it easy to bear cross and tribulation? Probably not. Cross and tribulation smarts. We groan beneath it. It seems to us to be an evil; and in itself it is an evil with which we are visited because of sin. And now our dear Savior Jesus Christ comes and bids us pray: "Deliver us from evil." The meaning of the petition is this: First, we should pray that God would keep many evils of body and soul, property and honor aloof from us, though we have well deserved them. Oh, and He does it! Secondly, we should pray that by His Holy Spirit God would help us to bear the cross which He imposes upon us for our benefit gladly and cheerfully, and that He would temper it, and soon take it from us, if such be His holy will. And, lastly, we should pray that finally, when our last hour has come, God would grant us a blessed end, and graciously take us from this vale of tears to Himself in heaven. "There'll be no cross, no smarting, no death, no bitter parting." There we shall be fully delivered from every evil. Thus fortify thyself with this petition, my dear Christian, against every trouble, against the devil, against every evil, against tribulation, against alarm and disgrace, against sadness, woe, and lamentation, against sickness, pain, dismay, against dejection, care, and trepidation, against every evil day. And may the Father's gracious acceptance of thy prayer always cast a comforting light upon thy path, until the blessed light of heaven shall dawn upon thee.

PRAYER.—So then, O my Heavenly Father, deliver me from every evil, for Jesus' sake! Give me Thy Holy Spirit, that I may know with the utmost certainty that every cross with which Thou dost still afflict me is not an evil, but an eternal blessing, and grant me grace to bear it patiently. Ah, my God, in fatherly goodness have compassion on Thy frail child, and deal mercifully with me! And lastly, O my Father, take me far, far away from every evil, into Thy blessed mansions. Amen.

Hymn 396, 8.

WEDNESDAY.

For Thine is the kingdom and the power and the glory forever. Amen.—Matt. 6, 13.

This is the conclusion of the Lord's Prayer. By adding these words we should mean to say to God in childlike simplicity that, being the Lord and King of the kingdom in which we have obtained citizenship, it is He alone with whom we should seek help; that He alone has the power to grant our petitions; and that, likewise, all glory, honor, and praise accruing therefrom shall be His alone. And then we should say: Amen. And this Amen we must not attach to the end of our prayer by force of habit, thoughtlessly, but it must be a conscious, strong, firm, believing Amen. For what is meant by the word "Amen"? Amen means: "Yea, yea, it shall be so." We should be certain that these petitions are acceptable to our Father in heaven, and heard; for He Himself has commanded us so to pray, and has promised to hear us. God says Amen to such petitions, and so we, too, should rejoice in faith and confidently say: Amen, Amen; yea, yea, it shall be so.—Dear Christian, study the Lord's

Prayer, and learn and consider what God bids thee pray therein, and what He thus promises to give thee. Thou wilt find therein an abundance of gifts for which thou mayest ask, and which God will give thee, and which will make thee truly happy and blissful in time and eternity. The Lord's Prayer is an open storehouse, full of treasures, and God shows thee the treasures and says: Ask me for them, and I will surely give them to thee. There open wide thy eyes, thy heart, and thy lips, and ask, and believe, and say: Amen, these treasures are mine! Amen.

PRAYER.—My dear Heavenly Father, I, a poor sinner, thank Thee through Jesus Christ, my Savior, that I may so address Thee. Write this Thy name Father into my heart by Thy Word and Thy Spirit. Let me be in Thy kingdom, here in time and hereafter in eternity. This is Thy gracious and good will; let this will be done in me. Also give me my morsel of bread. And graciously forgive all my sins, and grant me grace to gladly forgive those who sin against me. And let me not fall into temptation. And deliver me from evil at all times, and finally from each and every evil. Amen, my Father, Thou wilt surely do this. Amen.

Hymn 396, 9.

THURSDAY.

It is the power of God unto salvation to every one that believeth.—Rom. 1, 16.

Our Lord Jesus Christ by His holy, precious blood has purchased for us forgiveness of sins, life, and salvation, and also the Holy Ghost to kindle faith in us. These treasures of His grace He has laid down in the *Gospel;* and through it they are given to us. Thus the Gospel is the power of God unto salvation. And thus the Gospel is a *Means of Grace,* a means through which God gives us all His grace. And through faith, which God engenders through the Gospel, we enter upon the possession of the treasures of His grace which the Gospel contains. Thus the Gospel is the power of God unto salvation to every one that believeth.—As a treasure casket may contain three compartments filled with treasures, just so the Gospel has three parts by means of each of which the same gifts of grace are bestowed upon us. These three parts are *the Word, Baptism, and the Lord's Supper.* And so we may say that there are *three* Means of Grace. Baptism and the Lord's Supper are called *Sacraments,* or sacred acts. For Baptism and the Lord's Supper are sacred acts ordained by God, wherein, by certain external means connected with His Word, He offers, conveys, and seals unto men the grace which Christ has merited. The external means connected with God's Word in Baptism is water; in the Lord's Supper it is bread and wine. Through these visible signs the Sacraments make it very plain and visible for thee that God bestows upon thee, even upon thee, His grace, that is, forgiveness of sins, life, and salvation, and also the Holy Ghost. How lovingly concerned God is about us, and how much does He do to firmly convince us that He truly and actually bestows His grace upon us! Therefore, we should indeed freely take of it, and rejoicing in faith, we should thank Him with heart and word and deed.

PRAYER.—I thank Thee, my God, for Thy Holy Gospel, through which Thou dost reveal, give, and convey unto me the saving grace which Christ has procured for me. And I thank Thee for Thy holy Sacraments, through which Thou dost deal with me in particular, and dost seal unto me Thy grace by means of visible signs. I pray Thee, my gracious God, thus to make me firm and glad in faith, and altogether sure of Thy grace. Amen.

Hymn 436, 6.

FRIDAY.

Go ye, therefore, and teach all nations, baptizing them in the name of the Father and of the Son and of the Holy Ghost.—Matt. 28, 19.

To baptize means to wash, to wash with water. But Christian Baptism is "the washing of water *by the Word."* (Eph. 5, 26.) Dr. Luther therefore says: "Baptism is not simple water only, but it is the water comprehended in God's command and connected with God's Word." Christian Baptism has not been ordained by man, but by God. God has instituted it, God has commanded it. It is the water comprehended in God's command. The Lord said to His disciples: "Go ye and teach all nations, baptizing them." And God has united His Word with the water of Baptism. It is water connected with God's Word. The Lord said: "Baptizing them in the name of the Father and of the Son and of the Holy Ghost." This Word shows what Baptism really is. We lost and condemned sinners are baptized, or washed and bathed, in the name of the Father and of the Son and of the Holy Ghost. We are washed and bathed in what the Triune God reveals that He has done for us. We are washed and bathed in the grace and love of the Father, who for Christ's sake receives us as His children. We are washed and bathed in the bloody merit of the Son, who has made us righteous and good in the sight of God. We are washed and bathed in the sanctifying power of the Holy Ghost, which kindles faith in us and makes new creatures of us. Thus Baptism brings us into the gracious communion of the Triune God.—O Christian, thou art baptized! Thank God for the wondrous grace, of which He has made thee a partaker through this holy Sacrament!

PRAYER.—I thank Thee, Lord, Triune God, that Thou hast delivered me from the power of darkness, and hast translated me into Thy Kingdom of Grace, and hast made me a partaker of Thy grace. Grant, O Lord, that unto my dying hour in true faith I may comfort myself with this holy Sacrament, and thus obtain salvation. Amen.

Hymn 403, 1. 2.

SATURDAY.

The washing of water by the Word.—Eph. 5, 26.

What does Baptism, the washing of water by the Word, give or profit?—Just because it is the washing of water *by the Word,* it has a great and mighty power. It gives forgiveness of sins, life, and salvation, and the Holy Ghost to kindle faith in us. Or, as Dr. Luther expresses it, "it works forgiveness of sins, delivers from death and the devil, and gives eternal salvation to all who believe this, as the words and promises of God declare." And now let us show thee such words and promises of God through which Baptism receives its great and mighty power. The Spirit of God says: "Christ also loved the Church, and gave Himself for it, that He might sanctify and *cleanse* it with the washing of water by the Word." (Eph. 5, 25. 26.) And: "Repent, and be baptized, every one of you, in the name of Jesus Christ *for the remission of sins.*" (Acts 2, 38.) And: "Arise, and be baptized, and *wash away thy sins.*" (Acts 22, 16.) Thou seest that Baptism works forgiveness of sins. And Jesus says: "He that believeth and is baptized *shall be saved.*" (Mark 16, 16.) And the Apostle, by inspiration of the Holy Ghost, speaks thus of Baptism: "Baptism doth also now *save us.*" (1 Pet. 3, 20. 21.) Thou seest that Baptism gives eternal salvation. And the Apostle writes by the Holy Ghost: "But after that the kindness and love of God, our Savior, toward man appeared, not by the works of righteousness which we have done, but according to His mercy *He saved us* by the washing of regeneration and renewing of the *Holy Ghost,* which He shed on us abundantly through Jesus Christ, our Savior, that, being *justified* by His grace, we should be made *heirs according to the hope of eternal life.*" (Titus 3, 4-7.) Here thou seest that Baptism saves us, and gives us the Holy Ghost to regenerate and renew us through faith, that we should be righteous before God and heirs of eternal life. Take, therefore, O Christian, take the gifts of grace which God has given thee through Baptism! Take them and keep them securely through the grace of the Holy Ghost, who likewise is given thee through Baptism.

PRAYER.—Help me, O God, help me that in true faith I may securely hold the great and saving treasures which Thou hast given me through Baptism! Help me to do this through Thy Holy Spirit, whom Thou hast poured out abundantly in Baptism. Help me to nevermore lose forgiveness of sins and life eternal which Thou hast given me! Amen.

Hymn 400, 1. 2.

Week of the Thirteenth Sunday After Trinity.

SUNDAY.

The washing of regeneration.—Titus 3, 5.

Baptism works forgiveness of sins, delivers from death and the devil, and gives eternal salvation to all who believe this, as the words and promises of God declare. When a Christian who is not well grounded in the Word of God hears this, he is astonished and doubtingly asks: How can water do such great things? Thou knowest the answer. It is not mere water, indeed, that does them, but the Word of God which is in and with the water; this puts these things into Baptism. And faith, which trusts such Word of God in the water, takes these great things out of Baptism, and appropriates them. Dost thou fully understand this, my dear Christian? Without the Word of God the water is simple water and no Baptism. But with the Word of God it is a Baptism: a gracious water of life and a washing of regeneration in the Holy Ghost. Through His Word God has placed into the water of Baptism forgiveness of sins, life, and salvation, and the Holy Ghost for kindling faith in us. Thou art baptized. Thou believest. And so thou art regenerated. Thou art a child of God that possesses forgiveness of sins, life, and salvation, and the Holy Ghost. And the Holy Ghost creates within thee a new mind. Thou rejoicest in the possession of the great gifts of the grace of God; thou dost fear, love, and trust in God; thou possessest new life. Thus Baptism is a washing of regeneration and renewing of the Holy Ghost, whom God has shed on us abundantly in Baptism through Jesus Christ, our Savior, that, being justified by His grace, we should be made heirs according to the hope of eternal life, as St. Paul teaches, Titus, chapter third. This is a faithful saying.

PRAYER.—Lord, my God, my gracious God, I thank Thee for what Thou hast done to me in Baptism! Thou hast regenerated me. Thou hast given me forgiveness of sins, and thereby that righteousness which is valid in Thy sight. Thou hast delivered me from death and the devil, and given me eternal salvation. Thou hast granted unto me the Holy Spirit, who works and sustains faith and a new spiritual life within me. O my God, in the possession of such grace let me live and die, and awaken and live forever. Amen, for Christ's sake! Amen.

Hymn 403, 6.

MONDAY.

Therefore we are buried with Him by Baptism into death, that, like as Christ was raised up from the dead by the glory of the Father, even so we also should walk in newness of life.—Rom. 6, 4.

Through Baptism we Christians are made partakers of Christ, and of all the salvation which He has procured for us. "As many of you as have been baptized into Christ have put on Christ." (Gal. 3, 27.) Christ died and was buried for our sins as our Substitute. We are made partakers of this through Baptism: we are dead and buried unto our sin, so that it can neither damn nor control us. "Therefore we are buried with Him by Baptism into death." Christ, our Substitute, was raised up from the dead by the glory of the Father, and now lives a new life, free from the burden of our sin. This, too, we are made partakers of through Baptism: we have a new life, free from the burden of our sin. "Even so we also should *walk* in newness of life." What does this mean? It means that the old Adam in us, the sinful depravity which we have inherited from Adam, and in which we are born, should by daily contrition and repentance be drowned and die with all sins and evil lusts. Daily we Christians should repent of the sin which clings to us, and pray God to forgive it for Christ's sake. That kills the power of sin. And, again, a new man should daily come forth and arise, who shall live before God in righteousness and purity. Such a new man, a new spiritual being and life, is in us Christians through the grace of Baptism which we have received. This new man should arise within us daily unto a godly life and conversation. And this new man shall live forever, in eternal glory, freed entirely from the old Adam.—This is what our Baptism should signify to us Christians.

PRAYER.—Lord, my God, who out of great mercy, through the washing of regeneration, didst make me a partaker both of the death and of the life of my Savior, I pray Thee to bestow upon me the power of Thy Holy Spirit, that I may daily die unto sin, but live unto Thee and serve Thee, until in the life to come I shall be wholly renewed and in perfect bliss. Amen.

Hymn 403, 5.

TUESDAY.

Verily, verily, I say unto thee, Except a man be born of water and of the Spirit, he cannot enter into the kingdom of God. That which is born of the flesh is flesh.—John 3, 5. 6.

The widely spread Baptist sect—in fact, the entire Reformed Church, of which it is a branch—considers Baptism a mere outward ceremony, without regenerating power. And they say it is wrong to baptize little children, because, so they claim, little children cannot believe.—Are the children who are born within the Christian Church to be baptized in their infancy? Yes, indeed; for they are flesh born of flesh, having inherited the sinful depravity of their parents. And very solemnly does the Lord Jesus assure us of the fact that no one can enter the kingdom of God except he be born of water and the Spirit, that is to say, regenerated. And whom does Jesus command us to baptize? All nations. (Matt. 28, 19.) And, surely, the little children, too, are included in "all nations." And He emphasized it very particularly that the kingdom of God belongs to little children. (Mark 10, 14.) Hence also Baptism, which regenerates them unto the kingdom of God, belongs to little children. Were not the little children of God's people in the Old Covenant circumcised on the eighth day by divine command? And has not Baptism in the New Testament taken the place of circumcision? (Col. 2, 11. 12.) And also little children can believe. The Holy Ghost, who in Baptism is poured out upon them, kindles faith within them, though we do not understand how He does it. Jesus says of little children that they believe in Him. (Matt. 18, 2-6.) Thus out of the mouth of babes and sucklings has the Lord ordained strength because of His enemies. (Ps. 8, 2; Matt. 21, 16.) And John the Baptist was filled with the Holy Ghost already in his mother's womb, and believed in his Savior. (Luke 1, 15. 44.) O Christian, be not deceived, but comfort thyself with the Baptism thou hast received in infancy.

PRAYER.—Lord, help me, lest I be misled by false and fanciful doctrine. Grant me grace to comfort myself with the Baptism received in infancy unto my dying hour, and through the grace obtained therein to obtain life everlasting. Amen.

Hymn 252, 3.

WEDNESDAY.

Be thou faithful unto death, and I will give thee a crown of life.—Rev. 2, 10.

Dear Christian! Thou, no doubt, wast baptized in infancy. There thou didst receive the grace of God procured for thee by Christ. There the Holy Ghost kindled faith in thee. Hence there thou wast regenerated and made a child of God. Hence thou in fact didst thyself what thy sponsors did for thee with their mouths: thou didst renounce the devil and all his works and all his pomp, and didst pledge thyself to the Triune God, to be His own in life and death, in time and eternity. Since that time this Word of our Lord applies to thee: "Be thou faithful unto death, and I will give thee a crown of life." Didst thou always remain faithful? Or, having fallen, didst thou return to thy baptismal grace through faith in Christ?—Mark well what God's will and regulation .is with respect to His baptized little children. As soon as possible they are to be nourished with the Word of God, diligently, daily, and properly, that they may remain faithful. This is what Jesus meant when saying to Peter: "Feed my lambs." (John 21, 15.) This the Holy Spirit admonishes the fathers to do, saying that they should bring up their children in the nurture and admonition of the Lord. (Eph. 6, 4.) For this purpose well-regulated Christian congregations maintain Christian parish schools. To this same end our children receive special instruction for Confirmation. At Confirmation, which is a laudable custom of our Church, the children after due instruction, publicly, in the presence of the congregation, with their own mouths repeat the promise which once they made through their sponsors: to renounce the devil and all his works and all his pomp, and to remain true to the Triune God, even unto death. And this baptismal vow, this confirmation vow, should endure throughout life. Let him that reads this hear what the Savior says: "Be thou faithful unto death, and I will give thee a crown of life."

PRAYER.—O Lord, gracious Trinity, who in my Baptism didst regenerate me to be Thy child, I now repeat my vow that I will renounce the devil and all his works and all his pomp, and will remain true to Thee unto death. To this end grant me the power of Thy Holy Spirit, O Father, for the sake of Jesus Christ, my Savior, and finally give me the crown of life which Thou hast graciously promised me. Amen.

Hymn 400, 7.

THURSDAY.

For the work of the ministry, for the edifying of the body of Christ.—Eph. 4, 12.

Our Lord Jesus Christ has instituted an *office* in His Church on earth. An office is a service, a ministry, vested with certain powers, a service performed in the name and at the command of some superior person. Such an office, which is to be administered in His name, our Lord and Savior has instituted in His Church on earth. To what purpose? For the edifying of the body of Christ, that ever more people may be joined to Christ through faith, and be strengthened in such faith. What, therefore are the functions of this office? To preach the Gospel, to administer the

Sacraments, and to forgive or to retain the sins to individual persons. To His disciples Jesus said: "All power is given unto me in heaven and in earth. Go ye, therefore, and teach all nations, baptizing them in the name of the Father and of the Son and of the Holy Ghost, teaching them to observe all things whatsoever I have commanded you. And, lo, I am with you alway, even unto the end of the world." (Matt. 28, 18-20.) And again He said to them: "Peace be unto you! As my Father hath sent me, even so send I you." And when He said this, He breathed on them and said to them: "Receive ye the Holy Ghost: whosesoever sins ye remit, they are remitted unto them; and whosesoever sins ye retain, they are retained. (John 20, 21-23.) This office is called the "Office of the Keys," according to the saying of Christ: "I will give unto thee the keys of the kingdom of heaven." (Matt. 16, 19.) For by means of the Gospel, and the Sacraments connected with it, sins are forgiven. And where sins are forgiven, there heaven is opened. But if according to the Word of Christ sins are retained to any one, then heaven is closed to such a one.

PRAYER.—I thank Thee, Lord Jesus, Thou Most High, that within Thy Church on earth Thou hast instituted the ministry of the Word and the Sacraments, through which Thou increasest, strengthenest, and preservest Thy beloved Christendom unto eternal life. Grant me Thy grace, I pray Thee, that in this office I may always seek forgiveness of sins and the strengthening of my faith. And guard me, lest I belong to those whose sins must be retained through fault of their own. Amen.

Hymn 425, 4.

FRIDAY.

Verily, I say unto you, Whatsoever ye shall bind on earth shall be bound in heaven; and whatsoever ye shall loose on earth shall be loosed in heaven.—Matt. 18, 18.

Who are the "ye" in this text? To whom did our Lord Jesus Christ give the Office of the Keys and all the powers connected with it—to whom? Whom did Christ command to preach the Gospel, to baptize, to administer the Lord's Supper, to forgive and to retain sins? There is much dispute on this question. We will therefore look into the Bible, and so, very simply, get the answer from the Word of God. —At one time Jesus said to believing Peter: "I will give unto thee the keys of the kingdom of heaven; and whatsoever thou shalt bind on earth shall be bound in heaven; and whatsoever thou shalt loose on earth shall be loosed in heaven." (Matt. 16, 19.) So here the Lord gave to Peter the Office of the Keys. And now the Pope raves and asserts that the Office of the Keys belongs to him, on the further assumption that Peter was the first Pope. But the Lord gave the same office to the assembled disciples, both men and women, saying: "As my Father hath sent me, even so send I you. Whosoever sins ye remit, they are remitted unto them; and whosesoever sins ye retain, they are retained." (John 20, 21. 23.) Here many assert that the Office of the Keys was given to the pastors, which is foolishness. In the text at the head of our lesson the Lord says to every Christian, and to all Christians assembled as a Christian congregation at any one place: "Verily, I say unto you, Whatsoever ye shall bind on earth shall be bound in heaven; and whatsoever ye shall loose on earth shall be loosed in heaven." Hence to all Christians, wheresoever some of them may be assembled, whether they be few or many (Matt. 18, 20), the Lord gave the Office of the Keys. The Office of the Keys "is the peculiar church-power which Christ has given to *His Church on earth*," says our Catechism, in accordance with the Word of God.

PRAYER.—Lord Jesus, from Thy Word I know that Thou hast made me, too, Thy disciple and a member of Thy Church, to whom Thou hast committed the powers and duties comprised in the Office of the Keys. I beseech Thee to grant me Thy Holy Spirit that I may prove myself worthy of such honor, and faithfully fulfill such obligations on my humble part, that Thy holy name may be praised on earth unto the salvation of many. Amen.

Hymn 426, 9.

SATURDAY.

God hath set some in the Church . . . teachers.—
1 Cor. 12, 28.

If, as we saw yesterday, the Office of the Keys is vested in the Christian congregation, and all the powers connected with it, what, then, is a *pastor?* In a Christian congregation the Office of the Keys must be administered in public, the Gospel must be preached, Baptism and the Lord's Supper must be administered, sin must be remitted and retained. It is evident that not all members can do this in the same manner. Therefore God has ordained that each congregation should choose and call a man who is to perform the functions of the Office of the Keys publicly, in the name of the congregation and in its midst. Such a man is called pastor, shepherd, bishop, teacher. When he has accepted the call of the congregation, it is God Himself that has given him to that congregation, as our text shows. He then is the steward of the mysteries of God, as far as his public office in the congregation is concerned. (1 Cor. 4, 1.) This his stewardship he has received from God through the congregation. But the instructions, the directions for his stewardship of the Office of the Keys, he has received from God alone. For the functions of the Office of the Keys are ordained by God; no man is permitted to alter them in the least. If a pastor does not adhere to the divine instructions, or if it becomes evident that he is a wicked man, then, after due admonition, the congregation should remove him. But if he does adhere to the divine instructions; if he preaches the Gospel in its truth and purity; if he administers the Sacraments according to the institution of Christ; if he forgives and retains sins according to the regulations which God has laid down; and if he leads a Christian life,—then the congregation should know that God has given her that man to feed it, and he himself should also be well aware at all times that God has appointed him to serve that congregation. (Acts 20, 28.) It is a great and gracious gift of God for a Christian congregation to have a faithful pastor and teacher.

PRAYER.—Lord, my God, I pray Thee that Thou wouldst at all times give us, Thy Christians and Thy children, upright teachers and ministers of Thy divine Word, and keep them in purity of doctrine and rectitude of a Christian life. Bless them in their office, and bless their faithful labors, that through their Gospel ministry our faith may be strengthened, and every good work prosper among us. And give unto me and to my brethren and sisters in the congregation Thy Holy Spirit, that we may willingly accept and receive whatever they preach unto us out of Thy revealed Word. Amen.

Hymn 491, 1. 2. 3.

Week of the Fourteenth Sunday After Trinity.

SUNDAY.

Repent ye, therefore, and be converted, that your sins may be blotted out.—Acts 3, 19.

We all are poor, miserable sinners. There is no doubt about that. But there are penitent and impenitent sinners. Penitent sinners are such as sincerely repent of their sins, believe in their Savior Jesus Christ, and are willing to amend. Impenitent sinners are such as do not repent of their sins, do not truly believe in the Savior, and are not willing to amend. The Gospel is to be preached to all sinners, penitent as well as impenitent. But the application of the Gospel to the individual, the consolation of the Gospel applied to the individual, by which he is assured of the grace of God through Baptism and the Lord's Supper, and by which the absolution, or forgiveness of sins, is pronounced to him,—that is for penitent sinners only. For the sins of him who repents and is converted shall be blotted out. This is the divine rule which we know, and which our text teaches us. To the impenitent sinners the consolation of the Gospel is not to be given, nor that of Baptism, nor that of the Lord's Supper, nor that of absolution. Unto the impenitent sinners, when they become manifest as such, their sins are to be retained. And the Office of the Keys, with the public administration of which, on the part of the congregation, the pastors have been commissioned, is the peculiar, the especial, and singular church-power which Christ has given to His Church on earth to forgive the sins of the penitent sinners unto them, but to retain the sins of the impenitent as long as they do not repent. May God graciously grant thee, my dear Christian, at all times to be a penitent sinner, in order that thou mayest be filled with the consolation of the Gospel, the consolation that thy sins are blotted out.

PRAYER.—O Lord, Thou gracious God, do not let me fall into a state of impenitence through the deceit of sin! Take me into Thy gracious keeping, and for the sake of Jesus Christ bestow upon me Thy Holy Ghost, that I may repent of my sins, believe in Jesus Christ, and willingly amend my sinful life. And thus lead me to the fount of grace which Thou causest to flow for me in Thy Word and Sacrament, that there I may find abundant comfort. Amen.

Hymn 426, 7.

MONDAY.

If I forgave anything, to whom I forgave it, for your sakes forgave I it in the person of Christ.—2 Cor. 2, 10.

My dear Christian, when considering and meditating upon what the Word of God says concerning the Office of the Keys, what, then, must be thy faith, what, then, must be thy attitude with respect to the public administration of this office as performed by the pastor of thy congregation? Thou must then say with all thy heart: I believe that when the called minister of God deals with us by His divine command, this is as valid and certain, in heaven also, as if Christ, our dear Lord, dealt with us Himself. If thy pastor does anything without the command of Christ, then it is of no value. But when he does something by the command of Christ, then he does this in the person of Christ; and then this is as valid and certain, and is fully as valid in heaven also, as if Christ, our dear Lord, did it Himself. When the pastor preaches the Gospel in its truth and purity, this is just as valid and certain as if Christ Himself stood there and preached. Just so it is with Baptism and the Lord's Supper. And also with holy absolution. When thy pastor pronounces absolution, or forgiveness of sins, unto thee, then this is just as valid before God in heaven as if Christ, our Lord, Himself pronounced the absolution unto thee. Remember, the pastor does this in the place of the congregation, in the person of Christ. If, in the due order prescribed by Christ, the pastor retains the sins of a manifest and impenitent sinner, and excludes him from the Christian congregation, then this, too, is as valid and certain before God in heaven as if Christ, our Lord, had done it visibly, in person. And just so it is when the pastor again absolves such an excommunicated person, and forgives his sins unto him, and when the congregation again receives him into membership, that is, after he has repented of his sins and is willing to amend. Wilt thou consider all this well?

PRAYER.—Lord Jesus, I thank Thee that for our, Thy Christians', benefit and consolation Thou hast instituted within the congregations the holy ministry through which Thou art present in person, to distribute the treasures of Thy grace. I pray Thee to preserve such ministry in truth and purity among us and among our children. And grant us, O Savior, Thy Holy Ghost, that we make proper use of such ministry for the strengthening of our faith and for our eternal salvation. Amen.

Hymn 425, 1. 2.

TUESDAY.

Therefore put away from among yourselves that wicked person.—1 Cor. 5, 13.

The retaining of sins, the excommunication from the Christian congregation, the *ban,* as it is called, should be executed upon those members of the congregation who are wicked, that is, who are manifest and impenitent sinners. Their sin must be *manifest,* that is, a sin which is recognized by every one in the congregation as an evident transgression of the Law of God. But even this is not enough for the execution of the ban. The *impenitence* of the sinner must also be evident to all in the congregation. But how is this possible? Who can look into the heart? sayest thou. It is not necessary to look into any one's heart. Our Lord and Savior has indicated a way in which it can be known whether a sinner is impenitent. It is given in Matt. 18, 15-17. He that knows of the sin of a brother should go to him, and very lovingly, patiently, and forbearingly seek to convince him of his sin. If the sinner accepts the admonition, he has been gained, and all is well. If he refuses to acceept it, then—I shall now address thee—take with thee one or two more, that in the mouth of two or three witnesses every word may be established, and again admonish the sinner very patiently and forbearingly in the love of Christ. If he neglects to hear you, then, together with the witnesses, tell it unto the church to which the sinning brother belongs. This congregation should then try to persuade him to repent. If he persistently refuses to hear the congregation, then he is certainly impenitent; for the Lord Jesus, the merciful Searcher of hearts, says that we should then consider such a person a heathen man and a publican. Then the pastor of that congregation should execute the verdict of the congregation: he should retain the sins unto the sinner, exclude him from the congregation, and publicly announce this. But as soon as the sinner repents, he should be publicly absolved of the ban. For even excommunication is not intended for the perdition, but for the salvation of the soul.

PRAYER.—Lord Jesus Christ, I pray Thee to grant Thy Holy Spirit to me and all true Christians, that we may deal with our sinning brother according to Thy Word and will, lest want of discipline and worldly-mindedness spread in the churches, that, on the contrary, the sinners may be duly admonished and disciplined, to the end that God might bestow upon them His grace unto repentance and salvation. Amen.

Hymn 381, 5.

Week of the Fourteenth Sunday After Trinity.

WEDNESDAY.

If we say that we have no sin, we deceive ourselves, and the truth is not in us. But if we confess our sins, He is faithful and just to forgive us our sins, and to cleanse us from all unrighteousness.—1 John 1, 8. 9.

Intimately allied with the Office of the Keys is that divine service which we call *Confession*. Confession embraces two parts. One is that we confess our sins. We are poor, miserable sinners, and remain such unto our dying hour. "If we say that we have no sin, we deceive ourselves, and the truth is not in us." We should repent of our sins and confess them with heart and mouth. This is the first part of Confession. The term "Confession" clearly indicates this. The other part is, that we receive absolution, or forgiveness, from the confessor, from the pastor, as from God Himself. Thou understandest this from our devotion of the day before yesterday. We should in no wise doubt, but firmly believe that by it our sins are forgiven before God in heaven. For if we penitently confess our sins, God is faithful and just to forgive us our sins, and to cleanse us from all unrighteousness, as He has promised in His Word. And in Confession God does this through the confessor. To be sure, if a hypocrite comes to Confession and with his mouth only confesses his sins, but at heart is impenitent, he does not receive forgiveness of sins; for, not having faith, he naturally does not accept the grace of God, though it is offered to him, too, in absolution.—What a salutary act of worship Confession is! There children of God come to their heavenly Father and penitently confess their sins, and implore grace for Christ's sake; and the heavenly Father most mercifully and kindly forgives them all their sins. Do come to confession often, dear Christian! And there say the following confessional prayer, which is granted at once.

PRAYER.—O Almighty God, merciful Father, I, a poor, miserable sinner, confess unto Thee all my sins and iniquities with which I have ever offended Thee and justly deserved Thy punishment in time and eternity. But I am heartily sorry for them and sincerely repent of them, and I pray Thee, of Thy boundless mercy and for the sake of the holy, innocent, bitter suffering and death of Thy beloved Son, Jesus Christ, to be gracious and merciful to me, a poor sinful being. Amen.

Hymn 415, 5.

THURSDAY.

I said I will confess my transgressions unto the Lord; and Thou forgavest me the iniquity of my sin.—Ps. 32, 5.

What sins should we confess? Before God we should plead guilty of all sins, even of those which we do not at the time realize and know, as we do in the Fifth Petition of the Lord's Prayer and in General Confession. For there is not a single commandment of God which we do not transgress daily. And David prays: "Who can understand his errors? Cleanse Thou me from secret faults." (Ps. 19, 12.) And when we have offended and grieved our neighbor, we should confess our sins to him and ask his pardon before we go to Confession. He who is not willing to do this, thereby clearly shows that before God also he does not truly repent of his sin. What does the Savior say? "Go thy way; first be reconciled to thy brother!" (Matt. 5, 24.) But perchance we know and feel in our heart some particular sin which above others weighs upon our heart and burdens our conscience. Then it is very good, wholesome, and beneficial to go to Private Confession, that is, to go to our confessor alone, and privately to tell him our sins, get spiritual advice and consolation from him, and to receive absolution for just these particular sins. This greatly strengthens and comforts our faith. It is to be regretted that Private Confession, where absolution is spoken to each person individually, has fallen into such disuse. For the sake of our infirmity it is better for every one of us to hear the word spoken to him: "*Thy* sins are forgiven thee" (Matt. 9, 2; Luke 7, 48), though it is true that in the absolution spoken in the General Confession essentially the same is given.

Week of the Fourteenth Sunday After Trinity.

PRAYER.—My God, help me by Thy Holy Spirit that I may never deny a transgression of Thy Holy Law, nor cover up or misrepresent it out of carnal pride and obstinacy, but that I may freely, frankly, and penitently confess my sins. And then let me obtain mercy according to Thy Word, for Jesus' sake. Amen.

Hymn 414, 5.

FRIDAY.

Let us search and try our ways, and turn again to the Lord.—Lam. 3, 40.

Observe a dear little child when it has done something wrong, how it comes to its father or to its mother and begs forgiveness. Or remember how the prodigal son came to himself and said: "I will arise and go to my father, and will say unto him: Father, I have sinned against heaven and before thee." (Luke 15, 18.) Thus should we go to Confession. We must truly know and realize our sin. We must beware of going to Confession from mere force of habit, scarcely considering or knowing what or how we have sinned. We should first search and try our ways, and turn again to the Lord. We must search and try our ways in the light of God's Law. "For by the Law is the knowledge of sin." (Rom. 3, 20.) We should take up the commandments one by one, and in so doing search and try our ways. We shall then find enough wrong, transgression, and sin. We should also consider the station of life into which we have been placed by God, and in the light of God's commandments endeavor to discern where we have sinned with regard to it. And then we should arise and go to our Father, and in sincere penitence confess our sins to Him in the confessional service. He will then assure us of His grace through absolution. God grant thee grace through His Spirit for Christ's sake that thy confession may always be such.

PRAYER.—Heavenly Father, illumine me with Thy Holy Spirit for Christ's sake that in the bright mirror of the Law I may rightly see my manifold, great and grievous sins, and truly realize how terrible is Thy wrath because of sin, and how awfully Thou wilt punish all the impenitent for their transgressions. From the Gospel, however, let me also learn to know Thy kind fatherly heart, which through Christ is opened unto me, so that with a broken spirit and a contrite heart, but nevertheless not despairing, on the contrary, firmly trusting in Thy grace, I may come to Confession, where Thou wilt surely deal with me according to Thy fatherly goodness, and wilt forgive me all my sins. Amen.

Hymn 416, 1-3.

SATURDAY.

The Lord's Supper.—1 Cor. 11, 20.

Concerning the Lord's Supper the holy Evangelists Matthew, Mark, Luke, and St. Paul the Apostle write thus: *"Our Lord Jesus Christ, the same night in which He was betrayed, took bread; and when He had given thanks, He brake it, and gave it to His disciples, and said: Take, eat; this is my body, which is given for you. This do in remembrance of Me. After the same manner also He took the cup when He had supped* (after the paschal supper), *gave thanks, and gave it to them, saying: Take, drink ye all of it; this cup is the new testament in my blood, which is shed for you for the remission of sins. This do ye, as oft as ye drink it, in remembrance of Me."* So this Sacrament of the Altar, as Dr. Luther calls it, is *the true body and blood of our Lord Jesus Christ,* under the bread and wine, for us Christians to eat and to drink, instituted by Christ Himself. And what is the benefit of such eating and drinking? "That is shown us by these words: 'Given and shed for you for the remission of sins'; namely, that in the Sacrament forgiveness of sins, life, and salvation are given us through these words. For where there is forgiveness of sin, there is also life and salvation."—How holy is this Sacrament, and how salutary! Our Lord Jesus Christ, the God-man, the Truthful and the Almighty, who is now exalted at the right hand of God, but nevertheless is truly present with us, in this Sacrament gives to every one who eats and drinks that very body and that very blood wherewith on the cross He procured for us the forgiveness of sins. And He does this to make us altogether sure of the forgiveness of our sins, of life, and eternal salvation. Sinner, Christian, come to the Lord's Supper!

PRAYER.—Gracious God, dear Heavenly Father, I thank Thee that for our benefit, through Thy dear Son Jesus Christ, Thou hast instituted the holy and venerable Sacrament of the Altar wherein under the consecrated bread and wine He truly gives us His body and His blood unto the forgiveness of sins. Grant unto me and to all Thy children Thy Holy Spirit, that we may approach this Sacrament in true faith, make proper use of it, and be strengthened thereby unto life eternal. Amen.

Hymn 431, 1.

Week of the Fifteenth Sunday After Trinity.

SUNDAY.

This is my body. . . . This is my blood.—Matt. 26, 26. 28.

God in His Word has revealed unto us the things that are necessary for our salvation. If we do not rest upon this Word alone and completely, but permit our reason to interfere, then we shall surely err and do all manner of foolish things. Thus it came about that the Reformed Church, with all its various and variously named branches, says that in the Lord's Supper we do not receive the body and blood of Christ, but only bread and wine, and that bread and wine "represent" the body and blood of Christ, and are mere "figures," or "images," of Christ's body and blood. Why twist the words of Christ, and tamper with their plain meaning? Christ's words are plain, very plain, and every child can understand them: "This is my body"; "this is my blood." And Christ says that He gives us that body which was given for us, and that blood which was shed for us. And the Apostle says by inspiration of the Holy Spirit: "The cup of blessing which we bless, is it not the *communion* of the blood of Christ? The bread which we break, is it not the *communion* of the body of Christ?" (1 Cor. 10, 16.) And he also says: "Whosoever shall eat this bread, and drink this cup of the Lord, unworthily, shall be guilty of the *body* and *blood* of the Lord." (1 Cor. 11, 27.) Indeed, in the Lord's Supper Christ gives us His body with the bread and His blood with the cup. In place of the Sacrament of the Passover in the Old Covenant He has in the New Testament instituted the Sacrament of the Lord's Supper, where instead of the flesh and blood of the paschal lamb, which was but a type and figure of the coming Christ, He now, under the bread and wine, gives us the flesh and blood of the true Lamb of the Passover, to wit, His own. This is what His words really say. And who, merely to satisfy his reason, dares to undermine the words of the divine institution of a Sacrament and the words of the Savior's divine testament?

PRAYER.—Lord, Thou True, Thou Almighty, and Thou All-wise, help me to accept and believe all Thy words just as they plainly read, also those of Thy Holy Supper. Guard me against the meddlesomeness and the objections of my depraved reason, lest my faith be wrecked! Amen.

Hymn 436, 4. 5.

MONDAY.

The cup of blessing which we bless, is it not the communion of the blood of Christ? The bread which we break, is it not the communion of the body of Christ?—1 Cor. 10, 16.

It is disagreeable to be compelled to speak of false and seductive doctrine when contemplating the Gospel. But unless we do so, the seduction will spread.—The Roman Church, the church of the Pope, whose coming was foretold in 2 Thess. 2, teaches that bread and wine in the Lord's Supper is *changed* into the body and blood of Christ. But all Scripture passages treating of the Lord's Supper show that we are given bread and wine to eat and to drink, but that this bread and this wine are the "communion" of the body and blood of Christ, that is to say, that together with the bread and the wine Christ's body and blood are given us. Because the Church of Rome teaches such changing, or "transubstantiation," it also teaches that the bread and wine must be *adored*. But Scriptures nowhere say that the bread and wine are to be adored, but they everywhere command us to eat and drink the bread and wine of the Lord's Supper. And the Church of Rome furthermore says that the bread in the Sacrament, which, according to their false doctrine, is changed into the body of Christ, is to be offered as an unbloody *sacrifice* for the sins of the living and the dead. But this is an abomination and a profanation of the atoning sacrifice of Christ upon the cross. "For by *one* offering He hath perfected forever them that are sanctified. Now where remission of these (of sins) is, there is no more offering for sin." (Hebr. 10, 14. 18.) And lastly the Roman Catholic Church *refuses the cup to the laity,* that is, to the members of the congregation, saying, with blasphemous presumption, Why, the body of Christ already contains blood! But the Lord Jesus says: "Drink ye all of it!" (Matt. 26, 27.)—My dear Christian, abide simply by the words of Christ, and seek the forgiveness of thy sins in the Lord's Supper:— for that is given thee through the body and blood of Christ which thou receivest together with the bread and wine.

PRAYER.—My Lord and God, do not let Thy precious Word, the bright and unchanging light which now shineth unto us, be put out and taken from us. Guard Thy dear Christian Church against the specious seduction of the Antichrist at Rome! Continue with us Thy pure Word and Sacrament, and grant that therein we may seek and find the forgiveness of sins. Amen.

Hymn 430, 3.

TUESDAY.

Take, eat! Drink ye all of it!—Matt. 26, 26. 27.

The Lord's Supper is the true body and the true blood of our Lord Jesus Christ, under the bread and wine, for us Christians to eat and to drink, instituted by Christ Himself. This is God's Word and the doctrine taught by Luther. But to prevent gross misunderstanding and malicious misrepresentation, it is well to show briefly what kind of eating and drinking takes place in the Holy Supper. —Bread and wine are taken in a natural way, that is to say, in the same way in which we commonly receive food and drink. Together with this natural eating and drinking of the bread and wine with the mouth, we also eat and drink the body and blood of the Lord in a *sacramental* manner. What does this mean? It means that together with the bread and wine we receive the body and blood of Christ in a supernatural manner, in a manner wholly incomprehensible to human reason, in a way past finding out, in a manner such as takes place in this Sacrament only. Seek not to fathom and to comprehend this, my dear Christian; for thou wilt not succeed. Simply believe that together with the bread and wine thou receivest the body and blood of Christ, not in a natural manner, like the bread and the wine, but in a sacramental, mysterious manner. And to get the real benefit of this, thou must observe a *spiritual* eating in the Holy Supper. What does this mean? It means that thou must know and believe through the Holy Spirit that with the bread and wine thy dear Savior offers unto thee His body which was given for thee, and His blood which was shed for thee, in order to give thee forgiveness of sins, life, and salvation, and to make thee perfectly sure of the possession of these gracious gifts.

PRAYER.—Lord Jesus, true God and man, Thou glorified and exalted Savior, who in a way past finding out for us dost fill all things, grant me grace to firmly believe that with the bread and wine in the Holy Supper Thou givest unto me that precious ransom with which Thou hast purchased me, a poor sinner, namely, Thy body crucified, and Thy blood shed for me. Grant that I may receive it in true faith, glory in it, comfort myself with it, and boast of it in the face of sin, death, and the Last Judgment. Amen.

Hymn 433.

WEDNESDAY.

I have received of the Lord that which also I have delivered unto you.—1 Cor. 11, 23.

Thus St. Paul speaks of the instructions he received with regard to the Lord's Supper. The Holy Supper is the Lord's Supper in reality only when it is administered in conformity with Christ's institution as recorded in Holy Writ. For this the following five points are necessary. First there must be *communicants* who partake of the Lord's Supper. If thou wouldst be such a communicant, thou shouldst announce thyself to thy pastor. Without announcement he cannot know whether there will be any communicants. And it is his duty to see to it that no unbidden guests appear. Secondly, there must be *bread* and *wine,* grape-wine. The pastor must see to this. Thirdly, this bread and wine must be *consecrated,* that is to say, they must be hallowed and set apart for use at the Lord's Supper in this way that the minister of the Gospel pronounces over them the words which Christ spoke when He instituted the Holy Supper. Fourthly, the bread and wine must be *distributed,* and the communicants must eat and drink them. Fifthly, it must distinctly be professed that *this Supper is the body and blood of Christ,* as He Himself has said. These are the chief points from which thou wilt be able to tell whether the Communion celebrated in any church is truly the Lord's Supper or not. Everything beyond these five points is not essential to the Lord's Supper, and is a matter of Christian liberty. But beware of every so-called Lord's Supper which is not truly the Lord's Supper, which is not administered according to the institution of Christ.

PRAYER.—I thank Thee, dear Lord, that in these last days of sore distress Thou permittest me to find places of public worship where Thy Holy Sacrament is administered in its truth and purity, according to Thy institution. Grant me grace, I beseech Thee, to hold fast to such treasure, and to resist every falsification whatsoever of this holy Sacrament, lest I be cheated out of my salvation. Grant that in firm faith I may comfort myself with Thy gift of grace. Amen.

Hymn 436, 8.

THURSDAY.

Given for you. Shed for you. For the remission of sins. Luke 22, 19. 20. Matt. 26, 28.

It has already been briefly stated in last Saturday's lesson what blessed benefit is offered us through the Lord's Supper, and that we may understand the nature of this benefit from the words: "Given and shed for you for the remission of sins." In the Lord's Supper thou receivest that very body and that very blood wherewith on the cross Christ procured forgiveness of sins for all the world. The precious ransom with which payment was made for the remission of the sins of all the world is given thee for thy own individual possession. And hence forgiveness of sins is securely sealed to thee. And thus thy faith is exceedingly strengthened, the blessed assurance that thy, yes, indeed, thy sins are forgiven unto thee. And thou art fully assured of life and salvation; for where there is forgiveness of sins, there is also life and salvation. Do see, do consider! By shedding His blood and dying upon the cross, Christ has procured forgiveness of sins, life, and salvation for all the world and also for thee. Thou knowest this from the Gospel. But now, in the Lord's Supper, thy crucified Savior comes to thee and to thy fellow-Christians, and, giving bread and wine to each of you, says: "Take, eat; this is my body, which is given for you. Take, drink ye all of it; this is my blood, which is shed for you for the remission of sins." While thou eatest the bread and drinkest the wine, He offers unto thee His body, which was given for thee, and His blood, which was shed for thee. How canst thou doubt any longer that He means thee? How canst thou doubt that God gives thee forgiveness of sins, life and salvation, when He who is thy Righteousness and the Resurrection and the Life, with visible signs and gracious words lays Himself into thy very mouth and heart?

PRAYER.—O Thou Savior, full of love and tender mercy, what more couldst Thou do to assure me, a poor sinner, of the forgiveness of sins, of life, and salvation? Thy loving-kindness is unfathomable. Open my eyes and heart by Thy Holy Spirit that I may truly learn to know the superabundance of Thy grace and rejoice that I may comfort myself with it in life and death. Amen.

Hymn 435, 2.

FRIDAY.

For we, being many, are one bread and one body; for we are all partakers of that one bread.—1 Cor. 10, 17.

Since the Lord's Supper so greatly enhances our assurance of the forgiveness of our sins through our Lord Jesus Christ, it also greatly strengthens us to lead a holy life. For a godly life proceeds only from the firm assurance that by the grace of God we have received the adoption of sons. And the stronger this faith is, the greater strength we shall receive to lead a holy life. By partaking of the Lord's Supper we Christians become *one* body with Christ. If we firmly believe this, can we serve sin any longer? Shall we not then walk as it becometh the members of the body of Christ? And He who is our Head also gives us, His members, divine strength to lead a holy life. And His Holy Supper, too, is the very means through which He does this. A foremost characteristic of a godly life is brotherly love which Christians should show each other. This is strengthened through the Lord's Supper. For if we commune together, we become ever more convinced that, though being many, through it we become *one* body; for we are all partakers of that *one* bread, of the *one* body of Christ. What is natural kinship as compared with this spiritual and heavenly kinship? And what is natural love as compared with this spiritual love? The fellowship of the Lord's Supper, which we Christians have among and with one another is a testimony that, though many, we are *one* body, that is to say, that through *one* common faith we are most intimately joined with Christ, and through Christ with one another. Therefore we should eagerly maintain altar fellowship with those who with us confess the true faith; not, however, with those who have separated from us by adhering to a false doctrine.

PRAYER.—I thank Thee, Lord God Almighty, for the wondrous gift which Thou bestowest upon me in the Holy Supper. And I beseech Thy mercy that Thou wouldst cause it to strengthen my faith toward Thee, to make me abound more and more in true holiness and in fervent love toward my neighbor: through Jesus Christ, Thy Son, our Lord. Amen.

Hymn 431, 3.

SATURDAY.

Given for you. Shed for you. For the remission of sins. Luke 22, 19. 20. Matt. 26, 28.

If in true faith we partake of the Lord's Supper, we receive forgiveness of sins, life, and salvation. This is most certainly true. But how can bodily eating and drinking do such great things? Thus, with scorn and disdain, those enthusiasts ask who reject the Scriptural doctrine of the Means of Grace. And now we join Dr. Luther in asking this question, in order to arrive at a clear understanding in this matter.—Mere eating and drinking in itself surely has not the power to do these great things. There is no doubt about that. But through the words of Christ: " Given and shed for you for the remission of sins," yes, indeed, by the virtue of these words, forgiveness of sins, life, and salvation are not only contained in the Lord's Supper, but offered to every one that eateth and drinketh. Hence, beside the bodily eating and drinking these words are as the chief thing in the Sacrament. But only such actually *receive* forgiveness of sins, life, and salvation as eat and drink not only in a natural manner, but also spiritually, that is to say, such as believe the words of promise. Every one to whom the Lord's Supper is distributed in accordance with His institution receives the body and blood of Christ under the bread and wine. But the benefit, the blessed benefit of it, namely, forgiveness of sins, life, and salvation, is received by him only who believes the words of promise: "Given and shed for you for the remission of sins." Whoever eats and drinks unworthily, that is to say, without believing the words of promise, him God will visit in wrath and judgment.

PRAYER.—Lord Jesus, I thank Thee that in the words of institution Thou hast clearly and unmistakably stated what Thou desirest to give me in the Holy Supper, namely, forgiveness of sins, life, and salvation. O my dear Savior, grant me Thy Holy Spirit, that I may fasten mine eyes upon these Thy words, gathering comfort therefrom in true faith, and thus obtaining blessing lasting through all eternity by partaking of Thy Holy Supper. Amen.

Hymn 434, 4. 5.

Week of the Sixteenth Sunday After Trinity.

SUNDAY.

Let a man examine himself, and so let him eat of that bread and drink of that cup. For he that eateth and drinketh unworthily, eateth and drinketh damnation to himself, not discerning the Lord's body.—1 Cor. 11, 28. 29.

Dost thou note this earnest admonition of the Holy Spirit? Thou must examine thyself to see whether thou be worthy to receive the body and the blood of Christ under the consecrated bread and wine for the remission of sins. Who is worthy to do this? Fasting and bodily preparation, appearing with due modesty and reverence at the Lord's Table, this is, indeed, a fine outward training and a praiseworthy custom; but they are nothing but outward acts which even a hypocrite may perform. The right and true, in fact, the only worthiness consists in believing these words: "*Given and shed for you for the remission of sins.*" If thou approachest the Lord's Table regarding thyself a forlorn sinner, seeking forgiveness through Jesus Christ, and if then thou reliest upon the words: "Given and shed for you for the remission of sins," thou art worthy and well prepared. But he that does not believe these words, or doubts them, is unworthy and unprepared. For when God out of great mercy gives us the body and blood of Christ and says: "*For you!*" namely, for the remission of sins, He wants us to believe this with a glad and grateful heart. Thus thou seest that partaking of the Lord's Supper worthily is not effected by any external preparation, nor by thinking pious thoughts or by doing various deeds of your own choice or making. Thank God that it is not so. But if thou comest as a poor, miserable sinner who heartily desires to obtain salvation through Christ, which salvation is offered in the Lord's Supper, then thou art acceptable with God, the Merciful. Examine thyself with regard to this.

PRAYER.—O Lord Jesus, Thou callest not saints, but sinners, to the Supper which Thy grace hath provided, but such sinners as rely upon Thy gracious Word. Grant me grace to always approach Thy Table as a poor sinner, hungering after grace and trusting Thy Word which promiseth grace, and to receive the forgiveness offered me therein with a believing heart. Amen.

Hymn 441, 5-7.

MONDAY.

Let a man examine himself, and so let him eat of that bread and drink of that cup.—1 Cor. 11, 28.

How shouldst thou examine thyself, and according to what rule, when thou wouldst eat of this bread and drink of this cup? Thou should *first* examine thyself as to whether thou truly repentest of thy sins. A child of God is most heartily sorry for his sins. A child of God is controlled and moved by the Holy Spirit, and every sin is as intolerable to him as a mote in the eye. Thou shouldst examine thyself *secondly* as to whether thou believest in Jesus Christ. To believe in Jesus Christ is to have a correct knowledge of the great and mighty grace, ever new, which Jesus Christ has procured by His suffering and death, and which he has laid down in the Holy Sacrament and always offers thee there freely and without price, and to put thy trust in it, and comfort thyself with it in the face of all, indeed, *all* thy sins. Thou shouldst examine thyself *thirdly* as to whether it is thy sincere purpose and intention henceforth to mend thy sinful life with the aid of God the Holy Ghost. A child of God that is heartily sorry for his sins most assuredly is earnestly resolved to abandon those sins. And when this child of God has learned to truly know, and rejoice in, the superabounding grace of God in Christ, he will also gladly mend his life, and most earnestly strive to please God. Examine thyself as to whether these three things are found with thee. If so, even though in a small measure only,—for thou still hast the wicked old Adam,—then go to the Lord's Supper, and there again receive the assurance of the grace of God. That will strengthen thee spiritually.

PRAYER.—My dear Heavenly Father, I know Thou lov'st me still as Thine, though 'gainst me world, sin, hell combine. Grant unto me Thy Holy Spirit, that with heartfelt repentance for my sins, with true faith in my Savior Jesus Christ, and with a sincere purpose of henceforth mending my sinful life I may come to Thy gracious Supper. And then bestow upon me all the blessings which by means of Thy Word Thou hast treasured up in this Sacrament. Amen.

Hymn 436, 7.

TUESDAY.

Lord, I believe; help Thou mine unbelief!—Mark 9, 24.

Faith, the faith of a poor sinner in his Savior Jesus Christ, constitutes the only true worthiness when appearing at the Lord's Supper. But how about those whose faith is weak? May they approach the Lord's Table?—Who is to be called weak of faith? Why, one who indeed believes in his Savior, but whose faith wants strength, and whose spiritual life, accordingly, is also weak, but—note this well!—who deplores his weakness and earnestly desires to be stronger, a person who cries like the father of that lunatic child, tearfully perchance, and says: "Lord, I believe; help Thou mine unbelief!" May such a person go to the Lord's Supper? Yes, indeed. He particularly should partake of the Lord's Supper, that his weak faith may grow stronger by using this Means of Grace. O the Savior rejoices when such a one comes to Him there to be helped by Him. He says: "Him that cometh to me I will in no wise cast out." (John 6, 37.) Isaiah already prophesied of the Savior: "A bruised reed shall He not break, and the smoking flax shall He not quench." (Is. 42, 3.) And is not one whose faith is weak like a bruised reed and smoking flax? Ah, the weak in faith is so miserable, and feels himself so unworthy and meek. But "the meek shall eat and be satisfied." (Ps. 22, 26.) A person whose faith is still weak is sick, spiritually sick. The Lord's Supper is medicine, spiritual medicine. Shall he take it? Yes indeed!—Does this comfort thee, my dear Christian?

PRAYER.—Ah, my Lord Jesus, what am I? I am a weak, miserable person, like a bruised reed, easily shaken by the devil, the world, and the flesh, and my faith is but a smoking flax, not burning with a bright and lusty flame. I know this and deplore it. And Thou wouldst have me— and Thou wouldst help me and heal me and make me strong. For this I give thanks unto Thee, Lord Jesus! And behold, I come to Thy Supper and unto Thee to be helped and healed by Thee. Amen.

Hymn 441, 4.

WEDNESDAY.

Give not that which is holy unto the dogs, neither cast ye your pearls before swine.—Matt. 7, 6.

These are words of our blessed Lord. By "that which is holy" He also means the Lord's Supper, which is one of our "pearls." By "dogs" and "swine" He means such as are known to be ungodly and impenitent; for after the manner of dogs and swine they abuse this most holy thing which the mercy of God has devised for us poor sinners.

Is it not so? The Lord's Supper should be denied to such persons. They would eat and drink damnation unto themselves in the Holy Supper. They are unworthy of the Lord's Supper. And "he that eateth and drinketh unworthily eateth and drinketh damnation to himself, not discerning the Lord's body," says the Holy Spirit. (1 Cor. 11, 29.) And when a pastor knowingly and intentionally, out of indifference, from fear of men, or for the love of gain, admits such ungodly and impenitent persons to the Lord's Supper, then he flatly disobeys the injunction of the Lord and brings down upon himself the curse of God. And when church-members, for any reason whatsoever, demand that such persons be admitted to the Lord's Supper, they are in the same position. The Lord's Supper is instituted for Christians, for God's children, who repent of their sins, believe in Christ, and are earnestly resolved, with the aid of God the Holy Ghost, henceforth to mend their sinful lives. It is good and profitable for every one to take this to heart.

PRAYER.—Graciously grant, O Lord and Savior, that Thy holy Sacrament may be kept sacred among us, and be used by us for our soul's welfare, and that it may not be cast before dogs and swine. Grant me and all sincere Christians grace to come to a true knowledge of this Thy will and to take it well to heart. O let Thy worthy Sacrament be among us what Thy mercy has designed it to be: a table where wholesome food and drink is given to poor and griefstricken sinners who put their trust in Thee. Amen.

Hymn 441, 3.

THURSDAY.

They continued steadfastly in the apostles' doctrine and fellowship, and in breaking of bread, and in prayers.—Acts 2, 42.

To the heterodox, that is, to those who deviate from the Word of God in many points of Christian doctrine and believe and profess false doctrine, hence, to people who on account of such false doctrines have separated from the orthodox church, or who want to hold and teach false doctrine within the pale of the orthodox church—to such heterodox persons we must deny the Lord's Supper, nor must we partake of the Lord's Supper in churches teaching false doctrines. Why not? Is it because we must condemn every person who holds false doctrine? By no means! We know and rejoice in the fact that even among the heterodox God has dear children, souls that truly believe in Jesus Christ, but are not aware of the fact that they depart from, and contradict, the Word of God with their false doctrine. Why, then, must we not commune at the same altar with the heterodox? Because altar fellowship is an outward and visible manifestation of unity of faith, of faith and church-fellowship. Those who break the bread together, that is, who commune together, thereby confess before the whole world that they have *one* faith, *one* doctrine, *one* confession, or creed, in common, as did the first Christians, of whom our text speaks. To practice altar- and, in general, church-fellowship with the heterodox would mean to surrender that which is holy, and our pearls, and to acknowledge false doctrine, which we must heartily reject and condemn, because it opposes the salutary Word of God, to be true and right.

PRAYER.—Ah, Lord Jesus Christ, how sadly Thy Christian Church is rent asunder by false doctrine, sectarianism, and fantastic vagaries! Lord Jesus, I thank Thee that nevertheless Thou dost sustain Thy Christians, Thy true disciples, who believe in Thee and are saved, even in the midst of such manifold and strong delusion. I furthermore thank Thee that Thou hast granted me grace to know the truth. Give me, I beseech Thee, Thy Holy Spirit, that despite all contempt and calumny I may hold fast to Thy Word and guard against every fusion with false doctrine. Amen.

Hymn 278, 6.

FRIDAY.

If thou bring thy gift to the altar, and there rememberest that thy brother hath aught against thee, leave there thy gift before the altar and go thy way; first be reconciled to thy brother, and then come and offer thy gift.—Matt. 5, 23. 24.

Suppose that by a sin which thou hast committed, or by what appeared such, thou hast given offense to one or more or all of thy brethren in the congregation, so as to give them reason to think that thou art still impenitent, and, possibly, by thy bad example to cause weak Christians to be led astray. What must thou do then if thou wouldst be a true Christian? Thou must at once, quickly, with haste, eagerly and willingly remove this offense. And how shouldst thou do it? Thou must tell all who know of the matter that thou art heartily sorry for what thou hast done, and that thou humbly seekest comfort in God's grace, and with the help of God desirest to mend thy ways. And thou must not go to the Lord's Supper, nor should thy pastor permit thee to commune, until thou hast done so. The offense would be far greater if thou wouldst go to the Lord's Supper before doing this. God wants thee to first remove the offense in this manner. See what our text at the head of our devotion says. No offering, no prayer, nothing that thou mayest do, least of all thy partaking of the Lord's Supper, is acceptable with the Lord unless thou removest the offense thou hast given. But a true child of God, who is sincerely sorry for his sin, certainly is glad and willing to remove the offense he has given by his sin.

PRAYER.—Lord Jesus, I am Thine. Keep me from sin! Because I am Thine, I am Thy witness who is to proclaim Thee by word and deed, that Thy Christian Church may be built also by me. Graciously guard me against giving offense to others! And when, by reason of the weakness of my depraved flesh and the temptations of the evil spirit, I have given an offense, do Thou help me by Thy Holy Spirit to repent straightforth and remove the offense. And then let me be assured of Thy grace through Thy holy Sacrament! Amen.

Hymn 430, 1. 2.

SATURDAY.

Let a man examine himself, and so let him eat of that bread and drink of that cup.—1 Cor. 11, 28.

Thou art familiar with this word of Scripture. A Christian should examine himself before going to the Lord's Supper as to whether he be in the faith and therefore will receive this Sacrament worthily. For that reason we must not give this Sacrament to such as cannot examine themselves, for instance, not to those adults who as yet have not a sufficient knowledge of the Word of God for such self-examination. They should first be instructed in the same. Nor should we admit little children to this Sacrament, for though, through Baptism, they have been united with Christ in faith, yet they do not understand the Word of God sufficiently to be able to examine themselves. They should be instructed in the Word of God as soon as possible, and when they have arrived at a satisfactory spiritual maturity, they should be given the Lord's Supper. In our churches we therefore have the laudable custom of confirmation. There the children that have been instructed, publicly, in the presence of the congregation, give account of their faith, confess their faithful adherence to the Church of the true faith, and thereupon receive the holy Sacrament of the body and blood of Christ. Nor should the Lord's Supper be given to sick people that are in a state of unconsciousness, or to such insane as are unfit for self-examination. But in all this we must not forget that the Comforter, the Holy Ghost, surely sustains the light of faith within their hearts and makes them partakers of salvation, if they have not otherwise been unbelievers. And now, my dear Christian, examine thyself, whether thou be a poor penitent sinner who believes in his Savior and is willing to serve Him, and then approach the Lord's Table, where thou receivest such complete and glorious assurance of the grace of God.

PRAYER.—Help, Lord God, that I, a poor sinner, may sincerely repent of my sins, find true comfort in Thy merit, desire to mend my life, and thus at all times, unto my end, receive the assurance of Thy grace which Thy holy Sacrament so abundantly offers unto me. Amen.

Hymn 432, 7.

THIRD PART.
THE CHRISTIAN'S LIFE AND DEATH.

Week of the Seventeenth Sunday After Trinity.

SUNDAY.

Blessed are the poor in spirit; for theirs is the kingdom of heaven.—Matt. 5, 3.

True Christians, who in faith are sure of their Savior and of His salvation, are poor in spirit. They are poor in spirit with regard to all those things that do not concern Christ and His salvation. Spiritually, in their spirit, which is ruled by the Holy Spirit, they are poor with regard to these things. They do not regard these things; they do not set their hearts on them; they consider them quite vain and of no value. Their spirit, their heart, soul, and mind, is filled with the things they have in Christ; therefore their soul is free and unencumbered as respects all other things. When people praise them and call them happy because of any earthly and personal advantages, they smilingly shake their heads and think of the advantages which Christ has given them. Must not the light of the moon and the stars pale before that of the sun? The Apostle Paul was a man who was thus poor in spirit. He writes: " But what things were gain to me, those I counted loss for Christ. Yea, doubtless; and I count all things but loss for the excellency of the knowledge of Christ Jesus, my Lord, for whom I have suffered the loss of all things, and do count them but dung, that I may win Christ, and be found in Him, not having mine own righteousness, which is of the Law, but that which is of the faith of Christ, the righteousness which is of God by faith: that I may know Him, and the power of His resurrection, and the fellowship of His sufferings, being made conformable unto His death, if by any means I might attain unto the resurrection of the dead." (Phil. 3, 7-11.) Thus true Christians are poor, poor in spirit with regard to all that pertains to their persons and to earthly matters. But they are blessed, very rich and happy, for theirs is the Kingdom of Heaven.

PRAYER.—O my God, who for Christ's sake hast graciously given me the riches of the Kingdom of Heaven, make me poor in spirit through Thy Holy Spirit, that I may not set my heart on anything that is severed from Christ, lest I be again enchanted and ensnared by vain, fleeting, and delusive things, but that with all my heart I desire only that which will make me truly and eternally happy. Amen.

Hymn 83, 1.

MONDAY.

Blessed are they that mourn; for they shall be comforted. Matt. 5, 4.

True Christians, God's children, mourn here on earth. Why so? Their sin causes them to grieve and mourn. They are no longer rude and carnal-minded men that sport with sin. They are born again by the Spirit of God and desire earnestly to serve God with a pure heart and with good works that are pleasing in His sight; and it grieves them that sin still dwells within them and spiritually paralyzes them. Read the lamentation of St. Paul in Rom. 7, 14-24, where he finally exclaims: "O wretched man that I am! who shall deliver me from the body of this death?" The sin of others grieves them too, and they mourn because of it. What sad things they must see and experience! How the world does run into destruction! How many fall from faith! Nor are the Christians exempt from this earth's misery which befalls all mankind. And besides this, the hatred of the devil and of the wicked world is directed against them especially. And, moreover, they must crucify their own flesh, which causes pain, indeed. And in addition to all this, they experience the chastisement of God, which smarts, though it is gracious and wholesome. Yes, indeed, true Christians and children of God mourn here on earth. But they are blessed. For, being the children of God, they shall be comforted. They shall be comforted always, even here on earth. God Himself comforts them through His Word and Holy Spirit. God speaks words of tender love to their hearts, telling them that He loves them; that all their sins have been fully forgiven for Christ's sake; that He desires them to remain His dear children, though world, sin, and hell combine against them; that He will cause all, yea, all things to work together for good to them. Then the light of heavenly comfort burns bright within them. And in the blessed life to come this light of comfort will utterly and completely dispel all the darkness of sorrow. "Blessed are they that mourn; for they shall be comforted."

PRAYER.—Come, Lord Jesus, and do unto me according to Thy Word! Let me bear the sorrow of the children of God, but also give unto me the comfort which Thou hast promised them that are Thine. And after this life let me graciously enjoy the fullness of comfort in the mansions of eternal bliss. Amen.

Hymn 333, 2.

TUESDAY.

Blessed are the meek; for they shall inherit the earth.—Matt. 5, 5.

True Christians, God's children, are meek. They are not selfish, willful, quarrelsome, contentious, disputatious, vindictive, angry, spiteful. And when they are tempted by their flesh in this direction they are soon brought back to a state of meekness through the Holy Spirit that abides in them. The love of Christ rules within them; it makes them longsuffering and kind; it does not suffer them to grow envious, to vaunt themselves, to be puffed up, to deport themselves unseemly, to seek their own, to be easily provoked, nor to think evil; it makes them bear all things, believe all things, hope all things, endure all things. True Christians, God's children, gladly yield in all things pertaining to their own person. Only when the Word of God and their faith is attacked, they stand firm and unyielding. They rather suffer wrong than do wrong. They are ever ready to forgive. It is easy to get along with them. They are blessed people. For, says the Savior, they shall inherit the earth. They shall dwell on earth in that peace which is denied them that are not meek. For the Lord, their Lord, espouses their cause, and protects them, and sees to it that justice is done them. The Lord makes even their enemies to be at peace with them. They have the promise of the life that now is, and of that which is to come. They shall inherit the new earth, wherein dwelleth righteousness. "Blessed are the meek; for they shall inherit the earth."

PRAYER.—Thou meek Jesus, my Lord and Savior, who didst not strive nor cry, nor didst cause an angry voice to be heard in the streets, who didst suffer patiently, and didst make intercession for Thy enemies, and didst commit all to Him that judgeth righteously: make me, Thy disciple, to be like unto Thee! Espouse my cause on this sad earth, until Thou shalt bring me where I shall inherit the new earth. Amen.

Hymn 334, 2. 3.

WEDNESDAY.

Blessed are they that do hunger and thirst after righteousness; for they shall be filled.—Matt. 5. 6.

All poor sinners who truly believe in Jesus Christ have and possess with Him that righteousness wherein they can stand before God and be saved. For the righteousness of Christ is imputed to true faith, be it strong or weak. And this is valid before God and will avail before His judgment-seat, for it is a spotless and perfect righteousness. After this righteousness of faith Christians need not hunger and thirst; they have it, and they praise the unfathomable grace of God who has graciously procured this righteousness for them, and through faith gives and appropriates it to them. But now they hunger and thirst after another righteousness. They hunger and thirst after a righteousness which they are to practice in their every-day life. Just because they have learned to know and have experienced the wonderful grace of God, thanks to which all their sins are forgiven and in no wise imputed unto them, they continually hunger and thirst to do only that which is right before God and over against their neighbor, and what God would have them do. And it grieves them that they succeed so poorly. For their old Adam clings to them until they die. And so this hunger and thirst is with them until they depart this life. Indeed, the better Christians we become, the more this hunger and thirst increases, as well as the grief that goes with it. But for this very reason, just because we hunger and thirst in this manner, we are blessed people. For by the grace of God we shall then ever more succeed to do right. And when this brief time is past, when we fall asleep and awaken again, then we shall be perfectly righteous. Our hunger and thirst shall be satisfied.

PRAYER.—Give unto me, therefore, O merciful God, give unto me, whom Thou hast graciously received as Thy child, that hunger and thirst after righteousness which I should practice in my whole life, in everything that I may think or desire, speak or do. Increase this hunger and thirst within me! And satisfy it, O God! Satisfy it ever more and more by helping me to do what is right. Satisfy it fully when I shall awaken with Thy image. Amen.

Hymn 351, 2.

THURSDAY.

Blessed are the merciful; for they shall obtain mercy.—Matt. 5, 7.

True Christians, God's children, are known to be merciful. For their faith daily teaches and reminds them that it is only and exclusively by the mercy of God that they are what they are. And this light of divine mercy is reflected in their regenerated hearts. They also hear their Savior say: "Be ye therefore merciful, as your Father also is merciful." (Luke 6, 36.) And the Holy Spirit, the Spirit of the Father and of Christ, makes them merciful. And the seed of mercy germinates and sprouts and buds and blossoms and bears fruit within their hearts, which by nature indeed are sinful and, hence, unmerciful. For the new birth is mightier than the carnal birth. True Christians, God's children, are merciful toward friend and foe, toward fellow-believers and toward such as adhere to false doctrines, toward rich and poor, indeed, toward everybody. Mercy is the element in which they live, as a fish lives in water and a bird in the air. They are blessed. For they, too, obtain mercy, even in this present time, from God, their Father, and from their brethren and sisters in the faith. And one day, on the day of Christ's reappearing, theirs shall be a bliss inexpressible, when by God's mercy they shall bask in His never-ending mercies.

PRAYER.—Merciful God, in whose mercy I live and have my being, whose mercy shall one day greet and satisfy and enrapture me: make me, a poor sinner, I beseech Thee, ever more like unto Thee. My Father, I desire to bear Thy image, for I love Thee. And I would have all men know that I am Thy child. Make me merciful, even as Thou art merciful! Amen.

Hymn 362, 1. 3.

FRIDAY.

Blessed are the pure in heart; for they shall see God.— Matt. 5, 8.

The Prophet Isaiah says: "We are all as an unclean thing, **and all our righteousnesses are as filthy rags.**" (Is. 64, **6.**) God Himself says: "The imagination of man's **heart is evil** from his youth." (Gen. 8, 21.) Does this also refer to true Christians, to God's children? Most assuredly. The heart of true Christians is still smirched with sin. And just they, more than all other men, know this and sincerely deplore this sad fact. But their sin is forgiven unto them. " The blood of Jesus Christ, God's Son, cleanseth us from all sin." (1 John 1, 7.) And "now are we the sons of God, and it doth not yet appear what we shall be; but we know that, when He shall appear, we shall be like Him; for we shall see Him as He is. And every man that hath this hope in him *purifieth himself,* even as He is pure." (1 John 3, 2, 3.) There we have it. True Christians, the children of God, strive against all sin and uncleanness that dwells within them, and through the Holy Spirit that dwells within them they rule over sin. They are always mindful of the pure and holy God, who in Christ is their dear Father, and seek to be like unto Him. Art thou not familiar with this? And thus they, we, are blessed people. God shall crown our seeking with joy: one day we shall see God; then the glorious image of God shall be resplendent within our souls and be reflected therein in heavenly and perfect purity. Yea, "blessed are the pure in heart; for they shall see God."

PRAYER.—My God and Father, who through Jesus Christ hast adopted me as Thy dear child, and hast given me Thy Holy Spirit, that I may greatly rejoice in Him: give, O give unto me an abundant measure of Thy grace, that I may rule over all the unclean desires of my depraved heart and purify myself. And finally let me see Thy face in the everlasting light, and illumine me throughout unto perfect purity. Amen.

Hymn 343, 5.

SATURDAY.

Blessed are the peacemakers; for they shall be called the children of God.—Matt. 5, 9.

The most frightful and insane war imaginable is that which, in consequence of sin, the creature has declared against God, its Creator. Death immediately followed upon the first transgression. But God, out of great mercy, made peace through Christ Jesus. And God proclaims this peace through His Word and His Holy Spirit. And they who accept this gracious peace are the children of peace and of God. To them the Holy Ghost says: "If it be possible, as much as lieth in you, live peaceably with all men." (Rom. 12, 18.) And the children of God are always ready to listen to this. Being of the same mind, it easily impresses itself upon their minds. They endeavor to always live at peace with all men. There are always two parties to a quarrel. If any one wants to start to quarrel with them, they simply will not do so. They furthermore endeavor to make peace when they see others quarrel. They do not, however, desire to have and maintain a hollow peace, which would compel them to forsake the Word of God, the saving Truth, and to renounce obedience to God. No, that is impossible for them to do. But where only human beings and human rights are concerned, they are ready to make peace, there they draw round about them a circle of peace. "Blessed are the peacemakers; for they shall be called the children of God." Thus says the Savior. For by their peaceableness they prove that they are the children of God, the God of peace. And on the day of Judgment it will become evident before all men that the peaceable disposition which they showed here on earth proves them to have been the children of God.

PRAYER.—Gracious God, who hast given that peace which comprises all blessedness unto me, a sinner and rebellious creature, grant that this knowledge may make me peaceable such as Thou wouldst have me be. Give unto me Thy Holy Spirit, that I may always bear in mind that I am Thy child through Jesus Christ, my Savior. Amen.

Hymn 346, 5.

Week of the Eighteenth Sunday After Trinity.

SUNDAY.

Blessed are they that are persecuted for righteousness' sake; for theirs is the kingdom of heaven.—Matt. 5, 10.

True Christians, God's children, are righteous, upright, and honest in all their dealings, and they avoid and reprove all unrighteousness and dishonesty. For this reason they are an eyesore to the children of the world, who feel a sting in their conscience when they see them. And the world persecutes them, and refuses to tolerate them, and harms them. But they are blessed, for the Kingdom of Heaven, the blessed kingdom of the eternal God, is theirs. But *who* in this world is hated and reviled most of all? Jesus Christ. And *what* is hated and reviled more than anything else? The Word of Jesus. True Christians, God's children, stand by their beloved Savior, and they profess and proclaim and defend His Word, and follow Him in all things. And so the hatred and reproach which meets Jesus and His Word is turned against them. Men revile and persecute them and say all manner of evil against them. Ah, let them but see to it that there is not a grain of truth in all the evil things that are said about them. Then they may rejoice and be exceeding glad; for just so were the Prophets and the Apostles persecuted, the men who foretold the coming of Christ and witnessed of Him. Blessed are the Christians in such persecution. For then it is evident that the Spirit of Christ rests upon them, and manifests Himself through them, that Spirit whom the Christless world and also the false church cannot bear. And in heaven, which to them is no far-off dream, but a reality near at hand, they shall find abundant solace and reward for every contempt and persecution they had to suffer here on earth. (Matt. 5, 11. 12.)

PRAYER.—Lord Jesus, my only Salvation, help me to take my stand with Thee firmly, freely, and frankly, and to profess Thy Word, and to let it guide me into all righteousness in this world of unrighteousness, where Thou and Thy

Word are hated so bitterly. And if I suffer contempt and persecution on account of it, then give me courage and the solace of Thy Holy Spirit, that with great rejoicing I may wait for heaven, where my home is and the eternal rest awaiting me. Amen.

Hymn 351, 3. 4.

MONDAY.

Ye are the salt of the earth.—Matt. 5, 13.

Salt keeps meat from decay and ruin, and makes it palatable. The Savior has prepared and appointed His Christians to be the salt of the earth. They are to keep decaying and ruining mankind from eternal ruin, and to make God's children of them, in whom God takes delight. How and by what means are Christians to be the salt of the earth? By bearing witness of the Savior in word and deed. Every one that believes in the Savior should bear witness by word and deed that in Christ there is salvation and righteousness and true holiness. Every Christian should be a constant and active witness of mankind's only Savior. This is the exalted and glorious calling of the Christians here on earth. The Savior says this very distinctly. He says: "Ye are the salt of the earth." But if the salt have lost its savor, wherewith shall it be salted? The Savior Himself no longer sojourns visibly on earth. Nor does He send His angels to do this. When Christians become unfit for their calling, when, instead of being the salt of the earth, they become inveigled into imitating the ways of the world, then they are henceforth good for nothing; God will then cast them out to be fully trodden under foot by the world; they then become amalgamated with the Christless world and will perish with it. O Christian, be aware of thy calling! See to it that on thy part thou be the salt of the earth!

PRAYER.—Lord Jesus, I am Thine. And because I am Thine, I must be Thy witness. And Thou hast made me sufficient hereunto by giving me the Spirit of faith. Now help me, O Jesus, to rightly know my calling and to fulfill its duties sincerely and faithfully. And grant Thy blessing that through my testimony men may be brought to living faith in Thee. Guard me against losing my savor, like salt will, lest like it, I be cast away. Hear me, O Savior! Amen.

Hymn 366, 2.

TUESDAY.

Woe to that man by whom the offense cometh!—Matt. 18, 7.

The word "offense" really signifies an obstruction, a stumbling-block placed in the way which causes one to fall. In a spiritual sense it signifies a temptation, a falling from grace, a seducing from the path of righteousness to a life of wickedness. To "give offense," or to "offend," therefore means to tempt and seduce one to do evil, to become wicked. When it is said that "offenses come by" some one, it means that one tempts and seduces others to become wicked. No offenses should come by us Christians, by children of God; we should give offense to no one, offend no fellow-man. Neither by word nor by behavior, neither by speech nor by example, should we offend any one, that is, tempt, or seduce, one to become wicked, to fall into unbelief and sin, or to remain in unbelief and sin and be hardened therein. On the contrary, we have learned that we should be the salt of the earth. The Apostle says: "Let every one of us please his neighbor for his good, to edification." (Rom. 15, 2.) Hence, if we offend any one, we set ourselves in direct opposition to our Christian calling. And our Savior says: "Woe to that man by whom the offense cometh!" And furthermore: "Whoso shall offend one of these little ones that believe in Me, it were better for him that a millstone were hanged about his neck, and that he were drowned in the depth of the sea." (Matt. 18, 6.) Let us, therefore, beware of giving offense to anybody! And if by reason of the weakness of our flesh and blood we have in any way done this, let us hasten, *hasten,* HASTEN to remove the offense by a penitent and unreserved confession.

PRAYER.—Lord Jesus, grant Thy grace, I beseech Thee, unto me, a poor sinner, but who, nevertheless, is

Thy own by faith, that I may walk circumspectly so as to give offense to no one, but rather please my neighbor for his good, to edification. And if ever I have offended any one by word or deed, grant unto me Thy Holy Spirit that I may immediately confess my wrong and make due apology, and thus still prove myself a Christian. Amen.

Hymn 333, 1.

WEDNESDAY.

It must needs be that offenses come.—Matt. 18, 7.

"It must needs be that offenses come," says our Savior. In this wicked, bad, and sinful world it cannot be otherwise. By word and behavior, by speech and example, there are abundant, yea, thousandfold temptations and enticements to wickedness. Thou surely knowest this, my dear Christian. Art thou not surrounded by false teachers of all description, by apostles of unbelief and by scoffers, coarse as well as refined, by sects and fanatics of every hue and color, by followers of Antichrist, by men and women who lead a life of vice and shame, who drink iniquity like water? Must it then not needs be that offenses come? Most certainly! All the world is full of offenses, of temptation and enticement to evil. And thou art brought face to face with these things. But do not *take* and *receive* such offense! Even as thou must not give offense, so also thou must not suffer others to offend, that is to say, to seduce thee, to lead thee into sin. Arm thyself in faith with the Word and Spirit of God! Fight the good fight of faith, otherwise thou wilt be lost! Call upon the Lord; He will give thee power to conquer all thy spiritual assailants. Thou must also remember that offenses given thee are caused by thy own heart, by the members of thy own body, and by things most near and dear to thee. Pluck them out, cut them off, and cast them from thee! With might and main thou must renounce everything that would make thee wicked. It is better for thee to enter into life poor and afflicted than, enjoying all temporal goods to the full, to be cast into eternal hell-fire. (Matt. 18, 8. 9.)

PRAYER.—O Lord Jesus, offenses compass me about, but in Thy name will I destroy them. They compass me about, yea, they compass me about, but in Thy name will I destroy them. They compass me about like bees; they are quenched as the fire of thorns; but in Thy name I will destroy them. They thrust sore at me that I might fall; but Thou, O Lord, help me! O Lord Jesus, Thou art my strength and song, and art become my Salvation. And in the eternal tabernacles of the righteous I shall lift up the voice of rejoicing and salvation. Amen.

Hymn 347, 3.

THURSDAY.

Agree with thine adversary quickly, whiles thou art in the way with him, lest at any time the adversary deliver thee to the Judge, and the Judge deliver thee to the officer, and thou be cast into prison. Verily, I say unto thee: Thou shalt by no means come out thence till thou hast paid the uttermost farthing.—Matt. 5, 25. 26.

Every one against whom or in whose presence thou hast sinned, hence, every one who justly hath aught against thee, is thy adversary. Personally he may be ready to forgive and to overlook thy sin, possibly from indifference; but in the eyes of God he nevertheless is thy adversary and thy accuser. (Gen. 4, 10.) And thou art his debtor. Thou owest him an apology, and thou must remove the offense thou hast given; indeed, a truly penitent heart will prompt thee to do so. Pay him what thou owest! Agree with him! "Agree with thine adversary quickly, whiles thou art in the way with him." What "way" is meant here? The way to the Judgment, which, as far as thou art concerned is immediately consequent upon thy death. How much time, therefore, is left for thee to agree with thy adversary? Thou dost not know in the least. Death and the Judgment may come to-day; thy life or his may end to-day. And if thou hast not agreed with thy adversary "on the way," if, in impenitent willfulness, thou hast allowed the time while thou art in the way with him to expire, then thy adversary—or, let me say, thy guilt—will deliver thee to the Judge, and the Judge will deliver thee to the officer, and thou wilt be cast into prison. "The Son of Man shall send forth His angels, and they shall gather out of His kingdom all things that offend, and them that do iniquity, and shall cast them into a furnace of fire; there shall be wailing and gnashing of teeth." ·(Matt. 13, 41. 42.) And thou shalt by no means come out thence till thou hast paid the uttermost farthing. But then it will be too late, for then the time of grace will have been spent.

PRAYER.—O Lord Jesus, help me, a poor sinner, that sinneth so much against his neighbor, to repent this very day, ere sudden death take me away, and to prove my penitence by doing unto my neighbor as Thou hast commanded me to do. Let me not come into Judgment, O Jesus! Amen.
Hymn 55, 4.

FRIDAY.

But I say unto you, That ye resist not the evil; but whosoever shall smite thee on thy right cheek, turn to him the other also. And if any man will sue thee at the law, and take away thy coat, let him have thy cloak also. And whosoever shall compel thee to go a mile, go with him twain. Give to him that asketh thee, and from him that would borrow of thee turn not thou away.—Matt. 5, 39-42.

These words of the Savior are often ridiculed and badly misunderstood. Let us apply them to the life of the Christians, God's children, which they lead among one another.— Peradventure thy fellow-Christian, possibly by some fault of thine, is overcome with anger, and smites thee on thy right cheek. What then is thy Christian duty? Shouldst thou take revenge? By no means! Right meekly turn to him the other cheek also. Surely, he will soon see his wrong and love thee. And then all will be well, will it not? Or thy fellow-Christian, in the heat and zeal of disputatiousness, positively thinks that he has a right to thy coat, and would go to law with thee about it. Why, Christian, let him have thy cloak also! In so doing thou wilt heap coals of fire on his head and gain thy brother, which will the greatest gain. Or, perchance, thy fellow-Christian, with an importunity that savors much of arrogance, compels thee to go with him a mile. Go with him twain! That will tend more to make thy brother modest in future than if thou wouldst quarrel and remonstrate with him, or flatly refuse his request. Or thy fellow-Christian may be in trouble and wishes to borrow money of thee. Shouldst thou say: My money belongs to me, and I owe thee nothing? No, do not turn away from him in this manner, but give to thy brother! Dost thou note that what the Lord Jesus says here only emphasizes that brotherly love which is born of true faith?

PRAYER.—Lord Jesus, through Thy Holy Spirit grant me that tender consideration and heavenly wisdom of true brotherly love which is born of true faith in Thee, that I may not in any way be a hindrance to my brother and neighbor, but be serviceable to him on our mutual way to eternal life. Amen.

Hymn 247, 7.

SATURDAY.

Love your enemies.—Matt. 5, 44.

It is against our natural inclination to love our enemies. But we Christians no longer are what we were by nature. We no longer are natural men who cannot be subject to the Law of God, but we are new-born men, and through the Spirit of Christ that which the Law demands, all commandments, including that which enjoins us to love our enemies, has become our second nature. But since we still have the old Adam within us, our inborn sinful nature, therefore the Savior demands our second and new nature to come forth by saying: "Love your enemies." Ah, yes, just because the love of our enemies is so contrary to our old nature, we should remember all the more that we are new creatures, and should listen to the Word of Jesus: "Love your enemies." For, surely, we wish to do the will of God. It is the duty of Christians, God's children, to love their enemies, to bless them that curse them, to do good to them that hate them, to pray for them that despitefully use them and persecute them. They should be like unto their Father in heaven, who maketh His sun to rise on the evil and on the good, and sendeth rain on the just and on the unjust, yea, who caused His Son to die for His enemies. For if we love them that love us, what do we more than even unbelievers are doing? And if we salute our brethren only, what do we more than others? Do not even the children of the devil do so? We must strive after that perfection which we observe in our Father in heaven, and must love our enemies.

PRAYER.—Lord God, dear Heavenly Father, who hast made me Thy dear child through Jesus Christ, my Savior, and hast given me a new heart through Thy Holy Spirit, so that now I may know Thy holy will and gladly do according to it: help me to overcome the old Adam, the sin that clings to me, and quicken the new man within me through Thy Word, that the enmity of wicked men may not excite me to hatred, but that I may love my enemies as Thou didst love me when I was Thy enemy. Amen.

Hymn 205, 13.

Week of the Nineteenth Sunday After Trinity.

SUNDAY.

Take heed that ye do not your alms before men.—Matt. 6, 1.

Alms, in the first place, are gifts of charity given out of pity for the needy. But also such collections as are raised in our churches and congregations for the extension of Christ's Kingdom outside of their own circle may be included here. Now, if the Lord Jesus says: "Take heed that ye do not your alms before men," this first implies that we, His beloved Christians, should give alms. Love, which flows from faith, should impel us to give alms as our Lord would have us do. Hence, take heed that thou givest alms, and that thou givest commensurably with the respective need, and according to thy ability, according to the means the Lord has given thee. Furthermore the Lord here says that in giving alms we should take heed that we do it not before men, to be seen of them. We should not do as the hypocrites do, who cause a trumpet to be sounded before them in the churches and in the newspapers, that they may be honored by men. Verily, such people have their reward! They have what they paid for: the praise of men. They dare not look forward to the gracious reward in heaven promised by God to His children. Shall we be like those hypocrites? Therefore, when thou doest alms, do it lovingly, with singleness of heart, and let not thy left hand know what thy right hand doeth. Let thy alms be in secret! And thy Father who seeth in secret, and seeth thy love and compassion, the fruits of the Spirit of Christ, bud forth in thee, will, out of great mercy, reward thee openly, when that day cometh on which He shall prove, by the works the Christians have done, that they had a living faith.

PRAYER.—Dear Heavenly Father, who hast richly and abundantly bestowed upon me, a poor sinner, all Thy benefits and gifts of eternal mercy, help me by Thy Holy Spirit that I may glorify Thy mercy by likewise being merciful, and opening my heart and hand for the poor and needy in Thy Kingdom. Amen.

Hymn 358, 2.

MONDAY.

Lay not up for yourselves treasures upon earth, where moth and rust doth corrupt, and where thieves break through and steal; but lay up for yourselves treasures in heaven, where neither moth nor rust doth corrupt, and where thieves do not break through nor steal. For where your treasure is, there will your heart be also.—Matt. 6, 19-21.

Treasures upon earth are extremely perishable and uncertain. Moths corrupt costly garments. Mold and rust destroy palaces. Thieves, especially those great thieves called financiers and money-men, devise very shrewd plans to get other people's money and goods. Moreover, thy life on this earth, O Christian, is very short and always uncertain. Treasures in heaven are absolutely imperishable and certain. Jesus' blood and righteousness, the glorious dress wherein thou mayest stand before God, is ever new and good. The mansions in the Father's house, where Jesus has prepared a place for us, stand firm forever. The things God has placed to thy credit are unquestionably safe, and no one can take them from thee. Moreover, thy life in heaven, O Christian, is eternal. O Christian, hear what thy Savior says! Seek not, nor lay up, treasures upon earth, but seek and lay up treasures in heaven. For where thy treasure is, there will thy heart be also. If thou considerest earthly things desirable treasures, thy heart will be earthly-minded, and saving faith will die within thee. If thou considerest heavenly things treasures to be desired, thy heart will be heavenly-minded, and saving faith will gain ever more strength. Now choose, my dear Christian, where thou wouldst lay up treasures.

PRAYER.—I will lay up treasures in heaven, Lord Jesus! I will lay up those treasures which Thou by grace already hast given to me and ever wilt do so. O Lord Jesus, open my eyes by Thy Holy Spirit, that I may know that which is of true value, and desire the eternal treasures of Thy grace! And rid me, O Jesus, of the earthly-mindedness of my depraved and benighted flesh! Amen.

Hymn 363, 3.

TUESDAY.

Therefore take no thought, saying, What shall we eat? or, What shall we drink? or, Wherewithal shall we be clothed?—Matt. 6, 31.

Why should we take no thought and say: "What shall we eat? What shall we drink? Wherewithal shall we be clothed?" Because we cannot serve two masters. We cannot serve God and mammon. We cannot be God's dear children and at the same time wish for mammon as anxiously as if it were our god. Just because God is our Father through Jesus Christ, our Savior, we should not anxiously take thought for our food and drink and raiment. Will not our Father, who has given us our life and our body, also provide food and raiment? Will not He who feeds the fowls of the air and clothes the flowers of the field do this all the more for us, His children? O we of little faith! The Gentiles, who do not know God as we know Him, who are without God in the world, who are not the children of God, may indeed worry and say: "What shall we eat? What shall we drink? Wherewithal shall we be clothed?" But not we children of God. For our heavenly Father knoweth that we have need of all these things. And knowing this, He also gives us these things. There is only one thing about which we should be concerned, only one thing we should anxiously seek; it is this, that we may remain God's dear children and live and conduct ourselves as God's dear children; then our food and drink and raiment will surely be added unto us. All this is promised us by our Lord and Savior, whose lips speak nothing but the truth. And He says in great kindness: "Take therefore no thought for the morrow; for the morrow shall take thought for the things of itself. Sufficient unto the day is the evil thereof." (Matt. 6, 24-34.) Therefore take no thought, saying: "What shall we eat? What shall we drink? Wherewithal shall we be clothed?"

PRAYER.—Great and omnipotent God, Thou art my dear Father through Jesus Christ, my Savior, and I am Thy dear child, whom Thou lovest with a boundless love. Give unto me Thy Holy Spirit, that I may always firmly believe this wondrous truth. And grant me to fully and cheerfully trust in Thee in life and death. And root out of my heart all anxious cares for food and drink and raiment unbecoming Thy children. Amen.

Hymn 363, 1. 2.

WEDNESDAY.

Judge not!—Matt. 7, 1.

To judge means to form an opinion of a fellow-man, and to pass judgment on him according to the strict requirements of the law. My dear Christian, wouldst *thou* like to have others treat thee thus? Art thou so utterly without sin as to be able to say to every man: "Judge me!" and to God: "Judge me!"? Nevermore! sayest thou. Very well; then thou must neither judge thy neighbor, in order that thou wilt not be judged. For with what judgment thou judgest, thou shalt be judged: and with what measure thou metest, it shall be measured to thee again. If with respect to thy fellow-man thou steppest out of the sphere of compassion into which the grace of God in Christ has placed thee and thy fellow-man, and if thou enterest the sphere of the strict requirements of God's Law and judgest thy fellow-man according to it, then the Law will hold its strict requirements up to *thee* and judge thee. Beware, beware! Judge not! If thou judgest thy fellow-man, thou art like a man who beholds a mote in his brother's eye and says: "Let me pull out the mote out of thine eye!" and, behold, a beam is in his own eye. What beam, then, is in thy own eye? The beam of hypocrisy. What hypocrisy? This hypocrisy, that, though being a sinner a thousandfold thyself, thou undertakest to judge thy neighbor for this or that sin. Will not the judgment of God smite thee? Listen! If thou beholdest a mote in thy brother's eye, then beware, above all things, of the beam of hypocritical judgment, and then help, with the sincere humility of a poor sinner, to cast the mote out of thy brother's eye. Always remain within the sphere of the grace and compassion of God.

PRAYER.—My God, how depraved am I, how sin does cleave to me! I, who have burdened myself with guilt a thousandfold, am so easily inclined to judge my brother and neighbor. O God, for Jesus' sake forgive unto me this wickedness of my heart, and grant me grace through Thy Holy Spirit above all things, in true penitence, to see my own sins, and thereupon to help my erring brother in a spirit of true humility. Amen.

Hymn 346, 3.

THURSDAY.

Enter ye in at the strait gate!—Matt. 7, 13.

Our Lord and Savior says: "Wide is the gate, and broad is the way, that leadeth to destruction; and many there be that go in thereat." Why is this? Because the way to damnation, that is, unbelief and a life of sin, is so suitable, agreeable, and pleasing to our depraved nature, and hence wide, broad, and smooth. And "strait is the gate, and narrow is the way, that leadeth unto life; and few there be that find it." Why is this? Is God at fault here? Does God make it so hard for us to be saved? No, God makes it easy for us to be saved. God desires to make us lost and condemned sinners righteous before Him without any merit, or work, or anything whatsoever on our part, solely by virtue of the merit and work of Christ, our Substitute, which we should accept by faith. Hence it is His great mercy that saves us, grace alone. And what is more, He even tenderly urges us through His Word and His Holy Spirit to go this way that leads to salvation by grace. But, according to our old Adam, we foolishly block this way, this gate of grace. To our old Adam the Gospel of Christ is foolishness and a stumbling-block; our old Adam refuses to believe in Christ; he refuses to put his trust in the righteousness of another and in the merit of another; he refuses to be a child of God; he refuses to follow Christ. The way which God has made even, the gate which God has opened, is too strait, too narrow, too disagreeable, too annoying, yea, repulsive to him. But "enter ye in at the strait gate," Christians! Deny yourselves, depart from the broad way, go the narrow way that leadeth unto life! "Enter ye in at the strait gate!"

PRAYER.—Lord, I call upon Thee in the trouble which my own wicked heart has brought upon me, because it takes no pleasure in the way of grace which Thou hast opened and prepared for me with the blood of Christ. Break Thou the fetters with which sin has shackled me! O Thou God of mercy, set my heart free by Thy Holy Spirit, and

lead me, Thy child, in the way of life, and let me enter in at the strait gate of eternal bliss. Amen.
Hymn 544, 7.

FRIDAY.
Beware of false prophets!—Matt. 7, 15.

Of the salvation which is in Christ we know nothing, nothing at all, save what God's Word tells us. And this salvation does not become our own except through this Word. Hence this Word is the only means through which God reveals, and also gives, salvation to us. It is the only light in the darkness of death through which we must pass, the only remedy for the ravages of death. How highly we should prize this Word! How anxiously we should be concerned about having this Word preached to us and taught us in its truth and purity, unadulterated and unabridged. Therefore our Savior said: "Beware of false prophets!" By false prophets not those preachers are meant that manifestly preach barren infidelity; on the contrary, such preachers as "come to you in sheep's clothing," those who pretend to be Christian preachers, and perhaps put on very holy and pious airs, but who adulterate the Word of God, and teach doctrines that are not wholesome, but pernicious and disastrous to the soul. False prophets are especially those who teach the people to build their hope of salvation on their own works, their own doing and conduct, and not solely on the grace of God in Christ revealed and offered to us in His Word. Concerning these specious deceivers the Savior says: "Inwardly they are ravening wolves." They destroy faith and salvation. And the world is full of such false prophets. Most pulpits are filled by them. "Beware of false prophets!" How shall we know them? "Ye shall know them by their fruits," says the Lord. By what fruits? Their teaching. Watch their *doctrine*, not their name and their demeanor; then thou wilt know what they are,—but, mark well! provided thyself knowest God's saving Word.

PRAYER.—My God, my God, let us keep Thy wholesome Word, which out of great mercy Thou hast given unto us! Guard us against false prophets! Do not let them lead us away from the sweet comfort true faith gives us. Grant us grace to try all preachers with regard to their doctrine, whether they are proclaiming Thy Word. Let us follow Thy admonition, and carefully guard against false prophets. Forsooth, it concerns eternal salvation, both our own and that of our loved ones, O Lord! Amen.

Hymn 408, 1.

SATURDAY.

Not every one that saith unto me: Lord, Lord! shall enter into the kingdom of heaven; but he that doeth the will of my Father who is in heaven.—Matt. 7, 21.

In the Christian Church there are people who call Jesus their Lord and Savior, who call themselves disciples of Jesus and children of God, yea, who may even consider the Gospel to be the truth, and, moreover, display zeal for the cause of the kingdom of God, and yet they do not do, they refuse to do, the will of God declared in His holy Law. Yes, there are those who preach and teach the Gospel and the doctrine of Christ in its truth and purity, with great power and eloquence, diligently and indefatigably, who defend the same, convert others and convince them of the truth, and do wonderful works in the kingdom of God, and accomplish many things, and nevertheless are carnal-minded and disobedient to God. Let us remember that the saving power of God is not vested in the person of the preacher, but in the grace of God which is effective through the Word that is preached. Now, Christian, note this! All such people shall not enter into the kingdom of God. Our Lord and Savior has never recognized them as His own, He does not now recognize them as such, and He will not do so on the day of Judgment. They are workers of iniquity; they must depart from Jesus. For how does the matter stand? Jesus receives sinners. We are made righteous before God and saved, not by virtue of our work, doing, conduct, or merit, but solely through the merit of Christ, which we accept by faith. But whoever does this, and thus has become righteous before God, a child of God, and an heir of salvation, is so minded now that he delights in doing the will of God. Hence, whoever does not want to do the will of God is devoid of true faith. Thus thou wilt understand our Lord when He says: "Not every one that saith unto me: Lord, Lord! shall enter into the Kingdom of heaven; but he that doeth the will of my Father who is in heaven." Now take a good lesson from this.

PRAYER.—Lord Jesus, give unto me, a poor sinner, Thy Holy Spirit, that I may derive true comfort trusting in Thy merit, and rejoice and glory in the fact that by grace I am God's dear child, and, in view of this, do the will of God willingly, yes, gladly, as much as Thy grace gives me power to do. And acknowledge me as Thy own, O my Lord and Savior, here in time and thereafter in eternity. Amen.

Hymn 314, 10.

Week of the Twentieth Sunday After Trinity.

SUNDAY.

The harvest, truly, is plenteous, but the laborers are few; pray ye therefore the Lord of the harvest that He will send forth laborers into His harvest.—Matt. 9, 37. 38.

If thou takest a general view of the heathen world and even of Christian countries where so many churches are served by false teachers, in what condition dost thou find the people? They are famished spiritually, and scattered abroad as sheep having no shepherd. Is not that a sight to move thee with compassion? Can thy Christian heart see this and remain cold and indifferent? Jesus was moved with compassion when He saw a condition similar to what we see to-day, and, therefore said to His disciples: "The harvest, truly, is plenteous, but the laborers are few; pray ye therefore the Lord of the harvest that He will send forth laborers into His harvest." And He says this to us. We should pray God, beseech Him fervently to grant laborers,

Week of the Twentieth Sunday After Trinity.

preachers of the Gospel, who are to garner immortal souls for His Kingdom. For wherever sowing is being done, wherever the Word of God is preached, there also, without fail, will be a harvest, there men will be brought to faith in Christ and obtain salvation. For God says of His Word that is preached: "It shall not return unto me void, but it shall accomplish that which I please, and it shall prosper in the thing whereto I sent it." (Is. 55, 11.) But do we Christians pray God for laborers as the Savior bids us pray? Dost *thou?* Alas, we must confess to much coldness of heart. If we Christians truly prayed God to send forth laborers into His harvest, He would surely gladly and abundantly grant our prayer. Indeed, by such prayer God would open the heart of many a one to say: "Here am I; send me!" (Is. 6, 8.) It is our fault that there are so few laborers. God is willing to give, but we do not ask Him; God is willing to send, but we do not go.

PRAYER.—Lord, for Jesus' sake forgive unto me this sin, that with such coldness of heart I behold how all the world is famishing spiritually, that, though Thou dost command us to pray for laborers, I nevertheless pray so seldom and so poorly, and that on my own part I do so little toward sending out laborers into the field. Give unto me the precious gift of Thy Holy Spirit, yea, through Him, I beseech Thee, inflame the hearts of many Christians and move them with sincere compassion and unto fervent prayer and willing service. Amen.

Hymn 470, 1.

MONDAY.

Whosoever therefore shall confess me before men, him will I confess also before my Father who is in heaven. But whosoever shall deny me before men, him will I also deny before my Father who is in heaven.—Matt. 10, 32. 33.

With the heart to believe in the Lord Jesus and with the mouth to confess Him before men, these two are as intimately linked together as a light and the brightness it sheds forth. For flesh and blood, which still clings to us Christians, it often is a hard task indeed to confess our Lord before unbelievers, who mock or threaten or smile in derision. But the new man within us ever again comes to the surface and freely confesses his allegiance to his beloved Savior. Flesh and blood may so overpower a Christian as time and again to fall into the mortal sin of denying Christ. But when the look of Jesus quickens his faith again, bitter tears and a renewed confession always follow. And him who thus confesses Jesus before men, He, the Lord, will confess also before His Father in heaven; He will testify that he is His own through faith, and will be His in all eternity. Blessed is he whom the Savior thus confesses! But he that denies the Lord Jesus, he that is ashamed to confess Him before men, he that in the presence of Christians, indeed, acts as a Christian, but in the presence of unbelievers acts as an unbeliever, such a person has lost his faith, has ruthlessly cast it aside. Him will our Lord also deny before His Father in heaven and say: "I know him not!" And woe, woe unto him or her whom the Lord will thus deny!

PRAYER.—Grant unto me, O my Lord Jesus, the right and sincere faith in Thee, my only Savior, that I may steadfastly cling to Thee in true faith, and confess Thy name, though the world should look askance at me for it. Help me, Thy weak child in every temptation, lest I deny Thee! And acknowledge me as Thy own before Thy heavenly Father, and as worthy, through Thee, to remain with Thee in everlasting bliss. Amen.

Hymn 552, 6.

TUESDAY.

Think not that I am come to send peace on earth; I came not to send peace, but a sword.—Matt. 10, 34.

Thus says the Lord Jesus. And it is a very strange saying of the "Prince of Peace," who also, in the night preceding His death, said to His disciples: "Peace I leave with you, my peace I give unto you." (Is. 9, 6; John 14, 27.) And we know of a certainty that He brought peace unto us: peace with God, whom we had offended and provoked to wrath, peace with all the reconciled children of God, peace of heart and conscience. But this is a spiritual peace, a peace indissolubly connected with the truth of the Gospel and faith. Jesus did not come to send a carnal peace on earth, a peace that conflicts with the truth of the Gospel and faith. On the contrary, where the Gospel is preached in its purity, and where men truly believe, there sword and war loom forth—brought on by such as refuse to believe and accept the Gospel. And back of them stands the old Evil Foe. And, alas! such sword severs the most intimate ties. The unbelieving son is set at variance with his father and the daughter against her mother and the daughter-in-law against her mother-in-law. And a man's foes shall be they of his own household. And we must bear this. We dare not, for the sake of peace, deny our Savior, nor His Gospel, nor any word of His Truth, nor the faith in Him and His Word. He says: "He that loveth father or mother more than Me is not worthy of Me; and he that loveth son or daughter more than Me is not worthy of Me." (Matt. 10, 35-37.) My dear Christian, do not let such sword and discord shake thy faith and become a stumbling-block to thee. Stand firm! Thou nevertheless hast the true peace.

PRAYER.—My Lord and Savior, I thank Thee for having merited the true peace for me. But when discord arises and war is waged against me because of Thy Word and my faith in Thee, as once it did against Thee, then give me Thy Holy Spirit, that my heart may not be troubled nor afraid, but that I may cheerfully and firmly cling to Thee. Amen.

Hymn 109, 2.

WEDNESDAY.

He that taketh not his cross, and followeth after Me, is not worthy of Me.—Matt. 10, 38.

The cross of which the Lord Jesus here speaks is every hardship or tribulation that we must bear because we follow Him. If we follow Jesus, we shall have a cross to bear, for the devil hates us, the world persecutes us, and our own flesh and blood troubles us in many ways. The cross with which our Lord and Savior was afflicted casts its shadows, which cause pain and affliction upon those who follow Jesus. And whoever does not willingly take this cross, and does not follow Jesus steadfastly, is not worthy of Him, he cannot be His disciple, cannot be a Christian. For if we wish to be exempt from this cross, we can accomplish this only by no longer following Christ. If we wish to avert from us a part of this cross, it can only be done by partly surrendering our faith and our confession and the obedience we owe Christ. But can a Christian do this without altogether falling away from Christ? An old, well-known pastor, since departed, owned a picture which represented some cross-bearers who threw off their cross entirely, and others who sawed off a part of it. But they all ceased to follow Christ. Whoever would lead a life that is agreeable to his flesh, and would try to find happiness by throwing off the cross of Christ, will lose this very happiness and enter eternal death. But he that loses his life and happiness on this earth for Jesus' sake, will find it for all eternity. Follow Jesus, even when burdened with the cross! The Lord will regard thee with compassion and help thee.

PRAYER.—Lord Jesus, my Savior, without Thee I cannot have life, without Thee I am lost; I must follow Thee as a sheep followeth its shepherd and a disciple his master. Grant me this, O Jesus! And if then I must take Thy cross upon me, graciously help me, O Jesus, and give me true courage and boldness. Yes, do help me, O Jesus! Amen.

Hymn 334, 1. 6.

THURSDAY.

Whosoever hath, to him shall be given, and he shall have more abundance; but whosoever hath not, from him shall be taken away even that he hath.—Matt. 13, 12.

God's spiritual gifts are, mainly, a believing knowledge of the Word of God, peace and joy in the possession of salvation, and strength willingly and obediently to follow

Christ through this life unto eternal life. These spiritual gifts, by reason of their divine origin and nature, thrive and bear fruit. For they are gifts of the Holy Ghost who dwells within us; and the Holy Ghost cannot be idle and inactive within our hearts; He causes the seed which He has planted, and which through Him has life, to grow. Thus it is that ever more of this believing knowledge of the Word of God, of this peace and joy in the promised salvation, and of this strength willingly and obediently to follow Christ, is given to him who has these spiritual gifts, and in whose heart the Holy Spirit truly abides. This is what the Lord Jesus means when He says: "Whosoever hath, to him shall be given, and he shall have more abundance." On the other hand, if any one disregards the spiritual gifts of God, if he resists the Holy Spirit, who desires to work within his heart, and refuses to give place to Him, then at last the Holy Spirit departs from such a person; and when the Holy Spirit departs, all those things are likewise taken away from such a person, which in the first place were given him by the Holy Spirit. He is then without the believing knowledge of the Word of God, without peace and joy in the salvation of Christ, having lost it now, and without strength willingly and obediently to follow Christ. A vine withered and cast forth, is such a person. And this is what the Lord Jesus means when He says: "But whosoever hath not, from him shall be taken away even that he hath." A very, very serious word, which, alas! but too often comes true.

PRAYER.—Lord God Holy Ghost, forgive unto me the slothfulness and disinclination of my carnal mind wherewith I have hindered Thee from bestowing upon me the full measure of Thy spiritual gifts. O Lord, let me rejoice in Thy precious and blessed gifts, and give unto me, O Lord, an ever greater fullness of the same, to the glory of Thy name and unto my soul's eternal welfare. Amen.

Hymn 249, 1.

FRIDAY.

Who is the greatest in the kingdom of heaven?—Matt. 18, 1.

What we would say in answer to this question might be wrong. Let us see what the Savior answers. He says: "If any man desire to be first, the same shall be last of all and servant of all." (Mark 9, 35.) What does this signify? It signifies three things. First: It is right for a Christian to desire to be first in the kingdom of God, that is, to wish to do more for the kingdom of God than any other man, and also earnestly to attempt this. Secondly: But in doing this, such a Christian must consider himself nothing but a poor sinner, which indeed he is, and deeply deplore that he can do so little, but esteem every other Christian better than himself. Thirdly: In doing this, he again must serve all others and make himself their servant, for in the kingdom of God service alone is what is wanted. Whom, therefore, does our Lord call the greatest in the kingdom of heaven? *Him who uses his best endeavors to amount to something in the kingdom of God, but at the same time esteems himself less than others, and serves others with the greatest humility.* The Savior further answered our question by setting a little child in the midst of His disciples and saying: "Verily, I say unto you, Except ye be converted and become as little children, ye shall not enter into the kingdom of heaven. Whosoever therefore shall humble himself as this little child, the same is the greatest in the kingdom of heaven." (Matt. 18, 2-4.) Conceit shuts one out from the kingdom of heaven, for it is in direct opposition to the state of a heart that trusts in the Savior of sinners. Whoever, like a dear little child, serves his fellow-man, and at the same time, again like a dear little child, considers himself the least of all believers, he, yea, he is the greatest. A wonderful doctrine, and directly opposed to flesh and blood! But such a one the Savior loves.

PRAYER.—Lord Jesus, give unto me, and sustain within me, a poor sinner, the true faith, that I may be and remain in Thy kingdom. And grant me Thy Holy Spirit to serve

Thee gladly in Thy kingdom by serving my neighbor. And guard me against faith-destroying conceit and vanity! Let me be Thy beloved disciple in childlike simplicity and humility. Amen.

Hymn 365, 1.

SATURDAY.

Lord, how oft shall my brother sin against me, and I forgive him? till seven times?—I say not unto thee: Until seven times, but: Until seventy times seven.—Matt. 18, 21. 22.

Thus Peter asked, and thus the Savior answered him. Hence we must ever and again be ready to forgive with all our heart, actually to forgive. How often does God forgive us who sin against Him? Daily and richly. It cannot be counted. We always sin against God, and God always forgives us. How often does our brother, our fellow-Christian, sin against us? It is as nothing compared with our innumerable offenses against God. Again and again we should be ready to forgive with all our heart, actually to forgive. Should we sinners be less ready to forgive than the holy God Himself? Should we, who could not live and be happy without the forgiveness which God grants us, refuse to forgive others? Why, then we would fully deny the spirit of faith, then we would have lost our faith, then we ourselves could no longer look to God for forgiveness. The Savior teaches us to pray: "And forgive us our trespasses, as we forgive those who trespass against us," and says: "For if ye forgive men their trespasses, your heavenly Father will also forgive you. But if ye forgive not men their trespasses, neither will your Father forgive your trespasses." (Matt. 6, 14. 15.) No one can remain a Christian who places himself in opposition to this word of the Savior and refuses to forgive. Ah indeed, for flesh and blood it is difficult and often impossible to forgive, to forgive from our whole heart. But have we not been born again? Should the old Adam rule within us? No, the new man must live and rule. And we want to forgive, forgive again and again. My dear Christian, take this well to heart! It is a most serious matter.

PRAYER.—Lord Jesus, again I come unto Thee for help. Help me against my sin-corrupted flesh and blood! Help the new man within me! Grant that I may always be ready to forgive from my whole heart if any man sins against me, a sinner. By Thy Holy Spirit make Thy clear command a power within me! Preserve me in Thy grace! Amen.

Hymn 365, 3.

Week of the Twenty-first Sunday After Trinity.

SUNDAY.

It is easier for a camel to go through the eye of a needle than for a rich man to enter into the kingdom of God.— Matt. 19, 24.

When the rich young man had decided in favor of his riches and against the Savior, Jesus sorrowfully said to His disciples: "How hardly shall they that have riches enter into the kingdom of God!" His disciples were astonished at His words. But the Lord now said: "Children, how hard is it for them that trust in riches to enter into the kingdom of God! It is easier for a camel to go through the eye of a needle than for a rich man to enter the kingdom of God." And they were exceedingly amazed and said among themselves: "Who then can be saved?" The Lord said: "With men it is impossible, but not with God; for with God all things are possible."—It is said that one can buy anything for money. Yes, anything that can be bought. Hence the powerful charm that riches have. Whoever sets his heart upon them is charmed by them, is bound as with a thousand chains, so that he cannot believe, cannot come to his Savior and follow Him. Riches take such a firm hold of his heart that he cannot give it to his Savior. For it is either—or: he must give his heart either to his Savior or to riches; he cannot give it to both at the same time. And as we have said, riches take a firm hold of his heart. Only God, yes, He alone, can set that heart free and give it to the Savior. My dear Christian, examine thyself well as to how thou regardest riches. If thou hast riches, dost thou set thy heart upon them? If thou hast them not, does thy heart desire them? Consider what thou hast just read! Thou must give thy heart to thy Savior, and to Him alone, or thou wilt be lost!

PRAYER.—Lord, eternal, almighty God, who protectest all that put their trust in Thee, increase Thy mercy upon me, that, having Thee as my Leader and my Guide, I may regard the temporal goods, which so easily ensnare the soul, in such a manner as not to lose the eternal ones: for the sake of Jesus Christ, Thy dear Son, my Savior. Amen.

Hymn 385, 4.

MONDAY.

Whether of the twain did the will of his father?—Matt. 21, 31.

Hear a parable of Jesus. "A certain man had two sons; and he came to the first and said: Son, go work to-day in my vineyard. And he answered and said: I will not. But afterward he repented, and went. And he came to the second and said likewise. And he answered and said: I go, sir. And he went not." (Matt. 21, 28-30.) Now the Lord asks: "Whether of the twain did the will of his father?" Evidently, the first.—What are we to learn from this? Listen! In Christian churches there are many who are yes-sayers and no-doers. They hear the Word of God. God's Word says to them: "Repent, and believe the Gospel!" They say, Yes, we will. Of course they say yes. Are they not church-members? How can they be expected to say no? But never a thought of true repentance, never an impulse of true faith arises within their hearts. They are and remain indifferent, dead Christians, Christians only with their mouths, only as to outward appearance. Then there are also those who are no-sayers and yes-doers. At first they are manifest unbelievers and slaves of sin. The Word of God comes to them. God's Word says to them: "Repent, and believe the Gospel!" They say, No! They are obstinate. They cast aside the Word of God. They want to remain in their unbelief and serve sin. Later they recall to their minds this Word of God. The Spirit of God operates upon their hearts. And they are sorry for having said no at a previous time. And they repent and believe the Gospel. And they become dear children of God. Which, now, of these have done the will of God? The yes-sayers and no-doers, or the no-sayers and yes-doers? Surely the latter. And who will enter the kingdom of God? Ah, thou knowest. And now what of thyself?

PRAYER.—Lord God, dear Heavenly Father, who at all times, by means of Thy Word and through the Holy Spirit, dost call me to true repentance and biddest me to believe the Gospel, grant me grace to truly say yes and also to do accordingly. Guard me against hypocrisy which merely professes Christianity with the mouth. O let me not be numbered with those unhappy ones unto whom Thou saidst: "The publicans and harlots go into the kingdom of God before you." Let me be Thy dear child for Jesus' sake. Amen.

Hymn 417, 1. 2.

TUESDAY.

Be not ye called Rabbi; for one is your Master, even Christ; and all ye are brethren.—Matt. 23, 8.

Rabbi means Master. The word Rabbi denotes a person who in the Christian Church claims for himself a spiritual authority above others, and hence also honor and respect in preference to others, as the Pope does and his priesthood. But Christ does not want such Rabbis in His Church and in His kingdom. To those who hold an office in the Church He says: "Be not ye called Rabbi." And He furthermore says to them, as well as to the Christian laity: "For *one* is your Master, even Christ; and all ye are brethren." And to all His Christians He says: "And call no man your father upon the earth; for *one* is your Father, who is in heaven." (v. 9.) In view of this I ask: What of the "Holy Father" of the Roman Church together with his many "Fathers," the priests? In the worldly governments there are masters indeed, and there is authority, and due respect must be paid those in authority, and each according to his station, or the power he is vested with. There is also parental authority. But in the kingdom of Christ there is nothing of the kind. There all without distinction are brethren of one another. There Christ alone is the Master. He rules in this kingdom by means of His Word, and solely by means of this Word. If a pastor proclaims the Word of Christ to his congregation, the congregation should obey; but in that case it is not obedient to the pastor, but unto Christ. If the humblest and poorest and least respected member of the congregation speaks a word that Christ has said, the whole congregation should obey at once; for it is Christ, their Master, who speaks through this person. And if the pastor, or any church official, or the most highly respected man of the congregation says anything that is not Christ's Word, it is of no value. *One* is our Master, even Christ; and all we are brethren.

PRAYER.—Lord Jesus, Thou only Master of Thy Church, I pray Thee to protect us, Thy Christians, lest men rule us, Thy Christians, and subject us to slavery. Do Thou alone rule within Thy Church by means of Thy plainly written Word. And give Thy Holy Spirit to us, who are Thine, that we may at all times willingly bow beneath Thy Word. Then all will be well with us. Amen.

Hymn 461, 1. 4.

WEDNESDAY.

For as many as are led by the Spirit of God, they are the sons of God.—Rom. 8, 14.

Dear Christian! May God forfend that thou be beguiled to live according to the desires of thy flesh, according to thy old Adam, according to the evil lust that dwelleth within thee; for if thou livest so, thou art lost. But if with the aid of the Holy Spirit that dwelleth within thee thou mortifiest, daily mortifiest, thy old Adam, who would force the members of thy body into his service, thou shalt be saved. Why? Does this thy work save thee? By no means. Thou art saved solely by grace, for Christ's sake, through faith. By mortifying thy old Adam with the aid of the Holy Spirit, thou provest thyself to be a believing child of God. The children whom God has received through grace have this disposition, this God-given disposition, that, led and moved by the Holy Spirit, they mortify the old Adam and gladly and willingly serve their heavenly Father. Whoever does not do this is not a believing child of God. He, however, who does this is a child of God. As many as are led by the Spirit of God, they are the sons of God. And this leading of the Holy Spirit is no slavish constraint and compulsion, so that thou must live in continuous dread and be full of trembling, like those who are under the Law and know nothing of grace. No, this leading of the Holy Spirit is a sweet and childlike impulse within thee which causes thee to say: Abba, Father, gladly will I renounce sin and serve Thee; do Thou but help me! And when the Holy Ghost so leadeth thee, He always bears witness unto thee through the Word of Grace that thou art a child of God, His dearly beloved child, whom He has received into His gracious arms, and that thou hast forgiveness of sins and art an heir of eternal salvation through thy dear Lord Jesus Christ. Is not this a most precious truth? Being a child of God, art thou not glad to have the Holy Spirit lead thee thus?

PRAYER.—Almighty, eternal God, who out of pure and unmerited grace hast made me Thy child through faith in Thy dear Son and an heir of eternal life, I pray Thee, let the Spirit of Thy Son take possession of my heart, and effectually cry within me: Abba, Father! and by His tender impulse move me to renounce sin and serve Thee with all my heart, until at last, in the perfection of blissful eternity, I shall enter upon my blessed inheritance. Amen.

Hymn 258, 1. 2. 5.

THURSDAY.

And we know that all things work together for good to them that love God.—Rom. 8, 28.

"I will do this or that"—thus thou art wont to speak and to purpose in thy mind. Well said. In matters pertaining to this life thou, to a certain extent, hast a free will. And yet, God, who rules all things, also governs thy doing according to His counsel aforethought. "O Lord, I know that the way of man is not in himself; it is not in man that walketh to direct his steps." (Jer. 10, 23.) "What a strange accident!" some one may say when something occurs in a strikingly unexpected way, something fortunate or unfortunate. But, my dear Christian, nothing is accidental What might seem more accidental than the falling of a hair from off thy head? "But the very hairs of your head are all numbered," numbered by God. (Matt. 10, 30.) The almighty and wonderful God guides all things by His counsel, the greatest as well as the smallest, with absolute surety of purpose, as with a million reins. "What a misfortune!" thou sayest weepingly when something grievous befalls thee. But there is no misfortune for the children of God. Children of God receive all things, all things—hearest thou?— from the gracious hand of God. Hence nothing can be a misfortune. Everything must be a blessing. "As for you, ye thought evil against me; but God meant it unto good," said Joseph. (Gen. 50, 20.) "No trouble troubles me, and night is bright as day." Thus we sing, and rightly so. In short, all things must work together for good to them that love God, to the children of God, within whom the love to God is kindled through faith. All, yea, all things must work together for good to them; what they do of their own proposing, what they might call accidental, what seems to them a misfortune, indeed, even the sins they have committed, must work together for good to penitent children of God. Oh, be a child of God, love God, walk in His ways, trust His power and grace, and know that all things must work together for good to thee. For good? Yes, especially toward the end that thou abide in the faith and be saved.

PRAYER.—Ah, then, my God and Father, let me be Thy dear child and firmly and steadfastly believe what Thou sayest, that all things must work together for my good in time and eternity. Give unto me Thy Holy Spirit, my Father, that I may greatly rejoice in such certainty, never caring, never doubting, never troubling my mind, but, being Thy child, always hoping for Thy wondrous grace through Jesus Christ. Amen.

Hymn 507, 1.

FRIDAY.

Trust in the Lord with all thine heart, and lean not unto thine own understanding. In all thy ways acknowledge Him, and He shall direct thy paths.—Prov. 3, 5. 6.

Thou wouldst always like to do the right thing whenever thou undertakest anything. Is it not so?—whatever will insure thee true success and God's blessing. How must thou go about this? Use proper forethought and calm deliberation in everything. An old adage warns against "doing things with haste and repenting at leisure." Hence, make good use of the understanding God has given thee. But do not "lean unto thine own understanding"; do not trust in it. For the sphere of thy understanding, though it be ever so keen, is limited. Thou canst not comprehend all things. A thousand contingencies may arise to upset thy shrewdest calculations. Trust in the Lord with all thy heart and in a truly childlike manner beseech Him to guide thee and direct thy paths. And be His dear child through faith in thy Savior, in order that thou mayest be able fully to trust in Him and to call upon Him and to pray to Him in a manner becoming a child. Yea, and in all thy ways, in all thy undertakings, acknowledge Him who is thy dear Father to be thy God, and always let it be thy foremost concern to do what is well pleasing to Him, avoiding everything that displeases Him. Then He will direct thy paths. Then thou wilt be sure of always doing the right thing, the thing that will bring thee true success and God's blessing. Thinkest thou not, my dear Christian, that thy heavenly

Father will direct thy paths better than thou art able to do? Therefore, trust in the Lord with all thine heart, and lean not unto thine own understanding. In all thy ways acknowledge Him, and He shall direct thy paths.

PRAYER.—O my dear Heavenly Father, be Thou with me in all my ways, and direct Thou my paths for my welfare in time and eternity. Thou wilt do it, for Thou hast promised it. But it is also Thy will that I should trust in Thee and acknowledge Thee in all my ways. Grant me Thy Holy Spirit, the Spirit of childlike trust, that I may gladly do this, and walk those paths that are well pleasing unto Thee. And then bless me, my dear Father, and let me prosper in whatever I may undertake, for Jesus' sake. Amen.

Hymn 384, 1. 2.

SATURDAY.

My son, despise not the chastening of the Lord, neither be weary of His correction; for whom the Lord loveth He correcteth; even as a father the son in whom he delighteth.— Prov. 3, 11. 12.

Art thou a child of God through faith in Jesus Christ? Truly? Then every grief that befalls thee, every pain of body or soul, every sorrow, great and small, every tribulation, everything that may annoy thee, every anguish, every need, want, or hardship—it is all a kind, fatherly chastening and correction God gives thee for thy soul's welfare in time and eternity. This thou must firmly believe. It cannot be otherwise. For what else could it be? Chance? There is no such thing as chance; everything is under God's direction. Or did others cause thy trouble, or didst thou bring it upon thyself? That may be the immediate cause. But this, too, is under God's direction. Or is thy trouble to be looked upon as a just punishment of an angry God? Impossible! Christ has suffered that for thee. And God loves thee, His child, though thou sinnest much. No, it is all, without exception, a kind, fatherly chastening and correction which God wants thee to experience for thy good, for thy spiritual betterment. Therefore, my child, despise not the chastening of the Lord, do not murmur against it, do not reject it; neither be weary of His correction. For—mark well!—whom the Lord loveth He correcteth, even as a father the son in whom he delighteth. Ah, indeed, thou mayest weep and pray and cry: Spare me, O Lord! But at the same time trust in Him, and kiss the loving hand that smiteth thee. Nor inquire after the why and wherefore in each case. Say not: What have I done now? Art thou not at all times a sinner in need of correction? Fix thine eyes intently upon God's never-erring wisdom and His never-wavering love.

PRAYER.—My dear Heavenly Father, I thank Thee that I may rest assured that every grief that befalls me is under Thy direction and is a kind, fatherly chastening for my good, my soul's welfare. Grant me Thy Holy Spirit, that I may humble myself under Thy mighty hand, firmly believing that Thou wilt comfort me again and gladden my soul, O Thou loving Father! Amen.

Hymn 246, 4.

Week of the Twenty-second Sunday After Trinity.

SUNDAY.

I beseech you therefore, brethren, by the mercies of God that ye present your bodies a living sacrifice, holy, acceptable unto God, which is your reasonable service.—Rom. 12, 1.

Note this, O note this, my dear Christian! When desiring to admonish us Christians through the Holy Ghost to sanctify ourselves and to serve God, the Apostle Paul does not say: "Thou shalt!" as the Law does, but he beseeches us "by the mercies of God." Believing and remembering that one great deed of mercy and the thousand mercies of God in Christ Jesus which we have experienced, we should be willing to consecrate both body and soul to God and to serve Him. The compulsion exercised by the

Week of the Twenty-second Sunday After Trinity.

Law produces no results within us that are acceptable and well pleasing unto God. But when the Holy Ghost beseeches us by the mercies of God, and thus admonishes us to serve God henceforth, then we really do so, provided we do not belie the name we bear: children of God; and God will graciously accept what thus we do.—But how should we serve God? What should we do? We should offer praises glorifying the merciful God. What kind of praise-offerings? Fruits of the field? Tithes of all we possess? Something much better than that! We should present our bodies a sacrifice unto God; we should place our whole life, whatever we may do and purpose to do, at God's service. Wouldst thou make an exception with regard to anything? Is there anything thou wouldst not place at God's service? Surely not! Such praise-offerings we should bring in true faith, through the Holy Ghost, actuated by a fervent love to our merciful God. This, then, will be a living sacrifice, holy, acceptable unto God, though it may have many, yea, a thousand imperfections. This should be our reasonable service, the proper service of the heart and mind, but a service, too, that determines and regulates our every action. Permit thyself, my dear Christian, to be thus besought and entreated by the mercies of God.

PRAYER.—Indeed, O Lord, most merciful God, I, too, will do what is well pleasing unto Thee; I, too, will place my whole life at Thy service, and bring myself, both body and soul, as a praise-offering unto Thee. But since it is not in my power to do this, I humbly beseech Thee to grant me Thy Holy Spirit that through the Gospel He may illumine my heart to see the magnitude of Thy grace; and beseech and persuade me inwardly, through the glad tidings of Thy grace, to dearly love Thee. And graciously accept these praise-offerings of a poor sinner, for Jesus' sake. Amen.

Hymn 349, 1.

MONDAY.

Be not conformed to this world, but be ye transformed by the renewing of your mind, that ye may prove what is that good and acceptable and perfect will of God.—Rom. 12, 2.

Dear Christian, hear! Thou art no longer a part of the wicked, unbelieving world, which is ever intent upon doing what pleases the flesh. Surely, thou art a child of God through Jesus Christ; thou hast learned to know the wonderful mercy of God, and this prompts thee to serve God with all thy heart. Now, therefore, be not conformed to this world. Do not demean thyself as does the world, which is carnal and unrestrained in morals. Do not take part in the thousand things the world has invented to gratify the desires of the flesh. Be transformed! Be different from the wretched world! But let thy transformation be from within. Be transformed by the daily renewing of thy mind, by remembering every day that thou art a child of God. Therefore, prove everything, examine everything, but not like hypocritical Christians do. How do they prove everything? They prove it to see whether they may not do it, or neglect to do it, as the case may be, without being convicted of a manifest sin. What a carnal mind does this betray! Do thou institute an altogether different test. How so? Always prove what the will of God is with regard to the matter in hand. Always and in every instance inquire what is good, perfectly good, and therefore acceptable in the sight of God, thy dear Father. Where must thou inquire about this? In the Word of God. But in the Word of God thou must search and inquire with eyes that have been rendered keen by the new sense which thou possessest, the heartfelt desire to live in accordance with the will of God. Alas! the flesh still clings heavily to us Christians. And yet, all true Christians truly yearn to do God's will.

PRAYER.—Renew Thou me, O my God, by Thy Holy Spirit! Daily illumine my poor carnal heart with the light of Thy mercy, that from my whole heart I may desire to do Thy will, Thy good and acceptable and perfect will, in everything. Forgive my sins for Jesus' sake! Thou surely doest it. And because Thou doest it, grant me grace to love Thee all the more, and do Thy will ever more perfectly. Amen.

Hymn 350, 1. 3.

TUESDAY.

Be kindly affectioned one to another with brotherly love, in honor preferring one another.—Rom. 12, 10.

How does God want us Christians to be minded toward one another and to deal with one another? We should have brotherly love for and among one another; for we are brethren. We have *one* heavenly Father. We have *one* head, the Savior, and hence are members of *one* body. We have *one* Holy Spirit, who rules within us all. We are going toward that *one* house of the Father, toward *one* eternal home. Ties of blood-relationship are as nothing when compared with our spiritual relationship. Therefore we should cherish brotherly love for one another. And in this brotherly love we should be kindly affectioned one to another. We should deal kindly with one another. In a truly affectionate manner we should rejoice with them that do rejoice, and weep with them that weep. (v. 15.) And our brotherly love must be active, or it is not kindly affectioned. We should distribute to the necessity of the brethren, and be given to hospitality. (v. 13.) We should not let the weaknesses, mistakes, infirmities, and insults of our brethren embitter us. Are we better than they? We should respect the brethren. Each one should esteem the other better than himself. Thus we should in honor prefer one another. We should treat the lowliest brother just the same as we do the most prominent one. (v. 16.) If our brother treats us ill, we should not be overcome with evil, abandoning brotherly love, but overcome evil with good, with love. Thus we children of God should be minded toward one another; thus we should deal with one another. Let this be the goal for which we strive in the Holy Spirit.

PRAYER.—Dear Heavenly Father, teach me inwardly, through Thy Word and Thy Holy Spirit, to love the brethren. My heart, indeed, is depraved and selfish and hateful. But create a new thing within it, O Lord, and change it, so that brotherly love may sprout and grow within it, which, in yonder eternal home, will bear perfect fruit. Hear my prayer for Jesus' sake. Amen.

Hymn 260, 3.

WEDNESDAY.

Rejoicing in hope; patient in tribulation; continuing instant in prayer.—Rom. 12, 12.

Dear Christian, child of God, thou art an heir of eternal salvation. And thou canst and must be sure, yea, altogether sure of eternal salvation. Do but abide by the Word of Jesus in true faith; abide with Jesus! Then thou wilt be saved. Jesus says: "My sheep hear my voice, and I know them, and they follow Me; and I give unto them eternal life." Art thou troubled with doubts, my dear Christian? Thinkest thou that the devil, the world, and thy flesh might, after all, pluck thee out of Jesus' hand? Indeed they might, as far as *thou* art concerned, but not when thou considerest *Jesus.* He furthermore says concerning thee and all His sheep: "And they shall never perish, neither shall any man pluck them out of my hand. My Father, who gave them Me, is greater than all; and no man is able to pluck them out of my Father's hand. I and my Father are one." (John 10, 27-30.) Thou canst and must be sure of eternal salvation, indeed, of eternal salvation. What a blessed hope! At the end of thy earthly pilgrimage, which may be a very miserable one, this hope glitters like a beautiful, cheering, beckoning star, illumining thy heavenward path. Rejoice in hope, in this hope! Ah indeed, this hope, growing out of faith, cannot but make us rejoice, exceedingly so, yea, so exultingly as to make our body and soul fairly quiver with joy. God, O God, make us, Thy children, rejoice in hope. And make us patient in tribulation; yes, indeed, patient in tribulation. Tribulation will have to be borne for a brief time only, and then we shall enjoy that bliss which will endure forever. And tribulation works for thy good, for thy salvation. Hence be patient, right patient in tribulation! And continue instant in prayer! Pray to God for help against everything that troubles thee, and for everything thou needest for the eternal salvation which He has so solemnly promised to give thee. Will He deny to give thee what thou prayest for? That is impossible. Therefore, rejoice in hope, be patient in tribulation, continue instant in prayer!

PRAYER.—My God, my God, I see right well that Thou desirest me to rejoice in hope and to be patient in tribulation, continuing instant in prayer, and Thou art willing, yea, Thou surely wilt help me to enter eternal joy and bliss. Here, then, am I, O Thou gracious God; fill me with the fullness of Thy grace! Amen.

Hymn 503, 14. 15.

THURSDAY.

Him that is weak in the faith receive ye.—Rom. 14, 1.

Who is he that is "weak in the faith"? O Christian, a child of God is meant, who desires, yea, earnestly desires, to serve God, but who believes that in order to do this, he must abstain from certain things, though God has not forbidden them, and that he must by all means do certain things, though God has not commanded them. Hence, a person who thinks he must make certain props and crutches for the life he should lead as a Christian, notwithstanding God has not provided them, is weak in faith. In the first congregation of Christians in Rome, for instance, there were some who believed that they must not eat any meat nor drink any wine, because their body would become too voluptuous and consequently unfit to serve God as they should. They also considered it a duty to set apart certain days on which to study the Word of God and to pray in seclusion and with special earnestness. Similar dear Christian souls may be found to-day, though not as many as in the days of the Apostle. These are weak in faith. For what is the truth of the matter? Whatsoever God has not forbidden must not be condemned, and the use of it dare not hinder us in the service of God; and whatsoever God has not commanded is of no value in the sight of God, and the doing of it cannot be of assistance to us in serving God. Our Christian life must move within the limits which God has drawn in His Word, and in no other, and every day our whole life should be a constant service of God. If this is our faith, then our faith is right; everything else is weakness. But mark! we must not despise the weak in faith, but receive them as our brethren with sincere love and esteem. And we must not offend nor confuse them, nor tempt them to do something that in their opinion is wrong, and so to sin against their weak conscience, by inconsiderately doing in their presence what otherwise would be permissible. Read Rom. 14 attentively!

PRAYER.—Dear Lord, should I despise my brother when out of fervent love to Thee and from a desire to serve Thee he does things which according to Thy Word he need not do? Far be it from me! On the contrary, O Lord, forgive me my slothfulness in Thy service. And give unto me Thy Holy Spirit, that I may be fervent and diligent in Thy service, and esteem my weak brother better than myself. Amen.

Hymn 339, 3.

FRIDAY.

We, then, that are strong ought to bear the infirmities of the weak, and not to please ourselves.—Rom. 15, 1.

Here weak Christians are meant that are different from those mentioned yesterday, Christians who are weak with regard to their daily walk and conduct, who soon stumble and fall, who are easily led into some sin, or give way to sin, such as anger, untruthfulness, intemperance, and the like, or who do not succeed in breaking away altogether from some habitual sin, though they greatly desire to do so. Such Christians, indeed, are weak; they lack spiritual strength. And it must be admitted that it is their own fault.

Or wouldst thou say that it is God's fault?—The Church of God is full of such weak Christians. Now if thou art strong, if thou showest great spiritual strength to rule over the sin tempting thee from within, and dost not permit it to prevail with thee, but always overcomest and conquerest it, and always walkest steadfastly in the ways of God—. But wait! Let me put a question: Art thou really such a strong Christian? Or art thou, too, one of the weak ones? If thou actually art strong, what, then, should be thy attitude toward the weak? Thou must bear their infirmities. "Bear"? What does that mean? Overlook? Tolerate? Let them pass? More than that! Thou must help the weak in faith as any decent man will help the physically weak and infirm on the street. Thou must take the infirmities of the weak upon thyself and help them to get strong. Thou must not be pleased with thyself, not concern thyself about thyself alone, much less pride thyself upon thy strength, thou wretched man, who standest only by the power of God. Thy demeanor should be such as to please thy neighbor for his good, to edification. And humble brotherly love will teach thee how to go about this.

PRAYER.—Lord, my God, what shall I say? What shall I pray? If by Thy grace I have mastered a sin, and then see a brother that is weak, help me not to judge him, not to forsake him, not to leave him alone, but most lovingly to help him, as Thou dost help me, O gracious God! Amen.

Hymn 370.

SATURDAY.

Be strong in the Lord and in the power of His might.—Eph. 6, 10.

Strong thou must be, Christian, or thou wilt be lost; for thy enemies are strong. And since with power of thine naught can be done, thou must be strong in the Lord and in the power of His might. Put on the armor, take up the weapons of offense and defense which God supplies, that thou mayest be able to stand against the wiles of the devil, yea, of the devil. For we Christians wrestle not only against enemies of flesh and blood, but against principalities and powers, against the rulers of the darkness of sin in this world, against the wicked spirits that set themselves between us and heaven. Therefore, O Christian, take up the whole armor which God provides, that thou mayest be able to withstand in the evil day, and, having done all, to stand. Stand ready, enter the lists of spiritual warriors, having thy loins girt about with truth, having thy breast protected with the breastplate of righteousness in thy walk and conversation, and thy feet shod, prepared to run the way which the Gospel of peace maps out for thee. In short, be a true Christian in the power of the Holy Spirit. For if the devil notices that thou art dishonest and addicted to a sin, he will soon inflict a fatal wound upon thee. But above all, take the shield of faith, of faith in thy Savior, Jesus Christ, a faith kindled within thee, and made strong and an impenetrable shield by the Holy Ghost. With this thou wilt be able to quench all the fiery darts of the wicked. For if thou holdest this faith, God dwells within thee and encampeth round about thee. And cover thy head with the helmet of salvation, the helmet of the joyous, certain, and confident hope of victory and of eternal salvation. And then lay about thee boldly with the sword of the Spirit, which is the Word of God, and against which no devil can stand. Yes, one little word can fell him. And cry, pray, cry unto God to help thee! The victory will be thine.

PRAYER.—O God, Heavenly Father, Thou knowest the danger in which I am, Thou knowest my enemies, Thou knowest my inability. Therefore I heartily beseech Thee that Thou wouldst arm me with Thy Word and Thy Holy Spirit, that I may be strong in Thee and in the power of Thy might, that in the evil hour I may be able to stand, and to carry the day, and to obtain eternal salvation through Jesus Christ, my Lord and Savior. Amen.

Hymn 380, 1-4.

Week of the Twenty-third Sunday After Trinity.

SUNDAY.

And for me.—Eph. 6, 19.

"And for me"—what? The Apostle Paul desired that the Christians to whom he wrote should *pray* also for him. Indeed, all true Christians should do this for their pastors. And all faithful pastors earnestly desire their parishioners to pray for them. The devil hates no one more than faithful pastors. How necessary, therefore, is such intercessory prayer of their parishioners! Do pray for thy pastor, my dear Christian! Pray that God would put on him the whole armor of God, that he may be able to stand against the wiles of the devil. Pray that by the grace of God utterance may be given unto thy pastor, that he may open his mouth boldly, and that God may grant him grace to preach the true, pure, unadulterated Word, to make known the mystery of the Gospel whose messenger he is. For the Gospel is a mystery, wholly unknown to man by nature, but revealed and made manifest through the Word of God, and through it alone. This Word thy pastor must preach in all simplicity, in its truth and purity, unalloyed with any reflections of his own reason. To be able to do this is a gracious gift of God. Pray God to grant him this gift. Then the strength of God will be made perfect through his preaching. Pray God for this strength. And beseech God to bestow upon thy pastor also this grace that in all the requirements of his office he may cheerfully act and speak as he ought to act and speak according to the Word of God. Thy pastor has been given thee by God, and thou hast helped to call him. Ask the Lord to bestow His blessings upon him abundantly.

PRAYER.—Lord God, dear Heavenly Father, I pray Thee to keep my pastor, whom Thou hast appointed unto me, in true faith and in a godly life. Also give utterance to him boldly to open his mouth to preach Thy Word in its truth and purity, and at all times to speak and to act as he ought to do. Bless him, O God, and make him a source of blessing for me and for many, for Jesus' sake. Amen.

Hymn 485, 1. 2.

MONDAY.

Thine eyes shall see thy teachers; and thine ears shall hear a word behind thee, saying: This is the way, walk ye in it.—Is. 30, 20. 21.

It is a most gracious favor of God for a congregation to have a pastor who preaches and teaches the Word of God in its truth and purity and with all simplicity. God promises this as a gracious gift unto His people that wait upon Him, saying: "Thine eyes shall see thy teachers; and thine ears shall hear a word behind thee, saying: This is the way, walk ye in it." Is not this a mark of God's gracious favor, if thou, a child of God, desiring to go the way that leads to heaven, mayest see thy teacher and hear from his lips the Word of God which will unmistakably show thee the way which thou must go to reach heaven, and which warns thee against every deviation to the right or to the left? Tell me, if God is always with thee through the word of thy pastor, and leads and guides and keeps thee on the way His children should take to reach heaven, and always guards thee against aberrations—is that not a wondrous gift of grace? Therefore thank God unceasingly if He has given thee such a preacher of the Gospel. And obey and follow thy teacher and preacher, and do thy part towards making him do his work with joy, by readily accepting his instruction; and do not cause him to grieve over thee, for that is unprofitable for thee. (Hebr. 13, 17.) Yes, indeed, that is unprofitable for thee. For the Lord Jesus says to those who truly preach His Word: "He that heareth you heareth Me; and he that despiseth you despiseth Me; and he that despiseth Me despiseth Him that sent Me." (Luke 10, 16.)

PRAYER.—Help us, good Lord, my God, that we, Thy children, may at all times have among us true and faithful teachers of Thy Word, and that we may guard against false teachers, lest, being seduced into error, we be led away from Thee. Grant that with singleness of heart we may abide steadfast in Thy Word unto our end, and thus obtain salvation through Jesus Christ, our Savior. Amen.

Hymn 492, 1. 2.

TUESDAY.

Fret not thyself because of evil-doers, neither be thou envious against the workers of iniquity.—Ps. 37, 1.

Anger, wrath, fretfulness, and envy would insinuate itself into our foolish heart when we see the evil-doers and the workers of iniquity prosper in this life. Why, say we, should the wicked prosper more than we, who are the children of God? But, dear child of God, fret not thyself because of the evil-doers, nor be envious against the workers of iniquity. Fret not thyself because of him who prospereth in his way, and of him who bringeth wicked devices to pass. For listen! The evil-doers and workers of iniquity shall soon be cut down like the grass, and wither as the green herb; they shall be cut off; for yet a little while, and the wicked shall not be: yea, thou shalt diligently consider his place, and it shall not be. And where shall he be? Ah, the Lord shall break the arm of the wicked; the wicked shall perish; and the enemies of the Lord shall be as the fat of lambs: they shall consume; into smoke shall they consume away. Therefore, O child of God, cease from anger, and forsake wrath, and leave off fretting and envying, lest thou, too, be tempted to do evil, and thou, too, become wicked, and thou perish. For the children of God, who, it is true, are called the meek and lowly here on earth, but who in quietness and meekness wait on the Lord, yes, they shall "inherit the earth" (Matt. 5, 5), and shall delight themselves in the abundance of peace. A little that a righteous man hath is better than the riches of many wicked. The Lord knoweth the days of the upright; and their inheritance, yea, their inheritance and treasure, shall be forever. The Lord upholdeth the righteous. They shall not be ashamed in the evil time, and in the days of famine they shall be satisfied. Oh, remain a child of God, and fret not thyself because of the evil-doers, neither be thou envious against the workers of iniquity.

PRAYER.—Lord God, dear Heavenly Father, give unto me Thy Holy Spirit, that I may have great peace and joy in being Thy child and in resting in Thy bosom, and that I may not fall into a sinful passion because of the seeming prosperity of the wicked, nor envy those who soon shall be destroyed. O Lord, I want to be Thine own here in time and thereafter in eternity, through Jesus Christ. Amen.

Hymn 385, 1. 2.

WEDNESDAY.

The wicked plotteth against the just, and gnasheth upon him with his teeth. And the Lord shall laugh at him; for He seeth that his day is coming.—Ps. 37, 12. 13.

The righteous man who walks in the ways of the Lord, who escheweth evil and reproveth it, is a thorn in the flesh to the wicked, as smoke to his eyes, and a sting in his conscience. And the wicked plotteth against the just, and gnasheth upon him with his teeth, and draws out his sword and bends his bow, to cast down the poor and needy, and to slay such as be of upright conversation, and watcheth the righteous, and seeketh to slay him. But the Lord, who ruleth all things, shall laugh at him, for He seeth that the wicked is as nothing; He seeth that his day is coming, the day of his downfall. Woe unto him at whom the Lord laughs thus! The sword which he drew out against the just shall enter into his own heart, and his bow shall be broken. Therefore, O child of God, be not afraid of the terror of the wicked, neither be thou troubled. Wait on the Lord, and keep His way; depart from evil, and do good, and thou shalt dwell forevermore, and the Lord shall exalt thee when His time cometh, and it shall be well with thee. For the Lord loveth judgment, and forsaketh not His saints; they are preserved forever. The righteous shall inherit the land, and dwell therein forever. But the seed of the wicked shall be cut off. When the wicked are cut off, thou shalt see it. How often one does see this even now! David says: "I have seen the wicked in great power, and spreading himself like a green bay tree. Yet he passed away, and, lo! he was not: yea, I sought him, but he could not be found." (vv. 35. 36.) Yea, the wicked plotteth against the just. But the Lord will not leave him in his hand. The Lord will not condemn the just when the wicked judgeth him. Fear not!

PRAYER.—Lord, my God, I have Thee on my side. Why should I fear the plotting of the wicked? Do thou but help me to abide with Thee and to keep Thy way. Then Thou wilt keep me safely and let me abide forever, when the wicked and Thy enemies perish. Let me be Thine forever through Jesus Christ! Amen.

Hymn 495, 4.

THURSDAY.

Rest in the Lord, and wait patiently for Him.—Ps. 37. 7.

My dear Christian, thou knowest that sometimes the sea that bears thy life's frail bark runs very high in consequence of a heavy storm. Then all is dark as night. The tempest roars, the waves and the billows rise, and thy skiff is threatened with destruction. Thou canst not direct the course, thou seest naught but destruction. What then? What shouldst thou do then? Thou must know that the Lord is with thee. And then "rest in the Lord, and wait patiently for Him." This is precious in the sight of the Lord, if thou so resteth in the Lord, and waitest patiently for Him. That pleases Him. In each and every trouble commit thy way unto the Lord; trust also in Him; and He shall bring it to pass. When thy enemies, the wicked, unjustly condemn and persecute thee, then He, the Lord, shall bring forth thy righteousness as the light and thy judgment as the noonday. Rest in the Lord, and wait patiently for Him. Do not flutter and flee hither and thither, restlessly. Calmly stay where thou art; do good; faithfully do thy duty, do all in thy power. Rest in the Lord! Know that He is but playing with thee as a mother does with her child, as an eagle does with her young. What of the fiercest storm, the direst need, if He is with thee? Rest in the Lord, and wait patiently for Him! Yes, smile as a little child does that is about to fall, when first attempting to walk, because its mother is right near. Try to spread thy wings as young eagles do that are about to fall, but whose mother takes them up on her wings. Delight thyself in the Lord. He shall give thee the desires of thy heart: salvation, O salvation! Rest in the Lord, and wait patiently for Him!

PRAYER.—Lord Jesus, Thou art mine and I am Thine. And Thou lovest me, and Thou art almighty. And Thou art always with me. Therefore, when trouble arises, great trouble, then help, O help me, Lord Jesus, to rest in Thee, and joyfully and patiently to wait for Thee. Thou shalt help me. Amen.

Hymn 525, 1.

FRIDAY.

Such as be blessed of Him shall inherit the earth; and they that be cursed of Him shall be cut off.—Ps. 37, 22.

In the Lord's kingdom, which extends over all, there are such as are blessed of Him, and such as are cursed of Him. They that are blessed of Him are those whom from eternity, impelled solely by His grace, for Christ's sake, the Lord has chosen and predestinated with the purpose of blessing them, and whom in time He made partakers, through faith, of this blessing through His Word and the Holy Spirit, so that now they live and walk according to His Word as His blessed children, and wait for eternal life. All this is solely the grace of God and in no respect whatever to be attributed to any work, doing, conduct, or merit of God's blessed children themselves. Those who are cursed of the Lord are those whom the Lord from eternity, impelled by His grace, for Christ's sake, most earnestly desired to bless, and whom in time He sought to make partakers, through faith, of this blessing through His Word and the Holy Spirit, but who would not have this blessing, and would not have Him, so that now they live and walk according to their own imaginations and lusts as the cursed of the Lord, and dash headlong into their own destruction. And all this is entirely their fault and in no respect whatever the Lord's will or doing; nor is it because the Lord had neglected them in any way. Now, such as are blessed of Him shall inherit the earth. The earth on which they live is theirs by the will of God; it belongs to them. And when that saying shall become manifest: "I saw a new heaven and a new earth," then shall it also become manifest that the earth is theirs and belongs to them alone. But they that be cursed of Him shall be cut off. God permits them to live on earth a while yet, and is longsuffering with them. But he that continues in his evil mind shall at last be cut off, he shall not see the new heaven and the new earth; he shall be damned.

PRAYER.—My God, I give thanks unto Thee that Thou hast made me, the unworthy sinner, partaker in faith of Thy blessing through Thy pure grace for Christ's sake, and hast thus given me the sure hope of eternal life. I pray Thee with all my heart to keep me in the true faith, and to let me remain blessed forever. Amen.

Hymn 341, 4-6.

SATURDAY.

Mark the perfect man, and behold the upright; for the end of that man is peace.—Ps. 37, 37.

Child of God, blessed of the Lord, believing Christian, mark the perfect man, and behold the upright, and be thou likewise! Be not like unto the wicked that borroweth and payeth not again, but on the contrary, be merciful and give and lend gladly to those who are in need. Let thy mouth speak the wisdom which the Word of God teaches, and let thy tongue talk the judgments of God. Let the Law of

God be in thy heart. Then shall thy steps be ordered by the Lord; and He delighteth in thy way. Though thou stumble and fall, thou shalt not be utterly cast down and away; for the Lord holdeth thee by thy right hand, and raiseth thee and sustaineth thee. The Lord will not suffer thy footsteps to slip. The Lord helpeth thee. The Lord shall help thee and deliver thee. Trust in the Lord! He is thy strength in the time of trouble. He shall deliver thee from the wicked and save thee. The Lord blesseth thee. And knowest thou what David says by the Holy Ghost? He says: "I have been young, and now I am old; yet have I not seen the righteous forsaken, nor his seed begging bread." (v. 25.) The transgressors shall be destroyed together; the end of the wicked shall be cut off. But do thou mark the perfect man, and behold the upright, and be thou like unto him; for the end of that man is peace. Many a distress may come upon thee, if so be the kind will of God, thy heavenly Father. But in the end, yes, in the end, thou shalt see and experience and witness, even here on earth, that thy end is peace, if thou goest in the ways of God. And at the very last, mark well! these ways lead into heaven. And "all's well that ends well"; is it not so? Yes, "mark the perfect man, and behold the upright; for the end of that man is peace."

PRAYER.—Lord God, dear Heavenly Father, who hast made me Thy dear child, and hast so profusely showered blessings upon me, I pray Thee to help me to be perfect and upright as becometh a child of Thine, and as Thy Holy Ghost moveth me to be. Hold me by my hand and do not let my footsteps slip. Raise me when I fall. And let my end be peace according to Thy Word. And finally give me eternal life through Jesus Christ. Amen.

Hymn 349, 6.

Week of the Twenty-fourth Sunday After Trinity.

SUNDAY.

Dust thou art, and unto dust shalt thou return.—Gen. 3, 19.

This Word was meant for Adam. And for Eve also. And it is meant for all the children of Adam, for all mankind. And all the creatures of the earth fall beneath the doom of this word. With this word God created DEATH. Death is the wages of sin. Therefore death is nothing good, nothing nice. Death is a horrible and dreadful thing. We, the living children of men, created by God, shall return to the dust out of which we were taken. And death is the dark passage that leads to the final Judgment. "It is appointed unto men once to die, but after this the Judgment." (Hebr. 9, 27.) This is the worst feature of death. Many seek death in order to escape the misery of life. They are fools. At the first moment of our existence we have the germ of death within us. No skill can eradicate that. Uncounted myriads of the germs of death completely surround us everywhere. We eat them, we drink them, we inhale them, we absorb them. And innumerable other causes of death are ever near us. Though in the midst of life we be, snares of death surround us. And: While in the midst of life we be, hell's grim jaws o'ertake us. And: Into hell's fierce agony sin doth readlong drive us.—Where shall we for succor flee, lest our foes confound us? Who from such distress will free, who secure will make us? Where shall we for succor flee, who, O who will hide us? *Thou, O Lord Christ, Thou only!*

PRAYER.—Lord Jesus Christ, Thou only Savior, Thy precious blood was shed to win peace and pardon for my sin. And Thou didst conquer death and hell when Thou didst rise from the dead. And Thou callest me to come to life and to salvation through faith in Thee, through trust in Thee. I come, Lord Jesus! Here am I, Lord Jesus! Amen.

Hymn 527, 1-4.

MONDAY.

I have waited for Thy salvation, O Lord.—Gen. 49, 18.

Jacob the son of Isaac, the son of Abraham, was at the point of death. And by the Holy Ghost he prophesied concerning Christ. And then he said: "I have waited for Thy salvation, O Lord!" Even in death he waited for the salvation of the Lord, for the salvation which the Savior would bring. He hoped and trusted in the Word of God concerning the future Savior and His salvation. Thus did he depart. He was not disappointed in his waiting, in his hope, in his trust. He departed, and the Lord received him, the Lord, who in the fullness of time was to become Jesus Christ, the Savior. This was almost two thousand years before the birth of Christ.—We know more of the salvation of the Lord than Jacob knew. "What the fathers most desired, what the prophets' heart inspired, what they longed for many a year, stands fulfilled in glory here. Abram's promised great Reward, Zion's Helper, Jacob's Lord, Him of twofold race behold, truly come, as long foretold." In life and death, yea, in death we should wait for the salvation of the Lord, for the salvation which the Lord has purchased for us. We must hope and trust in the Gospel telling us of our Lord and Savior and His salvation. Thus we should depart this life. We shall not be disappointed in thus waiting, hoping, and trusting. Departing thus, we shall go to meet our Savior. And in the midst of death He will keep us and show us His salvation. He will let us taste His salvation. In the gloom of death we shall pass into a great light.

PRAYER.—Lord Jesus, my Savior, when my last hour is close at hand, and I must hence betake me, then let me wait, in faith let me wait for Thy salvation. Thus will I depart and go to Thee, Lord Jesus Christ. I will stretch out my arms to Thee. Peaceful and calm my sleep shall be, no human voice can wake me. For Thou, Lord Jesus Christ, wilt open heaven's portals for me and take me into Thy mansions of eternal bliss. Amen.

Hymn 529, 2.

TUESDAY.

So teach us to number our days, that we may apply our hearts unto wisdom.—Ps. 91, 12.

Everybody knows that he must die. No one, however, knows when he shall die. And death is so awful, so big with consequences! But who minds it? Most people are as unmindful of death as brute creation. Others, again, despair. Regenerate Christians should learn to pray as Moses does in the oldest of Psalms: "So teach us to number our days, that we may apply our hearts unto wisdom." For to do this is a gracious gift of God. To number one's days with a proper regard to death, and to truly apply one's heart to wisdom, no one can do of himself; God, through His Word and the Holy Ghost, must teach a sinner to do this. How should we number our days, that we may apply our hearts unto wisdom? What wisdom is able to help us against the assaults of death? We should consider that death is the wages of sin, and therefore leads us to Judgment; and we should be heartily sorry for having sinned against God and merited eternal punishment. But in numbering our days we should also consider that our Savior has redeemed us from sin, death, and the Judgment, and we should therefore flee to Him in true faith. If we thus number our days, we shall have applied our hearts unto wisdom, and found salvation from death. And daily must we so number our days; daily our hearts must thus be applied to wisdom; daily we must pray God to teach us thus to number our days, and thus to apply our hearts unto wisdom. For death may come any day. Such a meditation does not make us downcast and unfit for life here on earth, as some say; on the contrary, this makes us glad and courageous to run our course; for then we shall not fear death.

PRAYER.—Lord, so teach me to number my days, that I may apply my heart unto wisdom. Teach me to consider that by nature I am a sinner doomed to eternal death. Teach me to remember this with contrition and repentance! But make Thy grace in Christ Jesus precious and mighty within my heart, that I may at all times take true comfort from it against all the terrors of death and of Judgment. Give unto me, O Lord, the Spirit of faith, that I may be ready every day to meet death cheerfully: through Jesus Christ, my Lord and only Savior. Amen.

Hymn 544, 3.

WEDNESDAY.

Precious in the sight of the Lord is the death of His saints.—Ps. 116, 15.

Who are the "saints" of the Lord? All believing Christians, without exception. For God forgives all their sins unto them, imputes unto them the merit of Christ, and receives them as His dear children. Are they therefore not His saints? The Holy Spirit also dwells within them, and moves them to do holy and good works. But as long as they live on earth, their good works are imperfect. What, now, is meant by the words: "Precious in the sight of the Lord is the death of His saints"? When one of His saints dies, this is a great and important event in the sight of the Lord. That is what these words say. Hence it is certain that the Lord will not suffer any of His saints to die unless out of great love to them He has so decreed, and at no other time and in no other manner than He has determined it. The saints of the Lord are ever in the secret place of the Most High, and abide under the shadow of the Almighty. The Lord is their refuge and their fortress. He covers them with His feathers, and lets them trust under His wings. His truth is their shield and buckler. They need not be afraid for the terror by night, nor for the arrow that flieth by day, nor for the pestilence that walketh in darkness, nor for the destruction that wasteth at noonday. A thousand shall fall at their side, and ten thousand at their right hand; but it shall not come nigh them—unless the Lord out of great love to them would have it so. He shall give His angels charge over them to keep them in all their ways. If thou art a saint of the Lord, thou mayest defiantly boast in the Lord against all adversity. Nothing can destroy thy life unless the Lord so wills it. And when death comes, the Lord sends it out of great love to thee. And the Lord will deliver thee, and with eternal life will He satisfy thee, and will show thee His salvation. Indeed, precious in the sight of the Lord is the death of His saints. Therefore, be thou His saint and rejoice!

PRAYER.—O Lord, my God, number me among Thy saints for Jesus' sake, and protect me according to Thy faithfulness and love, and let my death also be precious in Thy sight. And finally give unto me eternal life. Amen.

Hymn 530, 2.

THURSDAY.

The day of death (is better) than the day of one's birth. Eccl. 7, 1.

This is very true. The day of death is better than the day of one's birth—for God's children. True, also for the day of thy birth, O child of God, thou shouldst and wilt praise God in all eternity. For God created thee and gave thee this temporal life that thou mightest obtain eternal life through Jesus Christ. But thou art conceived and born in sin, and certainly it is not God's fault. And thou art born unto work and toil on this sad earth which the Lord has cursed. (Gen. 5, 29.) It is not necessary to speak of all the spiritual and bodily misery into which we have been born, and the end of which is death. But now thou art a child of God. Thou art God's beloved child through faith in Christ Jesus. And when the day of thy death comes, thou mayest rejoice and say: "Lo! the sun of morn now rises, and the breaking day I see that shall never end for me." What day? The day of eternal and a perfectly blissful life. This day bends down to the day of thy death and consumes it. The sun of this day rises as soon as the darkness of the day of thy death descends upon thy heart and eyes, and thoroughly illumines thee with the most blessed light. Then there will be no more sin, no more curse, no more work and toil, no more misery, neither spiritual nor bodily. Then there will be naught but righteousness, naught but blessing, naught but comfort and rest, naught but bliss, both spiritual and bodily. Ah, indeed, the day of death is better than the day of one's birth. Therefore St. Paul writes by inspiration of the Holy Ghost: "I have a desire to depart and to be with Christ; which is far better." (Phil. 1, 23.) And therefore our own, never-to-be-forgotten Dr. Walther once said, with eyes a-gleaming: "The day of my death? Oh, I can scarcely await it; I rejoice at the approach of it; it will be the best day of my life!" The day of death is better than the day of one's birth. For then our true life will begin.

PRAYER.—Dear Heavenly Father, I thank Thee that through Jesus Christ Thou hast made me Thy dear child and an heir of eternal life. I pray Thee to give me Thy Holy Spirit, that by Thy Word I may overcome all the terrors of death, and look forward with pleasure to the day of my death, which by Thy grace must be for me the gate of life. Amen.

Hymn 547, 5. 6.

FRIDAY.

Thou shalt rest, and stand in thy lot at the end of the days.—Dan. 12, 13.

Thus spake the Lord to the Prophet Daniel through the heavenly messenger. Thus the Lord says to every one of His children. Thus the Lord speaks of our death. What, therefore, is the death of God's children? It is rest, sweet, peaceful, blissful rest, which is but faintly foreshadowed by the rest we enjoy when sleeping, though it be ever so sweet and peaceful a rest. When we are dead, we rest; our body rests and our soul rests. The soul rests in the arms of Jesus, and no torment shall touch it. The body rests in the earth in God's keeping. No man can call us, no human voice can wake us, no man can disturb our rest. Nothing, nothing at all, can disquiet us. In this world, in this life, alas! no rest can be found. But for God's children death means rest. While resting in death, we shall know nothing of this world, nothing of this present time. When resting peacefully in this life, we know nothing of what is going on in this world; hours of world-forgetfulness then pass as in the twinkling of an eye. However, this but faintly foreshadows that perfect rest in death, where we shall be entirely removed from this world and time. That rest will be like a brief blissful moment. And then we shall rise. We shall rise and stand at the end of days. The Savior will wake us. But we shall not rise, the Savior will not wake us, for renewed unrest. O no! We shall stand "in our lot." What is our lot? Eternal life. Ah, with what youthful vigor, with what cheer, and our soul full of bliss shall we stand in our lot at the end of the days, in eternal life! We shall rise unto fullness of life, unto an overflowing fullness of life, unto an ever new and eternal abundance of life. But this, too, will be perfect and joyful rest.

PRAYER.—O God, how my flesh doth dread death! But how eagerly my spirit doth long for that sweet rest which Thou wilt give unto me in death for Christ's sake! Oh, my Father, keep me, Thy child, in true faith, that I may go to sleep in Thee; and then let me rise with new vigor and cheer in my lot which Thou wilt graciously give me. Amen.

Hymn 540.

SATURDAY.

But I would not have you to be ignorant, brethren, concerning them which are asleep, that ye sorrow not, even as others which have no hope.—1 Thess. 4, 13.

Regarding our loved ones who have fallen asleep in Christ, and whose resting-place in God's acre we had to prepare with bitter grief and sorrow, the Apostle would comfort us, that we sorrow not as those do who have no hope extending beyond death and the grave. We children of God—thus does the Apostle comfort us—know and believe that Jesus died and rose again. Even so will God bring them with Him that are fallen asleep in Jesus; He will bring them up from the grave as He did Jesus. Yes, this is an unfailingly sure promise of the Lord, proclaimed by the Apostle, that all those Christians even who will be living when the Lord will come on the last day, shall in no wise precede those who are resting in their graves. For the Lord Himself will descend from heaven with a shout, with the voice of the archangel, and with the trump of God: and the dead in Christ will rise first. Then those children of God who will then be alive, together with the dead that have been raised, will be caught up in the clouds to meet the Lord in the air. And thus all the children of God, and we also, together with our loved ones who departed in faith, will ever be with the Lord. This the Apostle says unto us " by the word of the Lord." We comfort ourselves with this. We sorrow indeed when our dear ones depart from us. But we do not sorrow as do those that have no hope. Our loved ones but precede us; we follow after. And with the Lord we shall find them again and have them with us forever.

PRAYER.—Lord Jesus, in Thee all that are Thine are everlastingly joined together, everlastingly united. Though I must leave my dear ones here on earth, or stand at their graves with bitter grief, yet I know that I shall find them again with Thee in eternal life. Do but grant that we may be and ever remain Thine own, Thou faithful Lord! Amen.

Hymn 559, 5.

Concluding Meditation.

Here have we no continuing city, but we seek one to come.—Hebr. 13, 14.

"Here have we no continuing city." We all know that we cannot remain here. The children of this world are looking into a dark future; and they will be cast into eternal darkness. We children of God, believing the Word of God, are looking into a ravishingly bright future, and we shall be received into eternal light. "Here have we no continuing city, but we seek one to come." This is what we believe and confess; and joy and a joyful longing would fain possess our poor heart, which is encumbered with sin. For, after all, it is well that we have no continuing city here where there is so much sin, so much sorrow and misery in and about us. And it is well, unspeakably so, that a city, the eternal city promised us in God's Word of grace, beckons us, where our eternal and blissful home shall be. Why do we not rejoice more exceedingly, more exultantly, because we are to go there, away from here? Because our faith is weak. But still, the Spirit, the Spirit of God, who dwelleth in us, helpeth our infirmities. For it is plain, we do not know what we should pray for as we ought, considering the great things He has promised us; but the Spirit Himself maketh intercession for us with groanings which cannot be uttered. And He that searcheth the hearts knoweth what is the mind of the Spirit, because He maketh intercession for the saints according to the will of God. (Rom. 8, 26. 27.) We are only pilgrims here. Hallelujah! We seek the eternal city that is to come, and shall find it. Hallelujah! The Lord Jesus Himself, our faithful Savior, is our safeguard. He Himself is our rod and our staff. (Ps. 23, 4.) Hallelujah!

PRAYER.—Lord God, my Father, I thank Thee that Thou wilt take me from this world of sin, away from this valley of death, and into the city of eternal salvation. Lord Jesus Christ, I thank Thee that Thou hast prepared this city for me, a poor sinner, by Thy bitter suffering and death and by Thy glorious resurrection and ascension. Lord God Holy Ghost, I thank Thee that through Thy Word Thou hast given me faith and made me a child of God and an heir of salvation. O my God, take Thou my hand and lead me home, home! Amen.

Hymn 559, 1.

www.ingramcontent.com/pod-product-compliance
Lightning Source LLC
Chambersburg PA
CBHW020632230426
43665CB00008B/143